South Pacific
Diary
1942-1943

Mack Morriss

South Pacific Diary

1942-1943

Ronnie Day, *Editor*

THE UNIVERSITY PRESS OF KENTUCKY

Endpapers: G-2 map on which Morriss plotted his travels in the South Pacific. Map was drawn in late 1943 and includes his second tour, which took him to New Georgia.

Copyright © 1996 by The University Press of Kentucky

Scholarly publisher for the Commonwealth,
serving Bellarmine College, Berea College,
Centre College of Kentucky, Eastern Kentucky
University, The Filson Club, Georgetown College,
Kentucky Historical Society, Kentucky State University,
Morehead State University, Murray State University,
Northern Kentucky University, Transylvania University,
University of Kentucky, University of Louisville,
and Western Kentucky University.

Editorial and Sales Offices: The University Press of Kentucky
663 South Limestone Street, Lexington, Kentucky 40508-4008

Library of Congress Cataloging-in-Publication Data

Morriss, Mack, 1919-1976
    South Pacific diary, 1942-1943 / Mack Morriss : Ronnie Day,
editor
        p.   cm.
    Includes bibliographical references and index.
    ISBN 0-8131-1969-3 (cloth : alk. paper)
    1. Morriss, Mack, 1919-1976—Diaries. 2. World War,
1939-1945—Campaigns—Pacific Area. 3. World War, 1939-1945—
Personal narratives, American. 4. War correspondents—United
States—Diaries. I. Day, Ronnie. II. Title
D767.9.M67   1996
940.54'26—dc20   95-44095

Brodie
DEC 15 '42
TONTOUTA

For
Helen Morriss Wildasin
and
Howard Brodie

Mack would have wanted it this way

Contents

Illustrations follow page 84

Acknowledgments

A lot of people have helped make this work possible. Some, a great many, in fact, are either in the diary, the stories filed for *Yank*, or both. They made the history that Mack Morriss so faithfully recorded. Others who were not participants in or a witness to the events described in the diary provided me with insight into both the personality and character of Mack Morriss as well as the area of northeast Tennessee he loved so much. The reader can gain an appreciation of how much I owe each of them by reading the notes and the photo credits. I thank them all—for the help and for the privilege of getting to know them.

Some, important to the events recorded in the diary, were equally important to me in coming to understand *Yank* and Guadalcanal. They are:

Averbeck, Forrest W., 23rd Squadron, 5th Bomb Group (H)
Brodie, Howard, *Yank*
Bralley, Walter S., 31st Squadron, 5th Bomb Group (H)
Burns, Berton H., 23rd Squadron, 5th Bomb Group (H)
Chaney, W. Marshal, 147th Infantry
Classen, Thomas J., 72nd Squadron, 5th Bomb Group (H)
Debnekoff, Basil D., 23rd Squadron, 5th Bomb Group (H)
Douglas, Wayne M., deceased, 132nd Infantry, American Division
Jackson, Allan, International News Photos
Rothermel, James D., 14th Naval Construction Battalion
Schumacher, William H. 35th Infantry, 25th Division
Weithas, Art, *Yank*.

There are still others—not mentioned in the text or the notes—and I take this opportunity to express my appreciation to them here.

In the beginning, when I was not quite sure what I was looking for, Bob Carson of nearby Kingsport, Tennessee who saw Guadalcanal as a member of A

Battery, 1st Batallion, 11th Marines, made available to me his fine collection on Marine Corps history and pointed me in the right direction.

Along the way, a host of librarians and archivists helped me. At my own institution, Beth Hogan, inter-library loan librarian at the Sherrod Library, secured what I needed—often enough when the only reference I could give her was a hunch that the work existed. In the States, I must thank the staffs at the National Archives, including the Suitland Branch and the Still Picture Reference at Archives II, the Naval Historical Center, Washington Navy Yard (especially Bernard Cavalcante and Charles Haberlein), the U.S. Army Center of Military History (especially Verne Schwartz), and the Air Force Historical Research Agency at Maxwell AFB (and especially Archie DiFante). I also want to express my appreciation to the Guadalcanal Campaign Veterans and to Ted Blahnik, editor of the organization's publication, *Guadalcanal Echoes*. In the Solomon Islands, I want to thank the staffs of the Solomon Islands National Archives (especially Jackson Macramo, George Gwailau, and Esther U. Karibongi) and the Solomon Islands National Museum, both of which are located in Honiara, Guadalcanal.

Financial support is always appreciated, and in this regard, I want to thank the Center of Appalachian Studies and Services, East Tennessee State University, for two grants and the Air Force Historical Research Agency, Maxwell Air Force Base, for a research grant.

A number of people very important to the completion of this work helped in special ways. I want to thank Jackson Lea and Frank Haikiu for showing me around Guadalcanal and Tulagi and my good friend, Alfred A. Bisili of Munda, New Georgia, for all the many things he has done. I want to thank two other good friends, Peter Woodbury of Sydney, Australia, for sharing his own research with me and Naoko Suesada, formerly of Tokyo, Japan, for translating materials and being my teacher. My colleague, Colin Baxter, took time out from his own heavy research schedule to locate some needed documents in the Public Record Office, London; another of my colleagues, Steven Fritz, who works in the military history of the European Theater, shared information and ideas with me; and my former student, George Sherman, did research for me in the National Archives. Nobuhiro Moriya, Defense Research Center, Tokyo, obtained some very scarce historical works for me.

My father-in-law, Ronald Orcutt, suggested at the beginning that I become computer literate in order to handle the mass of material necessary for this project. He helped me to become so. Ronald and Bea Dotson of Winchester, Virginia, made my research in the Washington, D.C., area a very pleasant experience.

Finally, I want to thank three women who each in her own way made this work possible—Helen Morriss Wildasin, my friend and Mack Morriss's widow; Margaret Ripley Wolfe, my friend and colleague and distinguished historian; and Meg Day, my wife. Each knows the central role she played.

Editor's Note

Every effort has been made to keep the text as near the original as possible. On the rare occasions a word was not intelligible and had to be omitted or a word was missing and had to be added, this has been noted. I have corrected spelling and made it consistent and I have italicized the names of ships, books, magazines, and the like. When under the stress of nightly bombing Morriss's language becomes telegraphic, this has been left exactly as written; likewise his abbreviations such as *tho* and *'smorning*. Finally, Morriss frequently used ellipses ranging from three to five points; they are a stylistic peculiarity. In no instance in Morriss's text does an ellipsis indicate that the editor has omitted anything.

Introduction

Six months after Pearl Harbor, Mack Morriss was still uncertain as to what the war had in store for him. He had been in the army since September 1940, when his National Guard unit had been called up for a year's training at Fort Jackson, South Carolina. Like the majority of men called up in 1940, he had trained with enthusiasm for the first few months and then weathered the boredom and discomfort of the winter that followed, living in tents because there were no barracks. When spring finally came, he again mustered up enthusiasm for the gruelling 1941 summer maneuvers in Tennessee amid rumors that the Guard would be retained in service, and listened with the others on a hot, muggy day in July when Roosevelt called for the extension in a radio address. "The cultured accent of the President, our Commander in Chief, radiated from a hundred radios in the battalion," Morriss wrote in a story for public relations. "Soldiers paused in the company streets to listen. They were quiet until he was finished." Then the station returned to normal programming and the country group singing the favorite of the soldiers, "I'll Be Back in a Year, Little Darlin'," came on. The men began to grin, then broke out laughing. "They're going to have to change them words," a Guardsman said finally. "They don't fit no more."[1]

So that autumn Morriss ate his second Thanksgiving dinner in the army, standing in the rain to have the traditional turkey and fixings ladled into his mess kit. The division was involved in its second-large scale maneuvers of that year, this time in the Carolinas. The disappointment of the summer over being retained in service, was fading. The men speculated among themselves as to when they might go home for good, what the situation with Christmas furloughs would be, and whether the rumors were true that had the division moving to some tropical paradise in the Caribbean. "You know," Morriss wrote his father, "I've an idea the Army's morale question has just about solved itself."[2]

Two weeks later, the Japanese bombed Pearl Harbor. Morriss was work-

1

ing at the divisional public relations office on a story about the health of the men during the late maneuvers when he heard the news. "All of us knew this thing was coming, really," he wrote early next morning, "and now that it is actually here there is more a sense of relief that the war of nerves is ended."[3]

But new uncertainties replaced the old. Morriss did the one thing over which he had some control—he went home to Elizabethton, Tennessee, and married Helen Davis. The wedding had been planned for some months and as he had written his father the previous October, he and Helen didn't "want to lose whatever happiness we may be able to get before the world goes to hell."[4] During the next few months, as the new year ushered in nothing but bad news from the battle fronts, he toyed first with the idea of transferring to the Air Corps and then of getting accepted into Officer Candidate School. During his almost two years in the army, he had been in a rifle squad, a mortar section, and had been in charge of a machine gun section. Twice, during the Tennessee and Carolina maneuvers, he had done a stint in public relations and impressed his superiors to the point that one of his stories had been forwarded on to the War Department. He had risen through the ranks, first to private, then to corporal, and finally to sergeant. He was intelligent enough and experienced enough to realize that the army offered an opportunity to bright young men with ambition, but just what it was eluded him.

Of one thing, however, he was certain. He was sick and tired of the sand hills of South Carolina. As far back as the summer of 1941, when the extension of the Guard became a certainty, he had written his father that the men were more disgruntled at having to stay at Fort Jackson than they were about having to remain in the army. Then in April 1942 he had a run-in with a cop at a Negro dance in Columbia that provided all the convincing he needed that a change of scenery was in order. From a hospital bed the next day he tried to be nonchalant about the incident in a letter to his father. "Well, I guess the guy must have said 'shut-up' and I thought he said 'stand-up,'" he wrote. "Anyway, your son is probably the worst messed up young'un you've seen in some time." The fact was, he had ten stitches in his forehead, two black eyes where the night stick had caught him flush in the face, and an assortment of bruises and lumps from the blow and from hitting the ground unconscious. He was in the hospital for most of the rest of the month.[5]

For Morriss, the incident was the lowest point of his military career and one he never forgot. But fortune finally was about to smile on him. He was scarcely recovered and back with his unit when he got what he always considered to be the biggest break of the war. On 8 May 1942, he received orders transferring him in rank to the Detached Enlisted Man's List (DEML) with orders to report to a Special Services detachment in New York City. Two of his friends, John Hay and Ed Cunningham, received identical orders. Morriss and Hay left that same day; Cunningham planned to join them in New York the following Monday. "None of us know what this is about," Morriss wrote Helen from a hotel in Southern Pines, North Carolina, "but it must be something." Four days later, he wrote his wife that he, Hay, and Cunningham were "on the staff of *The Yank*, the Army's newspaper published by the Army and for the Army." The paper was so new that the official title had not been completely settled on (ultimately it was *Yank, the Army Weekly*) and the first job facing the men who reported to the sparsely furnished offices on East 42nd Street was to put together the first issue. Less than a month later, Morriss told a *New York Sun* columnist in Ralph's, a bar where the girls rehearsing for a show at the Music Box liked to frequent, that he was the "luckiest man in the army."[6]

Morriss found himself in as select a group of men as any assembled to wage a war in which the typewriter was as much a weapon as the machine gun. "The first job of this paper," the War Department committee that recommended establishing *Yank* wrote, "would be to arouse the fighting forces to a desire to fight like hell."[7] To do the job right, the army collected newspapermen, writers, artists, and photographers from across the country to serve as enlisted men on the staff of a paper that would carry the slogan on its masthead, "By the men for the men in the service," and announce in its first editorial, "Here's the YANK, brother." But while the staffers might wear stripes on their sleeves instead of insignia on their collars, most of them were well-educated and many had reputations already established. It was heady stuff for a young man of twenty two whose newspaper experience had been with a small town daily and whose formal education had ended with one semester at the nearby teacher's college. His assignment to *Yank* had been the blindest kind of luck, Morriss liked to say, and while luck played a part—it usually does—it was not blind. His work in public relations at Fort Jackson had earned him his chance. It had been no coincidence that Morriss, Hay, and Cunningham had all received identical orders on the same day sending them to *Yank*. Their boss, Lt. Robert M. White, II, himself barred from the paper because he was an officer, had recommended them.[8]

It was the beginning of an incredible odyssey through World War II. Just before Morriss left for the South Pacific on his first tour of overseas duty, his father wrote and asked, "Can you arrange for *Yank* to be sent to me so that I can follow you through it?" The arrangement was made, and in January 1943 the first stories began to appear in the paper, two dozen in all from the South Pacific, with such titles as "They Don't Joke on Guadalcanal When a Battalion Moves Up," "Bomber Raid Over Bougainville," and "Infantry Battle in New Georgia." Ordered back to the States in the fall of 1943, the stories continued with titles such as "There Were No Dramatics on the Dock When This Hospital Ship Came Home" and "Mental Breakdowns in the Army." Then it was back overseas again, and the stories followed the course of the war in Europe, "Inside the Siegfried Line," "How Aachen Died," and the next to last from Europe, "Berlin Death Rattle." Morriss's last assignment in the summer of 1945 was to attach himself to an infantry unit being redeployed to the Pacific and tell "for the benefit of the men who will follow them, what happens to a guy who is transferred from the ETO to the Pacific." The dropping of the atomic bombs and Japan's abrupt surrender canceled the need for the story.[9]

All told, Morriss saw a much bigger slice of the war than did most enlisted men. On the twentieth anniversary of his entry into the service, 16 September 1960, he started to write out his reflections on a legal pad. The manuscript was never finished, nor the part written ever edited or revised. But in a sentence that turned into a paragraph Morriss summed up what his three and one half years with Yank had meant. "The experience—whether it was living it up in Paris or London or New York or Honolulu or Auckland, New Zealand, or sweating it out in a foxhole in the Solomons or Germany or on some rock of an island with one tree 7,000 miles from home, or up 20,000 feet in a B-17, or on an LST headed for a new beach, or in a hospital with a guy shivering with malaria and a backful of grenade fragments, or in a wrecked schoolhouse with a dead GI in the doorway, or looking up at a guy standing in the door of a battalion aid station with an arm blown off, or looking at a man in the floor crying, or simply pulling guard on the motor pool with frost glistening in the moonlight—the experience had a lasting effect on me: It made me believe in this country and in us Americans."[10]

He believed above all in the infantry, and both he and the critics agreed that his best stuff was on the foot soldier. The affinity was natural. Morriss had grown up in the mountains of northeastern Tennessee and had been reared on the stories the 30th Infantry Division veterans had told of World War I. He was well aware that September, as he marched through the streets of Elizabethton with his company of the 117th Infantry, that there was a strong military tradition to be upheld and by the time his expertise with the typewriter outweighed his ability with the machine gun and he was ordered to Yank, he had achieved his objective of becoming an infantryman.[11] His familiarity with his subject paid off later when he was writing about the 25th Infantry Division in the Solomons and the 4th Infantry Division in the Huertgen Forest. Near the end of the war, when The Best from Yank, the Army Weekly was published, Ira Wolfert, Pulitzer Prize-winning war correspondent for the North American Newspaper Alliance, wrote of Morriss in PM that "there are few, very, very few indeed, of the internationally famous war correspondents who can match this youth's work in its passion for meaningful detail." [12]

The passion for recording the detail of what he saw and what he thought was a life-long habit. On the day he and his doctor discussed the fact that his illness was terminal, he typed out the conversation as he would have any other story. "It was a matter of fact conversation with E.L.," he added. "We might have been talking about the weather, a change of season. I felt nothing, no shock, no upset; I suppose that's why I'm recording this. It was a first-experience, however."[13] It is not surprising then that as a young man starting his first tour of overseas duty in the South Pacific he would set out to keep a record of his experiences. What is surprising is that he managed to do it, day by day making the meticulous entries under conditions that went from pleasant to horrible to exotic, once writing by the bright moonlight while the P-38 pilots who had just shot down Admiral Yamamoto celebrated nearby.

Morriss made the last entry in the diary, 19 July 1943, in Honolulu before he left again for the combat area in the South Pacific. From this point on, the black leather bound volume with its 291 pages of closely packed writing was on its own. While the trail of a loose-leaf diary that he kept in New Georgia can be traced from Honolulu to the War Department and on to the New York office, the adventures of the black leather bound diary remain a mystery. Morriss was covering the Ardennes counteroffensive in January 1945 when a friend at the New York office wrote that the diary had arrived in a package addressed to Mack but with no indication of where it had come from or who had sent it. Morriss could not believe his luck. The safe arrival home of the diary was like a close friend showing up suddenly after having been listed as missing in action. "I was so happy to know this impossible thing had happened," he wrote his wife, "that I helped Ed [Cunningham] and Reg [Kenny] murder a quart of scotch last night."[14]

Morriss himself arrived safely home for the last time in July 1945 and was discharged shortly afterward, a month and a few days shy of five years of service in the army. He worked briefly for *Life*, then quit to go home to Tennessee and write. Since the fall of 1941, he had been planning to write a book about his experiences, and after a number of starts finished a novel set in the European theater, *The Proving Ground*, which was published in 1951. The novel was neither a literary nor a financial success; Morriss's own frank appraisal was that it "got polite reviews and no sales."[15]

In 1956 he gave up trying to support his family on the sales of articles and short stories to magazines and went to work at radio station WBEJ, first as a newscaster and then as station manager. He stayed there for the rest of his life, his commentaries on the news becoming a regular part of the life of the people in Elizabethton and Carter County. While he was still living, a former classmate described him as "the poor man's Ernie Pyle;" ten years after his death another respected resident called him "the pulse of the community." Morriss had a strong sense of place; he loved his community and the community reciprocated. But the radio station, his growing involvement in public affairs—he was eventually elected mayor of his hometown—and the onset of his illness gradually pushed writing out of his life. In 1965 Morriss published his last story, a short murder mystery, and despite the encouragement of friends, he published nothing else. In a letter to one of his closest friends, Ralph G. Martin, the former *Yank* correspondent who had become a highly successful writer after the war, he wrote in the summer of 1973, "I have been a non-writer so long that I've lost my bravado, or what passed for confidence, and coming up on a major undertaking daunts me somewhat."[16]

During the years Morriss was active as a writer, he published nonfiction pieces on subjects as varied as a raid on a moonshine still and the growing fame of evangelist Billy Graham, short mystery stories, and travelogues—pieces connected only by their common southern Appalachian setting.[17] *The Proving Ground* was the only work he published on the war, and since it constitutes his sole public statement on the subject other than a Memorial Day radio commentary in 1958, it merits some discussion. The novel is set at Fort Jackson, in his hometown, and on the Western Front. It was released in July 1951, when the *New York Times Book Review* listed James Jones's *From Here to Eternity* as the number one best seller followed by Herman Wouk's *The Caine Mutiny* in second place, and James Michener's *Return to Paradise* in third (all, ironically, set in the Pacific). Herbert Mitgang wrote the short review and after some qualified praise he went right to the weakness of *The Proving Ground*: "An appropriate moral is tacked on to the fictional talk, sometimes unfortunately, giving the impression that the story is being explained, not just told."[18]

Morriss in fact wrote a prologue to the novel that is similar to the conclusion Paul Fussell came to forty years later in the last chapter of *Wartime*, called after Walt Whitman's statement "The Real War Will Never Get into the Books." Describing the reaction of the combat soldiers to the hype and hypocrisy of the home front with all the fury but not the language of a mountain preacher, Morriss wrote, "Said the warriors, finally, laughing, said the brave men, almost angry, said then all the combat soldiers of the things that had been fed them, of the pictures, of the pages, of the hot synthetic rages, said then all in voices sneering, said then at the frauleins leering, spoke then caring not a whit, said then with resounding wit, 'Now ain't *that* a crockashit?'" The problem with the novel lay not in the story but in the telling.[19]

Morriss was an intensely private man, sensitive and honest to a fault, with a strong streak of the moralist in his makeup. Howard Brodie, the *Yank* combat artist and lifelong friend who was with him every step of the way in the South Pacific, told him in 1947, "there was a time when I felt that your sensitivity and reluctance to come out with what was on your mind, was weakness. Now, I feel that it is one of your great strengths. There is a gentleness about you that is wonderful." James Jones, who did not know Morriss but at his request took a shot at assessing what went wrong in *The Proving Ground*, wrote, "just writing about simple bravery of humans is not enough, doesn't go deep enough. It may also be that you have some sort of psychological block of not wanting to look deeply enough into yourself to get at the very basic truth. One has to have a sort of peculiar compulsion, a certain masochism, to want—and need—to do that and then expose it in writing." It was admittedly a shot in the dark, but it seems to me that it hit the target. Morriss looked as deeply into himself as he could, but instead of exploiting the raw material he found there in his writing, he tended to analyze it intellectually.[20]

As one would expect, this tendency carried over into the diary he kept. In a revealing passage of 23 December 1942, the night before he and Brodie flew into Guadalcanal, Morriss wrote, ". . . I wonder why I'm writing this stuff sometimes—I write, as often as not, with the screwed-up attitude that somebody will just pick this thing up and start reading it as if it were a polished, completed work. What I should do is write with complete honesty, candor and a minimum of self-consciousness. Instead I seem to be doing this as if somebody were looking over my shoulder."

It was Morriss himself looking over his own shoulder, of course, analyzing what he was learning about himself. But try as he might, he could not keep the raw truth about himself, and by extension, about humanity, from surfacing in the pages of well-ordered prose. The shock of what he saw and experienced was simply too great. The facade he attempted to erect around himself fooled no one, as in the incident of the Japanese tooth recorded in the 23 May 1943 entry. Recalling it later, Wolfert, who was present, wrote: "Mack was very young then in 1943, both to living and to war, and long and thin, and it was plain to see that, while functioning as a journalist, he was as sensitive as an artist. He had reacted to the horror of war with such great horror that he was compelled, in order to keep himself sane, to overcompensate for it, so he carried back from Guadalcanal, as a memento, a big, snaggly Jap tooth, which he showed with an uneasy swagger."[21]

If all this fails to explain completely why Morriss never published anything else on the war, perhaps it does shed some light on it. Perhaps, too, since there is nothing in his papers one way or the other nor can his wife remember him ever discussing the matter, it leaves us a clue as to why he never seems to have considered publishing the diary—or even selections from it. The conclusion seems to be that for Morriss, the diary was a conversation he carried on with himself about the war, about himself in the war, and about the friendship he developed with Howard Brodie as they confronted the war together. It was an intensely personal, and private, conversation and remained so for the rest of his life, shared only with his family and Howard Brodie.

On more than one occasion through the years, Morriss either lent the diary to Brodie or else looked up information in it for him. In a very real sense, the diary was as much the chronicle of Brodie's experiences in the South Pacific as it was Morriss's. The two men had barely known each other when they set out on the assignment in the South Pacific. Until a short time before, Brodie had been sketching sports for the *San Francisco Chronicle,* and he ended up at *Yank* by way of a few weeks training in the Signal Corps at the suggestion of a former editor at the *Chronicle*, Bill Richardson, the first managing editor of *Yank*. Morriss, of course, had been in New York long enough to be happy to get away from what he called "a center of bickering, of meanness, of phonies."[22] The friendship that developed in the South Pacific continued for the rest of the war, and while they were never again traveling companions as they were in the South Pacific they worked together in the States and occasionally met up during their coverage of the war on the Western Front. After the war, although Morriss was in Tennessee and Brodie was on the move a great deal—he covered the Korean War and Indo-China for *Collier's*, the Near East and Vietnam for AP, and sensational courtroom dramas such as the Charles Manson trial for CBS News—the two men kept close contact until the day Morriss died.

In fact, it was a letter from Brodie that caused Morriss to get out the diary and the other materials he had on Guadalcanal in the summer of 1975, the last summer of his life. Brodie was working on a project and enclosed a list of questions ranging from the name of the river in which they had bathed (it was the Lunga) to whether they had flown out of Guadalcanal together when they had left for the last time in April 1943 (they had). "I spent hours this weekend (answering questions for Brodie)," Morriss jotted down in some notes that have survived, "re-reading Guadalcanal historical material and my own diary." [23]

What he read can only be surmised by looking at the inventory of his personal library. More has been written about Guadalcanal than any other battle of the Pacific war, partly because of its decisive nature and partly because it was waged at the extremities of each combatant's reach and so turned into a battle of attrition lasting almost six months, from 7 August 1942 to 8 February 1943. By the summer of 1975, when Morriss was delving back into the past, a half dozen books had been published, each in its own way a classic, that together constructed both the public's perception and the historical record of the campaign.

The first two of these were the work of journalists and appeared in the book stalls in the States before the fighting was over on the ground on Guadalcanal; Morriss and Brodie in fact were still covering the army infantry fighting over the hills west of the airfield. One was Richard Tregaskis's *Guadalcanal Diary*, an eyewitness account of the Marine landing and the repulse of the first two Japanese counterattacks at the Tenaru River in August and Bloody Ridge in September. The other was John Hersey's *Into the Valley*, an account of a skirmish along the Mataniko River in October. Both books enjoyed a phenomenal success. *Guadalcanal Diary* was excerpted in *Life*, selected by the Book-of-the-Month Club, and made into a movie by Twentieth Century Fox, while *Into the Valley* received wide critical acclaim and was recommended by the Council on Books in Wartime as necessary reading for those who would understand the war.

After the war, three major histories appeared, each of which met with wide critical and popular acclaim, and which together provided the standard historical interpretation for the campaign. Samuel Eliot Morison, *The Struggle for Guadalcanal*, a history of naval operations, was a volume in his semi-official *History of United States Naval Operations in World War II*. Samuel B. Griffith II, *The Battle for Guadalcanal*, focused primarily on Marine operations from August to December in which the author himself was a highly decorated participant. Thomas G. Miller, Jr., *The Cactus Air Force*, limited his history of the collection of air units, marine, navy, and army, that played such a critical role in the defense of Henderson Field and the battle in general to the first four months of the campaign.

Not a lot of notice was taken in the works cited so far of the army infantry units that fought there, beginning with the arrival of one regiment of the Americal Division in October and swelling to two full divisions—the Americal and the 25th—by January 1943. James Jones's novel, *The Thin Red Line*, the second in the trilogy that began with *From Here to Eternity* and ended with the posthumously published *Whistle*, did much to complete the record. Written from the author's own experience, *The Thin Red Line* was the story of one infantry company that took part in the assault on the complex of hills known as the Galloping Horse. Norman Mailer called it "so broad and true a portrait of combat that it could be used as a textbook at the Infantry School;" some would argue that it was the finest combat novel to come out of World War II.[24]

Of these half dozen key works, Morriss had three, *Guadalcanal Diary*, *The Thin Red Line* and *The Battle for Guadalcanal*. If he did indeed reread these, he left no notes to indicate what he thought. But years before in 1947, in a letter to *Salute* magazine turning down an offer to do a who-really-won-the-battle type story on Guadalcanal, he had sketched out his own overall view. It is a remarkable one for its lack of service-connected bias. "Altho I saw six weeks of pretty bloody stuff there," he wrote, "my arrival was after the Marines had done most of their work and were merely containing a couple of weak sectors while the Army did the final work. Thus my conception of the campaign is strictly one-sided, and while I have always believed that the Army got the short end of the publicity thing my belief is based on having seen the Army fight over terrible terrain in the jungle . . . and merely having walked over the less difficult ground occupied by the Marines. Too, there was a great psychological burden on the Marines in the early stages when they were short-supplied and poorly supported, fighting an enemy which at that time was still in good condition and being constantly reinforced."[25]

Morriss did write a brief commentary on the diary that stands for itself as his last statement on the subject.

"I was amazed to realize how much of a pacifist I was at age 22-23 in the middle of combat. I remember being sickened by pain and death, but one or two sentences in the diary intimates that I really blamed the country's leader-ship—not for having gotten us into the war but for not having avoided it some-how. I could not see how the body of a GI cut in two by Jap machine gun fire solved any diplomatic problem and I apparently equated Pearl Harbor's casual-ties in somewhat the same way altho the necessity of fighting & winning the war is not questioned. I saw it at the time, apparently, as a tragedy saddled upon my generation by all the ineptness of the great powers from WWI to Dec 7 '41 to achieve a peace. That there has got to be a better way to run the world is something I've known for a long time . . . but I didn't remember that it went back to Dec, 1942 on Guadalcanal. What I do remember from then, and even before then, and up to the last day of the war, was the spirit of the American combat man himself—regardless of service—who was a noble being. My 3½ years on *Yank* was spent trying to convey that message and had nothing to do with strategy, tactics, diplomacy, politics or anything except how Americans at the shooting level responded to the personal, individual demands of their war."[26]

Six months later he was dead. His hometown newspaper lauded him for being the champion of the common man, and across the state of Tennessee, others marked his passing with a tribute to his public service. All of this was true and would no doubt have pleased him. But what without question would have pleased him most was a statement in the *New York Times*: "Mack Morriss, a top combat correspondent for the Army magazine *Yank* in both Europe and the Pacific . . . ."[27]

"Going Overseas"

Tuesday, November 3, 1942. Here begins a record.

This morning at 11:45 we slipped beneath the Golden Gate and headed out to sea, bound for the South Pacific with a holdful of AC technicians, medicos, ANCs and what seems to be a small scale task force of all arms and services.

For most of us, the swells that lifted this Dutch East Indiaman while the southern tip of SF still gleamed white in the sun was the first taste of ocean sailing. Results were swift. The room marked "Troop Latrine" was a mess.

This is a tiny convoy—three transports with a Navy escort of one vessel. Blimps shepherded us until dusk, then turned back and floated toward the mainland.[1]

During part of the afternoon a group of AC men sang—sang the lilting, lusty songs men like to sing. In the evening the loud speaker system screeched Strauss waltzes and a few light classics. The music was better than the announcer, who told us the next number would be "Danlay Orientally."[2]

Brodie[3] and I feel sure neither of us have grasped the full impact of this thing. This is "going overseas"—that part of the Army which most of us have spoken of in awe—yet we find nothing terrifying about it. I feel surprisingly at home in the never-ending chow line, in the jammed hold where we sleep in triple-deckers just wide enough to hold a man. Most of the men aboard have been in camps, waiting, for such a long time that they seem relieved to be on the way.

Blackout at 6:00. Weather clear; easy rollers, wind.

Wednesday, November 4. Two seaplanes, one on either side, took up the

11

watch. They patrol a half mile ahead, turn, come back and turn again. Monotonous way to earn a living. I can see where this business of eating twice a day is going to get old. We breakfast at 7:30, dine at 4:00—all the coffee we want, but be careful to balance the table or some guys get their food in their lap. Current crack is "anybody who wants to go over the hill—go ahead." First wave of sickness seems to have died, but some of the men were truly ill. The sea is calm, old hands tell us. The Air Corps is at it again: a chaplain who made a stab at organizing singing gave it up. Spontaneous or nothing.

The two troop ships with us cleared their guns this morning and we on the *Tjisadane* got a ringside seat for the movement of tracers streaming skyward. Somebody burlesqued "Praise the Lord and Pass the Ammunition": somebody else suggested they save what they had—we might need it later.

Bill Boni has a bunk with us: he spent most of his time the first day trying to unzip the zipper on his bag. Said he was going to write the office to tell those people what lousy zippers they made. Strange that I should meet him under such conditions. He is of that group of AP men whom I considered old friends because I handled their stuff off the wire at home. We are not going to the same place.[4]

We saw the Sgt. Major this morning and he told us to come in anytime: Brodie needs to work, but there is nothing I can do and space is too valuable for loafing. The sun is better.

A physical description of this ship is impossible for me, because I don't know anything about terminology. A corporal last nite said she looked like an inter-island passenger-freighter and I guess that's as good as any. It strikes me she is pretty dirty topside, but that's our fault.[5]

Boni did a broadcast over the PA system, condensing news picked up by radio at sea.

The men listened attentively, seemed keenly interested in announcements in the Solomons; however news of what seems clearly a U.S.N. victory caused only a ripple of applause.[6] Bill did a workmanlike job on the announcing. Later I heard a soldier in the hold describe him as "that guy who advertised over the radio." First time I've heard that since I left Tennessee—I'd almost forgotten.

Talked at length to a Sgt. in a weather outfit. He was just recovering from mal de mer. A Californian not long married, he felt, as I have heard so many other guys express themselves, that, "We haven't yet really jumped into this fight yet. We aren't mad. Sometimes when I hear guys griping I feel like standing up and telling them. . . . ." When I reminded him that he would only be laughed at, he shrugged his shoulders and said "Sure—don't I know it!" He stoutly maintained that he "had nothing against the Army," but his story revealed he had been kicked around on repeated attempts to get into the air. He said his color vision was bad. He tried pilot, weather officer, RAF, gliders and wound up forecasting local atmosphere although he held a private license and has a number of hours flying time.

To do anything aboard this ship, you stand in line—mess, PX, latrine. Average wait for mess is half hour to 45 minutes. Soldier who bunks next to me came in with armload of groceries which he bought after waiting more than three hours. He gladly sold me candy, gave me crackers and most of a can of deviled ham.

After dark a medico brought his concertina topside and a group sang to his very bad accompaniment: old drinking songs in university German, familiar songs of peace and happy times. The old sentiment.

We set our watches back one half hour tonight at twelve.

Thursday, November 5. This morning we were joined by a converted aircraft carrier and another transport. We are now six troop ships, the cruiser, the carrier and another vessel which is either a destroyer or a sub-buster; it never got close enough for me to say definitely. Soldiers, too, manned the 20mm AA guns and the 4 inchers fore and aft. I understand we were 600 miles out this morning, and that the extra ships joined us from San Diego.[7]

Saw a Cpl. Harry Belgrade this morning and did what I could to help him set up a ship paper. I am to do a piece on the history of the ship, which should be a definite piece of deathless prose. Belgrade, a former English instructor, is an enthusiastic-type fellow, but I'm not sure I can be of much help. Not that a mimeograph sheet is above my journalistic talent—ha—but I somehow seem to have lost the spark of "Betsy Flasher" technique.[8] I'll do what I can, but I don't intend to run around with a pencil behind my ear—or perhaps I should say I'll do a little but not much. I'm a lazy bastard.

The loud speaker has begun its evening concert—"La Golondrina"; then "For Me and My Gal"—"The bells are ringing for me and my gal"—a touch of loneliness for Helen (so soon)—"the birds are singing for me and my gal" . . . . . ."Moonlight and Roses"—what are these people trying to do, make me crack down in a sentimental jag two days out of port?

Talked to a Medical Corps Sergeant today who whined that I "certainly had a racket."[9] Earlier I had heard him say he had been in service only since April, so I let him have it: told him if I sat on my can for the rest of the war I would still have a clear conscience after 18 months in the infantry at Jackson. Actually, that's not so—but it sounded good and he seemed impressed. "Jackson's a hole all right," he agreed. I let him keep on thinking so; it's a paradise compared to some.

Friday, November 6. Went to work in earnest today on the ship's paper, snapping out of a lethargy which seemed to have me slug-nutty since we put out. Interviewed the skipper—Capt. Burger—and got a story on the *Tjisadane's* background. She's a romantic old crate, has cruised all the movieland places in the China Seas. More interesting was a view of the 1st class accommodations on the upper decks. Luxury compared with this ant hill below decks—luxury with paneled cabins and lounges and dining salon and a sun deck. Strangely enough, recognized a lieutenant this morning as the same one who did the work for us on the Dirty Fighting Pictures. He was giving exercises, so didn't speak to him. May not at all.[10]

As I write a harmonica artist has been ranging his repertoire from classics to swing, with a good deal of the Spanish stuff thrown in. He plays well. The only sounds are the clinking of change in the poker game on the deck below, the whir of the ventilator, and the sharp breathing of the harmonica. Everybody is busy doing nothing—lying, reading, fighting off boredom, calmly sweating it out. The barracks bags tied to the posts beside me rock to and fro with the roll of the ship. Now a soldier has started to sing a timeless ballad to no one in particular, lying flat on his back and looking at the roof three feet above him. His voice clashes with the thin strains of some song Allan Jones did with Jeanette MacDonald in a movie version of an operetta years ago—what was it? "Donkey Serenade?" The ventilator whirs monotonously. The attitude is like our old "Order of the Day—Rest." Don't let your mind go backward, and don't let it reach forward. I'm comfortable after a shave and a change of clothes, comfortable with a bag against my back and my feet on a warm blanket—so what the hell. Why worry when there's nothing here to worry about? Why look for trouble, dream it up? Nobody here does.

We had our first boat drill today at 2:00. It consisted of going up on deck and smoking cigarettes. Everybody had a laugh looking over maps and "computing how far we'll have to swim." We set our watches back another half hour tonight.

Friday (continued). Because I'm not ready for sleep, I'm falling back to the old Army pastime—pitching a bitch. I went looking for Bill this morning and having found him on the sun deck, asked him to do a roundup for us. As I was talking to him an Air Corps captain came up and began a conversation of his own, just as though I hadn't been there. Earlier, the Chaplain came into his office which he had given us as a "city room" and brought two nurses[11] whom he introduced as helpers on the mimeographing of his Sunday service program. After the introductions which, I think, Belgrade and I managed to get through in a gentlemanly manner, His Highness the Chaplain smirked that we "of course will find boxes and give these ladies the chairs." Little things—sure—but these things get under my skin. It's like having a man offer cigarettes around to everyone but you, or some such feeling. I thought New York might have knocked out some of that bitterness, since we paid little attention to officers in general, but I find return to "active duty" has already resulted in my curling a lip at pomp and circumstance—mostly circumstance. Oh well—There are worse things than officers by act of God, I suppose.

Saturday, November 7. (Invasion of North Africa)[12] The heavy set soldier with the dark stubble sat on the head and made plans to sleep on deck tonight. He said sleeping on the hard boards would help his back.

"Hell," he explained, "I used to have planks under my mattress. I hurt a vertebra when I fell off a truck one time. Sleeping on a hard bed will do it some good over a period of time—say two or three years.

"Sure, they drafted me this way . . . . . but I'm in the medics—a non-combatant outfit. This isn't my idea of the Army, though, emptying piss pots. I thought they gave a man a gun and let him go. Closest I've been to a gun are to those on board ship.

"Funny thing about my outfit. You line up ten men, strip 'em and let 'em do a few calisthenics, and if three of them are Medical Corps men I guarantee you I can pick 'em out. We get the worst of the bunch. Why, I'll tell you . . . . .

"We got a boy in the outfit who's had spinal meningitis. The kid weighs hardly ninety pounds—he hasn't any strength at all. Hells bells, the poor guy's good hearted and tries hard—but I've seen him pass out time after time. He couldn't protect himself if he were in danger—he couldn't even run away. He can hardly walk. He tries to get along, but he's a detriment. Sure he's going overseas with us—he's right on this boat.

"I was drafted in Boston. They'll take anything up there—all the rummies and drunks and whatever turns up with the right number. We got a poor kid who doesn't know enough not to play with himself. You see him lying on his bunk and he'll say 'me no jerk—me no jerk,' and God damn he goes right on and does it, on and on. It'll drive him crazy sooner or later. He's a foreign kid. Why the hell don't they do something about it—why don't they stop him?"

The chunky guy with the game back pulled up his pants and flushed the salt water down.

"And the funny part of it is . . . . . we got some of the best specialists in the East as officers in the outfit, and a bunch of enlisted men who are university graduates. It's a screwy outfit."

-0-

Gunnery practice for the 20mms today. Plane from the cruiser towed a sleeve over and one of our port crews snapped the cable with a bullet, bringing it down. The whole boat cheered. It made me feel good—even proud—to see it float down with tracers still hitting it after the first burst canopies over the decks. It's getting hot in the sun. Final work on the first issue of the paper.

What a stinker. More work than meets the eye. Reading L. Hughes' *Big Sea*. Red Cross ditty bags.

Sunday, November 8. A confused day, with nothing definite except the heat which gets worse as we near the equator, and the smell which grows with the heat. Neither is really bad—yet.

Bull sessions at sea are like bull sessions in tents or any where else. Talked to Walter Kennedy, who was on the *Washington Times-Herald*; he knows Hosfeller, having once been a news man. We drank five cups of coffee each and talked shop.

Met an interesting character—if true—who dropped in to say he had procured a pint of Bourbon. He's a DEML Corporal on his way to join MacArthur's staff of administrative men. During the course of the conversations—there were several—he disclosed he had: a) crossed the Atlantic 18 times, b) been consul in Chicago for San Salvador, c) mastered three or four languages, d) worked as foreign news editor on the *Chicago Journal of Commerce*, e) never learned to field strip the .45 he was carrying. I held a class on the nomenclature of the pistol. Strangely, even here I find myself a soldier of comparatively "veteran" status in length of service. Held a loud and ridiculous argument, in which 5 guys took part, with a Harvard boy who had to be convinced by innumerable examples that the Army is the least democratic of all American institutions. He has been in only three months. Perhaps the question is silly, but I am beginning to wonder where are all the guys who pulled their time in the doldrums before Pearl Harbor—overseas already, training new men . . . . . or just sitting as we did so long? I have found things which have worried me, and I have found other things which gave me confidence and pride in the Army. The spirit and the general high level of these men—amazing. Utterly unlike Jackson and pre-Pearl Harbor. We turn back watches tonight one half hour. A million stars.

Monday, November 9. Today—of all days—I worked like hell and that hat box we've labeled "Editorial Offices" has been a steam bath. Took off my shirt and just sweated. Am trying to make this issue of the "Taffy" a super-dooper publication with emphasis on the art rather than the writing, which God knows is stinking. The idea is of course a rather mature high school organ, but we are some troubled with the philosophers and poets. A drunk KP came in and said we "wouldn't print the truth; that's why there are men like Walter Winchell to tell the truth—you're afraid to print the truth." He was, I believe, bitching because at some time the officers have had steak and we haven't. A sober poet submitted a poem titled "My Blue Heaven" which Belgrade had him read to us because his handwriting was impossible. The poem concerned the man's wife and child, whose "Daddy has gone to the War." It was so corny it was pathetic, but not half as pathetic as the sincerity of the guy who wrote it—he almost cried as he read. Harry treated him gently; told him to try again, this time for rhythm.

I begin to realize that the paper is taking all my time—I was on deck only twice all day, and then briefly. Of course I have nothing else to do, but it might be better to lay out in the sun and get back into the feel of the real Army again. What was it Kipling said about losing the common touch—not that I have walked with Kings. Anyway, I think I'm going to take some time off and watch the water again. It's silly to keep on being a desk soldier in the middle of the Pacific.

The PA played "I'll Never Smile Again" tonight and I got that old feeling. That song will haunt me as long as I live. Today's news from Africa was wonderful. Praise the Lord. . . . . .

Tuesday, November 10. Tonight I had my first drink aboard ship, three swallows of Bourbon supplied by Corporal Wiel. He paid $5 for the pint, buying from the sailors. I understand our little bearded "Mystery Man" gets $6. The bastard.

The hold tonight—as every night—is full of poker games: wherever there is space for two or three men, they sit on the boards and watch the cards fall. Some pots are abnormally high—$50 and $60. I can see where a lucky man could retire when we reach port.

Work on the paper—with all its art—was slow and tedious. I shouldered the responsibility for the printing and cooked in my own grease. Next issue of the "Taffy" is going to be simple and pure typing. No more fancy stuff; the experiment failed as far as I'm concerned. The hell with it.

Cleaned up tonight and decided to give my mustache one last chance. If it doesn't look like a mustache the next time—tough. Last time I tried that was exactly a year ago on maneuvers: no luck. Incidentally, orders today were that every man shave at least every other day.

This is my last day as a 22-year-old, and things constantly rise up before me to remind me that mine has not been the life of travel and adventure which I dreamed of as a kid. Of course, the war has helped me realize some of my ambitions, but the years ahead offer so much more. I have only to turn to any of several people aboard—holding much less "glamorous" jobs than mine—to realize how pitifully lacking is my own education, formal or otherwise. If I have a son, he'll go to college if I have to drag him—but God forbid him a Harvard complex, or its equivalent.

We turn back watches one-half hour at midnight.

Wednesday, November 11. Twenty-three today. Congratulations all around and Boni gave me a pack of Luckies. I can't remember a birthday having passed with less thought on my part. It used to be that each Armistice Day to me was a step nearer to manhood, but now I find myself almost holding back—or trying to hold back—the years. Perhaps that is silly for one so young, but I had a head start in life and I want to keep it. The phrases "youngest editor" . . . . . "youngest man on the staff" are precious. I think youth traded for maturity is a poor swap, however inevitable. With the years will come, I suppose, the broadening of scope, the depth of knowledge and experience, which I so much desire; but with them will come the closing down of avenues of life and vents of expression. In youth there is flexibility; a true adult is too bound by convention and responsibility—I welcome it—but when there is too much, and the mold is formed, it is difficult to get out from under. Perhaps the solution is to stay young as I grow older—never lose the ability to sponge up new ideas. But the fear of age is for me at best a long-range emotion, and at this stage definitely silly. Silly as hell.

The Chaplain held a short service commemorating Armistice Day. He said the only two things he could possibly have said: that in the light of history today, peace 24 years is a hollow mockery; but that Armistice Day is a symbol to all the people that peace, freedom, victory came to us then as it will come again. He added that to those aboard who fought before us, the phrases "Make the world free . . . . ." and "Armistice" are humiliating because they left the job undone—they and their contemporaries—but that Armistice Day, '42, serves as a day to remind us that this time we have to finish the job right down to the ground. I have said before—and reaffirmed it today—that no son of mine will ever lift a gun if I can help it . . . during this war or anytime after.

As the finale for his service, the Chaplain asked that we all stand and give the pledge of allegiance and sing the National Anthem with accompaniment by the band. I have rarely seen as embarrassed bunch of men as we were during the pledge. Some held out their hands in the traditional grade school manner; some even gave the Boy Scout sign. But the public school system has done its work well—at least we all knew it. Weird is the word for our singing of the "Star Spangled Banner." Some stood at attention, some saluted, some didn't, most of us just stood. While I have snapped up to salute in many a dark New York theatre balcony, today I stood with my hands on my hips and looked around me while others tried to follow the band and the way-off key Chaplain. It was pretty lousy as a show of patriotism in the grand manner . . . . . a la Hollywood or average America, even, for that matter. I think most of the boys felt as I did about it: that coupled with a putrid musical rendition, our presence aboard an Army transport bound for a combat zone should be ample reason to remain silent, or at least apathetic. Actually, the band accompaniment was more nearly the real reason: we were caught a little flat footed, and a little disgusted, simultaneously. Let him who doubts our love of country know that no man aboard this ship has indicated anything but an intense desire to get into this war, get it over with, and get home. Why do men fight at all? To go home!

The second issue of the "Taffy" "went to press" and was received with due comments to its improvement over the first issue. Even so—no more PM makeup for me.

The news has been so good lately that Boni has been accused of sugaring it for the newscast. Today's Africa situation is music to us: Darlan a prisoner, Oran captured, moving on Tripoli . . . . . on toward Rommel. Hi-yo Silver!

Thursday, November 12. (Second Battle of Guadalcanal, Sea) This afternoon at 1:37½ o'clock we crossed the Equator; in a split second we swapped hemispheres and Autumn became Spring. Boni wrote a skit and it was presented over the PA—a script dealing with King Neptune and his Piscatorial Realm. Nobody seemed over impressed with our crossing—the card games under the canopy went on.

Strangely last night and tonight—as we steam through the heart of the torrid belt—the breeze has been cool and fresh. Tonight, from the Southeast, it came like a caress just at sundown as I went forward after toasting on the after deck for an hour after dinner. Strange too is the sudden darkness; there is no twilight, no softening of the day into night.

Belgrade, Brodie and I went into an argument today. I was called upon to present my philosophy of life—which I couldn't do, because my philosophy is too nebulous for me to put into concrete, defendable, words. I'm afraid I left them with the idea that I favor simplicity in living—the average things. Such is not the case at all, but, then, what are the "average things?" What is simplicity, or complexity, or average, or unorthodox? I wonder. I don't know, yet.

We spoke of our post war world. What kind of a country will we come back to? Will we be able to have a say in the reconstruction of our lives, or will "they" be reluctant to turn loose power? Belgrade foresees the possibility of civil war, or else the masses controlled by capital—"Think my way or starve." I don't think so: I have faith in people who ask only an even break in the fight to keep afloat and get ahead—who ask only that, but will fight for and die for it if ever were to be denied. Supposed they are denied—civil war? Perhaps, but who would deny those rights?

We can't possibly make the same old mistakes—again.

Friday, November 13. (Rickenbacker Rescued) The "Taffy" office is a savior—a sanctum for the few of us who stay there and pass judgment on the stream of characters who drop in and out through the day. I don't know what I would have done if it had not been for that little cubicle with the beautiful view of the sea.

The people, soldiers all now; but before that—what? Today we had three; but one was like a bolt of lightning.

Vito Burnetta, a second generation Italian from Brooklyn, came in to give us the names in the boxing tournament. He stayed to tell us the story of his life in the jargon of Canarsie—"hoid" and "thoid" and "moider."

Vito, who bears a faint resemblance to Benito Mussolini, "wasn't bad—just rowdy." He and his mob ran things their own way. Once in high school some kids from Flatbush got fresh with Vito's sister on the car coming home. Vito found out, and the kid making passes finished in the hospital with a fractured skull. Anybody wanting something from his kid sister saw Vito or one of the three bigger brothers first. Vito weighs 192; the old man is 6-3, and he's a bruiser.

Like the rest of the mob, Vito liked a good time. He used to do a little gambling and then he drifted into the numbers. Most of Vito's friends worked the numbers and it was legitimate. "You pay me two cents, I pay you two dollars if you win. Who's the loser there? Me." The guy who ran the racket was well known and everybody liked him. That is, everybody but Vito's older sister (she's a nurse in Ireland now) and she said the guy eyed her funny like. Well it was a tough mob and occasionally somebody got bumped off, but mostly the cops took their cut and the numbers paid off in cold cash and were protected in their winning because the orders were that the mob leave the winners strictly alone.

Then came the blow-up.

"Lucky" Luciano was indicted and unmasked as the head of the white slave syndicate, and a good friend of Vito's was rapped in the cleanup of Murder, Inc. Well, Vito's father—the families were old friends—put up bond for the boy and then the boy took a powder because he was afraid of what the mob would do to him if he appeared for trial. It was a desperate situation because Vito's old man would be ruined—he manufactured men's clothing—if he had to pay off that $10,000 bond. So Vito and the kid's brother found the kid and put it to him straight. "Hell, if you're guilty, that's the way it is: think of my mother—the ruin and the disgrace." The kid stood trial. He got the chair.

Vito got an $800 cut when the numbers racket broke up after Lucky got his. Vito didn't want the money then because he nor any of the rest of the mob knew that Lucky was mixed up in the vice stuff. But the $800 wasn't filthy money—it was the numbers money split up among the mob, and a lot of it went to the poor people. Lucky may have been a vice king but he used to be poor himself and he always helped the poor. There was one down-and-out family and they got $1200; they built a new home.

Vito was in the National Guard—he put in a year and a half at Fordham but a girl got knocked up and although he was cleared by the girl he decided to quit pre-med, although Coach Crowley wanted him to stay—and so he went to the Army in October, 1940. Since he is married and has two kids at 26, he got out last year. But he's glad he's in again and straightened out. Hell, one brother's in the Navy, and the other two are in the Army.

You wouldn't know Brooklyn now it's so quite, Vito says.

Saturday, November 14. It would seem that we're getting into that part of the South Pacific where there could be trouble. The Chaplain casually remarked tonight that "we're in dangerous waters now." We had two abandon-ship drills and Brodie says he understands we can expect them at any time of the day or night. Noticed for the first time today that we zig-zagged, but I think our changes in course were only convoy practice. If we are in a danger zone (this voyage has been like a pleasure cruise so far, except for the strictly enforced blackout restrictions), it certainly doesn't show on anybody on board. We had steak for supper, tough, and everybody was a damned sight more interested in that than in the war. Extra life preservers were placed in the companionways over the ship and some of them were promptly missing. The Sgt. Major raised hell. Card games go on exactly as they have since the first day out. I think if we were torpedoed some of the games wouldn't break until the order to abandon had been repeated. There is no tension whatsoever. We are due into the "first port" a week from tomorrow.

Boni had no usual news summary because of the electrical disturbances last night, but he managed to pick up a newscast from San Francisco and pass it on. When he flashed the break of Rickenbacker's rescue after three weeks on a raft, the boys all yelled. It was swell news. Everybody recalled his wife's stubborn disbelief that he had died. Whatta a woman.[13]

No work today. Too many interruptions.

Set 'em back another half hour tonight.

Sunday, November 15. I missed writing on this date and am catching up Monday night. What happened yesterday? I'm trying to remember. Every day is very much like the next. Eat, loaf, work perhaps, eat, sleep. Yesterday was calm. The sunset was beautiful—the first one I've noticed particularly—brilliant red, rimmed with gold and spread all over the sea. Everybody talked about it. We spent quite a lot of time idling along on a plate glass sea while the cruiser wet nursed one of the ships which dropped far behind, presumably because of engine trouble. For the first time noticed a real feeling of boredom; the monotony got a grip on me—that's why I didn't write last night. It seems others feel it too: heard of at least two fights.

Monday, November 16. Funny how you start off some days—today woke with the idea of getting something done and shook off the indifference which all of us have had since the last paper came out. We completed and ran off five stencils today. May do one more issue after the one tomorrow, if we have time. Everybody has evidenced the fact that the brass has worn off: even Belgrade's enthusiasm is all but gone. He concentrates more on his peculiar aptitude for converting conversational phrases into more or less humorous puns . . . . . i.e.— "what is a duck—now that's a fowl question." It's an affliction of his. Brodie's sketches printed surprisingly well, and he was amazed. Wiel brought in a half pint which we killed in two drinks each. Helluva nice guy, and regardless of whether his tales are true he's a remarkable character. Boni's newscast told of 30 Jap ships sunk or damaged in the Solomons.[14] I was impressed by the seriousness with which the boys receive the broadcasts. They drop everything to listen. We are supposed to be within 500 miles of Samoa today. Found the *Mademoiselle* issue today. The boys got a big kick out of it.

Tuesday, November 17. At 12:45 today the cruiser, the carrier and four transports left us and headed westward, apparently in the direction of New Caledonia and Australia, possibly the Solomons. Shortly afterward, the two remaining ships went off southeastward, apparently toward southern ports of New Zealand. We are left alone.[15] On the after deck we watched the six ships drop away over the rim of the sea and it was a little like seeing a friend of brief but intimate acquaintance go away. We felt we had lived much with the flat top and the others, and tonight the ocean seemed strangely vacant, even more vacant perhaps than it would had we never been in convoy at all. As we watched the moon play on the open water, I felt a little as a man does on the first night he goes to bed without his wife.

Before I was hardly awake this morning, Brodie told me that the convoy was to break up in the afternoon. Everybody aboard knew it—the radio operators from Scott had caught the blinker messages. Further intelligence from the same source is that we are to pick up plane escort for the rest of the trip in.

Spent most of the day on the after deck, read Hemingway's *Winner Take Nothing* and experienced my first sunburn in almost a year. I don't know how far south we are, but the sun is fierce; tonight the breeze was cool. The combination of sun and wind is giving me a wonderful salt-air tan. I love it.

Printed and distributed the "Taffy" and Brodie was congratulated all 'round for his sketches. For a mimeograph outlay they were actually amazing. We decided to do one more issue in a hurry, and quit.[16]

Had a wonderful meal tonight—roast beef and potatoes. Also an argument between Chaplain Sloss and Belgrade on religious beliefs and concepts, ending in a wild discussion of the differences between psychological and mental influences. The old class-room brawl; always the same.

Belgrade makes a good agnostic. He says he'll believe anything proven to him. He doesn't argue against religion; he merely asks to be shown. He has a sharp and penetrating mind—certainly nobody's fool, but he amuses me some-

times by slipping back into his lecture course technique. Occasionally I don't
listen to what he's saying, but become acutely aware of how he's saying it. He is
the college prof, coaching the debate team.

Something is going on here. I find myself doing the very thing I despise
in other people—spouting too much about what *I* think, about what *I* was
doing then, about how *we* did it at Jackson, about what *we* did in New York. I
find myself fighting to come up with something that tops whatever the person
talking just described. How it is, I wonder, that I do these things when they are
what infuriate me in other people.

I held sway tonight for fully 45 minutes on Bob Neville. It was shear
monologue, and although Bob to me is one in a million and the boys seemed
impressed, I don't think the discourse was quite justifiable. But it uncovered
one thing—that Belgrade knew Merle Miller quite well in Iowa. Belgrade and
I compete for the floor in the office—we are both egoists.[17]

In that respect, Brodie doesn't help me curb myself much. He was in
favor of my mustache—strictly a self-satisfying venture—and he deplored my
shaving it off. He draws attention to things I do, seems interested in my views
on things. The latter is purely a hobby on his part, but I am used to such
attention only from Helen. Brodie is a keen and very accurate observer. He is
well aware that I am conscious one way or the other of his study of me, and
feeds me here and there with remarks drawn from whatever mental notes he is
making. He has impressed me several times with his extreme sensitivity, and at
the same time he is prone to complicate things in which, until he spoke, I
found no complexity. He has a passion for drawing out whatever is in your
mind, comparing ideas and testing them. He can be acutely candid, and often
is; about himself or anybody else. He's no simple character, Brodie.

Wednesday, November 18. Brodie ran into someone else he knew today—
or vice versa, as it was—a fellow named Thompson who runs the PX. He
didn't know Brodie, but knew his stuff. Brodie and I were invited up to his
quarters tonight for a couple of drinks in a room that was so thick with smoke
that finally neither of us could keep our eyes open. Thompson introduced us to
the little steward, Thomson, an Australian who looks like Popeye with Gable's
ears. Between the two they told us a good deal about Australian ways of life,
which didn't help much: they did show us Australian money and tried to teach
us how to handle it. I found that a shilling is a bob and a few other things, too;
but I am reserving a day after we land to learn rates of exchange and the values
of notes and coins. Last night I was more interested in the little Australian who
took this run, he said, "for a nice, quiet cruise." He went along when the
Marines landed in the Solomons. He has been "over the side three times in this
war, an' it ain't so bad if there's someone there to fish you out of the bloody
water." Beyond that I couldn't get much out of him.

Boni passed along a joke he heard from an officer at blackout boat drill: The bride and groom registered at the hotel and the groom said to the clerk, "We're newly weds, y'know." The clerk smiled and asked, "Then wouldn't you prefer our bridal suite?" The groom turned to his wife, who had been standing off and thinking thoughts of her own. "Bridal suite?" he asked her.

"Oh no, dear," she told him, "I'll just hold onto your ears until I get on to it."

We cross the Date Line tonight, so tomorrow is Friday. We sighted a fishing boat today. I saw only sails.

Beautiful sunset. I wrote Helen by V-mail.

Friday, November 20. You can feel it in the air—the awareness that we're almost there. Everybody writes letters and argues whether you print or write addresses. Nobody knows. We can get two V-mail blanks each at the library. Chances are none of the letters we write will ever get home, because they can't be posted until we land and the confusion then will probably be terrific. I understand everybody disembarks and cargo is unloaded for units at the "first port" and then reloading and re-embarkation begins for the outfits that go on. We expect to be in at least by Sunday, but heard no "official" confirmation today. We were supposed to pick up our plane escort sometime today, but the weather was all the way down and they didn't show. I was waked this morning by the Dutchman explaining that all hands were to be at general quarters—off the decks—when the planes were sighted and to remain off until identification had been established. These people take no chances. Alone like this we have been weaving all day long, and an albatross has been on our tail. Beautiful flyer, that bird. Two whales, male and female, passed us but I missed them. We see more and more gulls.

I found myself tonight almost regretting that this must end. It's been so damned much fun—I feel like a kid playing war and knowing all the time it was just in fun. Sitting in the office tonight, watching Bill type "Hasta la Vista" and then "30" at the end of his round up for us, I was overcome by the idea that everybody in the world is good and fair and pleasant—and how I wish it were really so and not just a poignant thought brought on by a brilliant sunset and a recording of "I Love You Truly" and the memory of a grand guy who always said "Hasta la Vista" when he left the tent at night a year ago on maneuvers. It takes only a second for a thought like that to pass through your mind and be gone, leaving you grinning at yourself and wondering when you'll be Queen of the May.

We were gypped out of a day of our lives last night—this should be Thursday. O well, we can pick it up on the way home. Turn 'em back a half hour tonight.

Saturday, November 21. Sighted a school of whales just before sundown, and a Dutchman on the bridge shouted over the PA that "they're big ones." We zigzagged in their direction but never got close enough to get any idea of their real size. The Dutch have been nice about that sort of thing—once before they told us of a school of porpoise off the port bow.

Due into port tomorrow.

Sunday, November 22. I am writing now as we move slowly in to dock at Auckland. We have been watching the shore since early morning—a lot like California's. The PA is playing marches and everybody's topside, leaning on the rail and waving to people in the tiny sailboats which float by us in the harbor. Auckland from the sea seems very nice. The weather is good, but thunderheads threaten in the distance—but nothing could really mar this entrance. It is almost 4:00. I am not in the least excited . . . . . I'm in a hurry to set down these impressions and square away for landing if we actually are to go ashore today. We don't know yet. Impressions? Yes, possibly a relief that the trip is over, although I'm certainly not crazy for the sight of land. I've enjoyed all this. More immediately concerning is who is the Commanding General, USAFISPA, and where the hell we'll find him—and then what? I haven't started the goodbyes yet . . . . . won't until the last minute. The guys have all been swell.

We have just docked. It was pretty wild.

An Australian band on the wharf played us in, starting with a march and following it with "Beer Barrel Polka" . . . . . everybody sang with them on that, and on the next one "Amopola." Then some more marches as we jocked in (with a tug) alongside. A pleasure craft cruised by with girls in bathing suits. Everybody went wild. On shore are a bunch of U.S. and Australian officers, Army & Navy, and at least one Bobby who looks like something out of Punch. In the middle of the music and yelling, the PA droned "Last call for chow . . . . . this is the last call for chow." Somebody yelled back, "throw the stuff overboard." Somebody else, as a parting shot to the PA and its function aboard, monotoned, "Attention, 20mm . . . . . Attention, 20mm . . . . . Unload and cover."

Men at the rail, as soon as we were within earshot, shot questions to the sailors on shore. First question they asked concerned whiskey; second, women—or maybe it was the other way. I missed the reply on the women, but I gathered whiskey just couldn't be got.

The band played a number which was either the "Star Spangled Banner" or "God Save the King." If it was our anthem, they added some new twists I've never heard before: we saluted, regardless.

We have arrived, 1700 of us, after crossing 6,124 miles of Pacific Ocean. The time is 4:35.

Tonight there is a full moon and the harbor is a pool of light: the New

Zealanders apparently think little of blackout restrictions on the waterfront. Perhaps it is an illusion of brightness after the black nights at sea. Auckland in the moonlight looks even better than in the afternoon sun—soft and mountain-rimmed and self-contained. War seems a million miles away.

We eat at 5:30 a.m. tomorrow and debark.

This is our last night on the canvas boards in the *Tjisadane's* hold . . . . . not such a bad place as it seemed 21 days ago.

Monday, November 23. Brodie and I debarked in the middle of a madhouse. We were given a truck and instructions to report to Victoria Park. A Lt. McCain there told us to see the Special Services officer at the Dilworth Building. He took us to see the Chief of Staff, as tough an old bastard as ever wore an eagle. He shifted us to G-2, and from there we went to the Exec Officer, Col. Skates. He sent us back to Victoria where we were told not to unpack—that we were leaving. We got bunks in one of the 4-men hutments . . . . . monuments of comfort after the *Tjisadane*.

Our hut-mates were two regular army crewmen on B-17s, back to this "Paradise of the Pacific" for a ten day rest after 11 months of combat. They took us to town and bought us drinks at the Royal Hotel bar. There we ran into Frank McCarthy, UP correspondent, and Jack Dowling of the *Chicago Sun*. They are just back from Guadalcanal.

After a couple of shots, we kept our appointment with Commander Gifford, Naval PRO. His yeoman spoke for him—we can't get accredited here, must go on to Poppy and get credentials from Lieut. Commander Gene Markey.[18] We tried to get clearances for a cable to the office, but couldn't. Censorship wouldn't permit it, the telegraph people said, but Mac said that had been lifted. Our only out is to send a story which I will tomorrow. I couldn't write my name now. Too hectic.

Went back to the Royal. Jack and Mac bought us more drinks and we had dinner with them and some dates they procured for us. Brodie went out to a dance hall and I took mine home. I had a terrific headache, and didn't feel like fooling. It was a wild day.

I've been in a daze since we landed. I just can't absorb this all at once. It's fantastic—like something out of a movie or Hemingway.

Everybody here is crazy about Auckland. They refer to it as the last outpost of civilization, and a wonderful town to come back to. The women, they say, are easy and from what I saw in the lounge of the Royal, it is so. Gin is plentiful, some Scotch and wine and beer.

But the people we've seen are the most amazing. In the Royal: A staff sergeant with a wild eye, a punchy expression which couldn't have been natural or intoxicated, ate lunch with us. He had been "up", he was going back. I'm trying to think of something he said: he didn't say much of anything. Maybe that's why I remember the look in his eyes.

A master sergeant, one of our hut-mates, explaining that the Japs have a neat trick of wiring their gear, so that when the dead are searched a grenade explodes. He advised that Jap prisoners be made to search them—if there are any prisoners.

A staff sergeant of Marines, very drunk, who insisted on joining our party in the lounge. I have never seen a man with that little regard for convention. Nobody would say much to him except Mac, who very bluntly told him to stay out. The Marine did—for a couple of minutes, and then back again. We didn't know what to say: the guy was just back from "up north." He had a picture which he handed around, telling us it was his wife whom he hadn't seen in over a year. We looked again. It was a snapshot of Betty Grable.

A drunk New Zealander who wandered over to our table, bellowed something, shook hands all around, and wandered off.

The group of young Air Corps officers and man who moved in on four girls, laughed a little while and then moved out with them. One man had a hand in a cast.

The women in uniform, the little waiter who does "anything just for you, Mr. McCarthy," the hodgepodge of uniforms on the street—practically none of them New Zealand. The ads in the *Herald*, on the front page, "in memoriam, in memory of so-and-so, beloved husband and father, killed in action Nov. 23, 1941, in Libya."

Auckland is the backlog of the war. The streets are jammed with men who have seen this war, and now want to see some peace. They live high, wide and handsome while they can.

Tuesday, November 24. Perhaps it would be well to start at the beginning.

At nine o'clock this morning we woke up. Last night we had drunk, in this order: gin, beer, Scotch, double gin, sauterne, Scotch, cherry brandy, double gin. We woke at nine. Outside, men had barracks bags packed and on the ground. I went seeking information. The lieutenant wanted to know "why the hell you didn't stand reveille? Don't you know we have reveille around here?" "No, sir." "Well, if you'd stood reveille, you'd know what to do—get your A bag and fall in here." "Yes, sir"—"sir, what about the other bags and supplies?" "Name of God! Put 'em over there!" "Yes, sir." Very unpleasant guy, the lieutenant, when he's ruffled.

Neither Brodie nor I had unpacked, except blankets and toilet articles, so we jammed them in, put one bag on the "B" pile and took the other with supplies. We loaded them and marched in column to the ship, reclaimed our bags and loaded. That was about noon: we had approximately 24 hours in New Zealand. Our orders read, "upon arrival at Auckland, you will report to the

Commanding General, USAFISPA (pronounced "usa-fis-pa"). The CG isn't here. We are going to him. What the office said *might* happen, *has* happened. We arrived right in the middle of it.

We are aboard the *U.S.S. Tryon*, a troop transport going "up" and a hospital ship coming back. It is immeasurably cleaner than the *Tjisadane*, much bigger, and with a navy crew.[19]

Incidentally, in the wild scramble to get our stuff together and ourselves aboard, I left our orders laying in the hut. They are important, but not so vital since this outfit has copies and our records. Most needed is that letter from Knox authorizing us, and my warrant and right to cable collect. But now I don't care. I'm past giving a damn. I carried that folder 10,000 miles and I think that's far enough. The hell with it. I may get it back since the lieutenant sent a man after it, but if he can't find it then it's just gone. I can't leave the ship.[20]

I have to write according to the way I feel at the moment, and right now I'm purring like a kitten. I've just had a hot shower—the first, honest-to-God bath since S.F.—and I feel like a human being. Then too, I took advantage of the latrine situation to wash socks, underwear and hand kerchiefs that have accumulated in the barracks bag I happened to bring aboard. On top of that, we can smoke in quarters and tea is just in the next compartment. This is a new ship and is clean as a pin.

But not to get too happy:

From every human I've talked to, I've heard that our destination is the ass hole of the Pacific. I've heard there's nothing there, that the chances of getting anything out are practically nil—all kinds of bad news. Will just have to wait and see. We heard some pretty terrible things about New Zealand, too. Of course this will be worse, but then Auckland is a pretty modern little city—a great deal like a Southern town, perhaps a Texas town—but there is really nothing in the states quite comparable to it. It has a character all its own, although being here isn't at all like being "abroad." The people, exactly like anybody else, except for their speech and the cut of their clothes. We really weren't around long enough to notice any marked difference—but of course there is. One thing we noticed that we weren't warned about is that in ordering from a menu, you order one thing at a time and when it is served you order the next thing on the list. Seems a little silly. Brodie says the dance hall he went to is just like an American whore house—with the dance floor downstairs and private rooms upstairs. Traffic on the left and wheels on the wrong side of American-built cars are strange. The cigarettes are awful, the beer weak. The girls we were with were "not bums," and they were no beauties either. They weren't groomed to my taste. But they had the same old line of chatter which was in no way enhanced by accent; they were well up on American films— *Reap the Wild Wind* is on now. In the lounge, U.S. music played on a sort of musazk arrangement—mostly standard stuff like "Begin the Beguine" and "Indian Love Call."

Tuesday (continued). But of all the people and things we've seen, McCarthy and Dowling are top characters. Mac is dark, with crisp black hair and circles under big eyes. Jack—son of Eddie Dowling—is smaller, with a baby face, tow-headed, but with an air about him that suggests he can take care of himself. Both men show the strain they've been under . . . . . I can't explain exactly how, but perhaps in the way they speak to men they met up there, and in the way Jack drinks at the bar and looks down at his drink most of the time. Both of them are going back with us aboard ship.[21]

Mac told me of the various places in the Pacific, using code names or cities in his conversation so that I had to ask often where it was he meant. It might have been romantic were it not that I'll be seeing these spots myself under conditions which hardly appear romantic at this distance.

Both of them were here for some months before they went up. They were on Guadalcanal six weeks, I believe. Some of the things they told us sounded pretty bad, and I imagine are actually worse than they described them. This is going to be no picnic.

Mac drew me a diagram of the Solomons situation and explained how and why things are as they are. I understand a lot I didn't before. While he was talking, a soldier came by and said to Brodie, "You can believe what these guys tell you. They were there with us, and they know." I consider that as high a tribute as a man in this racket can get.

I suggested that their offices should give them a break and let them go home for awhile. Jack replied a little insincerely, I thought, "Who the hell wants to go home?" Mac said he'd like to go back just long enough to wake people up to the fact that this war is "big league stuff."

At dinner came the crack of the evening from Dowling. In an announcer's voice he boomed, "The cry up and down the Pacific—got a light, bud?"

Wednesday, November 25. It would seem that the chips are beginning to be shoved out on the table. We shoved off this morning—back by the same dreary shores we just passed on the way in, and the motors of this troop ship make the springs on which I'm writing vibrate constantly. We are moving into dangerous waters, although not so dangerous as those north of our destination. We're heading into something about which I have only the vaguest sort of conception. This is all virgin territory for me.

I find it hard to analyze my feelings. Yesterday I was pretty disgusted—one of those moods I suffer when a lot of petty grievances pile up. Today I've shaken that off—it's a bad thing to pucker up when everything does go just so. But to my reaction:

Just now a weird conversation took place. The boys were discussing our chances in this compartment if torpedoed. One said we were too high. "Hell, have you ever seen a ship torpedoed?" "Hell yes—two of 'em." "Well you ought to know it knocks a hole just about three feet above the water." "Yeah, but how about the concussion?" "Well hell, a three-inch AA shell will knock you out of your seat in a plane. One went off about 50 feet from us once and you should have seen that plane—went every which way."

I'm trying to realize just how green I am in this business—but I know I can't. I'll just have to wait and see.

The thing that impresses me is the calm way in which these boys discuss the action they've seen. Bob Hall, a G-2 staff sergeant, said this morning that it all depends on the man—that some take it lightly when they get back, and others are strained and morbid. I have found a certain attitude of fatalism, and in almost all cases a what-the-hell way of living ashore. Those boys don't give a damn for anything—why should they? You can catch that spirit in almost anything they do, the men who are going back.

Brodie is inclined to be optimistic—he's a steady sort of guy and I'm glad of it. I can at least hang onto him when things start piling up. Maybe we can lean on each other if we start banging against stone walls somewhere along the line.

Thursday, November 26. Thanksgiving Day! Didn't even realize it until church services were announced over the PA this morning. Brodie and I tried to attend, but the deck was so crowded we couldn't get close enough to hear the chaplain. That is the first time I've ever seen an Army church function crowd anybody out.

We had a big dinner—turkey, but no cranberry sauce. Last year we ate Thanksgiving Dinner under canvas on a rain soaked Carolina maneuver area. We were in the woods somewhere near nowhere, as I remember. This is my third Turkey Day in the Army; the first dinner was a country club affair with napkins and table cloth in the mess hall at Jackson.

Standing in line—which is worse if anything than on the *Tjisadane*—I saw a lieutenant shove a boy down the stairs. First time I've seen an officer lay a hand on a man in the Army. The boy, a corporal, seemed a little bit too taken back to say anything. A staff sergeant told another officer about it and he raised hell with the lieutenant. It was a trivial thing, but new to me. I don't know whether the shavetail is supposed to be tough or what. I'm going to watch him to see what happens as we go along. He's the same one who got on me about reveille the other morning. I think he's more bully than man: can't tell yet.

We had our first General Quarters last night during supper, but it was a false alarm. We didn't even stop eating, except to put on life belts.

A sailor told me yesterday he "hated the transport jobs," and I'm beginning to see why. It must be one thing to be on a warship, and quite another to play wet nurse to a lot of soldiers. Most of the crew are just kids—one told me it was a "shake-down" run for him. But boots or veterans, they'll knock you down on their way to battle stations.

Thank God our stay on this ship is short—there's nothing to do except eat and sleep. Brodie has been teaching me some card games—anybody with luck at cards as bad as mine should certainly be a helluva guy with the women.

There are infantry soldiers aboard, and I find the language of the infantry the same here as anywhere else. In a line outfit, things are pretty basic. The conversation ranges from women to liquor, back to women. Except for that—and how to get off details—nobody says an awful lot.

T'were ever thus.

Friday, November 27. At 3:30 this afternoon we inched past the brilliantly white lighthouse which marks the break in the coral reef girding the harbor of Noumea, New Caledonia. Noumea is a city of color from the bay, little as I had pictured it, but the spectacle was not the city. The bay itself held more attractions—jammed with ships. My first thought was that this would be a happy hunting ground for Jap bombers: another Pearl Harbor if they ever broke through. Here in the bay lay at anchor an aircraft carrier, a battleship, I don't know how many smaller warships and transports.[22] Just after dark we had another General Quarters. We heard all sorts of rumors after "secure" was sounded, but apparently a group of returning planes had come in unidentified. From the sea, New Caledonia is all mountains, lesser ones which rise from the water, and big ones which tower in the background, their tops with a helmet of clouds. Noumea is nestled among them, its bright colored buildings scattered on and between hills which look just as barren and as rugged as the foothills of the Rockies. The approach to the bay is the most beautiful I've seen, but I haven't seen much yet. On the ocean side of the reef the water is a deep blue; on the bay side it's a jade green. The line of demarkation is a lazy ruffle of white surf.

Finally located McCarthy and Dowling as we were coming in: they said they had been trying to find us since yesterday. Mac pulled his "rank" to crash the soda fountain line and set us up to ice cream sundaes—so we enjoyed the pleasures of a drug store cowboy and a soldier on a South Pacific cruise at the same time. Both guys are really wonderful to us—have been since two minutes after I barged in on them at the bar in the Royal.

As I write, the first sergeant is sitting on a head, bemoaning the trials of his job as nurse maid to some 600 guys in this outfit. He wants to go back to his old outfit in a mechanized battalion. He has his troubles.

There are a thousand things I could write—the AC boy who flew with Ronald Reagan in making *Rear Gunner*, and did the shooting for Burgess Meredith—the argument going on now about an Army baseball game played in 1928—the tales of Auckland women—but right now I give it up. I'm trying to figure out how to get around all the red tape that I'm expecting when we get ashore. Mac said today "they fight a phoney war here: get out as soon as you can." But will have to wait and see—no use borrowing trouble. We debark tomorrow. Hope we can get settled down for awhile—at least long enough to notify the office.

Saturday, November 28. Apparently we won't go ashore today, so I'll take this morning to set down some of the bull session chatter which has kept this compartment from becoming an air cooled chamber of boredom. Best of them all was related in the sincere North Dakota accent of a Pfc. who was evacuated from the Solomons with tonsillitis. He said the Marines there swore the palm trees were the property of the Palmolive Soap people, and that every tree destroyed in the fighting would cost the government ten bucks.[23]

This AC staff sergeant is the character of the compartment. A gunner, he fought over London, at Midway, over the Philippines and in the SPA. Somehow he managed to cram in a short hitch in California where he flew with the ships the Army loaned Hollywood for the picture with Reagan and Meredith. He has real respect for Reagan's flying—said "he'd turn you every way but loose up there."[24] He didn't think much of Meredith—called him a "dried up little sissy who wore packs over his eyes to 'keep the dust out'"—but he had several things to say about the women. He said on the last night on location, the movie people brought in dates and whiskey, and turned them loose. The Army went Hollywood.

Also in our group is a guy with one hitch in the Regulars—he wears no chevrons—who can turn a rifle "every way but loose." He explained there are 150-odd movements in the Queen Ann manual, and demonstrated a few of the fundamental ones with the same flashing and spinning motions as a drum major uses his baton. Said he picked it up in the Regulars back when there wasn't anything else to do.

Another man—a corporal—is on his way back after stopping machine gun bullets in the leg while on a B-17 mission over the upper Solomons. He's a gunner; says he's damn lucky he got hit—the rest of his crew got knocked down a couple of weeks ago. Still another guy is on his way back after having a piece of shrapnel split the top of his head on Guadalcanal.

An ex-newspaperman, now company clerk for this outfit's duty section, said he had seen no copies of the paper in New Zealand, but his outfit liked it in the States. The canteen manager in Auckland said they had received only one shipment of papers. A lieutenant told me he had seen none in New Zealand, but had up north. Our two AC men at Victoria said practically the same thing.

Practically everybody at least knows about the paper, however.

It's siesta hour in the compartment now, so perhaps there will be quiet enough in here for me to tell a story of tragedy in the Solomons.

It begins in the States where the 164th, a National Guard infantry outfit, had in it a big soldier who knew his stuff and had plenty of nerve in a fist fight. In the same outfit was a kid who did a lot of worrying about the war—he was a nervous type.

The 164th went overseas. Then they moved into the Solomons.

On the first night on Guadalcanal, the nervous kid was the calmest one of the bunch. The closer he got to war, the less it seemed to bother him. But with the big guy it worked the other way. In the dark, he thought he detected Japs crossing the river. He went wild, grabbed his BAR and ran back to where his corporal and this kid were sleeping. He swung the automatic around in a nervous frenzy: the kid all the time kept talking to him, trying to keep him from blowing his top. "Put that gun down—you know me—put it down—you know who we are—take it easy." The big guy was too far gone . . . . . his nerves had gone back on him in the dark with the Japs close around. He opened up with the BAR and the kid went down with a row of slugs across his chest. They sent the big guy back to be put under observation, but he persuaded the medics to let him rejoin the outfit next morning. The CO took him down to Regimental CP and said he wouldn't keep him in his company. They sent him back to the States. Maybe he'll make an instructor. He can handle weapons.[25]

-0-

We went ashore Sunday, November 29, just at dark. In the sage words of Dan Harrison: "If there is any way for a thing to be fucked up, the Army will find it. Sometimes they'll even fuck it up when you'd think it's impossible." We sat all day in the harbor and landed so late that we had to eat and pitch a squad tent in the dark.

Noumea harbor is picturesque and beautiful, like a Fitzgerald travelogue, although to military intents it isn't so hot. Our ride through the town left all of us grasping for words. It was like something out of this world . . . . . foreign and unreal, and yet too real—the people, the dirt, the houses. Here is a place ancient and modern at once. On top of a hill is a bastion with the tricolor floating over it: like a desert fortress in *Beau Geste*.[26] It is a city of color, both artistically and actually—bright flamboyants are all over. Javanese stand in doorways and stare. I haven't seen a woman—there are some females here, however.

Monday, November 30. (Battle of Lunga Pt.—3rd Solomons Sea)[27] It begins to look as if the fears I've had about our reception here were so much wasted worrying time. After our first day here, it looks almost too good to be true. We were ushered in to be interviewed by Col. Sherman, the G-2, and he gave us the promise of all the cooperation we could ask of any man. We hit a temporary snag this afternoon when we went to the AG to have our orders amended;

Captain Freeman, the PRO, took us over to see it through, but the thing was lodged on General Harmon's desk, and, as the captain said, "you don't hurry the general."[28] We had been scheduled to see Lt. Comdr. Markey for our Navy accreditation but the short-stop at the AG messed that up.

This place Noumea gets more fabulous every time we look at it. The G-2 offices are crowded into a building in town, so we were in and around the streets most of the day. We had "lunch"—a ham sandwich and passion fruit juice (whatever the hell that is) at a place rather obscurely titled the Snack Shop, presided over by a plump French woman with hazel eyes and well-groomed hair. The food wasn't too bad, and it was cheap. We visited a sort of general store affair, and then went to the New Caledonia version of a drug store, complete with a juke box. The "juke" was a record player behind the counter which operated in accordance with the sign reading: "Latest American Hits—Boogie Woogie, Praise the Lord and Pass the Ammunition . . . . . " and something else I don't remember. A French waitress took the orders of some soldiers who were afraid they hadn't made themselves understood. She replied "Me sorry." I wonder if she speaks only pidgin English. Almost as unusual to me as the native population—the Charleys with their hair dyed red, the Javanese, the ragged looking whites—are the Free French with their gaudy hats and barefoot black sentries. The New Caledonia native men—black as the ace of spades—are beautiful physical specimens. The women, those I have seen, are just specimens. One of the boys who has been here some time says they "get whiter every day." But regardless of everything, this is certainly a place of natural beauty. There is a beach a short distance from camp that is strictly from the travel folders. A Red Cross worker in the RC service club said YANK went over big. She called Noumea the "Paris of the Pacific." So this is Paris![29]

"Christmas Day
on Cactus"

Tuesday, December 1 Saw the PX officer for Poppy this morning and he gave us an idea of the troubles of circulation and distribution. Recommended air transportation for the paper if possible. Issues on sale now are September's. Back room space crowded with packages unopened pending sell out of earlier ones. Walking into that place is like going into a display room we might have ourselves. Copies strung all over the walls, posters up, and a huge sign on the counter plugging for us. You couldn't ask any more of the guy. The boys read it . . . . . admitting the fact it is virtually the only reading matter on the whole damned island. *Saturday Evening Post* is here, too, I'm sure. But I've seen more copies of *Yank* stuck in pockets here than anywhere else. I want to get up to Button and Roses and over to Fantan; it is supposed to have good distribution there too.

I can see here and now that we will want to get out of here on "junkets" as the Colonel calls it. In the first place, we are about to see our way clear to start moving here, in the second place, the office is going to want some stuff pretty soon, and in the third place—if we have to spend many more days like today in this place, I'm going to start tightening up. There is less to do here than any place I've ever been, and less to do it with. Or maybe I'm just griped because I tried my first cup of New Cal coffee and found it to be half coconut and half ether. Putrid stuff! But the cocoa is okay at the Snack Shop. I heard rumors of Pernod, somewhere.

Wrote Dad and Helen air mail today. Hope it gets to them in time for Christmas. That's all the present I can give them.[1]

Our orders, now thru the CG, now read "for special service" with G-2. We have the freedom of the Army in this area. Now for Navy accreditation, and we should be set. I expect to have to repay the people here with PRO

35

work to a certain extent, but it will be worth it as long as I can get exclusive stuff back to New York.

Went swimming at our beach this afternoon and watched a Pacific sunset right out of this world. I can see where this would be a wonderful spot for some guy with a persecution complex. He could get away from it all.

The guys don't yelp to go into town as they ordinarily would—why should they? On the streets everybody just walks around, occasionally stopping in one of the few shops still open. But there's little to buy. Sandwiches and drinks do the business.

Wednesday, December 2. Took the afternoon off and proceeded to get sunburned on the back—the second time I've little enough sense to stay out in the open in these parts. "Mad dogs and Morriss. . . . . "

Nothing new. Letter to Major Forsberg on circulation. Saw Walter Black, now a master, whom I'd known at IAC.[2] Same old "ham actor."

Thursday, December 3 Talked things over with Capt. Freeman today, and it appears that we are going to operate on a "give and take" basis, as he put it: we will get the authority of this office and all that goes with it in return for some PRO work on the side. I think it's a pretty fair situation, altho I will be involved more than Brodie. If I can be given the opportunity of getting around freely, I'm willing to do extra work for it—as long as the *Yank* stuff is exclusive. . . . . and I'll see to it that it will be. Ways and means of getting stuff back are still a little confused, but that can be worked out. As I understand it, we are not to put too much stress on the *Yank* correspondent angle, but are to tell people we are working for G-2. I'll see how that works first, because I don't particularly like the idea, regardless of its points in getting around.[3] We are to have credentials from this office which will help. We also went with the Capt. to see Lieut. Bassett[4] at Navy, and he said we would not need Navy accreditation—that a letter from USAFISPA would fix us up. It certainly doesn't make any difference to me as long as we can get what we want. I put in a bid for Cactus today, so we may be going up shortly. In any event, I don't think we'll be here much longer. I hope not—what a hole. Two MPs were wailing this morning that the Navy & Marines have all the beer they want, while the Army must drink this "butterfly brandy" which is strictly poison. Said it was bad for morale. I agree it's pretty tough to watch, as I did yesterday, while sailors inhaled case after case of beer and we dog faces just had to ignore them. But those boys supposedly were back from action, so I suppose that makes it different.

Sometimes I think a Grade A gripe is justified in the Army, and although there is no denying things could be immeasurably worse, my subject for today's treatment is based on principle. It has to do with the movies we attended for a time last night at an open air theatre on the side of a hill. I would certainly have liked to have had out here the man who picked the stuff for us. The first masterpiece of cinematic technique was a little number entitled *Brother Golfers*. It dealt with the Tunesa brothers—six of them—who play golf. In the film they played golf—18 holes of it—and the cameras followed them faithfully as they drove and putted and so on. The camera would get back 100 yards from the green (to get in the club house in the background) and the announcer would scream: "He's measuring the distance, he's a deliberate golfer and it looks like he's determined to win..... it's a 20 footer..... he missed!"You could see tiny forms moving in the distance as this was going on. Well, it wound up with a champagne party and everybody was happy. Every soldier in the place was disgusted and said so. The feature was an old moth eaten thing, *Mother Carey's Chickens*. Now Mother Carey and her chickens might have been all right for a public which some time back was being fed a "back to home sweet home" movement, but to several hundred soldiers the sight of the quiet family life in which the most exciting event was when the little kid fell face down in the dust, it was a little out of place. With all the pictures Hollywood turns out, it seems the big shots could do better than that. As one Marine said: "Who the hell wants to see chickens?" A horse-opera, Grade C, would have been a great deal better. But, out here, you can either take it or leave it alone. We left it alone.

-0-

We had good chow tonight, pork chops, but the talk was of some of the previous meals which weren't so good. One guy spoke up: "The guys on Corregidor ate horses." Everybody shut up.

-0-

Palla, the boy who was on Guadalcanal with Freeman,[5] knows someone by the name of Cole from Tennessee. Described him as heavy-set and with a brogue. I'm looking forward to seeing ceders again.

Friday, December 4. Met Ralph Morse, the *Life* photog who wanders around from task force to task force looking for trouble. He was in the third wave that hit the Solomons, got some beautiful action stuff as the beachhead was being established, went aboard the *Vincennes* with the stuff he'd shot—and had everything go to the bottom that night.[6]

Tried to find Dowling and McCarthy at the Pacific.[7] I certainly don't envy them their quarters.

Saw Lieut. Bassett and was told that we had to clear island stuff thru a Colonel Stead, G-2 of U.S.F. in New Cal. Asked him about Bob Montgomery, who is here. Am sitting on the Eddie Rickenbacker thing, but hope to clear something later on. Morse flew in with him, but can't say a word. Tough.

Did my first stuff last night—color—as a test on the local censorship. Capt. Freeman thinks it will clear, but I don't know. Brodie is working on illustrations.

Sunday, December 5. Went up to Tontouta air base with Palla and Robertson[8] to see what I could kick up. Ran smack into the first rain since we got here and into some feature stuff that is beautiful. The rain was a blessing because it kept us indoors where the bull was going strong. Here we were back in the hills in a spot about as remote as anything I've seen—and there was beer and brandy which the guys were mighty free with. I pulled the first drunk since we left the States . . . . . on two bottles of Australian beer and not too many sips of brandy. Palla and Robby went out last night, but I hit my bunk long before dark. Didn't want to get too far gone, and it's a good thing I had that much sense. Robby came in this morning (I'm writing Sunday) to report there was a certain Javanese woman. . . . .

At the field the weather was closed down and Gen. Harmon was coming in from Fantan in a B-17. We were in the operations room, where the rain on the tin walls and roof almost drowned out conversation, but believe me people really worry when a two-star is upstairs trying to get down. He made it alright. The Lt. Col. who was piloting him will probably be a Colonel tomorrow.

But let's shoot the breeze. . . . .

Joe Melton, a solid master sergeant with a GI haircut plus, lays under his mosquito bar and offers us beer from a sack under the table. There is no opener so he pulls back the slide of his .45 and flips off the caps. He's been in the Army 14 years and you learn tricks like that.

So we drink Joe's beer and listen to Joe talk while the rain drones on the tent outside. Joe has been on the Canal, but now he reclines in his underwear like some drawling Pasha; he laughs easily and we laugh with him, because he can tell things well.

About the night the Jap battleship shelled them . . . . .

"Well, sir, I was asleep when the fust un hit and just sort of instinctively I found myself out of my bunk on my hands n' knees. Thought it was an explosion of some kind—gasoline or something—but then here came four more. Hell, I knew t'weren't no explosion when the dirt from them fust ones started fallin' on the tent, but when the next four hit I just zzztt! into that foxhole. I ain't sayin' I was fust, but I'll be damned if I was last."

You have to hear or see Joe to appreciate him. He makes it sound like he was scared to death, but you can take one look at him and tell he'd been a helluva man to stop once he got started. . . . .

"This lieutenant come up to me on the beach and says 'Joe, I got a radio out back there—let's go fix it.' I looks at that jeep he's driving and says, 'How far back?' and he says, 'Oh, just a little piece back—come on, let's go fix it.' So I get in with him and we started up toward the front and pretty soon I hear this tat-tat-tat-tat off in the trees somewhere an' says, 'What's that?' and he says, 'Oh, that might be one of our machine guns' an' I says, 'Whatta you mean—it *might* be?' an' he says, 'What's the matter, you scared?' and I says 'Well I ain't sayin' I am, but I'll be God damned if I'm sayin' I ain't.' An' he says, 'Well, it ain't but a little further on' and just then tat-tat-tat-tat right up close and he says, 'That's one of ours,' and I says, 'I'm mighty proud it is' and then we get to the set. About that time I hear something go 'boom' and I look back an' there's two branches fallin' and dirt a-flyin'—them Jap bastards had put a mortar shell in there and this lieutenant wanting me to do a highly technical job under conditions like that. Well, sir, these boys were all standing around and they musta thought I was a miracle man, because I put my hand right on the trouble. Just luck—I started to shake them little resisters[9] to see if there was any loose connections and one of 'em came apart in my hand. Just burned up. So I patched it up and I said to the boys, 'Where's the Japs?' And they said 'right over there' and I looked and couldn't see nothing, so I says, 'let's go. . . . . '"

Joe had a Jap mess-kit and canteen on the table, and he gave us some Jap canteen checks.

"If the Japs didn't know before, they know now what the American Army's fighting for—it's souvenirs. Up there they'll shoot a Jap and he'll jump in the air and before he hits the ground they'll be all over him, frisking him for souvenirs. God-damnedest bunch of boys I ever saw. One time the Japs tried a push and we mowed down about 3,000 of 'em and them boys were all over 'em before the last shot was fired. One Marine was searching a dead Jap and started to roll him over and the Jap hit at him with a bayonet. I was with this other Marine one time and he pointed off in the trees an' said, 'Let's go way back there,' an' I said, 'What's back there?' an' he said, 'Japs' an' I said 'Live ones or dead ones?' an' he said, 'Well, some of 'em are dead.' An' I said 'Let's wait until they all die.'"

Palla prods Joe with questions about people they both met on the Canal and Joe tells stories about them as we listen. About the boy who, right in the middle of a bombing, speaks up and says to whoever's in the foxhole with him: "You know, right now I'd like to be just stretched out on the beach, taking it easy and talking to Dolores." Joe says, "Hell, I'd like to have been on the beach with Dolores and I don't even know Dolores." And he imitates the high squeaky voice of one soldier and the fast clipped accent of another as they lie in a hole listening to the Jap motors overhead: "Sounds like a four-motor bomber to me." (fast) "Now you know Goddam well that ain't no four-motor bomber!" (squeaky) "Hell it ain't." (fast) Joe comments dryly. "Hell, that kind of stuff gets on your nerves while you're a-listenin' to them sticks walking up on you."

But Joe and the boys here do everything they can for the men who fight. Joe got his share of souvenirs—a flag, rifles, bayonet, helmet, an officer's sword— and he gave them away, what he isn't going to send home. He gave Palla a rifle and Palla took it down to Noumea and sold it for $30, then gave the $30 to the liquor fund this outfit has for the men up there. It used to be they sent stuff up marked "Spare Parts" but the Marines caught onto that so now they have to do it some other way.

-0-

After we talked to Joe, we went over to a shack. There was Markel, who unscrewed the fuse of a live bomb before it had time to explode. There was Vaughn, who is up for the DFC. There was Dorsey who did something to a propeller that will save the government millions.[10] There was brandy.

Sunday, December 6. Joe brought out his sword—a beautiful thing—and a battle flag which is pure silk and inscribed with good luck messages by Jap soldiers. He also parted with three or four more bottles of beer—we have no right to drink them, but we shared around. And he gave us some more material. Joe's from Texas and he was on the Canal two months so he's a fountain of color and material. Palla gave me a tip which is worth something—that on the Canal people are too busy to fool with you much, but down here they can sit back and talk and take time to go over things which happened. Here, Palla insists, are the people who have seen it all and are willing to tell it—so what difference the background. My only point is that eye-witness stuff is better than second hand stuff, but there is such a wealth of material here—enlisted man's angle never before touched at all—that I can't just go off and say "Oh I can do better than this when I get there." Perhaps I can, but I doubt it; and why should I get caught with my pants down? Here enters a little trouble—I'd like to get all the feature material possible—just flood the office with it—but I'm under obligation to Capt. Freeman to turn in some stuff for him. I'm going to have a hard time deciding what I'll give the paper and what I'll give him. I don't want to ruffle feathers at either end. There must be a medium. My plan now is to do a story on souvenirs with pictures of Joe, do a story on Markel, another on Dorsey and another on Vaughn—all for *Yank*. What the hell does the Captain get?

-0-

This camp itself is something. It may or may not be typical in the islands—I don't know yet—but it is the one I hear the most about.

Here is the 67th Fighter Squadron,[11] nestled almost under a mountain which towers high in moisture-heavy clouds behind them. Pyramidal tents are pitched in a grove of white, mealy looking tree trunks, and the ground when it rains is trampled and rutted into a mire of coal-black mud. Some of the men live in shacks they built themselves—native looking structures put together with packing boxes and native material. The administration offices are soldier-built, but the pride of the Squadron is its day room built, the boys tell me, by the Chaplain single-handed. In the day room are seats & tables, a magazine rack, a phonograph and a GI radio set. It's cozy. The mess, with one open shack for the men and another for officers, is across a creek bed. Inside the tents, things are pretty nice. The boys have been here long enough to fix things up—tables, shelves, dressers, etc. At the entrance, pointing upward toward the tent & shack area is a stenciled sign reading "Used Beer Department." I'm not sure where the urinal trough is located, but it must be in that direction.

-0-

Joe told us of his woman at a secret air base. One night the Javanese family's house burnt down nearly and Joe collected clothes for the old man. Joe told him he'd be up at his house, a pretty good distance away, and so when he arrived the old man & his woman left, leaving the young Javanese girl alone with Joe. Joe said she didn't say a word—just pulled off her clothes. He said later he worked an arrangement with the old man so the girl would meet him twice a week at a bridge. Said he didn't have to walk so far then.

Monday, December 7. Well, it was a year ago today.

Since the Japs are a date-happy bunch and like to report big doings on special holiday occasions, we were on an alert last night and today. Same goes for tomorrow, I hear. This outfit doesn't pay too much attention to alerts—too many have come and gone before—but they had to turn out at 3:15 to get their ships on the line. Palla and Robby and I tried to follow up on the parachute jump the Marines were going to stage but the weather closed in and it rained like hell. We are rained out all the way around.

Was told an amazing story today by the boys who experienced it—13 of them are in this outfit out of the original 67 who left the States last November as volunteers in the AVG. They were 7 days out of Pearl Harbor this time a year ago, bound for the Philippines and then China. They turned off to Fiji and then Brisbane. In Australia they were inducted into the Army at the point of a gun—one of the damnedest things I've ever heard of. It's a long story and from their standpoint an ugly one, but in any event I'm going to try to get it back to the States. If what they say is true, and they all told it the same way, they've had the rawest deal ever dished out. I don't know how much I can say, but I'm going to say something.[12]

Tuesday, December 8. Am writing by flashlight and listening as San Francisco comes in by short wave. Heard a Jap broadcast by a guy with an English accent—he said Japan staged a helluva celebration. Then heard an American commentator say the U.S. didn't celebrate but launched 27 ships and kept on working.

Palla went back to Noumea this afternoon; suppose Robby and I'll go back tomorrow. Wanted to get something on Whizzer White, but I understand he's still with his raider outfit at the Canal. But we are just about finished at Tontouta as far as I can see.

Deliver me from letting these boys down on inaccurate stories. I've taken too much of a beating from them on some of the stuff we've already done, and I'm beginning to see just how ridiculous it is to a man to read crap about conditions he himself has experienced. If the office could spend a week in the mire and mosquitos with these fellows, there'd be no more cute off-the-cuff stuff about conditions in the field.

The boys aren't bitter, exactly, but they've been away from the States a long time—since March—and it makes them mad as hell—pisses them off, as they say—to swallow things that do not conform to their opinions on the war and things in general. They feel they're in a position to pass judgment on anything going on in the Pacific, and I guess if anybody has the right, they do.

I'm listening to a commentator quoting a communique from MacArthur's headquarters. Here they refer to him as "Dougout Doug."

Best crack of the day came from Markel, who was talking about the prop trouble which Dorsey fixed. "There was certainly something wrong with the thing. Hell, even the pilots could tell that."

Next best was about a Marine who prodded a reluctant Jap with a bayonet. Said the Jap: "Don't pull that shit on me—I'm from Ohio State myself."

-0-

This place is a hive of rumor manufacture. With everything centering on the hope of relief and going back home, something new makes the rounds every day. The boys take it with a grain of salt but they want to believe some of the things so badly it's pathetic. They use the usual jokes: "What's the latest? Don't know—haven't shit this morning." Sometimes they speak with disarming seriousness: "Were you out there when the DC-3 exploded this morning? No—guess it must have made quite a blow with all the HO it packs around. Yeah, littered the runway for quite a ways." Nobody even lifts an eyebrow.

-0-

Am listening to a Special Service rebroadcast of one of Fred Waring's programs. Homesick for—of all places—Jackson & Crockett.[13] But most of all for Helen. I can sweat out all this stuff until I have seen the things I came here to see all over the area—but after that I'm afraid I'm going to have a hard time convincing myself or anybody else that I wouldn't rather be in her arms than anywhere else in the world—war or no war. Right now I'm mighty curious about Cactus and some other places—but that will get old. Wrote her today; can't really say anything, damn it.

Tontouta and the 67th Fighter Squadron, AAF, is to me representative of the glory of war. The glory is in the States—there is no such thing here. The only things here are an airport circled by mountains which are bitches. The Squadron is camped at the foot of the biggest one. The good things are the quiet, the day room, the lights at night. The routine for the ground men—and everybody in a fighter outfit except the pilots are ground men—is a pretty dull business anywhere outside of actual combat. In combat the excitement comes in keeping alive and trying to do a job at the same time: it doesn't include shooting back. Here at Tontouta for men who have been here since March, everything is familiar. Packing boxes serve for houses in cases where men prefer anything solid around them to the canvas flimsiness of the pyramidals. Since I've been here it has rained almost constantly and that hasn't helped. And it wouldn't be the Army if everybody didn't gripe. They do—they bitch about everything a soldier can find wrong. But one thing the outfit can thank the stars for is the 1st Sgt., Bill Hereford. Bill can handle things, and does. I haven't heard anybody complain there, nor about the Chaplain—Smith of Smith's Corner, Ky, or some such place. The day room is nice—damn nice considering—but it has its limits. If a man is content to spend day after day reading the same magazines, listening to the same records, passing baseball, playing ping pong, writing letters and sleeping, this is the spot. For anybody else, I wouldn't recommend it. As it is, it is better than Noumea, or at least some phases of Noumea. Sometimes there are amateur shows and an occasional movie—the whole sector turns out for that, I hear. Town—Noumea, that is, is 35 miles away. Strangely enough we can get nothing to drink in town but the boys here have a drag with a Frenchman nearby and he can get them Australian beer and brandy that is good. But that is only rarely, and in no great quantity. If there is a woman even a horny nigger would touch in the whole damn sector, I haven't seen her; but I haven't been around. Nobody here discusses local stuff and that's a pretty sure sign there isn't any here. I have heard some terrible stories about native and local concoctions—Aqua Velva, Andy De Gaulle with opium in it, butterfly brandy with kerosine content, etc. If anybody can show me anything glamorous or glorious about this, I'll try to be convinced. When I get back to the States maybe I can make somebody believe it's "all very romantic," but I'll have to be an awful heel to even make the attempt. Sherman knew his stuff. And this isn't even war—perhaps it would be better if it was. Some think so.

Wednesday, December 9. Back to Noumea to run smack into a situation which almost scares me. I don't have the details yet, but there's something in the wind and I'm afraid it means the shutting off of things which made this setup as good as we could get. If it does I can attribute it to my own big mouth and to human nature—I remember telling Capt. Freeman how Neville was lifted from the staff by Eisenhower and it might be that I put a bee in his bonnet—a bee that will sting hell out of me.[14] There has been some sort of change here and I don't yet know what the score is, but if these people think I traveled 10,000 miles to get a screwing they're crazy. Here's where I gird for battle.

Thursday, December 10. The plot thickens.

Friday, December 11. Well, it wasn't as bad as it might have been. All of Brodie's stuff goes to the BPR in Washington with the stipulation that that marked for *Yank* will be forwarded to N.Y.; and that the stuff he does for Freeman will carry the credit line: by Howard Brodie, *Yank* staff artist. Drawn for PRO USAFISPA. My stuff goes direct to Spence.

Funny thing how it's worked out. Could be much worse. I wrote Spence how it is.[15]

Did four stories—Markel, Dorsey, Grey, and Chaplain Smith—for PRO and four others for us.[16]

Saturday, December 12. Took our stuff—Brodie's sketches for the Noumea color stuff—to be cleared for *Yank* thru Col. Stead, G-2 1st Island Command. Stead wanted to have the sketches photographed and sent by his bunch to Washington. I said no. Told him we had copyright. He said, "Sergeant, the War Dept. is supreme!" I got mad but got out of his sight before I popped off. We got Capt. Freeman to get him off our necks. The trouble with the Army is it isn't fucked up enough—somebody is always trying to go 'em one better.

Sunday, December 13. Went out to the fighter strip on the beach with Palla & Robby to get shots of a P-39 strafing. A Lieut. Lynch did the business at about 425 mph. Later on, a Lieut. Hansen went up and did the same thing—and the Colonel grounded him.[17] Palla & Robby covered him by trying to take a couple of extra shots and say that Hansen was strafing and doing slow rolls for publicity. I don't know whether Col. McNeese will swallow it or not. Markel and some of the boys—they moved down from Tontouta the day after we came back—had two quarts of "Andy De Gaulle"—anisette—and some Noumea beer. They pulled one for the book in cooling that stuff—put it in a bucket of 100 octane gasoline—and it worked. The Andy wasn't too terrible mixed with water; tastes like licorice. The beer was pretty weak. Markel and a boy named Red got in a fight—the screwiest piece of foolishness I ever saw—and Red literally knocked Markel on his ass. Markel had one terrible right eye. It really wasn't either's fault—just a little misunderstanding brought on by Markel's being 2/3 drunk.

But the day's hot business was this: before Lynch went up on his flight he was talking to a couple of other pilots. One of them I knew I'd seen before so I asked him if he was from Tennessee. He said yes, so I asked if from Johnson City. He was, so I shook hands with Bill Hart, now a 1st Lieutenant and a P-39 pilot, whom I haven't seen since Teacher's College days.[18] Bill said his outfit hasn't been in action yet, altho he's been over here 10 or 11 months; he's been in Australia most of the time. He saw Robert Lee Davis down there while Rob was still in a bomb outfit, but doesn't know how he finally ended up. He said he merely heard he'd gone down.[19] I can say Bill has changed one helluva lot since I last saw him. He used to be a great kidder at school, but now he refers to his position as "shit for the birds." He says they've all been yelling for action—no dice.

Monday, November 14—December rather. Today things began to look like something—even with a hangover. We were issued orders to visit stations at seven different points in the islands—Efate, Santo, Guadalcanal, Fiji, Bora, Tonga—and Auckland. We get $6.00 per diem and there's no limit on the time. Looks like we're set for a junket that will really be something. We plan to go to Button for four or five days and then on to the Canal. It won't be long now.

Funny situation tonight. Major Shope[20] found out I have no typewriter, and almost simultaneously found out the G-2 at Button has no typewriter—their whole office equipment was sunk on board the *Coolidge*.[21] So Shope gave me the only available machine—a portable—saying he was "taking care of his men." Well, I gave it to Lt. Cohen—the Asst. G-2 who is here now pleading for stuff—but Shope doesn't know it. I signed for it and "when I take it with me" to the Canal it becomes expendable so when I come back without it I won't have to pay for it. Cohen will actually take it back with him to Button. I figure the winning of the war is more important than my writing about it—but I'm not being noble entirely. I also figure that to have a G-2 at Button on my side is as important as anything else—and I can always borrow a typewriter for a little while someplace.[22]

Got my first letter from the States today—from Sgt. Al Hine 33072447, DEML Detch., Spec. Serv. Div. APO 6823 NYC. It was mailed November 15 from Miami Springs, Fla., cleared San Francisco November 18. Al must be in England now, or in North Africa.[23] Anyway, it's mighty good time: would like to hear from Helen before we leave, but guess that won't happen because she didn't know my address. Dammitt.

Finally got my stuff off to the office—four stories: B-17 crackup, color sketch, Melton's bull and the alert—all in one package. Hope it gets there.[24]

We leave for Tontouta & then Button tomorrow at 0800.

Tuesday, November 15—December it is. Tontouta again—and rain again. We leave for Button Wednesday at 1300.

The story of the war is being told by men who fight it; chapter after chapter rolls out in the casual, self-effacing jargon of shit sessions such as the one tonight in the transient barracks. Men back from weeks and months of combat sit on bunks and slap mosquitos and retell their tales of action—stories which bring war so close and yet wrap it in a mist of unreality. They talk of death and destruction as if these things were disconnected sidelights of something more important: furloughs to New Zealand, swimming holes, beer, malaria mosquitos. More often than not the things they did or the things done to them are buried in their appraisal of their own reaction—but always they speak with nonchalance of fear: nonchalance and humor, yes, but they never evade the presence of it, nor the awful awareness of it.

Tonight for instance:

The B-17 gunner with the tiny black mustache grinned boyishly and talked of the ack-ack he had known: "you can talk about all that bravery and crap but believe me I chewed my fingers the first time they opened up on us. Fact is, I think I had my whole hand in my mouth once. Believe I'll take the Zeros to ack-ack. With them you've got something to do, but with AA you just have to sit there and sweat it out. It'd be better if you just had a magazine to read or something. There's a hell of a lot of boredom up there, but there's also some concentrated excitement."

Another B-17 man—a tail gunner with whiskers and goatee—didn't have too much to say, but what he said was with quiet vigor. They talked of enemy opposition: "Jap naval AA is a helluva lot worse than their ground stuff. When you go over ships they throw everything at you but the decks. We don't bother with their ground stuff. Zeros? We can keep 'em off of us. They're getting so they don't jump us unless there's a bunch of them; if there's just a few they usually don't bother us. The fighters keep 'em off, or if they come in we get to work on 'em. But they're good."

They bulled about dishing it out:

"Remember that battlewagon we hit? Three right across its ass—four distinct explosions————" and then it was Wednesday. . . . . .

Espiritu Santo. From Tontouta to Button in 3:15, or maybe it was 3:00 flat. It looks good. Sounds better. Nothing here but "the implements of war." That's enough, for the time. Saw Major Curran, G-3, Capt. Fuller, G-2, and Gen. Rose, CG. All swell guys—the Major is okay.[25]

Thursday, December 17. From the general's kitchen a few yards away, I hear the sergeant telling a native boy: "We make um little fellow cake." He meant hamburger.

Well, that's part of Santo.

The Army is part, the Navy, the Marines—and the natives. There are a number of them here, not so big or so muscular as the New Cal natives, but every bit as black. They were recruited from surrounding islands; from the plantations come many of them, already contracted. They work for a shilling a day.

The flora and fauna here is like nothing I've seen. It looks like the first pictures of Guadalcanal. The island command headquarters is in a grove of coconut palms, and everywhere are a species of tropical tree whose trunk twists into the ground like the flying buttresses of a cathedral. Vines writhe from their tops to the ground.

There isn't much else to Button. No town at all, no real action except with the bombers. Even they aren't what they were—everything has moved up. We seem always to be met with: "If you'd been here a couple of months ago. . . . ."

We are disappointed in what we saw today, primarily because we saw nothing that really hit us in the face. Perhaps we didn't look far enough. At our present location, quartered snugly in navy-built quonset huts, we can't see a damn thing—we are planning to move in with the 11th Bomb[26] in order to get the idea of what's going on. We've got to do something.

Friday, December 18. Today we did a couple of things, neither of which amounted to very much. In the morning we saw the wounded Jap prisoners and in the afternoon we went with the Navy on evening patrol.

The prisoners gave me my first close up of the Jap. I didn't feel any hatred, because they have never torn into me personally with shrapnel or killed a friend before my eyes. I looked at them as I would animals in a zoo—with a sort of detached interest and a somewhat indifferent curiosity. They were wounded and one made a show of pain: I felt no compassion—I thought rather that he was putting on. Perhaps he wasn't. We gave one a cigarette: another handed me an ashtray when my own butt burned low. The doctor says they're being treated "like human beings," which is obvious: they get the same attention our men get—plus armed guards. The sentries serve a dual purpose; the doc says some psych cases back from the Canal have presented a problem: they want to finish the Japs off. Battle psychology doesn't end when the last shot is fired. The Japs look subdued, the kind of look anybody has when they're bored with being in bed and waiting to get well. They're dead pans—one particularly, but before we left they had all laughed and cracked jokes and tried to help the doctor with his Japanese lesson. They're lucky bastards—lucky because they're not dead, and lucky they're not still fighting this war. They eat well, get regular medical attention and lie on GI cots in a quonset hut that's snug and dry. All the fight's gone.

As we were leaving, some casualties from the Canal were coming in. One boy had a stained bandage on his shoulder. It was the first blood I've seen in this war—after almost 2½ years as a soldier.

Our evening patrol in a Navy Kingfisher was a complete bust.

Three hours to see the sea. At least it was beautiful from the air—the coral and the surf, the emerald and the blue. Picture book stuff until you remember the flies.

Saturday, December 19. Nothing—just nothing.

Two stories, one for Freemen on Small Bong, the mess boy, and one for *Yank* on the Japs. The Jap story comes under the heading of "fascinated by the sound of own words dept."[27]

Sunday, December 20. The Sunday before Christmas.

Yuletide in the Pacific war zone, where B-17s roar up to seek the enemy and on the rich sodden floor of the jungle men try to seek peace.

Christmas carols in the tropics. The band in fatigue clothes standing in mud. Where are the old spit and polish days. Stand in the mud and hear the music.

"Joy to the world, the Lord is come
let Earth receive her King. . . . . "

The words come back slowly, but the music is easy to remember. A carol in the jungle, where the Chaplain preaches peace and the men sweat to win a war. It sends shivers up your spine—the old familiar carols amid the mud and vines and trees. The band plays on.

"O come all ye faithful, joyful and triumphant
O come ye, O come ye to Bethlehem. . . . . "

Where is Bethlehem? Bethlehem of Judea—in the Middle East. Is war there too? It's a long way from the palm-woven shacks and the moisture of the islands to the arid plains of Palestine. But a man's faith stretches further than that. A man can stand in the mud and see Judea when the music plays. A man can believe in peace in the midst of war.

"Silent Night, Holy Night,
All is calm, all is bright. . . . . "

It rained all night last night. The rain came down, warm and steady and soothingly. A nice night to sleep.

"Round yon virgin Mother and Child
Holy Infant as tender and mild
Sleep in heav'nly peace. . . . . "

This morning the sun beats down through the trees; here and there things begin to steam. It gets hot in the jungle quickly—and the sweat comes and won't go away. Sunday in the tropics and carols just before Christmas. Time out and then work goes on. Win the war. . . . .

"Sleep in heav'nly peace."

Monday, December 21. My first wedding anniversary—and a helluva place to be celebrating it, 10,000 miles from Helen. I wrote her and tried to sound nonchalant and all, but I didn't feel exactly the way I wrote. I have found myself, for the first time in my life, struggling to write home because I'm afraid to say what I think—the loneliness I feel—because it would upset her. I wonder if I am a convincing liar.

The occasion today was marked by a toast from the boys in the general's mess—a toast of cherry brandy, and only two swallows apiece of that. It was the property of Sgt. G. Maynard, who had been saving it to celebrate his own anniversary yesterday. George has been married a year and away from his wife for 11 months. What a mess.

-0-

One thing I forgot to mention that happened Friday. We had donned our U.S. collar insignia and gone off to be war correspondents in the grand manner. It worked all right—too well, in fact. Every enlisted man we saw "sirred" us—us, two half-ass sergeants. We took the damned things off. The whole thing almost turned Brodie's stomach, and I felt like an idiot. It was a good idea—but just won't work.

Tuesday, December 22. This morning I saw something that would, a year ago, have stirred one to emotional tears—but today it left me a little cold. I don't know why.

I saw 438 decorations handed out to men of the 11th Bomb Group by Gen. Harmon, with Gen. Ross and Gen. Fuller and Comdr. Crackenkish attending. The guys were in three ranks and they marched down Bomber #2 and stood before a massed formation of troops and faced the brass. It wasn't screwed up badly.

There was Blondie Saunders and Edmundson (looking like a college sophomore—he's a major) and Lucas[28] and a mob of guys who got the DFC & clusters, the SS and clusters, the PH, the SM and ribbons for the Air Medal. A Negro boy received the SM for a piece of work I did a story on in N.Y. months ago.[29] He wouldn't give 'em that old "shine" grin for the pictures—I don't blame him.

Somehow it all left me feeling there was something to be desired. Perhaps it was the fact that there were too damn many people cluttering up the place for pictures. I realize pix—at least those Robby & Co. took—are necessary, but Robby wasn't alone and it seemed there were so many people screwing around taking shots.

Sad Sam Oppee, our famulous 1st Lt. roommate, did the movie stuff and sat on a jeep which Jackson drove backwards in front of the brass to opt a dolly shot. That took more brass than the generals had.

Anyway, Gen. Harmon pulled a smart trick when in his speech he said the ground crews didn't get the medals but their work was just as important. The guys who did get them certainly deserved them for my money—I hate this crap I hear occasionally about "Now what the hell did he do?" These guys have fought a pretty damn good fight. And out there today they didn't look very heroic—just ordinary guys.

Wednesday, December 23. Last night I decided something—I swore it to myself. I'm going to do a story here—when it can be released—of one of the most beautiful examples of mass Americanism anybody has ever seen. It'll be long, but it'll have the stuff in it. I was told last night that Ralph Morse, the *Life* boy, almost cried about the thing—I don't know whether because he couldn't get it cleared or not—but I think not for any reason so material or so crass.

This story is about the 6,000 men of the *Coolidge* who landed on this island Oct. 26 (the day we left N.Y.) with not a damned thing. Some didn't have clothes on their back. The *Coolidge* came all the way from S.F. without escort and then was sunk coming through our own minefields in the harbor just off shore. She was hit twice near midships and sank in an hour & 15 minutes. Two men—a capt. and a man shutting off valves in the bowels of the ship—were lost, everybody else got off, oil-soaked & naked. Everything they had in the way of equipment went under water.

That combat team—the 172nd—is still on its feet. Last night I saw them put on an amateur show and everybody howled with laughter. The band played with borrowed instruments and the boys performed with whatever was at hand—one was a "trained horse" thing that actually was funny. You couldn't tell anything had happened to those guys, except when you see some of them still wearing Navy & Marine clothes. They say the Navy really took then in—gave them the shirts off their backs, literally—when they came ashore. Imagine 6,000 men coming out of the sea with—nothing. And it rained for three days straight, naturally. The men were fed—short rations for everybody—but they were fed. Imagine a soldier spending his first night in the jungle with nothing but a pair of pants—no tent, no blankets, nothing, in the rain. That happened— not once, but in scores of cases, hundreds.

The CT is gradually being re-equipped. They are still in pretty bad shape, but the stuff is coming in. When they are a fighting force again I want to do their story. It's got to be done.

Brodie and I had another one of those damn fool discussions today on life and our work and high aims and that sort of thing. They always leave me confused, and they somehow keep jabbing me with the idea that I am not yet capable of setting down any straightforward, really healthy attitude toward my future. They also leave me with a hangover after the intoxication of talking about myself. God, I'm an egomaniac. And by the same token I wonder why

I'm writing this stuff sometimes—I write, as often as not, with the screwed-up attitude that somebody will just pick this thing up and start reading it as if it were a polished, completed work. What I should do is write with complete honesty, candor and with a very minimum of self consciousness. Instead I seem to have been doing this as if somebody was looking over my shoulder. I have tried to be honest and candid—have been as I know—but there is evidence of an increasing trend toward this glamour pants stuff. I hope it's just a passing fancy, because I'd hate like hell to fill a book with a lot of pretty phrases and not much else. Then, too, I feel that a good deal of the stuff lacks the guts it really should have. Perhaps that's not justified and perhaps if it is, even, it's because my idea has been all along that the closer we get to Cactus the closer we are getting to the real thing. Sometimes I must have had the idea that it just didn't mean a thing until Guadalcanal. I suppose that's a result of the second-hand war we've been living so far. On the other hand, I've tried in spots to capture moods and in other spots to picture situations. Often as not I've gone into a lot of my own petty bitchings—like this one—but perhaps some day I can take it all and reconstruct an overall picture from this jumble of inconsistencies, if they really are inconsistencies.

I have written this as I used to write letters home—as a vent, yes, but primarily as a medium of setting down in so many words what I am thinking. It helps me to think a little clearer.

Brodie and I are set to be at Operations in the morning at 6:15 to grab a hop to Cactus. I'm glad to get out of here. Pretty disgusted with the way I've bitched things up—two stories in a week. My omnipotent ego tells me I've been a dope—that my handling of news sources and everything in general has been wrong.

December 24, Thursday. This is the hottest Christmas Eve I've ever spent. We're on Guadalcanal. We thundered in on a B-17 and landed at Henderson Field. My first impression was of the heat—we started sweating as soon as the props quit turning. Later on it rained and cooled off—and muddied.

The Canal wasn't exactly what I expected—but we could see where the first pictures made here were taken. There are bomb craters here and there and the palms are eaten with shrapnel. But on the field nobody seemed to have an idea that the Japs were anywhere within a thousand miles—they're about four.

We ran into the press again—including a newsreel man I worked with on the TD story at Hood.[30] Our tent is fairly near theirs. Think I'll go over and listen to some wild tales. Sleep is better.

December 25, Friday. Christmas Day on Cactus.

This morning at dawn I woke to hear a band playing Silent Night and Adeste Fideles. It was a Catholic mass, so I understand, but I couldn't hear the father. At breakfast we found the mess shack decorated with red and green rope and Christmas tree balls and spangles. The boys complimented cook on his art; they talked about egg nog and asked each other what gifts they'd got. Some had thrown Christmas Eve benders—the whiskey had "just appeared." None has appeared to me yet, although Dowling had some gin yesterday. He, incidentally, has a hangover today—he lost his passport & $300 last night.

I'm sweating as I write and my hands are trembling because, I think, my nervous system doesn't react well to this atabrine we've taken. A grain yesterday and a half grain today.[31] I used to think men's hands trembled because of battle nerves, but now I know different. It's getting worse, so I'll quit for awhile. We eat turkey at three.

We haven't seen anything yet, haven't done anything. Washing Machine Charley didn't put in his scheduled appearance last night, so I haven't heard my first bomb fall. From our first 24 hours on Guadalcanal, we can't tell this is where the war is after all. Occasionally we can hear artillery in the distance, but it sounds very dull and very far away.

It's evening, and I'm sitting at the end of a coral cliff—one of those, I'm sure, which must have been a Jap strongpoint when the Marines first landed. In front of the cliff, about 30 yards away, are two bomb craters, one little one, and a huge one that somebody has half filled with tin cans. The trees around me here are eaten with bullet holes and shrapnel. To the right is the very tip of Henderson Field and beyond it are the palm groves.[32] Overhead, planes are coming in and going out constantly. But for their motors, it would be quiet. There are thousands of birds here, noisy critters. They fly in formation and when you first glance up you think they are planes. There are a million flies— they bite at your ankles and elbows and eyebrows.

The sun is coming in at a long oblique across a field of green grass that borders the bomber strip. It looks like a lush meadow. Diagonally across it is an unpaved road, soggy and rutted, and jeeps and two and one-half ton trucks loaded with shirtless men roll across it to, I suppose, the river. In a few minutes it will be dark.

From what I've seen of Cactus—and that's precious little so far—it's all jungle except the clearing and the field. I mean where there are trees, other than the palm groves which have been cultivated by some unfortunate soul, there is jungle—and a dense one.

One thing I've noticed which is utterly different from any other Army installation I've seen, is the equipment lying around. I'm sitting on a perfectly good oil treated raincoat which I found folded here. Down off the cliff are blankets and a helmet. A haversack, looking brand new, I saw lying in the mud not far away. Over at the far end of the field are a bunch of Grummans bunched together. From here they look like salvage and they must be; they were here yesterday. One, off by itself, is stripped to the fuselage. Driving across the field itself yesterday I saw several planes wrecked & burned to hulks. There is Jap stuff, too—hundreds of mats, some shovels and pieces of equipment. I saw the Jap steamroller, now scrap. War has been here. That it is still here, I have to find out.[33]

December 26, Saturday. I have just come back from my first trip to the front—or as close to the front as two British and two American reporters with a Marine driver named Bill could get in a jeep.

It wasn't exactly what I had expected. We of course had been told that in jungle warfare you couldn't see anything at all. We could. We went over the worst roads I have ever traveled in all my life, sincerely, the worst, to a Bn CP of the 132nd Infantry—the "Men of Illinois"—sitting at the edge of the jungle on top of a hill. On the way up we were passed by, first, a casualty with blond hair leaning unconscious on the arm of a boy in a jeep, and, second, by stretcher bearers carrying a dead soldier down the hill. The first boy was pale; the second's face was covered, but his pants were covered with blood. He was the first American I've seen killed in action. I don't know what I thought as they brought him by—not much, except that he was dead because his face was covered. I went on up the hill. There were men who were filthy dirty and from the look of most of them, tired. They were serious and, I think, mad. A patrol of theirs had run point blank into a machine gun. The CP is on top of a hill and men were dug in on the slope—a hell of a spot to be in. The jungle was thinned a little at the edge, but deeper in it was just a tangle of trees and vines. The advance positions were 300 or 400 yards out in that direction; they pulled back last night to let artillery shell Jap positions.

From the hill is a beautiful view of the sea, with Savo jutting up to the left and Florida lying low to the right, and Tulagi barely visible at its top. As we looked across the terrain westward we could see the Jap-held ground. We were shelling it and through an OP scope we could see shell craters on a forward slope of a hill. I traversed the scope over the ground between us and them and saw the Marines and infantry troops. I saw somebody standing on top of a ridge, stark naked, bathing. There wasn't much to see except terrain and occasional smoke shells. We apparently were shelling two different positions, one at intervals. In the distance along the rim of the island we could see beached Jap transports and some landing boats. They were shot to hell and gone. The beaches were bare.

From there we went back over the same awful road, passing artillery batteries firing over our heads at the positions we'd seen. We could feel the concussion and hear the shells whistle overhead.

We went on down to the palm grove and over to the river—I can't spell the name—where Jap tanks had tried to come up the beach. They didn't make it. I think there were six in all—two in the river, three on the beach, and one on the beach behind the guns—rusty now and shot to pieces. The scene of desolation around our guns was something—everything gave evidence of one hell of a fight, the sand-bagged positions, the empty shell boxes, the barbed wire, the ground itself and here and there parts of clothing and equipment lying around. The palms across the river from the guns were literally blown to pieces; those still standing at all were just stems with their tops gone. I noticed a mound with two sticks for a cross with a helmet hung on. There was no name.[34]

Both here and on the hill there was everything that looked like pictures and stories I'd seen, but the realism of it hit me at once. Bright yellow grenades snapped to belts or laying in boxes, rifles, ammunition, chopped off leggings, empty cans of tin rations and a box of rations with half the cans gone. The Sgt. Major on the hill was making out the strength report for the battalion. I looked over his shoulder and read names followed by the terse abbreviation "FR DUTY TO MIA." From duty to missing in action.

I passed Brodie coming up as we were on the way back. I'm going to do some kind of story today on what I saw—which actually wasn't much at all—but I know I can't get into it the naked reality of the thing. I can't even do it here, but my reaction to death and to tired men with grimy faces wouldn't be of interest. You can't describe discarded equipment and wounded blonde boys riding over bumpy coral clay roads. I'm too new at this yet—I'd make it sound too bad, I guess, or not bad enough. I couldn't see how it was with the Japs. Our boys wish they could do that, too. They shoot a bunch of Japs at night and when morning comes they look for bodies but the Japs always take their dead back with them.

December 27, Sunday. For me nothing; for Brodie, his baptism of fire. He was at an advance position doing sketches and a sniper located him. He hit the ground and scooted behind a log, covering the drawing he was doing with mud. I want him to send it back as it is—with mud on a half-finished sketch. He said he was scared only when he had to walk back by himself to the CP.

While all this was going on, I was on a wild goose chance at Lunga, watching cans plough around on a sub alert. Didn't even see an ash can tossed. The action in harbor and on shore convinced me that Guadalcanal is firmly held. The Japs may try again, but things are too far along here for them to ever hope to regain what they've lost. Keyes, the London man,[35] was telling me how things were when he got here—not so secure.

Wrote my first story and asked Bob Miller[36] to look it over. He said he thought it good—said if I "got the stuff out" before it all became routine to me I'll have damn nice copy. I know he's right.

Walked all over Henderson Field just to see what it looks like, and after chow went down to the river with Tex Litman & Brodie for a bath.

-0-

Two tents away there is a battery radio and I can hear the Andrews Sisters. They sang "Beer Barrel Polka" and "Apple Blossom Time." I think it's Command Performance—last night we listened to Crosby & Hope and Ginny Sims.

But the strangest coincidence of them all happened this afternoon. "Alabama" Givens,[37] tentmate, got some Mobile papers. I was thumbing thru and suddenly a picture hit me right in the eye—Major Harry C. Hathaway—the Little Skipper, my old company commander in the regiment back home. There was a badly written story along with the picture—it was just a sketch in a personality series of officers at Brookey Field, but there was Elizabethton, Tenn., in print and the Skipper looking big as life. Made me feel good.[38] Somebody is singing "When the Lights go on Again."

December 28, Monday. Went with Bob Miller out to a Marine CP—Col. Arthur—was introduced as "Mister," drank two bottles of the Colonel's beer, met his staff plus two very human generals, and ate at the Colonel's mess. That kind of stuff is not what I'm out here to do, but the beer was good. So was the Colonel. I got the material for two stories, but I'll have to grind them out.

As an enlisted man—even a misrepresented one—the thing I appreciated most was a report by a major whose battalion ran into trouble yesterday and last night. He was red-headed Major Ewell Scott Love—"Scotty"—a former insurance agent from Seattle. I'm going to do the story from a soldier's standpoint, because it does a man good to know his officers don't hog the credit. "Scotty" was a pretty worn-out fellow, but the way he told how his men fought made me want to throw an arm over his shoulder or something. Sounds silly, but I felt that way. No wonder the Marines are good.

One incident he told me was strictly from Hollywood, but without attending heroics. There was a machine gun crew. A mortar burst got four. The fifth man—not a gunner, an ammo bearer—went crazy. He turned the gun on Jap held positions, but couldn't get a clear field of fire. So he picked a .30 caliber light machine gun up in his arms and fired it from the hip. He continued to fire, picking the gun up again each time the concussion would force him to the ground, until his own men threw a poncho over his head and dragged him down. We couldn't get the man's name, but the Colonel told Scotty to "recommend him"—probably for the Silver Star.

The other story the Colonel gave me—debunking the Jap superman angle. He said the stories MacArthur let out from Bataan were partly to cover a bad situation there and that they had had a pronounced effect on new men going into the line for the first time. We are fighting veterans of Malaya & Bataan and China here, and they've pulled some dumb tricks.

December 29, Tuesday. Last night hitched a ride on a PBY to Munda. We bombed, got a little ack-ack I didn't see at all...it was on the other side of the ship. Did the story. Not so hot.[39]

December 30, Wednesday. Went up to the 2nd Marine front. They'd been under mortar fire, but nothing happened while we were there. Those men had been in combat 142 days. They wonder how much longer.[40]

December 31, Thursday. Did a put together story on the "Jap is no genius" angle which I half-way hope never sees print. It's straight quotes from two people—one of them the Colonel who gave me the stuff Monday. The other was a boy in the 2nd Marines I saw yesterday. But still. . . . . I thought it should be done, and now I don't know whether I have the courage of my convictions on it. It's like Hipple says: "One day you hear the Japs are supermen, and next day you hear they aren't. What the hell." But, hell—if I'm writing this stuff I might as well say what people here think—they're supposed to know. Trouble is, everybody doesn't think the same which makes life interesting in the long run.[41]

"Whatta Racket"

Friday, January 1, 1943. Awfully, awfully drunk last night. It was funny. Dowling, marooned or submerged at Button, sent two cases of gin up by plane. It arrived at the last minute in a jeep driven by a Navy pilot who roared up yelling, "Where's the Press Tent?" like a knight errant in search of a battle. The boys had gotten some medical alcohol & grapefruit juice in case Jack didn't come thru. We hit the gin. Robby, too drunk to know what he was doing, swiped three quarts—and returned them today, as embarrassed a guy as I ever saw. We drank them tonight. Brodie was so drunk and so sick he sat balls naked on the coral & vomited out the tent.

Saturday, January 2. Today I got my baptism of fire—and I saw things I don't care if I never have to see again. Brodie and Jackson and I talked a major out of the general's jeep which Brock and Ralph had turned in when they left yesterday. We went up to Grassy Knoll where the 132nd made their long awaited push this morning—the first day under command of Col. George, the peep troop man. Nelson, the regimental CO, was relieved of his outfit, George took over, and things happened.[1] They took Hill 27.

I decided to do a story on medical evacuation, starting at the beginning and going all the way back. So we went all the way up—to within 150 yards of the action—and I stayed until a casualty was brought in to Bn Aid, then followed him back to the hospital—even to watching his operation.

Right now I've got the jumps—right here in my own tent, of all things—I leap at the least noise. I've seen things, too many in one day: a man cut in two by a machine gun, my "own" casualty with a hole in his gut—and his incision and suture—a Jap with his face mangled with a .50, his left eye hanging down across his face—men scared and so exhausted and stunned they just sat and starred—the Guadalcanal, or 1000-yd, stare.

And we had sniper trouble. The first time he opened up I started looking for cover, but a kid made me feel foolish by pointing out that on your first time under fire you think every bullet is aimed at you. Later on I actually got mad— I was surprised to discover I really was—and looking for the little bastard, as though I could have hit him with my .45. Once or twice I swear somebody shot off firecrackers. The fire up there—we were blasting at a pillbox—was terrific, but I believe the Japs tried their firecrackers trick at least a couple of times. It's hard to tell, tho. The boys said there were several snipers in the woods around us, and I know fire came from at least three places where we had no men—but in that mess it's impossible to see anything. I saw smoke from the first firing but couldn't see a damned thing. But even so, I think Jackson must have seen more than we did—he went the extra 150 yds. In any event, I'm satisfied with as much of it as I saw—it was really rugged.

Sunday, January 3. Washing Machine Charley finally came back last night, and I heard my first bombs drop. That made yesterday a pretty full day. Something must have screwed up our radar, because we had almost no warning at all—I was standing on top of the ridge (on my way to the dugout) when he let loose two. They didn't whistle or whine, which surprised me, but sort of swished down. They hit quite a distance away, and I think they were small bombs—100 pounders. We got him in the lights and he buzzed around until we got disgusted. He didn't drop anything else, so we went back to bed. He was still buzzing.

There were supposed to have been Jap destroyers off shore last night, but nobody is sure they landed troops. The PT Boats say they didn't, but might have floated in some food.

Worked three hours today on the evacuation story and nothing happened.

Monday, January 4. Tried to finish the story and still didn't. Diggory Venn, Marine combat correspondent whom I met Saturday, was over with copies of his work—straight stuff and very gutty—good.

Brodie spent the day at the front. He was around while a couple of mortars opened up and seemed to have been in on more auto fire than we were Saturday. Robby went up another trail and had a pretty full day—brought back a filthy Jap cap. All while I sat on my ass and tried to do a story.

Venn said this morning that he hoped Brodie didn't get too much of the war here because he (Venn) knows what it can do and he knows Brodie is a sensitive guy. They are old buddies: used to work together on the *Chronicle*.[2] I noticed when Brodie came back he looked more tired than usual and didn't say a hell of a lot. I told him not to go back up there for awhile. Don't know how much effect that it'll have on him, but he said he wouldn't.

Tuesday, January 5. Finally finished the story on evacuation, altho it took me longer than anyone should require on such a thing. Luckily, my man pulled through okay and was evacuated. Now I have to get it cleared. Cromie made me mad by saying it was a "dirty trick" to use the man's name because the story might beat notification of the boy's people. I contend it is better for them to learn of it through a complete story than thru a brief WD message.[3] Washed clothes.

Wednesday, January 6. This is one of those low days when I am hamstrung by the idea that I'm not doing anything—or not doing enough—or not the right thing. It's like going to a three-ringed circus and staring at the peanut vendors. As I write, somebody has a radio turned on and we're getting some beautiful light opera—and even that screws me because here I am writing in my little book and listening to music when up on Hill 27 men are wondering where the next shot is coming from.

The brass is beginning to wear off, I'm afraid. I'm beginning to be less overawed at being on Guadalcanal. I think I'm mad at myself more than anything else. For one thing I think I talk too much. I tried to tell Jackson how I thought he should handle his PRO work and I don't think he liked it very much. I was sincerely trying to help him, but he has a mind of his own and I think I overstepped. Probably do well to handle my own job.

We are here on Guadalcanal to cover the American soldier in action. I have a feeling I'm not holding up my end. I have done two stories on "action"—one was Navy—and yet I haven't gotten around yet to even seeing a soldier shoot at a Jap. What in hell kind of business is that? I'm not even sure I've actually been under fire—I think I was, but I'm not sure. I didn't actually hear the bullets hit around me. What the hell's wrong—am I scared, or what? I've been close enough to the front several times to come under fire, and I've been scared, but did I have reason?

This seems to be a regular thing with me in the Army—its happened so many times before—when I turned down Co. Clerk to be a field soldier, when I quit Corps to go back to the line—when I asked to get out of the office and see the war. Does that make me a glutton for punishment, or does it make me one of those poor fools who's afraid somebody will say "Hell, boy, you've never done anything in your life?" Or does it make me a coward trying to prove to myself I'm not?

So many factors enter into a thing like this. I'm out here to do a job. Deep inside me something keeps pushing me into going up, attaching myself to a squad and fighting like a soldier, living like a soldier, going hungry and all that stuff. Something keeps telling me to do it and yet something else—just as deep—is holding me back. I can think of all kinds of good practical alibis—away from training too long, out of shape for physical strain, unfamiliarity with this kind of combat (or any other kind), too great to risk for comparable return in story form, undue exposure to malaria—a thousand of them. But, in the last analysis, I'm afraid I'm scared of getting hit. That's a hell of a thing. Is it fear of fear, or just plain fear period?

I've had a mere glimpse of what war really is—just a bare taste of it and I don't like it. It's ugly and filthy and hysterical and a lot of other things—but the damn stuff keeps challenging me. I know I haven't really seen anything yet—haven't experienced anything—haven't done anything. I want to, and again I don't want to. It isn't that I think I could scoop the world on a story—that's not it at all—it's a personal thing that keeps gnawing at me. It rained the day I came off the front and I kept thinking that night of these poor sons of bitches up there beating off Jap counter-attacks and lying in the mud. And yet then—with me ten miles away and on a bunk—I kept feeling my stomach turn cold every time I heard a noise. Nerves—reaction from the tension and the blood—sure, but what would have happened if I'd been up there with them? I think that's what I want to find out. Why? To test an ego.

Wednesday, January 7. [Editor's note: This is actually Thursday, 7 January, confirmed by the letter he wrote his wife.[4]] Got my first letter from Helen today—dated Dec. 10—telling me, among other things, that I'm sure to become a father. I've known that since a week before I left New York, but wasn't actually positive until the letter today. Should be sometime in June. I don't like to think about that until I'm back in the States—but for gosh sakes there's no sense in that. Having a child to raise is one thing I have about as much knowledge about as flying a P-39. Talk about a bull in a China shop! Well, there's one thing: it's something to work for, something to really buckle down for from now on. I think that's certainly for the best. I wish I could be with Helen. But she's a dandy.

Out to the extreme right flank at Point Cruz, first time there. Nothing doing. Snipers supposedly, but no evidence. Saw Jap skeleton, skull; started to bring back skull, changed my mind. Walked down beach to tanks—then we were told by Marine whole beach mined. I walked back in somebody else's footprints—very lightly. This was first outing for Allan Jackson INS photog in yesterday. Very dull. Wrote Spence three pages, wrote Helen.

Can't get over being father to be. I'll be damned.

Thursday, January 8. [Editor's note: Almost certainly Friday.] Nothing, absolutely nothing. Down to the docks to look at some Jap rations picked up afloat and brought ashore. I'd hate to try to live on pressure-packed oatmeal cakes. Tried to start wheels rolling on engineer story; not much luck.

As I write I can hear "Hi Neighbor Program," Benny Goodman, "Gal from Kalamazoo," etc. Wrote Helen yesterday, saying I don't like to listen or read. That must have puzzled her and, I'm sure, made her a little sad. I wish I hadn't said it, but it was true when I wrote it and is true most of the time. I guess I'm a whole hog or nothing guy—when I'm home I can't get enough of that sort of thing, but here I don't want any of it. The complete incongruity of it ruffles me. Saw part of a movie *Pride of the Yankees* (with everything backwards on the screen) and now & then artillery would go off not far away—loud. That's what I mean.

Friday, January 9. [Editor's note: Almost certainly Saturday.] Toured the Guadalcanal road net with Col. Gillette, Corps Engineers. But you can't get a story on engineers by driving over the ground with a colonel—particularly one who harps on little stuff and speaks in broad terms. All I got was jeep cheeks.[5]

Saturday, January 10. [Editor's note: This entry could be either Saturday, 9 January, or Sunday, 10 January.] Got two letters from Dad. Felt wonderful about it—he sent me $15 and some airmail stamps. I can't spend the money and the stamps immediately stuck together, but still felt wonderful. There's nothing like mail from home.

Sunday, January 11. [Editor's note: Almost certainly Sunday, 10 January.] Up to the front where the new 35th Infantry made a minor push.[6] Snipers had gotten three and were way the hell back of the lines. Everybody trigger happy. Damnedest situation I ever saw. Something else funny—this morning heard aerial machine gun fire, looked out, saw plane on another's tail; the first was smoking. I didn't hear anymore about it, so I guess I'm getting the Guadalcanal jumps. After we were at the front, came down and went swimming in the ocean. We could see shell bursts in the hills and up the coast, and yet our beach was like a Hollywood set except for cases of food piled up. Pitched a can in the water and shot four rounds (near misses) my first on the island.

Monday, January 11. Screwed up on dates. Now correct. With Artillery most of the day. Two alarms last night. First one, early, was fake; second, about 3:00 a.m. wasn't—damn stick was already down before radar even knew Jap close. Must have followed plane in. Cans off shore for second time. Lost two PT boats. Did they land troops? Nobody knows.[7] Hello, hello—what kind of war is this? Scuttlebutt says Charlie's sneak got one man, injured 12. They were close. Then 155s pounded all night.

Tuesday, January 12. While Cromie and Jackson and Robby were on the front with a ringside seat of the war, I labored on the artillery story, got mad and persuaded Brodie to spend most of the afternoon on the beach. I didn't even know the damn guys were up until they got back, each with a couple of lurid tales. So I was still mad—for missing out.

But if I missed that, I caught something else flush in the face. A kid came in under the wing of a major, CC. The boy was loaded down with Jap souvenirs and the Father—whatever his name is—was gushing and calling him "one of my boys." The story was pretty sordid. The kid was on the front, bringing up grenades, when he saw a Jap private lying wounded. He cut off the Jap's head and then heard another Jap groan. Going over to the second one, he found an officer with sword, etc. As I got it, the kid reached for the sword and the Jap grabbed him—either in the desperation of a dying man, or at the end of the usual possum act. Anyway, the kid went wild—partly, he said, because he'd had a buddy killed, and partly, I think, because he was scared to death. He broke loose, grabbed his knife and stabbed the Jap in the gut, chest, back, cut off the left cheek of his ass and then decapitated him. All this the kid told me as Brodie did his portrait. Okay, so the kid went crazy and cut a couple guy's heads off. C'est le guerre. But what got me was the Father. While the bloody details were being related, the padre kept needling me with: "Nothing can stop the American boy;" "My isn't he blood-thirsty;" "Nothing the American boy won't do if you get him mad"—then to the kid: "Stand steady there for your picture, boy, or I'll whip you good"—to me, punching—"He knows I'll do it, too." Now what in hell kind of stuff is that? I felt like pushing the fat bastard over the cliff. It's not my conception of a chaplain that he should glory in blood and sort of buzz around like a school kid in the dubious fame of a guy who killed a couple of Japs—wounded or not. The whole thing disgusted me, particularly when he asked me to take a picture of him holding a Jap scarf. He put his arm around the kid's neck and grinned like an idiot. He wants the negative—I suppose so he can show it around in the States. I'm glad it was a double exposure. Nuts.

Wednesday, January 13. Finally finished two stories—on artillery and on the kid who killed the Japs.[8] I did a putrid retouch job on the kid, giving him the benefit of doubts I hold that he deserves a damn bit of credit. The Jap might possibly have been really playing possum. Actually the story hinged on the fact the kid once studied for the priesthood. Some change. I tried to do the stories at the press tent but had to give it up in the confusion. Took Miller's typewriter to the tent and banged 'em out right away. Got awfully mad at those guys, but after all it is their tent. Dowling's working on a play— "Tokyo Express"—no wimman—and Cromie is still wrapped up with his Rolliflex. Miller's working with the PT boats out of Tulagi; Hipple has malaria; Jackson & Brumby[9] are just sort of hanging around. To tell the truth, if everybody scurried around as much as Jackson & Robby the wires couldn't hold the stuff. Of the press, Cromie works hardest and Jack probably can sling the best copy. But he sweats it out. I think his play is about the Guadalcanal Press Club.[10] Robby tells me they plan leaving around the 16th; their month is up then. Brodie's supplies are running low, but we've still got lots of work to do. I really sweated on that artillery story—I don't know a damn thing about it and, vital as the guns are, there just isn't a helleva lot to play up about a bunch of guys around a gun shooting at something they can't even see. Wrote Dad long letter couple days ago, got by with a lot more than I thought. If he didn't know where I am, he will now. Swimming yesterday with Brodie, shot two clips—missed every darn time. Brodie got one hit. Swimming again after chow—damn good chow: steak and *coffee*—first coffee for supper since I've been on the island. Last night had such a yen for it built a fire and made some. Boys in tent had can hams, potatoes: we had a regular banquet. Invited guest was Stewart Island boy, 20, who came overland with two British. He spoke good English, learned in 6 years from missionary. Told us some interesting things about his home, how they stole their wives if the old man wouldn't say yes and lot more of the authentic South Sea stuff. We almost talked him into making some native whiskey—but not quite.

Thursday, January 14. Got so fed up trying to get transportation, decided to see Col. Crawford, G-2, 25th,[11] and stay up for awhile. He said okay for tomorrow. Don't like the idea of sleeping on ground in rain—but looks like that's the answer. I'm doing too little work and trying too hard to do that. Trouble is I get mad and can't do a damn thing when I get the opportunity—and more wild goose chases. Robby, Jackson plan leaving tomorrow morning. Killed story on kid who killed Japs. Talked to Cromie and he said the thing got better every time he heard it. I gave boy benefit of doubt how bad Jap hurt—Cromie said he had a hole in belly.[12]

Too much.

Friday, January 15. Last night was pretty hectic—three air raids and the damn radar missed them all. I can't see any excuse for that—they're sure batting a thousand with it; haven't hit one right since we've been on the island. The first raid was at dusk—the plane circled around over and then came back. Brumby, Jackson & I, suspicious, went up on the hill. Somewhere around the airport somebody yelled air raid. No siren, nothing. Then the damn plane made its run and laid a stick down the beach. Nobody down there, of course, had any kind of warning at all. Six killed. Ten minutes after the bombs fell the alarm went off—everybody cheered. We had word DDs and AKs coming down. Then three or four Jap planes came over and the AA opened up. Helluva mess—bombs, flashes, concussion. No warning then except sound of planes. We were in dugout when Cromie, Robby came in: they had been developing in the dark room, got caught in jeep halfway here on second raid. We went to bed—I in Miller's bunk because night promised lot of getting up and obstacle course leading off Cactus Heights too much for me. We half asleep, waiting bombing or shelling, when siren again. Got up, shoes on, waited. Plane buzzed around 15-20 minutes, went away. No bombs. Late at night, we all asleep, 105 opened up, jarred us almost out of bed. We thought shelling for sure. Everybody keyed up. Finally sleep.

This morning nobody knew for certain whether transports came in or not. Heard lost one PT; also heard two cans sighted afire and running at slow 20 knots. Pathetic thing happened. At NOB, officer told sailors during 1st raid to clear beach: he must have thought the worst, yelled Lunga invaded, ran. It developed into general stampede. One kid ran naked from Cub 1 to airport— heard some got as far as here at division. Father Gehring, we talked to today, said he tried to stop them, pushed off road.[13] No more than can expect. Man can't put faith in air warning system—never knows what the hell to expect. Bad situation for morale, worse for nerves. I not nervous last night, but got butterflies today. Took full grain atabrine, may account for it. That stuff really gets me sometimes. Went out to look for damage this morning, came back to find man looking for Brodie & I to take us to the front. Brodie went. Here I am. Got nothing. Tremendous barrage this morning, most big stuff. Understand Kokumbona got six Bns artillery concentration. If Japs landed, I pity them. Must be big stuff on front. Think bigger stuff brewing for whole island— looks like they're feeling us out to try the big push we been waiting for. I'm going to try to find way to the front this afternoon. Frustration getting me.

Saturday night, January 16. This ink is diluted by the water of the Mataniko. It's late and we've already had our nightly alarm—a fake naturally, because we got some warning (or am I being bitter?). Anyway I find it impossible to sleep— think I'm too tired—so will try to record the happenings of yesterday and today without going so deeply into it that the mood of the story I want to write will be affected. I got up front okay, stayed last night and returned late this afternoon. It was unquestionably my best experience on Guadalcanal—by far. I'm so excited about it I think that might be why I can't get any rest, because gosh knows I need it. I came in tonight more tired than I can remember being in months—sunburned, soaked all over, absolutely filthy and crazy for coffee— which I finally had to brew for myself.

When I came back yesterday & found Brodie already gone I was so mad— at myself—I couldn't think. Then a captain came to the Press Tent saying he was going to the front—manna from heaven. We went to the 25th Div. CP where Col. Crawford, the G-2, transferred us to his jeep with a strapping MP named Sykes and we hit for tall timber. It was raining like hell. We went as far as possible and then hit a jungle trail like nothing I've ever seen before. It was wet & slippery and I think we were three hours getting to our destination—the 35th Inf. Their position is so inaccessible it has been necessary to drop supplies in by plane. Native porters are bringing stuff in now—there must be about 200 of them; they are the only people who could get it thru.[14] We had no sooner arrived than I located Brodie and the story began to move. I'll skip that for now.[15] Col. Crawford and I came back this afternoon—down the river. Boats take wounded from as far up as our positions extend down to a collecting point at the nearest peep road. We brought down three malaria patients—an experience I'll never forget. It took us an hour & a half, the Col. and I both in the water ¾ of the way down. The only way the boats can get down is for men in the water to push & pull them down. We helped the regular crew. Most of the time the water was from knee to chest, but quite often it was over our heads and we had to hang on and swim it down. The physical strain of walking an hour & a half on a rock bottom, fighting to keep that damn boat from snarling on logs or rocks, was about enough for me after running around on the front.[16] I was pooped—and am—but we got the son of a bitch in. That colonel is one helluva guy. I brought back a Jap bayonet, a clip of .25 ammo for Brodie who came back earlier the same way to do sketches—and a hip pocket full of literature of one kind or another. All of it got soaking wet. My greens stink to high heaven—I never got so filthy in such a short time in my life. And for a minute I thought it was all for nothing—I lost my notes but a boy who had them gave them back. The story—prisoners & the prospect of a great many more—should be a dandy. I saw the best picture today of the war—a soldier carrying a Jap piggy back down the ridge trail. Poor Robby—he'd have given his arm.

I am too full of the things I've seen to trust myself. What an outfit up there—the "Pineapple Division"—all regulars and service from one to four years, average. They have done wonderful work, which to me isn't a damned bit spoiled by the fact the Japs they're fighting are in pretty bad shape. They've pocketed them & pounded them until the Japs would be absolute idiots not to give it up and come on in. This is the first outfit I've seen that was more willing to take prisoners than to go on killing. I saw a Jap ear some dope had cut off. It was passed from man to man, and none of them liked the idea. It's like a captain said, "Why should we do the heroic thing and wipe them out if we can get them to surrender?" I heard men say it was a shame to waste ammunition on them.

Brodie, who had only just arrived when we got there, helped carry a PA system up over which Capt. Burden, Japanese interpreter, broadcast a surrender appeal.[17] Brodie was even dirtier than I; he had lugged stuff up on his chest and was covered with mud. He must have been dog-tired. Coming down this afternoon he said he asked for food at an aid station and the officer in charge thought he was a casualty. He did have about a four-day beard and looked like he'd been on the line a month. We were both a mess.

-0-

Second air raid tonight was a dud. Somebody yelled air raid & everybody dugoutwards in a hurry. Seems terribly silly but the way things are becoming it seems the smartest thing to seek shelter at any alarm. Why? Because the other night, when there was no siren warning, somebody yelled air raid. An MP, under orders Lt. O'Roark, went around telling people lights out. Got to G-2, and they bawled hell out of him—"There is no air raid until we are officially notified"—wham—wham—wham—the damn plane laid a stick down the beach. Feel awful dope running to hole on false alarm. Actually inside a dugout only twice here. Building new one near tent—won't have to get up.

Sunday, January 17. First draft on story. Press conference Gen. Patch[18] showed the old man concerned over communiques in states about Cactus. Doesn't think they do soldiers justice—which they most certainly don't. From his end, he says, there'll be some changes made. Still so tired can hardly walk—feet hurt—next time I wear rubber boots on an excursion like that . . . . . Wrote Helen (No. 6.)—got two.

Monday, January 18. Finished "The Story of a Battle" but not satisfied with it although Brodie thinks it best yet and Miller said it was "damn good"—a little politely, I think. There are spots in it pure corn, other spots amateurishly handled. Don't know what's wrong with me—I sweat blood to get the ingredients of a helluva good yarn, and then I don't seem to be able to wrap it up as I'd like. Maybe the rewrite desk can help it—it's way too long and written to be cut, so I guess they can speed up the drags. One thing too many names, unnecessarily cluttering it up. But names are the difference between a color story and a news story: this was meant to be both. Anyway it's what our orders said we should do: "fighting stories." This one has the guts. Or does it?[19]

Dowling, Cromie, Jackson were on the Marine front, came back green at gills from seeing too many dead Japs. They said it awful. I fail see how this can last much longer. By actual figure there are 51,000 of us here and something like 8,000 Japs—all of which aren't effectives—and this still drags on. It must be incredible to people who have never seen this place. But I wouldn't be surprised if we're not still rounding up strays a year from now unless they all starve to death. It isn't the Japs so much as it is this god-awful terrain: but at the same time the little bastards are as hard to get rid of as a dose of crabs. They dig in and come hell or high water they won't come out unless you drag them out. They're fighting the worst kind or war there is— a sort of fatalistic desperation. They must know they haven't got a chance, but apparently they mean to die hard. But they're beginning to break.

This thing wouldn't have to drag on if some of these men had any sense. It's disgusting. Higher headquarters is breaking a leg to get all prisoners possible, but look at all these incidents.

On the Marine front last night a Jap came in with his hands up, saying "Me sick, me sick." The major, knowing there were other Japs watching, motioned him to come on in—told his men not to fire. One Marine raised his rifle and the major knocked it down—but on the other side of him another dope brought up a shotgun and blew the Jap apart. The Japs watching melted away—they'll never give up as prisoners now. Things like that are always happening—guys get trigger happy or think here's a good chance to kill me a Jap and let'em have it. As long as this situation exists, the Japs will naturally fight to the last man.

On the Army front the men had sense enough to know that if they shot a man who would surrender they were just making it hard on themselves—and they haven't done it, at least, not the 35th. Those Marines must have been trying to live up to their reputation. It's not a matter of humaneness, but purely a matter of practical military operation.

I've heard some pretty bad stories of savageness on the part of our boys. Dowling said they shot a sniper 100 yds. from him and before he could get there they were kicking his teeth out for souvenirs. That was the Marines, a bunch of kids who get ferocious in a fight. The Army is a little different. At the 35th I saw a Jap ear passed around. The men didn't have much stomach for that. But then there's the case of my young "killer priest" who hacked off heads for the fun of it or something. When the bars of civilization come down, they hit with a bang. I can understand part of that, but there are other things I don't get at all. Perhaps that's because I haven't seen enough.

But in either event, war in my book is a lot of crap. Even up on the 35th, where there weren't but two casualties and we had everything our own way— like in the movies—I still got a bad taste in my mouth. It was the exact opposite of our experiences with the 132nd—infinitely a cleaner, more glamorous type fighting—but I still keep thinking "What's the use?" I mean the isolated things— taken by themselves—seem not worth the effort.

Tuesday, January 19. Got up this morning and had to make a run for the head. Looks like I've got it. Turned in story on battle, not fully satisfied with it by any means. Scuttlebutt says Japs in full retreat toward Kokumbona. Miller & Brumby came back from Koli Point with a case of beer. Had one bottle, gave another to John Frommell—together with a bayonet scabbard—for package of matches friend of his sent up from Button. Understand cruiser, 6 DDs on way down—Tokyo Express. Japs taking a terrific beating—don't see how they stand it.

Am planning to devote about week on stuff for Freeman. Don't think Jackson covered stuff that will see print, so intend to try my hand at the little things on theory that home town papers will grab it as they did on maneuvers. Trying 132nd first to check commendations, etc., as Marine combat reporters do. Owe Freeman something and now that Robby and Jackson have gone feel I'd better start producing.[20]

Wednesday, January 20. Up this morning and crapped right in my pants before I could take a step. Guess I must have left the spigot open. Most embarrassing. To hospital for paregoric. This is my first real case of diarrhea; been lucky, I guess. Must have picked it up on the line somehow. Last night thought sure taking malaria—fever and aching—but doc said that goes with my trouble. Hate like hell being even a little sick this damn place. Feel like awful idiot, afraid to leave because never know when must take quick trip. Used ground this morning, sprayed liquid like squirt gun. Amazed me.

Tokyo Express failed to show last night. Dowling said this morning the reported Jap rout was more on the order of orderly retreat. Sometimes I think, "Well . . . . . " and then again I don't know. Brodie's tent, as of a couple of days ago, now Artists & Writers Club. I moved in.

Now I'll believe anything—just ran into Louie Kinch. Louis—still dark and bright eyed and quick to laugh—the guy I used to almost worship in those old days of my growing up back home: the man who was my scoutmaster—seems rather funny now—the man who for a time I lost faith in but could never really dislike. The man who took my wedding pictures—the man who shaped my life the winter & summer I was 12. How long ago it seems, and yet how little Louie had changed. He was in the back of a jeep which drove up after chow; the sailor driving was trying to locate some Col. Louie didn't say anything until I noticed him sitting there. My God—of all people—we both thought that. He thought I was still in New York. When I last heard, he had gone into the Navy as a CPO, sometime after Christmas, '41. He's been here working on the *Curtiss*[21] at Santo. He came up on a B-17; he's doing aerial photo map work. He lives only a couple of tents away. Sometimes the coincidence of such things staggers me . . . . . from Elizabethton to Guadalcanal—ten thousand miles, from overnight hikes and camporees to war in the islands. Louis Kinch—scoutmaster, printer, jackleg photographer, struggling to get ahead, wearing shabby clothes, jumping from one thing to another, never very successfully. Louis, the man who made bad cuts and got them to us late—us a small town paper with a deadline and a smart skinny kid editor who by God had to have better service than that by God or you don't get any more business from us, Louie. Louie of the ghost stories at Oceola, Eagle Scout, church worker, hiker-camper extraordinary. The guy who ran me out of the scout hall for saying, "Spots on the Wall by Who Flung Dung" when I was 14. Now taking pictures from a B-17. Fantasia on Cactus.

Thursday, January 21. Secretary of the Navy Frank Knox, with Halsey, Nimitz, Wood[22] and a bunch of other brass, arrived this morning on a PBY.

The press—eight to a jeep—got to the plane in a photo finish—Cromie had gone after gas and gotten back late. We introduced ourselves and when I told him *Yank* he said "Oh, yes, yes, *Yank*," so I suppose he knows all about it. Not much at the field, except a Marine colonel who didn't want to let us thru. He grabbed Miller, but nothing happened. Knox said they were bombed at Button last night—eight bombs—so apparently the Japs know he's here: that's the first time Santo has been hit, I'm pretty sure. Knox said he was sleeping on deck on the *Curtiss* and "when the first one hit I was on my elbows." Hipple asked him if it was the first time bombed in this war; he replied, "Yes, but it was familiar sound." The press has all shoved off to follow him on a tour of inspection this afternoon: there wasn't room for me—which is always the way it is when something of note happens—makes me feel a little like a bastard child, especially have to sponge on their typewriters too. I know I'm too damned sensitive, but having to depend on somebody else for everything doesn't set very well. It makes me mad when I get crowded out, and at the same time I know I'm foolish to get peeved: I'm just spoiled.

There will be a press conference tonight, I understand, which I want to cover for Freeman. Brass on Guadalcanal is no *Yank* feature. Ned Burman[23] and I, both missing out on the tour, may get to sit at the feet of the big fellow. Knox was wearing khakis and a sun helmet; he's red faced and what I'd say is the personification of robust health, although looks like he could stand a little sun. We had air raid warning—fake—just before he came in and since they hit Button last night I'd lay 20 to 1 we see some fun before he leaves tomorrow.

Sometimes at close range, in the maze of petty things which edge themselves into our operations here, I become jammed up inside—confused and bewildered and mad. Not discouraged, but in the vernacular of the Army, pissed off. I wonder how many more years it will take me to rise above inconveniences—how long it will take me to realize that if my every wish isn't gratified it is not a personal affront. Other people seem to ride more or less smoothly along, but I find myself damned near always ready to bitch about something. I rarely say anything at all, but inside I'm yelling, "Well hell fire . . . . . " I won't say anything because I don't want to be forever complaining, and it seems that when I haven't got anything bothering me I try to think up something. Dammit all. I'm the guy who once dedicated his life—in the infantry—never to give a damn about anything. And here I am—doing what? I had intended going over to the 132nd on a story for Freeman but of course Knox coming in stymied that. Now, with the jeep gone, I'm toning up my tan. It's at least a beautiful day. I wonder, if I had a jeep at my disposal, whether I would be satisfied? No, I'd of course want a typewriter. Perhaps then I could think up something else to screw me up. If I had produced as many stories on Guadalcanal in ratio to the energy I've spent worrying about how I was going to get them and where I was going to write them, I'd have flooded the office by now. It's a damn good thing

I'm not tied down to routine as I once was—I'd go nuts. I think I must still be trying to get that out of my system—perhaps that's the answer. One thing I know—when I'm working here I'm happy. When I'm not I'm worrying about what I'll do next, and how. Whatta racket.

Friday, January 22. Eight hours condition red last night, finally four hours sleep. Sons of bitches buzzed around here like flies from about 8:30 to 4:30—must have worked in relays of two. Ack shot & shot, heard rumor of one downed. In and out of foxhole until finally too sleepy & too moskey bitten to give a damn. Last time woke up to hear plane almost overhead: stepped outside tent and heard bomb on way down. Beat it to dugout, but was waylaid by a tent rope and almost flipped over backwards. Cut arm. Funny to run like hell and hold breath at same time. Spent more time in hole last night than all previous time put together by far.

This morning hear reports Jap task force on way. All sorts evidence preparations big doings. Artillery emplacements under our hill: 132nd going on beach defense. Looks like it's going to hit the fantail all right. This should be a dandy.

Press conference last night okay, but Knox said nothing much. He doesn't think much of night fighters but maybe he changed his mind by this morning. Nimitz sat in on conference.

Read in *Life*[24] yesterday Vandergrift's letters home to his wife in Virginia. Knowing what it must have been here when he was writing, I admire his casual ability to take it easy in his correspondence. He must be a very simple, very fine man. All the boys here are crazy about him; I can see why.

At 132nd this morning was given carton & 4 packs cigarettes from among the belongings men killed in action: sort of felt a little funny about smoking the first one.

Saturday, January 23. Another long condition red, almost as bad as night before. This is getting damned annoying. Haven't had a really good night's sleep in a week.

Long talk with Louie last night. He hasn't changed a bit, except that he cusses like a sailor. I was mistaken that he was just arrived on Guadalcanal. He was aboard the first B-17 that set down on Henderson Field, had been in and around here since before operations started.

He's still the same guy, with plans already made on what he's going to do after the war. He seems to be doing all right as it is, making $175 with flight pay & taking in some on the side.

Sent off the first six stories to Freeman, not counting the Knox story yesterday. Still have 14 to go, which will do tomorrow provided can get some sleep tonight.

Understand Kokumbona was taken today,[25] that the first Jap officer prisoners were captured—and that two Chinese, supposed Hong Kong business men, were brought in; they're supposed to have been in some kind of labor battalion.

Norman (?) Lodge of AP is in, together with Brockhurst,[26] off the *Saratoga*. Big doings coming off up north. Lodge, who was a little high on brandy, didn't impress me very well. We didn't meet.

Scuttlebutt says night fighters arrived today. Hope so—this night life is getting me down. (Ed. Note—fighters didn't show.)[27]

Dowling says new order from Halsey bars the press boys from traveling by air—which is certainly one hell of a note. Jack said they "were thinking about" leaving and letting the place cover itself. Of course they won't, but I don't understand such an order. Don't think it will affect us, however.

The softening up of Munda is supposed to start tomorrow. The *Saratoga*, the *Enterprise* and three converted jobs reported at Tulagi.

Did precious little work today—got up too tired to move and tried to catch up on my sleep this afternoon. One story. Feel like a dope sweating out these damn raids, especially since spend about 95% of the time at the hole waiting for bomb swish to send us piling in. Stand around half asleep with the plane buzzing around up there—hear it fade and hope the bastard gone—hear him buzz in again—stand and wait, too grouchy to admire even a beautiful moonlit night like last night. If AA opens crane neck and wish they'd get him. Then sweat out falling shrapnel. It would be so much easier to forget the whole thing and stay in the sack—some do, some don't—but every time I get in bed and hear him coming he sounds directly overhead. Figure the percentage of getting hit by bomb or shrapnel, decide best thing to do is go to sleep. Then get up and stand by hole. Disgusting, but one thing—always got plenty company. Our new hole jammed last night, think liked cave better. If it weren't so hard to get to would be okay.

Sunday, January 24. Third straight night. Twice close bomb hits. Second time was sound asleep, awoke to hear 'em on their way down. Rolled out of bed, taking blanket, mosquito bar and all. Had to crawl under bunk and outside of tent to get back on my feet. And yesterday I wrote a "funny" story about a captain who tore his tent down. Ha! They got fuel dump last night—brief fire. Managed to get more sleep, don't feel so bad today. Press tent 'smorning talking about sleeping raids out—agreement foolish, as Cromie said, "piling up per-centages." Think quite a few changed mind about bed after last night, altho times so sleepy doesn't make a damn.

-0-

Funny to see how busy is area with idea of improving the grounds for air raid purposes. Allan, our Polynesian boy, got to work on the cave—we can at least get down there now. I drug out pair of leather gloves for mosquito purposes, also headnet. Don't give a damn if all of this love's labor lost, however. Trade it anytime for a good night's sleep.

Twelve stories off to Freeman today. Just bang them out, but I think the kid's mothers back home may be a little proud to see what her Johnny did way out in Guadalcanal. Handling that stuff is simple, but a lot like work. I'd have been lost without Delancy's typewriter. What a dope was I!

Met Mr. J. Norman Lodge last night, but he'll never remember it. Drunk or sober that guy must be a stinker. He was vaguely nasty to me, but not too bad. Boy, he loves himself. Got carton of Camels, issue. Was running low, even with the PMs from the 132nd.

Have just read an article in the Dec. 27 S.F. *Chronicle* by E.E. Hutshing, writing for *This World*, which impressed me as being a damn good thing and I intend writing the office to that effect. Hutshing is raising hell because no real fighting song has been written for this war and I know in my own heart that he's certainly right. There have been times in States when I would have liked to have kicked the teeth out of the song writers—the stealing bastards—who turn out music for a nation at war to sing. Certainly nothing has been written that soldiers out here will sing, nothing but a lot of drivel that usually is a steal from something else and always about as shallow as a coat of paint. What we need is a gutty song, one that has some bounce to it and at the same time says something without smirking. A man has to blush to sing about two thirds of the stuff from Tin Pan Alley and the rest of it is so damn insincere that you feel like a fool. Most men sing because the tune is easy to handle. They don't pay as much attention to the words, unless the words happen to reflect the man's feeling. Nobody is going to own up to the silly sentiment most of this crap oozes out. The Australians have a song that made a pretty big hit with the boys and I've tried to locate the words. It's a simple rising & falling tune, almost a chant, and begins, "There's a troopship that's leavin' Bombay, bound for old Blighty's shores . . . . . " the refrain goes: "There'll be no promotion this side of the ocean, so cheer up lads—fuck'em all." In polite company that could be changed to "bless'em." The song isn't a fighting song—it doesn't yell blood & thunder, but people sing it. It has guts. Even the simple little one about "I'd rather be a pimple on the ass of a whore, than a first class private in the Medical Corps," has a certain quality to it.

The men who are fighting here aren't a damned bit refined. They're guys who shoot a Jap in cold blood and then knock his teeth out with a butt of a rifle. They are the guys who are going to win this war for the song writers back in New York, and somebody it seems to me should be able to write a song for them, put some words to it that don't drip with phoney patriotism or cry for some dame's soft young arms, and turn it loose for the inspiration—not the entertainment—of everybody concerned. I think everybody wants something like that because they try so hard to make something real and genuine out of these fake jobs. An honest-to-God, simple, rousing fight song would be a god-send to the Army.

Monday, January 25. First good night's sleep in a week. We had an alarm, but it didn't pan. So I blossomed out with my first piece of poetry. I guess Guadalcanal has got me—never thought I'd stoop to this. A copy of my epic may or may not be inserted in the book for safe-keeping. Depends on how I like it tomorrow.

Am now back in my usual state—no typewriter and looking for something to do. Don't know whether to work on a PRO feature or try to get that engineer story out for *Yank*. Frankly not over energetic this morning. My sudden burst of poetry must have sapped my "creative genius." Ooof!

Brodie says it is "close to art." Not very close; he's too kind. The thing stinks.[28]

Wrote Helen yesterday—No. 7. Japs sent 78 planes over today. Fighters shot down 5, bombers never did come in.

Tuesday, January 26. Went up to Kokumbona, past one of the worst scenes of havoc imaginable, past decomposing bodies which smelled to high heaven, past blasted Jap installations and weapons, to the place we've been trying to take for so damn long—and that the Army just walked in and grabbed. I think this must be Japan's Bataan.

Ran into Walter Bullock, now a Sgt. in Co. B, 27th Inf., whom I used to play ball with when we were kids. Haven't seen him since Jr. Hi. days. But recognized him, even with mustache. I don't try to explain a memory like that—or a coincidence.[29]

The Kokumbona story is good, but I think I'm going to lay off ground stuff for awhile—except that damn engineer thing. I'm going to get "Fire in the Hole" down on paper, and that's a promise.

Saw Col. Sherman who said our stuff clearing all right—but added a very subtle hint to get hell on the ball with some Air Corps stuff. I still have my ideas about whether our stuff is actually going to *Yank* or not. If I thought we were getting the double-cross, I'd raise hell. If we only would hear from Spence. Sherman said too that Freeman is swapped to combat intelligence, and that Shope is head man, with a new officer in to help him. I believe a man just in from the States. That may be a new problem.

Letter from Jackson just received. Not very encouraging. Seems to be censorship trouble on prisoners & other stuff. O, hell. What's the use—and why bother. I'll write it and forget it.

Wednesday, January 27. Two raids last night, first by two planes, second by six. They dropped a mess of stuff—all of it too far away to whistle. But once the concussion in our hole was so much my ears were ringing. There seems to have been some sort of naval action. Scuttlebutt says something may be happening today. Was so sure we were going to have a raid last night that I went to bed with my shoes on, but I didn't think they'd wait until 3:00 this morning. All clear about 5:00.

Thirty-eight planes this morning. Took blanket, detective book, helmet, to foxhole, determined to at least spend the time doing something. The bombers didn't get in, but I hear they got a P-39 & a Grumman. Too early to know yet. Later heard score 16-7.

To river for much needed bath. I'm peeling and after that jeep ride yesterday—I stunk. Could still smell dead Japs last night.

Finished story on Kokumbona Push, which, I think, will be my last infantry story for awhile.[30] Saw pack mules this evening so that must mean artillery and it should make a nice story with Brodie's drawings. Want to do an AA story—plus that damn engineer thing. Going after the engineers tomorrow if possible: have tentative arrangement to go with Col. Reeve, 25th Eng. officer.[31] Hope I can make some kind of story, because feel their work here deserves all kind of credit. The more I think about it the more I believe it would be unwise to stay with one outfit and do the routine name-conversation piece. Better to take another look-see & do general picture as started. Glad I talked myself into that.

Cromie got letter from Jackson, enclosing my $15. That's fine because when we leave we'll probably go to Suva and I'm flat broke.

Cromie & Dowling will be leaving on the first ship out to make room for two other correspondents. Travel by air is *not* authorized for them, so they'll probably pull out with the 2nd Marines. I wonder if that damn order concerns us—we have our orders that say by air—but I don't know. On board ship is where I wish the hell I were an officer. Some bastard stole my pistol out of the jeep at K., I discovered.

Thursday, January 28. Raid last night around midnight, but all of us slept it out. Johnny got up to see what the score was, couldn't find anybody in bed so came back and went to sleep. We all too sleepy to care. No bombs anyway. It was dark & raining but if there had been bombs we'd probably all have broken legs, literally, to get to shelter. Bad combination: sleep, darkness, mud.

Breakfast 'smorning heard another of these strange tales that make the Jap a character incomprehensible. The general's driver—wish I knew his name— was up yesterday and saw on the beach 1,000 yds. above them 20 Japs marching along in close order, 4 abreast. They put an artillery shell 500 yds behind them and the Japs never wavered. Then a battalion of artillery opened up—just for practice—and blew them to hell. I have every reason to believe the boy was truthful, because on the beach at the Tenaru 1,000 Japs marched down in close order against the Marines one night. This incident happened yesterday, so it might have been a defiance in the face of our push up there. What people those Japs can be.

A prisoner was brought in yesterday that I was almost glad to see because he proved that our drive hasn't been against a bunch of half dead sick men. This guy was in good shape, his uniform fairly clean and complete to the peaked cap. Someone said he had malaria but he looked okay to me. His face was round—not peaked & pinched as some are.

Beaton came in last night and said Col. Brown had liked the Kokumbona story very much. I don't remember his exact words but I appreciated it. Beaton almost gushed about it because he said almost any compliment from the Col. was something. Brown looks more like a football coach than a staff officer. He wears an aviation flight cap and smokes a pipe—he reminds me of a combination of about three coaches back home; has that same quiet manner & speaks with that slow careful choosing of words.[32]

This afternoon we really hit the jackpot. For the record I'll take an inventory to determine exactly how much mail we did get. It came in about this order: a letter from Jackson, telling me my stuff is clearing okay; a package of matches from Jackson; a V-mail letter from Helen dated Dec. 8. Second delivery: a batch of stuff from the office, including circular letter very complimentary on stuff from Tontouta; a couple letters from Helen—Nos. 5 and 6 (Dec. 29-31), Brodie got several letters & Dec. 30—Jan. 6 issues of *Yank*. Third delivery: letter V-mail from Dad (12-8-42), letter AM from Dad (12-31-42), letter straight from Hilton (12-16-42). I've never gotten so much stuff in one bunch in my life. Also, in last delivery, got Jan. 13 copy of *Yank* with story & pix Joe Melton played page one by-line. Wonderful. Never been so hopped up over anything—all the mail—in long, long time. Hot damn!

Now to digest some of the stuff. Having read them all over again, the best news is that Helen seems happy and in swell health and reports $225 in one letter plus $50 in another. If my first $105 allotment for December has been received, then things are looking up financially. God it feels good to be out of debt, even out here. Next thing is Forsberg's and then Spence's reports that something new has been added in the way of "correspondent's ratings" for staffers in the field. Spence said to all that it will "help *most* of you" in getting around. In a way that doesn't sound like a dream come true to me because I don't think if we were 4-star generals we could have any better travel orders than those we have and should the office's well-intentioned idea screw us up I'd have a helluva type thing on my hands. But the thing must entail some sort of promotion or something because it is intended to "change our status." If that doesn't mean promotion, but merely stronger operating orders it won't be much help. But we can't tell what situations we may run into, so the more paper we can flash the better off we probably will be. Frankly, in a combat zone it doesn't really make a helluva lot of difference about our ratings as long as we can bluff a little, but back in the areas where they fight the war on paper we need all the rank we can get. It gravitates to a very simple thing. In Noumea an officer can buy drinks at the bar; an enlisted man can't. I'd just as soon buy drinks at the bar and leave the Andy De Gaulle alone.

Friday, January 29. This morning at dawn I saw my first Jap plane at fairly close range, and five minutes later it became the first plane I've seen shot down in flames. The siren went off about 4:15 and Brodie & I lay down on his sack while somewhere far out something buzzed around. Then, as it got light, we heard a burst of .50 cal and AA fire from the fighter strip; we were up just in time to see tracers streaking past a plane that banked & turned over the trees at the hospital and apparently headed up toward Kokumbona. We figured he must have sneaked in to strafe the field—he was very low, a medium bomber, I think. While we talked that over a P-38 dropped out of the clouds and loafed in over the field, doing nothing in particular, apparently. Then he headed out to sea—we didn't pay any attention. Then Allan—who has eyes like a hawk and something close to an infallible radar ear—said "Look!" and pointed. At first we could see only the 38 in the distance, but then, beyond it, another plane. The P-38 came down on him in a diving turn. We could see a tiny stream of black smoke sailing out behind him. The plane in front was going hell for leather diagonally across him and then suddenly it just disappeared in a terrific burst of flame—just like the sudden flare of a match, same orange color. The ball of fire kept going, and then dropped out of sight into the drink near Savo. The P-38 came whistling back over the fighter strip and zoomed lazily up. When the Jap went to blazes we all yelled like bastards; somebody who had been in the office below said Col. Long[33] chuckled:"Bagged one before breakfast" and everybody on Cactus Heights took it up, grinning. Made me feel damn good. That pilot must have felt like a million because it was a beautiful show—one pass, one 3-second burst—and bingo! Good thing too, it happened almost in front of Kokumbona and the boys up there must have had a helluva kick.[34]

There were two other warnings last night—neither panned.

Finally sweated out that Engineer story yesterday. What a grind, but it proved one thing to me: that the experience we've had here on the line, etc., can come in handy. I talked to Col. Gillette again and then just filled in from what I've seen. It was no masterpiece, however Hipple said this morning Col. Brown had told him about it and thought it was good.[35] Col. Brown is my buddy, altho I don't think he knows me when he sees me. The boys seemed to think the Melton story okay.

Cromie and Dowling left this morning to board ship for Noumea. I was sort of sorry to see them go because I believe it's the start of the busting up of the Guadalcanal Press Club as I knew it. I have never yet been able to quite understand Jack. He and McCarthy were nice as hell to us in Auckland, but up here, he hasn't said fifty words to me since the day we got in. He doesn't say a helluva lot to anybody for that matter, but I still don't get it. I must have done something to him, but damned if I know what. He was damn cordial in saying so long. I like the guy.

Bob and I got to be good buddies. He became much more friendly, I think, after our trip up to the 35th. I think I understand why, because he had a near monopoly for awhile on the rough stuff. Perhaps that's silly, but it worked out that way. I can get some funny ideas, particularly since the 35th trip was actually more physical exertion than danger altho we did come under fire out there and I finally got the front line story out of my system. I was in much worse shape emotionally on the 132nd push, mainly I suppose because we couldn't see a damn thing in the jungle and I didn't know from nothing about what really was going on. That first sniper shot up there aged me a couple of years, but after that it wasn't so bad even tho what we walked into was the worst mess I've ever seen—or want to see. The slaughter & stink at Kokumbona didn't hit me as hard. I'm still finding out that all the things I've gone thru—the emotional evolutions—and am still going thru are certainly not peculiar to me. Deep inside, I think everybody feels the same: it crops out in a lot of ways in men.

Brodie told me something this morning I sensed but didn't actually understand. The guy had something chewing on him, as I did for awhile, and he had to get it out of his system. He wanted, for the record, to study at close range the dead. As background and experience he felt that he should have a knowledge of how men look when they're left for the flies & land crabs.

At Kokumbona the other day he found out. I missed him almost at once and didn't see him until we got back to camp. Today he spilled it. He got off the road and went looking for bodies. He found them—they were all over the place—and did brief sketches of "the curious positions of the dead"—putrefying, maggot-eaten, shell-torn Japs, some of which could hardly be told from a lump of bones and uniform. Brodie is, as I've said too often, sensitive and probably has a delicate stomach—so I admire him for going against his every natural instinct to do a job he thought should be done. He waited, he said, to see how the after-effects would hit him before he told me about it. He said it hasn't seemed to bother him. One thing I know—that the smell of dead men and the sensation of riding calmly over a rotten body in the road is tough on sensitive natures.[36] I also know that to stare at the remains of Japs, parts of them, what's left of them, is not nearly so frightening to me now as such things would have been a year ago. Like everybody else, I did it with no emotion whatsoever. At Kokumbona a Jap washed to shore and kept floating face down & spread-eagled in the water, each time almost being left on the sand but each time washing back on the next wave again, like the pendulum of a clock. The Jap's skin was absolutely white and the body was bloated so it seemed a pin prick would have exploded him. The back of his head was burnt coal black by the sun on his exposed skull. He washed back and forth on his belly and men came down to the beach looked at him and went away. Nobody changed the subject of their conversation except to make an initial remark about the body. There was something infinitely lonesome about the waves and the man, even if it was a Jap.

I've been writing these two pages almost as tho the campaign of Guadalcanal were ended. I'm premature. Perhaps I've been trying to summarize our first month on the scene of action, a month I'll never forget because it's changed my outlook on things. I've undergone some of the strongest emotions of my life here. But that ain't nothing. Elmer Stone the Marine interpreter is pulling out. He just told us: "We've been on Guadalcanal only three months, but it's been 13 months since I've seen a white woman."

Saturday, January 30. Another reveille alert, but no bombs. Went to QM and drew four pair wool sox, one de-loused set of greens. Wrote Helen and Dad yesterday, Helen No. 8. Got two more letters—one from Dad dated Christmas; one from Helen dated our anniversary. Press boys trying to inveigle new jeep. Old Faithful, veteran of Guadalcanal from day one—Aug. 7—finally has gone ka-phloony. Somebody supposed to have shelled Kokumbona last night; scuttlebutt has rumors of Jap action vicinity of Beauford Bay. More talk Jap thrust Cactuswards—also more talk our air, navy strength. When this one happens it ought to be good. Did story on condition red in my best college professor writing. The office will either think it funny or the most idiotic piece of crap ever.[37] I wonder which. Gave a coverall stuffed full of clothes—filthy clothes— to Allan to wash for me. I don't care what he charges—there's nothing I hate worse than scrubbing those things. Heard the Japs occupied the Russell Islands today; what that means and if whether it's true I don't know yet. Brodie and I discussed for the first time tonight how much longer we will stay. He says he has one more set of drawings and then he'd like to take a break. He's worked like a horse and the strain, plus occasional lack of sleep, is beginning to tell. If I'd worked as constantly and as conscientiously as he, I'd be a nervous wreck by now. As it is I'm ready to pull out and knock around the Pacific for awhile, then come back with a re-opened mind if and when things start to break. I know damn well the fur's going to fly pretty soon—either on our new offensive or theirs but can't tell when because nobody around here knows anything. That's not this island's concern. Brodie says ten days for his drawings and I have a couple of air stories to do to clear my conscience and keep people off my neck. I want to try to make Hawaii.

Sunday, January 31. Somehow, even on Guadalcanal, you can sense the feeling of Sunday. I've noticed that around headquarters, but on the front it's like any other day. I believe it was a Marine interpreter who told me that a Jap he questioned was disillusioned by the fact that Marines fight just as hard on Sunday as any other time, which was contrary to the information apparently given out by Jap officers. The office wants a story on a chaplain on the line and I think I'll ask the 25th about it. I know for a fact that Father Finnegan of the 35th was in the middle of it because I saw him up there. He and Father Gehring of the Navy have bolstered my faith in the cloth after a couple of pretty unwholesome instances I've run into in others. There are Chaplains and Chaplains, I've found out.[38]

This morning at breakfast the boys were talking about officers. There was Beaton and other boy from 164th and an MP. The things they said were things I've heard before by men out of almost every outfit in the Americal Div., and I record them here for the sake of noting that an officer bears a terrific morale responsibility and that being an officer in no way releases a person from the job of proving himself first a man.

First, the boys criticized National Guard officers in general. They claim almost every outfit is run by politics and that too often the ranking brass is shot with incompetence. Beaton pointed out the regimental exec officer was a small town barber, etc. The MP expressed the opinion that the National Guard as it now exists should be abolished completely after the war, or that the officers should be entirely Regular Army, carefully chosen. I've heard that idea advanced before, once in particular by a very well bred selectee who maintained the Guard picked the biggest prick in each town and gave him the highest rating. That might have been an unjustified beef, which is certainly not a correct blanket statement. However, I have listened to a hundred men chow talk of outfits and officers, and everyone of them has had a story to prove that if the officers are good the outfit is good and if the officers are poor the outfit isn't worth a hoot in hell. I used to think that non-coms make an outfit, but now I know that isn't so. Good non-coms can hold a poor outfit together but it's the officers who set the standards and who form the structure on which everything else is built. In the Army there are two classes of people—officers and enlisted men. Non-coms will side with the enlisted man invariably if the officers are no good, because a non-com is an enlisted man first and a sort of second-hand leader without the authority to mold things.

Some examples picked up this morning: the 182nd has been screwed since the day it went into action for such reasons as this. A Colonel ordered a lieutenant to move forward and spot enemy gun emplacements. The lieutenant said, "Sure, Colonel, come on and go with me—the two of us together will draw twice as much fire." The Colonel wouldn't go. Another time the outfit had walked from hell to breakfast in the heat of the day. A Colonel rode up to an 81mm mortar section and told the men to get the hell moving faster. A boy just dropped the mortar he'd been lugging and said, "Colonel, suppose you carry this awhile." One officer of the outfit actually was put on trial for deserting his men in the face of the enemy. He was acquitted, but there was something wrong or such action would never have been taken. Too, the men tell of cases in which the officers stayed behind and ordered the men forward in a hot spot. I know of the case in which Col. Nelson of the 132nd asked to be relieved of his command because he got to the place on Mt. Austen that he didn't know what to do, or how to do it. Col. George took over and the next day the outfit took Hill 27. Those are the things which completely destroy men's confidence, make them utterly useless in combat. They are infinitely more serious than the idea the men have that promotions are based on politics.

On the other hand I've seen some magnificent examples of officer leadership, Nat'l Guard, Reserve, and Regular Army. On the Horse's Neck with the 35th the officers went down ahead of their men. This Captain Cagwin was all over the place; the men swore by their battalion CO, Major Mullen.[39] I swear by Col. Crawford who took us up there and pushed a boat down coming back. At Kokumbona with the 27th I never heard a bunch of men voluntarily praise an officer as highly as they did Capt. Bowen[40]—and the praise wasn't only from men in Bowen's outfit. Capt. Burden, the interpreter, went way the hell back in the bush with patrols to try to talk Japs into surrendering (and Col. Brown rightly raised hell with him when he got back). The boys this morning told of listening to a BAR raise hell all night and when morning came they found it was a lieut. col. firing. A reservist Lt. Fitzgerald with the 35th was a right guy all the way and I've already recorded the story of the Marine Major Love who reported his Bn's action to Col. Arthur.

So there are good officers and bad. But the Nat'l Guard seems to have a burden of bad ones. I'm convinced the lousy showing of the 182nd was a result of poor officers alone, and that the 132nd had unnecessary losses and a bad start for the same reason. Fact that their CO, Col. Wright, was killed on patrol the first day didn't help at all. The 164th had trouble when it first came in, but later won the reputation of one of the best outfits on the island. Gen. Collins of the 25th is a fighter if there ever was one and his outfit shows it every day.[41]

I know from experience of 18 months in the 117th that the proportion of poor officers was fairly high and that the outfit for a long time was run by West Tennessee politics. It's difficult in the Guard to draw the line between personalities and military qualifications. Sometimes it was hard to think of a man you liked personally as being a poor officer. Out here the men think of some officers as "good civilians" and let it go at that. There was a great deal of favoritism, and I can remember clearly a Colonel having ridden to the head of the column and gotten out, half drunk, with the declaration that he could "outwalk any man in the regiment." I remember Tom LeMay having climbed in a command car and ridden past us on a march back to camp. Tom, I understand, later became a good officer, but he had a lot to learn then. Altho I hated to see it done from a personal standpoint, it was good that the old 117th was busted up as a clannish regiment. At the same time I refuse to condemn our regular officers—Ritts, Crumbly, Bowen, Mottern—because I know they'd have gone thru hell with us in action. I have often thought A company would have made a helluva swell combat outfit here—but perhaps I'm still prejudiced by the old Army pride.

Anyway, I have seen it proven beyond all possible doubt in my mind that a good officer personnel is an absolute basic necessity for an Army organization. I've seen one outfit whose officers weren't so hot and I've seen another whose officers were really leaders. There was all the difference in the world, not only in the performance of the men but in the accomplishments of the outfits. There was a definite difference in the training background of each, which also reflects on the officers primarily, and no badly trained bunch of men are going to transform suddenly into combat wildcats.

In the making of officers in the Guard there was the original sin of trying to make silk purses out of sow's ears. In the Regulars there are the West Pointers who form the structure and who take the Reservists in hand. I don't think it possible for a bad teacher to produce a good pupil, and in the Guard there is too much phoniness at the top in too many cases, and it filters down. In the making of new officers it must be absolutely essential that a candidate has proven himself as an enlisted man, otherwise the situation becomes even worse. It is the same thing as taking a third stringer and making him coach. An officer has got to be a leader—an intelligent, courageous leader—before he is anything else.[42]

These references to the situations which occur and have occurred too often in the Guard go against my whole background as a Guardsman. It is not an indictment against every Guard outfit or every Guard officer, nor a defense for every soldier in the line who might use his officers as an alibi—and sometimes does. I'm just writing of what I've seen.[43]

"I'd Write Hallelujah!"

Monday, February 1. Givens came back from Button yesterday and brought four bottles of gin, which we went to work on last night. Hangover this morning. I am now definitely conscious of a change in me as a drinking man—I talk too much. It used to be that I kept my mouth shut—was even noted for it back home—but I became aware in New York of the fact that my tongue was getting oily. Then when we pulled that terrific bender New Year's Eve and the lesser one the next night I found myself prattling away like a house afire—saying all kinds of damn fool things. And last night Givens and I got into an argument which was absolutely ridiculous, at least my part of it. We were talking about the things entered on the three previous pages, and I think I must have set myself up as something of an expert. After a little less than three months overseas and a little more than five weeks of action, a man still has a long way to go before becoming an expert on anything—much less on so complicated a thing as the Army or so many-angled a thing as combat. Hereafter, and this is a promise, I'm either going to control my talk while drinking, or else do my drinking on a lone wolf plan, or quit getting drunk. If there's anything I despise it's a talking drunk.

I paid Allan $2 to wash all those clothes, which he brought back yesterday semi-pressed and looking almost as if they had been dry-cleaned. He did a wonderful job—and it was worth a good deal more than that to me. I don't like to wash clothes and I'm not at all ashamed of the fact.

Read three plays by Eugene O'Neill this morning, with a slight interruption—*The Emperor Jones, Anna Christie,* and *The Hairy Ape.* Enjoyed them very much. I'm taking a break now while the ground situation seems to be petering out, before I do the Air Corps stuff, and doing such things as reading a pocket book of famous detective stories and Mercury Book of O'Neill's plays is as good a way as any. Wrote Charlie Hilton and Lee Wilson yesterday.[1] Tried to send Charlie a piece of Jap notebook, but doubt it will get through.

The "slight interruption" this morning was a strafing-bombing by five Jap twin-engined jobs. We got Condition Red and were all standing around the cave when the damnedest racket opened up on the other side of the hill. Haven't heard so much fire since the push on Hill 27. Anyway, we got in the cave and Frommell and I who were closest to the door looked out to see, I think it was, five planes helling from the direction of the field, out over the palm groves. There had been a lot of machine-gun fire and some bombs, and there was still a lot as they went up the beach, ours & theirs. The ack-ack opened up on them but didn't get close, altho they couldn't have been more than 1000 feet, if that much. They were going too fast. It was a beauty of a sneak raid and you've got to hand it to those bastards—it took guts. I heard we got some of them, a bomber and a few of the Zero escorts but I don't know exactly. Too soon to get complete tabs at chow.

One bad report: we lost three B-17s and some SBDs up north this morning. Zeros jumped the 17s. Beaton says 20 DDs and some more stuff coming down, due in after ten. The Tokyo Express was reported last night, but I don't think it showed, so maybe the two will join. There should be some naval action.[2]

Another raid this afternoon, but it was intercepted. We lost a can off Savo which sank in two minutes, but the Japs lost 20 planes. We couldn't see a damn thing, but I wouldn't have seen it anyway because I took a blanket & a January *Reader's Digest* down with me and read until I almost missed a steak supper.

Jackson & Hipple and Miller must have had a field day. They went up this morning before I even ate breakfast and while there they got strafed, watched a can shell Jap positions and then saw Jap dive bombers sink the can—the lucky bastards.[3] And me on my ass again. Think will start on AC stuff tomorrow— can't stand this sitting around; gets on my nerves and makes me feel bad. And I write too much in here.

Tuesday, February 2. Last night was a rat race from way on back. I haven't had a raid so get on my nerves as the one's we had, and the whole thing is a study of the confusion of a man's makeup.

We were knocking off the rest of Givens' gin at leisure, with the conversation running easily when I suddenly sensed a plane. For not much of a reason I said, "Let's check this plane" and everybody stopped talking. Just then he let 'em fly—close—and the lights went out as everybody hit the deck. We crawled from the tent to the dugout by dead reckoning; I wiggled over the sand bags & down in headfirst. So did everybody. Brodie banged his knee. Came the All Clear, we went back to the gin. During the first one, in all the wild scramble on the ground and after we got inside, I noticed I was calm as a cucumber whereas when all the fire opened up yesterday morning I was pretty shaky for a minute after it was over. I thought that strange. We were back on the gin, with the lights on, when the second alarm came and everybody was on his feet and in the shelter in nothing flat. This time they were also pretty close. All the time we had word of a naval engagement and we fully expected to be shelled. So everybody decided to go below. We stayed below until after midnight and nothing happened so we turned in. The condition was still red so I kept my shoes on. We heard a plane and after about five minutes Brodie put his clothes back on and went outside. He was right. The AA opened up so we made for the hole. (I'm writing now from the cave—we just had a Red). That was the final visit of the evening but by this time it was beginning to tighten up. Before Brodie went out we had heard a plane which I thought was Jap so we had all gotten up, which is how keyed up we were. It was our own plane, with lights. Anyway, on the last one the Charlies buzzed around and around, always close, and dropped a few now and then. They were shooting for this pocket. The AA raised hell at first and then laid off, apparently trying to lure them in. When I really got the jumps was when those bastards circled directly overhead, no AA against them, and we were waiting for the swishes to duck low. Actually for the first time I literally sweated a raid out—my heart pounded like a trip hammer. All the hits were close, or seemed like it. We didn't like the dugout and after his third pass we made a run for the cave. By the time the All Clear came at 4:00 I'd had enough. Swallowed my pride for the sake of some sleep and slept on the coral until daylight.

This, I think, is the fourth day I haven't done anything, and it's beginning to get on my nerves, but I've noticed that as long as I'm doing something—as long as the incentive is okay—it doesn't bother me. It's not good to just fluff around—makes a man feel a little like a GI lounge lizard, even on Guadalcanal. The hell of it is I want to do this AC stuff and then again I don't want to do it. Can't get hepped on the thing for some reason. I honestly feel we've done justice to the ground stuff and I know a couple of good features on the pursuits and one on the bombers would pretty well square us away. Maybe I can talk myself into it as I go along. But I can't seemed to get enthused on it like the infantry stuff. But hell—I have to do something—can't just sit here. Nine stories in five weeks should be enough to hold 'em awhile, but when we shove off I want to leave feeling we wrapped things up as well as possible.

The CR this morning didn't pan. I think the final box on yesterday and last night was 29 to 11 planes and 5 to 1 cans. But the hell of it was they landed troops, possibly 3000 and that just means that much longer. There's something wrong at Wing on the plane operation, that's in the air. Those people should never have gotten in here.

Talked to Major Ash today and he's working on what he thinks will be an entirely new type airplane with some kind of opposite cylinder revolution that will mean noiseless propulsion and the doing away with the wing & the prop as it now exists. It was too technical for me—aerodynamic principles of lift and

Morriss's sketch of his first encounter with American dead and wounded during his visit to the front on Guadalcanal in late December 1942. Morriss Collection.

(*Above*) The photograph taken on Guadalcanal that Morriss later saw in Jim Bassett's office. Front (left to right): Bob Cromie, *Chicago Tribune*, Jack Dowling, *Chicago Sun*, Bill Moscowitz, Marine driver; back (left to right): Morriss, Allan Jackson, INP, Roberts Jackson (probably), Army PRO, and Bob Brumby, INS. Allan Jackson. (*Below*) Morriss and Brodie with the 35th Infantry on Hill 44 (the "Sea Horse"), 16 January 1943. The machine gun points toward the enemy and in the background is BAR man, Ray Flemm, mentioned in Morriss's story, "Jap Trap." *Yank*.

Brodie's sketch of G.I.s on the "Sea Horse" carrying a Japanese prisoner, which was included in his spread, "Last Days at Guadalcanal," *Yank*, 19 March 1943. U.S. Army Center of Military History.

Brodie's sketch, "Road to Kokumbona," of the Japanese corpse that Morriss described in his diary as "tough on sensitive natures." U.S. Army Center of Military History.

(*Above*) B-17s of the 23rd Squadron, 5th Bomb Group (H) preparing to take off from an air field on Guadalcanal for a bombing mission. Basel Debnekoff. (*Below*) "The Skipper," in which Morriss and Brodie flew a mission with the Berton Burns crew to bomb Kahili on the night of 9-10 April 1943. Basel Debnekoff.

(*Above*) The Burns B-17 crew. Standing (left to right): Lt. Art Cohen, a Capt. Bailey or Bradley, Maj. Berton "Tex" Burns, Lt. Radar Forsberg, Walter Sidler; front (left to right): Forrest Averbeck, Basel Debnekoff, Ross Henderson, Anton Schmidt, and J. W. Weaver. Basel Debnekoff. (*Below*) Vice Admiral Marc A. Mitscher greeting the first of the Classen B-17 crew to arrive back at Guadalcanal, 11 April 1943. Left to right: Lt. Robert Dorwart, Lt. Balfour C. Gibson (shaking hands with Mitscher), Capt. Thomas J. Classen, the TBF crew member, Delmer D. Wiley, and Mitscher. USMC.

(*Above*) The "Old Japanese Hangar" at Henderson Field as it looked when Morriss was gathering information on ground crews for his stories for *Yank*. The five-hundred-pound bombs on the ground have been brought up from the ordnance area nearer the beach and have had their box-fins attached. U.S. Navy. (*Left*) Lt. Walter S. Bralley, 31st Squadron ordnance officer, who showed Morriss around and provided him with information for the story, "Ground Crews," which *Yank* never published. Walter S. Bralley. (*Below*) 31st Squadron ordnance encampment on Guadalcanal as it looked in the spring of 1943 when Morriss was working on the ground crew story. Walter S. Bralley.

(*Above*) The Tojo Ice Co., which Morriss described in his story for the 21 May 1943 issue of *Yank* as "one of the best known of all Guadalcanal landmarks." Walter S. Bralley. (*Below*) The cemetery at Guadalcanal as it looked in the spring of 1943. By September 1943 when Morriss visited the cemetery again on his way back from New Georgia, the chapel built by the Solomon Islanders had been dedicated. James D. Rothermel.

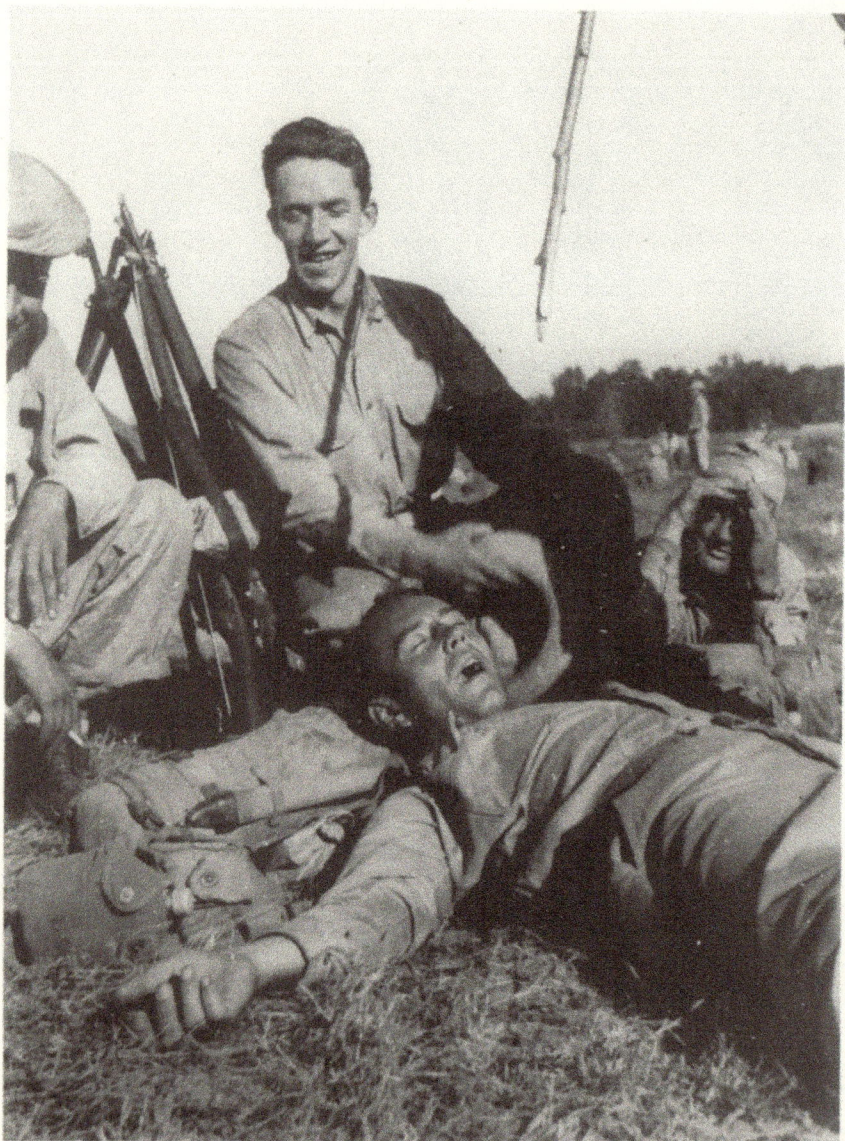

In April 1943 Morriss visited the cemetery and stopped at the grave of Cpl. Ervin Bickwermert (shading his eyes in this photograph taken during the 1941 Louisiana Maneuvers), whose last words had been "hold that hill." Sgt. Wayne M. Douglas (laughing, center) was awarded the Silver Star and a Battlefield Commission for his role in holding Hill 27. Mrs. Wayne M. Douglas.

drag and air foil etc.—but he thinks he's got something. Could be, because he's had a few things in that line before. He had some mail for us—pencils for Brodie, mainly.

Jackson wants us to put the bee on Major Shope to send him back up here, so I think I'll write the Major and tell him we plan shoving in a couple of weeks and that Bob should be sent back up. Dammit, I can't get going on PRO stuff at all. I just don't like the ideas anymore and anyway they seem to be satisfied.

Heard we getting some new planes in 24s and 38s and such, so that should be interesting.

Wednesday, February 3. Went to bed early last night, trying to catch up on sleep, but at 8 o'clock another Nip sneaked in. Woke up to hear 'em bustin'. We live right in Bomb Alley, between Henderson field and the fighter strip so they sound close to us either way. After they dropped and the siren made itself foolish by howling as it does in the bombs' echo, I said the hell with this noise and went below. Had to have some uninterrupted sleep last night, regardless. So I got in my blanket, left from night before last, and slept like a log—on a log.

Woke up just before dawn, decided to come up for last couple hours on bunk. Started around the tree, put my hand on the trunk, then saw it about two inches from a snake. Sprang back, lost balance, fell. Stayed watching him, then saw him with triangle head much closer, heading my way. Got the hell out of there, went long way around back to tent, got Gene's jungle cutlass. Back at tree saw snake twined in with roots, hit him, he disappeared. Thought he was either cut in two or I'd missed him and he'd gone to other side down below. Went down, saw whole snake working along, cut his head off. Saw another snake overhead in tree, threw cutlass at him as Bong taught me, missed him. Woke Allan, still asleep in tree-cave. Then saw snake working through brush, hit him three or four times, knocked him down. He already had cut on him, so must have been one hit in tree. Snakes long, slim, dark, but with pointed heads and slim necks, so if the Handbook for Boys was right they both poisonous. Final score, one down, one probable. First experience snakes on Guadalcanal— have now seen everything.

To fighter strip this morning, ran into feature on pursuit pilots which is about the usual stuff. It's been done before but it's always good. Bomb damage over there heavy for just four bombs. The place was lit up like a Christmas tree, so he couldn't miss. Got pieces of P-40 shot to hell; pilot is okay but don't see how. Learned how those 3 17s lost; they broke from formation and went on own—Zeros hit 'em hard & fast.

Letter from Jackson 'smorning most heartening. Says stuff thru okay— also that Shope doesn't want us to do PRO work which is wonderful. Also says Miller, Bushemi in Noumea to do story on N.Z.E.F. Why I don't know.[4]

Australian George Doling says snakes 'smorning are Diamond Heads, poisonous; that they have them in Australia, too.[5]

Am now waiting for someone to finish with their typewriter.

Thursday, February 4. I hate to have to admit it—and I mean I really hate it—but I'm afraid I'm getting bomb happy. After three nights ago my nerves have been shot to hell. We had a CR last night and I went to the little dugout for the first pass; then everybody went below so rather than stay there alone I went too. The next pass was with a stick of four or five—the closest I've felt. They really rocked. But the hell of it is, I got the shakes. My muscles are beginning to tremble and there's not a damn thing I can so about it. If getting mad would do any good I'd be all right, because I cussed and swore at myself last night and the night before until I was blue in the face, and then spent a half hour outside the tent after All Clear last night listening to a motor which rose and faded in the distance. I can truthfully say I'm not actually scared, but somehow my reflexes won't let me settle down. There was a time when I could sleep thru a CR or go to the dugout and come back to bed immediately after the bombs fell, but it looks like now I'm the first guy in the hole. Yesterday we had a CR and we were all out the outside of the cave. I heard the swish of a Grumman coming in behind us, thought sure it was a bomb, and almost ran over Brodie getting inside. Pure imagination. It's a little like being skittish in the dark. A helluva thing, but I can't let this thing lick me. I've seen Brodie pass thru this stage already and after the other night Gene has been pretty jumpy too, which is unusual for him. I think it must have been Monday night that got the wind up in me, when Gene kept saying, "He's right overhead, fellows," and then "Duck!" when he heard the swishes. After all, tho, that's perfectly natural—it was just my reaction then that screwed things up, and by golly I couldn't help it. I think I would have been infinitely better off if I hadn't slept in the cave night before last, for two reasons: one being that I kept seeing snakes before I went to sleep last night. There's no use pampering a nervous condition—just have to bow my neck and snap out of it. The hell of it is, it makes me so damn mad at myself.

Finished the story on fighter pilots, finally taking advantage of Miller's absence at the front to use his typewriter. He & Hipple went up. Four companies of 147th[6] been pushing since Kokumbona, now at Tassafaronga. Hip says the jungle pretty rugged. They swam out to beached transport.

Understand Tokyo Express due in again tonight—hope to hell the Navy gets at 'em just to prove to the Army there is a Navy around here.

Friday, February 5. Charlie & party came over last night at 8:00 and didn't go home until five o'clock this morning. I must say he wore out his welcome. He made at least six bombing runs that I know of and a couple that I slept thru.

Everybody spent the night in the cave, fighting mosquitos, trying to sleep. Slept thru breakfast this morning and walked boldly into officers mess for coffee. Got it too.

The Tokyo Express came in all right and I don't think it got hurt. Col. Brown estimated this morning Japs have landed up to 3,000 troops in last two tries. "We know they're coming, follow them right on down—and yet they get stuff ashore. They're outsmarting us—that's all." Something seems to be wrong.

Allan Jackson got off this morning for Button. Two things Allan is proud of: being on Guadalcanal for a month, longer than any other photog (and in fairness, doing less work), and his practice of total indifference to air raids. Allan is the perpetual ski enthusiast.[7]

If I had anything to do about it, Bob Miller would get the DSC. Uncle Bob—the unquestioned dean of the Guadalcanal Press Club—and one of the grandest guys I know—doesn't mind risking his neck for a story and he makes reports to G-2 that are more complete than a lot they get from other sources. Bob went out with the PT boats Monday night—he was gone three or four days—and last night was in a PBY that bombed the DDs. He reported to Brown 'smorning and I know it was the only intelligence G-2 had on what happened. I once made a report to G-2 on something that happened at the front which made me think highly of myself for a couple of hours, but Bob makes that kind of foolishness look silly.

I sneaked a look at his diary he was working on this morning and read how he was "as close to death—in my own mind—as I have ever been" during the PT business when they spotted what everyone believed to be a torpedo headed dead into them. Bob said he knew the danger but "I kept watching the horizon for a look at the damn fool Jap who would waste a tin fish on a PT boat." He noted that only after the threat—a school of porpoises in the dark— was past he reacted to fear. Then he said the relieved feeling was intense—"as in a man after spending a great passion."

Bob is a student of the psyche of fear in battle, and Guadalcanal is his laboratory in which he studies men in the field, or a correspondence course in English grammar in the Press Tent. Gen. Vandergrift has said "Bob Miller is a good Marine." I say Bob is a good newspaperman.[8]

The scuttlebutt this afternoon is of a Jap task force—this time the Big Train—headed down with three aircraft carriers, one battleship, three cruisers and God knows what else.[9] Everybody is set for some rough sailing. Bob Brumby came back this noon from Button with the news that there's nothing down there, which I assume means our task force is out. If all we hear is true, then another terrific naval engagement is on the griddle. Eddie Ackley made the statement in the Press Tent that he "had no faith in the Navy whatsoever, that the Japs have planned this carefully and we plan our strategy off the cuff" or something like that. Eddie, in my opinion, is a nice enough guy which suffers him his broad A's and his talk of a wealthy fiancee, but he isn't much of an officer, even as a second looie talking among friends. Admittedly, the evidence has been that the Japs have been infiltrating a big force down from Truk, feeding it in slowly and sneaking in here with cans. But my idea is that the Navy is hep and that the fact they let the cans in is a come on for the bigger stuff. From what Halsey said, I think the Navy is trying to draw them out for a showdown fight, and I think we can knock hell of 'em. If I didn't, as I told Bob & Hip, I'd have left on the afternoon plane. Of course nobody can predict the outcome of a thing like this, and we here may take a shellacking—we assuredly will if our force doesn't contact them—but my money is on the Navy.

Brodie is all steamed over not being able to produce—"three tired little drawings" he just now yelped. "Shit!" Well, hell, between lack of sleep, mosquitos bites, Tokyo Expresses, short supplies and having to remember minute details of something he saw two weeks ago, I don't see how the guy could draw flies.

He has just been telling me some of the things the[10] boys have told him about conditions as they exist at Noumea—spit & polish, reveille, salute the officers, MPs all over the place. Boy, what a life. The Army must be the Army, no matter what. That galls me at this distance.

I swapped Beaton's rifle for a quart of Old Crow which Olin Clements of AP got out of a souvenir-minded bomber pilot—the sap. I don't think we'll hit it tonight, however.

Saturday, February 6. Last night I took two blankets down to the cave and laid them out, took a machete and chopped away some troublesome roots. Atkinson took down an extra bunk for a bench outside. Bob Cohn raided the kitchen for crackers, salmon, fruit juice which we stored inside. Everybody had his own anti-mosquito arrangements made when he went to bed, ready for instant service. And—we had no air raid.

The intrigue that went on last night for possession of the Old Crow was a kick. After I brought it up, Cohn said he wanted to swap Beaton a Jap flag, a Jap rifle and a German rifle for it, but Beaton wouldn't swap unless I said okay. Cohn said "Put in a good word with Beaton and I'll give you my watch." It's a cheap watch, but I needed one so I said I'd see what I could do. Then Beaton came up and tried to talk me into the idea of swapping, so I said I thought it might be a pretty good idea and anyway it was Beaton's whiskey, not mine. So Beaton swapped, got a battle flag he's been trying to get for a long time; I got a watch, and I think we've got a couple of quarts on the fire for the flag or the rifles. And Col. Timboe drank the whiskey.[11]

Talked to Lt. Ray today as a feeler for a story on the C-47s and found that the Army does have some sergeants flying them. SCAT is a combined Army-Navy-Marine operation which should make a good angle, altho this story will probably require three or four days to be done properly.[12] Sometimes I think I haven't either the temperament or the personality of a newspaperman. I don't think Ray liked the idea of my intention to play up the Army side of the Marine setup, and I had to follow him around to get an interview for tomorrow morning—which made me mad and I didn't try to conceal the fact. SCAT is certainly one of the best air stories here, but I don't like to lick a man's boots to get something. Well—what the hell?

The Jap task force—or forces—is still fiddling around. So are the rumors.

Read over some of my stuff today and came to the conclusion I at least tried hard, but am convinced went overboard a couple of times on names and several times bad construction.

The C-47 story should be good, if I can get it; then one on the bombers. By that time Brodie will either be finished or out of pencils, or both. And the naval engagement should have happened, one way or another.

Bob Miller and I were talking about Dowling tonight, and I told Bob the things I've already noted here, about my not being able to fully understand Jack. Bob replied by saying "there is one thing I pride myself in and that's having a fair understanding of the human mind and it's workings—altho there have been times when I've wondered—but to me Jack is a genius." Bob speaks simply and flatly of such things. "Jack is highly sensitive and being what he is his spirits are sometimes way up and sometimes down—the least thing can set him off in either direction. Yes, I consider Dowling a genius—and I've been around plenty of them (I presume in H'wood) so I know how they work." I knew Bob thought Jack the best writer on the island, but I didn't know he felt so definitely that Jack is not of the mass. I would certainly have liked to have read that play of his in the rough. Bob himself constantly amazes me. He's reading "Storm" and getting a great kick out of it—because, as he said, "I've gone out in the pastures and looked for rain—the weather used to mean a lot to me." Bob is going home in a month or so. I don't think he should have ever left it.

Sunday, February 7. Brodie and I, after a general discussion, decided this morning that we will leave Thursday. I had really wanted to stay two full months, but seven weeks is okay. Brodie is at the end of his string from an art standpoint. He has, as he says, just enough pencils and just enough energy to finish his present set of drawings which he intends finishing Wednesday. He wants to go away for a rest—which he actually needs badly—and then come back to tackle it again. From my own angle, I'd like to get out of here as badly as he for the very simple reason that the pressure is beginning to warp my perception and is in no way helping my writing. That story on fighters had some good material but I didn't do it justice—I couldn't get it down.

This morning I went over to SCAT and watched as a plane was unloaded, loaded again and cleared. I talked to a Marine kid, Lt. Morehouse I think, who gave me the names of some of the old timers. It became obvious to me then that catching those guys here would require weeks, probably, whereas I might be able to get them in a bunch at Tontouta. This afternoon I went back to SCAT to ask about transportation and saw several things that would have to be done from this end. I still have to talk to Ray because he's running the thing and while I don't think his impression of me is any too high after the other day & vice versa (pressure point there) he is the guy who is holding down this, the business, end of it. My idea this morning was to go from here to Button and then Noumea, but now it appears wiser to go to Noumea and back to Button because there are a couple of things there that will require time. One is to mingle with a bomber crew, come back up here with them for their operational stint and then return. I think that is a better way to do the story and it will give me a chance to get my feet back on the ground. Right now I don't feel up to going out on strikes with a B-17, a fact which I hate to admit but which is nonetheless true. Actually I have no desire to return to Noumea for several reasons: one, that I don't think I'll like the place now any better than I did before; and, two, I'm afraid of being short. Stopped down there before we can get going on our projected tour. But the cold facts are that Brodie cannot operate until he gets some more supplies from New York, so there's no use in our going anywhere until he is set again. We both could stand a good night's sleep and a damn good drunk, but we have no guarantee of the latter anywhere west of Suva or north of Auckland. Getting drunk in a wilderness is no fun anyway.

Only one thing mars our leaving at this time, and that's this damn naval action. It screws the deal, but royally. The truth of the matter is that at this date nobody seems to know the score—first it's off and then it's on—but everybody has a pronounced case of the jitters. The worst I've seen among the boys, and I know now it all dates from the night I tightened up. Nobody seems to have been the same since then, altho we've had no CR for the last two nights—which just aggravates the situation, strangely. Today noon the scuttlebutt was that Tokyo had boasted "Guadalcanal will be in Japanese hands by the 15th." Other things have happened which screw the nerves, but they're beside the point. The facts are that another attempt to retake this place appears imminent. A naval engagement to Brodie or myself means nothing, but a landing—that's different. I'm firm in my belief that no landing will be made, but of course that's in the hands of the Gods. Quien sab?

Monday, February 8. To SCAT for long discussion their operations which think can probably make into good story, but plan tread carefully because sense rather than see a veiled move to obscure Army's part, even tho SCAT is a Marine baby and must be treated as such. Am going to have to check carefully at Tontouta to round up loose ends. Am still casting around for some kind of story so as not to lose my average but I seem to have gotten to the point where I don't know a story when I see one. Col. George has been wounded and a personality story on him would be good, but I have been told it's tabu—but I think I'll try it this afternoon. As a short, think I'll tie in some of the trick names around here for a color angle altho it will be strictly off the west wall. After reading Ed's story on the bombing of Rangoon I'm even more convinced that ever that any story I do on B-17 bombing mission is going to have to be something more than jumping on a plane, bombing, and jumping off. Bomb missions are too much alike for a really good straight eye-witness to follow Ed successfully.[13] I think that best approach is the Button idea of living and flying with the crew, up here and back. Another approach would be picking a plane that would be shot down and later rescued, which is a little uncertain, and for which I have no great stomach.

Miller came in 'smorning with the cheerful opinion that he'll be home by April because it is his firm conviction that the Japs on Cactus are really washed up. Two days ago I heard the scuttlebutt that they are evacuating men. Today Beaton—my G-2 string man, says deserted boats have been found at sea. So the Tokyo Express may actually have been taking them off instead of putting them on. The Express was down last night again, but for the first time without Charlie to screen for them. From a practical standpoint it seems the only sensible thing the Japs could do because George's outfit has long since landed behind them and the squeeze is on. The 161st, which relieved the 147th, is driving right on up, meeting occasional resistance only. So it would seem logical that the Japs, who have lost a lot of material, should get the hell out while some of them still can. But, somehow, I don't give the Japs credit for being logical. Their task force is still moving around. It's remotely possible they may be covering the evacuation. The whole thing smells faintly of a feint one way or the other.

Tuesday, February 9. This morning at chow nobody could understand how and why we have been allowed four consecutive nights of uninterrupted sleep. The consensus is that something is afoot—but nobody can figure exactly what. We all feel much like the lighthouse keeper who's signal cannon misfired, waking him up to demand, "What was that!"

Yesterday morning the place was full of rumors, which prompts me to believe that the further a man could get from a high headquarters the better off he would be. One tale was of a landing by 1500 Japs eight miles above Koli Point. That turned out to be our own troops fooling around. Another was of the loss of the Big E, which is equally groundless. Another of a B-24 believed to have been sabotaged—it crashed at Button, killing 11 and destroying a ton of photo material, when all four motors cut out at once.

Bob and I drove over to the new fighter #1 last night and it is a beauty.[14] They were supposed to set the first planes on it last night. We also went to a

Seabee PX and I made my first purchases on the island . . . cigarettes, soap, tooth paste, candy. Brought back a carton of Pall Malls to Brodie, who was delighted to get his favorite brand for the first time since we left the States.

Talked to Col. George yesterday—the poor guy. He had an inch and a half of shin shot away. Just a case of too much guts—but how his boys love him. It will take him six months to get well, which is a helluva blow at this time.

Went over to the Signal outfit and Sgt. Bruning turned over some prints to us of shots on the 35th terrain. Also talked to some of the boys in the Special Services outfit under Capt. Cook, one of whom came up with the observation, "Whatta a racket." I have long since learned that men who have the least work to do in this man's Army are the ones who invariably take that attitude. One of the boys there has just begun a mimeograph job called the Sun Setter which may in a small way help fill a terrific need for reading matter here. They told me there that Gen. Patch had turned thumbs down on an Army PX, which the SS was supposed to have operated. That just makes any attempt to get *Yank* here so much the more difficult—dammit it to hell.

I'd write Hallelujah! all the way across this page if I could just get it into my head that this afternoon at 4:30 the forces moving west and the forces moving east on the north side of Guadalcanal met and that between them there were no Japs. Is this fact—something we've been fighting for (I use the editorial we) since I've been here—to be interpreted as the final securing of the island? Corps is happy—people are going around with grins on their faces—but I wonder if this is really the end of organized resistance. On it's face it could be nothing else. Where could any more Japs be—further around the coast on the South Side? It doesn't seem likely. In the hills? Possibly a few. Then it would seem that Guadalcanal, scene of the first U.S. offensive blow, is at last really ours after six months and two days. I wonder if the general will announce the thing that way, or whether he'll be prudent and wait. The natives pushing up from the South report no Japs. So it appears, then, that the 37 x 90 mile strip of coral on the bottom of the Solomons is actually in U.S. hands. If so, this is the end of the beginning.[15]

I've been considering for two or three days doing a think piece on Guadalcanal, but now I don't think I'll do another story at all. The fact that the island is secured, if it is, is a straight news thing and not, I believe, a subject for feature. People on this island will be willing to forget a lot of things that have happened here and already I can almost sense the fermenting tales that will be spread. I think I'll get a few facts for reference but if I make a story at all it will be on a report to Spence. I don't want to gush. I don't think it's smart—there's too much ahead. And the boys here don't want to be reminded of that—they want to go home. The story now is that a captured Jap asserted, "We may not retake Guadalcanal, but you'll never get Pearl Harbor back."

Did the story on Col. George. My biggest regret is the lack of any pictures at all. With pix I believe it would be a honey. George the man is half the story.[16] There have been times here when I'd have given anything for a camera. As great as Brodie's work is—and he does things with a pencil no camera could touch—still a photo is sometimes the only answer.

It now appears more evident than ever that Brodie and I will have to concentrate for a time on Air Corps exclusively, because for them the fighting goes right on. We were lucky to get here when we did.

I'm going to pick up as much info as I can tomorrow in order to have some kind of chronology on the thing from the beginning. The paper can get the chronology from official sources, but it will be up to me to fill in. In my head and in here are stories that can make the inserts on a rewrite man's rehash of the campaign. I'm not going to do it. I'm arguing myself out of it right now.

Now it is twilight—or the nearest thing to twilight in the tropics—and the way the sun slants across the field and into the palm grove is beautiful. It would be a horse laugh to a soldier if he read "Guadalcanal is beautiful." But the truth is, Guadalcanal at sunrise and sunset *is* beautiful, particularly at sunset. I've seen some of the most gorgeous sunsets here, and the air after a rain is cool. The mountains in the background are jungle covered and far away, but they look almost like the mountains at home. When a man is bitten by a million mosquitos, sloshes around in mud, eats from greasy mess-kits or out of cans, goes thru hell on the front and comes back to do fatigue labor when he is supposed to rest, when he gets bombed at night, when he thinks how long it's been since he's seen a white woman or had a drink out of a glass with ice, when he wonders how long before he sees home, he's not apt to think any place is beautiful. Who could blame him?

If I were writing a think piece, the first thing I would say is that it is easy to be wise when looking backward. The second, that it is easy to be foolish looking ahead.

October 13 was the date of arrival of the 164th Inf., the first Army outfit to see full scale combat—offensive combat—in the war. The 164th made its reputation and each outfit that followed followed its pattern—screwed up at first and straightened out later. Some outfits never straightened out. A great many mistakes were made, mistakes of a very human nature and mistakes of a military nature. Sometimes the two went hand in hand. There will be a great deal of glory-hogging, a great deal of lying, a great deal of genuine disgust born of Guadalcanal. But a small part of the Army of the Pacific has been blooded, and that is the important thing. The men here, most of them, have been over-seas for some time—the Americal came to Caledonia on March 12; they left the States Jan. 19, '42. The 25th Division has been the Pineapple Army for a long time, being RA men in foreign service. A good many of the air units, notably the 11th Bomb and the 67th Fighter Squadron, have been in the Pacific since shortly after Pearl Harbor. These men, for better or for worse, want to go home. Tonight everyone is happy, wild hopes and flaring up—tomorrow the rumors will be rife. But can these men go home? It's a hard thing to say, but they alone with the men we have in New Guinea are the only U.S. troops who have been under fire—they are the only seasoned troops we have in the Pacific. The human thing to do would be to relieve those men and ship them home. The military thing would be to use their experience again and again until every man who fights here will be on a par with the already veteran Japanese, and until the new men coming in have been given their baptism of fire at the side of men who already know at least some of the tricks of the trade. I hate to think that this must be so—but I'm willing to bet it will be so.

If we are to fight an island to island war then we must be prepared to pay a terrible price. Moving North from Guadalcanal will not be easy—it may be a repeat performance of this campaign at every stop on the way. There is a constant search for some indication of an easier way to win this war than to jump from here to New Georgia to Bougainville to New Britain and on. Through China would give us a chance to try out our strength on open ground. We don't like the jungle—I wonder who does—and there will be beachheads and jungles from here to Tokyo, if we have to go that far. The idea here is that we are suffering at the expense of the ETO. We think that with the full weight of our strength could be directed here, we'd mop up. Who knows?

One thing I know—that the war on Guadalcanal has not been fought by the book. The basic things hold true here as anywhere else, but in the actual operations and the handling of men if the book had been truly the Army's Bible then we would probably have lost the war. We have had to learn to meet situations as they arise, and sometimes that learning has been hard. Men have died here, as in all wars, because of other men's stupidity. The first Army units to fight have had to learn as they went along. The 25th had jungle training, and showed it.

We learned a lot about ourselves, and some about the Japanese. We learned that the Jap is a fighter, but often a dumb one; we learned to watch him as an unorthodox, tricky, cunning, cruel killer. We found that tho he may have been trained for offense he can fight a defense. And we know that, sick and hungry, he may crack but he may just as easily die hard. We think his tactics are screwy, but we have trouble combating him—he is rarely a pushover. We think his artillery is his most misused weapon—and I think he lives in fear of ours. He should—we once turned 83 guns on him at once, 5100 shells. We learned his snipers are lousy, his mortars good, his concealment excellent.

Of ourselves we proved that there is no training like a battle and no substitute for courage, not even brains.

Wednesday, February 10. The Artists and Writers Club, Cactus Heights, Bomb Alley, Guadalcanal, Solomons, in short, is a mess. Brodie and I are in the process of tearing down all we've built here and that we had so much junk is a matter of deep mystery to me. We leave at 6:30 in the morning, via SCAT. Brodie drew Frommell's and Burchfield's portraits as a parting gift and gave Beaton one of his unfinished sketches. I haven't much to give.

This day has been a full rush—urgent frantic—with me scurrying around to get last minute facts on the campaign. Wish I had more time for that, but was lucky in hitting a couple of people who knew what they were talking about. Brodie has had his hands full too, getting his stuff organized. But we both took an hour off for a bath at our favorite log in the Lunga.

To put the stopper on things, I got a letter from Miller asking for some info on malaria control, so I had to walk over to the 101 Medics and talk to Col. Friend, then type it out. Merle wanted sketches, too, but that was impossible. The stuff won't get to Pearl when he wants it, but at least I tried.[17]

Still have some work to do—

Somewhere below a trumpet player makes the music soar—"Natchez to Mobile—Memphis to St. Joe—Wherever the four winds blow"—he plays big time. This is the first time I've heard him. He is playing from the ridge across the way and outside the moon filters down, a struggling quarter moon trying to give more light. Strange, but I catch the same feeling for music—starvation— that I felt on the last day of maneuvers. I remember that night the problems finally ended when we sat around fires and listened to recordings over the PA. Less than two weeks later we were at war. But tonight I long for music.

Said goodbye to the boys at the club. Hipple got drunk last night in celebration—and lost the jeep. We all said we'd meet again. I expect we will.

This hitch on Cactus has been a great experience in my life.

Thursday, February 11. I'm writing aboard a DC-3, Marine flown. We have just slipped around the SE tip of Guadalcanal, headed straight thru to Tontouta. We took off from Henderson at 9:00 AM. Guadalcanal from the air looks a damn sight different than it does from the ground. (We are passing San Christobal). When we were no more than 500 feet off the ground, Pt. Cruz looked close enough to spit on and the island all the way to Esperance seemed less than a two minute run. Mt. Austen was under us almost immediately and we headed out to Koli Point. It all seemed so damn simple to see those places and spot them from the air, but nobody could be more deceived than the ordinary pilot who never goes into the bush to study terrain from up close. East of our place on Cactus lie miles of meadowland, shielded from the sea by palm groves and occasionally by the jungle. Beyond the meadows are the mountains, all jungle covered with here and there a hunk of bare coral jutting out. Along the shore, in the palm groves, we saw occasional plantation houses, invariably red roofed, snuggled in among the trees. At the island's tip there are atolls, and once or twice I spotted the thatched roofs of a native village. I'll bet those people don't know a war is going on across the way—and I'll bet they don't care. I was impressed again by the beauty of the beaches from the air, where the coral shines thru from the deep blue and graduates in elevation and color until it breaks the surface—blue, turquoise, green—with the slow roll of the surf stripping it brilliant white.

Somehow when we shoved off I felt almost sorry to be leaving, altho will be coming back. Jim and John drove us down to SCAT, then took us back again for breakfast—fresh made coffee and pancakes. That gang in the tent has been swell all the way through—we were lucky as hell to be in with them. They were half the fun we had. Last night Frommell appropriated a box full of canned stuff for a farewell dinner. We ate like kings. They gave us letters to people we probably can't find, but we should get in good if we do—at least a good meal & something to drink.

At the moment I'm happy about the whole thing—everything up here smells clean, it's cool, and outside the world is blue and white. Somehow you get the feeling of being completely detached from all earthbound things—the sweat, the dirt, the sticky air, turning your ankles on coral, fighting flies; and war, too, seems far below and long removed. But with all that the prospect of returning to Noumea doesn't make me leap with joy. I hardly know what we can expect down there, except I'll lay odds we'll be bucking people who are fighting their own private little phony war—which is worse for us than the real thing.   At least on the Canal we were allowed to enjoy all the privileges we could handle by ourselves—I mean if we wanted to go anywhere or to do something it was all right as long as we managed to do so under our own power. Of course we had to wheedle and borrow and steal a little, but that was part of the game. I wonder how it will be elsewhere. I long since learned that the closer men are to combat the less inclined they are to be such bastards on occasion. That goes for everybody from a buck private to the CG, all along the line.

Along that line too, I want to swear an oath right now that, having been seven weeks on Guadalcanal and having seen in reality only scattered bits of action and only fragments of that, I will not commit the unpardonable sin of becoming a military expert or a battle-wise veteran. God forbid! Brodie and I have seen combat, we know conditions, we understand a few things that perhaps we didn't understand before. But we certainly didn't experience enough to set ourselves up as authorities on the subject. I feel in my heart that our work from Guadalcanal has been good. I don't think either of us, however, was too much impressed with the absolute wonder of it all. Under the circumstances I believe we did the job we were sent out to do and in a few instances we might have done a little more than was actually required of us. But God knows we didn't do any more than anybody else—immeasurably less than some. We didn't fight—we watched others fight. That was our job.

Not that our work is in any way over. Guadalcanal, like the war in the Pacific, was more the beginning. I can't get over how lucky we were to get here in time to see some real action—the Hill 27 kind of action—and to stay until it was over. If we had taken it by easy stages, going everywhere else before we came to Cactus, we'd have completely missed the boat. And it would have been completely pointless to have arrived only after the last Jap was gone—like a buzzard sailing around until the last life is gone and then coming in to pick at the remains.

As to what lies ahead—who knows. A tour of the islands. I'm looking forward to that as a sort of busman's holiday, but it entails one disadvantage— we will have to glean what we can from places that may offer a wealth of color but not a helluva lot of actual material. I honestly believe anything short of battle is going to be a letdown. And there may be censorship trouble. But the fact remains that even yet there are a lot of men who are doing their duty as soldiers even tho they've never fired a gun in anger (neither have I) and they shouldn't be forgotten. On the other hand I refuse to pull the unsung-hero stuff. So, bluntly, I plan to get as far as I can and as much as I can out of this junket while we have the opportunity. I have never been able to shake the old infantry idea of taking full advantage of any good situation the Army should happen to offer.

The entire field of combat aviation lies before us. When the ground action begins again we can come back to that. I know myself too well not to realize that after enjoying some sort of vacation I'm not going to relish the idea of going back into the jungles. (The altitude is screwing my pen). On the other hand I rather believe we'll be so bored and fed up with fooling around that we won't mind it. I have this SCAT story to complete at Tontouta before doing anything else. Then perhaps we'll start on the circuit—or return to Santo and join up with the bombers. The beauty of this situation is that we got the ground action while it was still in full sway—and we can always fall back on the Air Corps. If I sound smug on the way we handled it—okay. I'm proud of at least a little foresight on the thing.

Friday, February 12. We hit Tontouta at 10 to 3:00—less than six hours out of the Canal. Got a ride straight in to Noumea, and somewhere along the way I had to misplace my pistol belt with everything on it. But it was as Brodie said: the trip wouldn't have been complete if I hadn't lost something. So now, both pistols are gone. Got in last night and squared away at Barnes.[18] Saw all the gang who got a kick out of my long hair and made awesome remarks about how much weight I lost. The silly bastards—I don't think I lost more than a couple of pounds, I looked this way when we left. But I let them have it their own way. Barnes has changed a hell of a lot for the better but there is still no mess hall and we all eat off the ground. Funny place. And are they going in for military life in the grand manner—inspections & formations, etc. Brodie and I got gigged this morning for having "barracks bags too close to beds." Now isn't that something! We got a good laugh. I worked most of the day on a report to Spence that got considerably out of hand. We horsed around with Jackson & Robby who took us to the Victory Bar where some little French slut stared at me in about as frank a manner as I ever saw. Ooh-la la! Jeepers—what a bitch. Noumea itself has blossomed out—the French have come out of their holes and the Army PX system has widened a little. I hear you can get two bottles of beer if you sweat out the line long enough. Ate lunch with Jackson at the Hotel Sevastopol—one buck for a dish of spaghetti, some cucumbers and potato chips, coffee. I'll eat at camp. Col. Shope and I had it round and round about that damned typewriter. I'm not taking the rap for that, too, after all the trouble it caused me up there. Saw the Jan. 27 issue which spread USAFISPA all over two pages. Okay. Got new canteen cup, so I can still have my morning coffee. The weather here is swell—dry—but, boy, the mosquitos.

Saturday, February 13. Bob Hall, Jackson, Robby, Brodie and I drank a quart of Andy DeGaulle and two quarts of wine last night, sitting in the park. Got pretty high—almost lost trying to get from the entrance at Barnes to my tent. Slight hangover. It's good to get tight in good company. We had fun. Brodie & I delivered Gene's letter to Marie. We saw her yesterday and came back today with the letter for her. She's a cute kid, half Arabian, and plump. Went around to Bassett's office and ran into a bunch of the guys, including 'Enry 'Awkins[19] and Keyes—that bastard. Keyes I don't like—we hardly spoke. Both AP and UP men—I didn't get names—were there asking about Miller & Hipple. I told them both were planning to leave. Saw Jackson—looking debonair in a MacArthur hat. The poor guy got shortstopped in Button and had to come down on a boat. Met Frank Shapiro again. Nice guy. Saw Van Hoerbeck, Frommell's buddy, and asked him to expedite that gallon of medical alcohol Johnny was sweating out. Finished my report to Spence—the biggest lot of crap I ever saw. And Col. Shope finally put the finger on the man who engineered the typewriter deal . . . . . Major Gates, supply. He absolved me, thank gosh, and insinuated religion played a part in it. I assume he means Gates & Cohen are Jews. Okay. Wrote Helen yesterday and forgot to number it—No. 10. But the kick was this—Jackson knew I was going to become a father. Miller or Bushemi had told him and I think Spence is at the bottom of it all. At first I was furious that the secret was out after I'd guarded it so carefully—even from Brodie—but then I didn't really care. I just wanted to keep it to myself until it actually happened. No matter.

Funny the way neither Brodie nor I can get used to peace again. Every time we hear a plane we get that old feeling, and a siren on the docks yesterday had its effect. I don't want to get too civilized here.

Sunday, February 14. Wrote Helen—No. 11.

My watch arrived and I picked it up at the PO—it's a beauty—15 jewel Elgin, serial number E 317739, waterproof.

Kicked around town, trying desperately to find something interesting. The beer parlor had something like a grand opening, and there was a double line around the block. Five bottles per man—it had been two. I wouldn't sweat out such a line for ten bottles of beer, served in frosted glasses.

The mess hall opened at Barnes—a really nice affair. Brodie and I sat at a table for lunch for the first time in two months—and there were no flies.

Last night I tried to get started on a Guadalcanal roundup, but there was so much noise at G-2 and so little feeling for it on my part that I didn't get to first base.

Tonight tried again—assembling my facts and so on—but just couldn't get started. Finally two and a half pitiful pages of pitiful writing. I haven't energy enough to dig into it. This is one story I'm forcing myself to write. And I don't know why except that I'm just not in the mood. A newspaperman is supposed to be able to write regardless, but sometimes it's like pulling a tooth for me to do anything with words.

After three days here I'm getting fed up with this place all over again. While Barnes offers comfortable living, a nice mess, lights in the office at night, and a wonderful beach within five minutes' walking distance, Noumea itself is still a hole. Crowded with soldiers and populated by indifferent French and unkept Tonkinese, the place just doesn't offer any sort of wholesome relaxation. Anywhere, that is, but on the beach—and even there, as beautiful as the place is, the few women who come down are surrounded by their "Fighting" French gallants while a hundred soldiers pass back and forth just to get a quick look if the girl happens to be anything the least above homely average here. I've seen possibly three fairly good looking women in this town—and I wouldn't call any of them any starry-eyed beauties. Oh, well . . . . . [20]

Monday, February 15. Last night I couldn't sleep, so took a stroll down to the beach—there was an officers' dance of some kind at the French Place, and some corny band was making some noise. People seemed pretty drunk. Walked back down the beach and came upon a couple of people knocking off a piece on the sand. I didn't say anything and they didn't, so I came back by in a few minutes and they were still at it. My curiosity aroused, I sat down at a discreet distance. After a half hour or so, they got up and started to leave. "You know I'm done in," said a woman's voice—one of the Kiwis, I think, and the man said, "So am I." They were walking toward me and then the girl, seeing me for the first time, I guess, exclaimed, "Well!" I almost laughed in their face, but they skirted around behind me and headed back toward camp. It was a dirty trick, but I got a certain pathological amount of fun out of it—purely sympathetic toward the lucky son of a bitch who can get his nuts cracked in this dump. Sex on Guadalcanal was something if thought of at all was discussed in the same abstract manner as the weather. I was less troubled by sexual desires up there than I have ever been before since I reached the age of puberty. But down here, where there are women—of a sort, but still women—the thing is beginning to rear its ugly head. From the time we left Noumea until the time we got back, Brodie and I didn't see a female, black or white. Damn, a man's human.

Spent all morning on the beach, took my notes down and tried to go ahead with the roundup. Wrote one paragraph. To Noumea this afternoon; Brodie and I called on Marie with negative results on whiskey. She was our ace in the hole, too. Ran into the Sgt. Major and two boatswains from the *Tjisadane*—they told us they got 27 days liberty in San Francisco when they got back. Nice job—with overseas pay. And they really get around. Saw Bill Hereford of the 67th and he said he'd get us some chute kits if I'd talk Robby into making up a set of prints of the stuff taken on the Squadron. Fair enough. Up to Shope's office and nobody said a word. The air of pent-up something or other is terrible—Jackson has snarled since we got here. He's terribly bitter about the way his job has worked out.

Band concert and movie now in progress. Shall attend.

Wednesday, February 17. Missed yesterday. One day like the next. This place would drive a man to drink, if he could get any. We could buy two bottles of beer last night, which was a nice interlude even if we did have to convince three people who we were.

Brodie and I decided this morning to go to Auckland. We can neither rest nor work here. Both of us are just as tightened up in Noumea as we were on Guadalcanal, tho for a different reason. What we should do is pull a good drunk, or several good drunks—get it out of our systems—and then get back to work. I've all but given up the idea of a roundup—I just don't seem to be able to do it, altho I'm going to make a supreme effort to finish it before Saturday, when I think we'll be able to get the hell out of here. Shope and everybody here seems to be in perfect accord with the idea—they all say we deserve a rest. Which makes me wonder when those bastards on the Canal are going to fall within their scope of sympathy.

Went to Tontouta this afternoon to try to promote those chute kits from Hereford, but couldn't get them. Said would have them for us Friday. Did get a beautifully done rooster insignia of the 67th—their Disney design done on leather. Took Bill the copy with the Melton story and the Jan. 20 copy which arrived today—with the cover and a double page spread by Palla, and my little stinker on the alert. It was quite a haul. The layout made Palla's pictures, but they looked good. Palla is showing his pleasure with his usual reserve. Capt.

Freeman, who got the credit line, was apologetic to him and pleased as hell otherwise. Sometimes the office does funny things.[21]

Had to bum back from Tontouta & missed chow. No more of that. Sometimes even Noumea has its nice moments. Tonight a native walked along the street strumming a uke and singing something with the tune like "Marie Elana," only it wasn't. Some native thing—he hummed it. The moon was ¾ and came down on the street. Romantic?—Nope, not in Noumea.

Thursday, February 18. Started on report to Spence last night and found it 3:30, so wrote Helen and Dad and by that time it was daylight.

Found we leave tomorrow morning for Auckland—at 5:15. Orders specify only two weeks—we wouldn't have stayed longer, but I'd rather they hadn't limited us. Rush to get everything done. Drew Dec. & Jan. pay—$84.70. Couldn't get to Tontouta so had to give up the idea of the parachute kits. Borrowed Palla's to leave in; damn nice of him, too.

Am little punch drunk at moment—losing sleep doesn't appeal to me. Up early.

Friday, February 19. Six and one-half hours from Tontouta to Auckland.

Saturday, February 20. This is the Army's liberty town and nobody bothers to make anything else out of it. When we came in yesterday we were given a long official song & dance on what we could & couldn't do, but it didn't mean a thing. We reported in at Victoria Park and were told that we could stay at a hotel if we liked, altho the sheaf of instructions we were handed said such was absolutely prohibited. So is the buying of liquor by officers for enlisted men, but it's done. Se we registered at the Royal—all we have to do is report to the top sergeant at Victoria every morning before 11:00. Our first night passed with only a mild drunk—very mild. Ran into Dowling—he gave us gin & scotch. We couldn't seem to really get started, even with gin and beer by the gallon. It was wonderful to sit down to a meal—a real honest meal—with chinaware and silver. Oh boy!

Sunday, February 21. I am writing on my bed—clean white sheets—at 12:15 a.m. This has been the damnedest day I've spent in months. I'm so full of solid food I'm almost popping—what a place this joint is. Perhaps I should start at yesterday noon.

Brodie & I were in the lounge when we spotted two wenches giving us the eye. We invited them to lunch. After eating they took us to their apartment. We had already drunk until our eye teeth floated, altho we never did get drunk, but we drank more there and pawed around awhile. The babe I had was married and she expected her husband, so Brodie made a date with her friend for

8:00 and I was to come back this morning. So we came back to the hotel, Brodie & I, ate and lay down. Naturally, we slept thru Brodie's date—oh, boy was he burned up. I was supposed to wake him—ha. Anyway, this morning we went around. To make a bad story short, we got it. I have never seen anything like these women—my God, what animals. I'll believe anything. Not to go into the gory details—I probably established a world's record for fast work . . . . . me and the rabbits. Four months layoff does things. I was not, shall we say, exactly pleased with mine—she was as evil minded a bitch as I ever saw—both of them—they had sex books of the dime variety all over the house. For pure carnal knowledge, which was all we had in mind, they were all right, but I couldn't stand a steady diet of that stuff. Phew!

This day has been one round of meals—we eat like kings. New Zealanders are meat lovers and that's down my alley—steak & eggs, fillet, pork—anything. I'm stuffed—and on top of that there's the beer. After three tremendous meals and a gallon of beer, we went out a few minutes ago & got an order of steak and eggs.

Reported in to Victoria an hour and a half late 'smorning and found we were wanted by the flight surgeon but it was too late. Suppose it concerns malaria. Seems like everybody here has it. Took a pro, the first in a year and a half. Have the usual mental hangover, to be expected.

Auckland seems to be everything everybody said it was. It seems strange to see a crowd on the streets—a civilian crowd. Equally strange to go into shops and buy stuff altho the merchandise is limited to an extreme: "Can't get that these days" is a stock phrase. No matter. But everything we could want is here—a bed, food, drink, people who speak English. We had heard the blackout was lifted; it wasn't. The place is full of unattached women, people in all kinds of uniforms, marines and sailors. Not so many soldiers. Here in the hotel is a B-17 combat crew, and they're raising hell—politely but thoroughly. Fact is, they're surprisingly well-mannered, but they are having all the fun they can crowd into every minute. Had dinner with one who had a hangover and a morbid state of mind at once. These crews stay in combat operations for three months and then get ten days. He didn't think he'd live to enjoy his next ten days. I can see how it is that men coming back here to rest, get drunk, and brood. It gets you, if you let it, much easier here than up there, I believe.

We haven't seen enough of the place to pass judgment, and Saturday afternoon and Sunday is closed-house anyway, but from what we've seen there can't be any place like it in the Pacific—in fact, there can be few places like it in the world today, I suppose. It actually gives me a helluva kick to see people having a good time, because I know most of them have been through their share of the rough stuff and they deserve to let their hair down and go wild. This is the place to do just that. Actually, Brodie and I haven't been drunk yet—don't seen to be able to get that way. I had heard it takes a couple of days to get in the groove. Jack says Cromie is in the hospital—malaria—may be there six weeks. We are still taking atabrine but the malaria business is serious here. Seems that everybody from up north gets it—regardless. I got my watch looked at—broken spring due to temperature change. Bought huge wallet for credentials—about $3.50 American. Clip?

Monday, February 22. The battle of Auckland, which opened with a reconnaissance in force, has settled to patrol action—feeling out positions & strength. One should never underestimate the opposition—especially here. Brodie & I saw the flight surgeon 'smorning—nice guy. I weighed in at 134½, so have dropped about ten pounds somewhere. We shopped around a little; I bought a shaving brush and a wooden comb, the only kind to be had in the city. Got my watch back, but don't know whether it's fixed permanently. Springs are another thing we can't get for love or money. Cabled Helen for 2 and 6.

I challenged Brodie to a drink-for drink contest of double brandies and he drank me under the table. I'm slipping. Slept it off this afternoon. Undressing, I caught three women in the factory across the way watching me. Have heard of everything else but that was a new wrinkle. When they call this the Land Down Under it implies that a great many things are in reverse—even to the sex of Peeping Toms. Damn. Anyway, they seemed to enjoy it, and I certainly didn't give a damn.

Brodie is off for another round with his woman. Beats me.

This whole place snows me under. The people are so damned nice—they want to see the soldiers have a good time—and even the Army people stationed here seem actually anxious to do what they can to smooth things along. We haven't run into any of the orthodox baloney we might have expected. Men on rest leave are the nearest things to free agents the Army will allow—and it certainly should be that way. I feel a little guilty being here, but certainly a million less than I would if we were stationed here. It would be heaven to live here, but I honestly don't think I could stand it.

Tuesday, February 23. Accomplished the feat of twice getting drunk and sobering up in the same day. Tonight went to Peter Pan and Shortland Club, but couldn't get an edge on. Pan is Auckland's de luxe nightclub, dancing and soft drinks.[22] Band plays jitterbug and cuts off lights for the sweet music just as at the Country Kitchen. Not a bad place; the joint is crowded with women trying to make pickups. With that exception, it's like any similar roadhouse in the States. The Shortland Club is wild—we got there just as a fight ended. A sailor was on the deck—out. Nice joint. They serve drinks.

Wednesday, February 24. Spotted a leather traveling bag and a camera I could use, so wired the office for $75. Had to go thru the usual red tape. Went to a movie tonight, not for lack of anything else better to do, but because I wanted to sit down and see a show and because there were other things I didn't want to do.

This is our fifth day here and altho I've generally had a good time I haven't really let my hair down and raised as much hell as I might have. Dammit, I want to and then again I don't want to. I can't explain it exactly, but I seem to be generally depressed—or rather, repressed. I don't know whether it's better to be that way or the other way. I guess it was that first flash that screwed the detail—that was a distasteful happenstance if I ever got into one. Am going to have to make up for that fiasco, if for no other reason than to preserve in my own mind the honor of Auckland's womanhood.

In walking up and down the street yesterday and today I found positive proof there are some swell looking babes here by anybody's standards. And didn't I pull a lemon out of the hat!

Thursday, February 25. Orders for our return Monday came out today and I promptly saw to it they were changed. No trouble—just a misunderstanding. Started on brandy before lunch and wound up throwing notes out the window at a cute blonde across the way. Negative results. Swapped over to gin and slept thru supper. Woke with hangover, but recovered.

Brodie and I had our first row today and it happened, as I was certain it would, when we were both a little pipped. I don't remember it too clearly, but Brodie started out with one of our sessions of discussion and out of the clear sky charged me with failing to hold up my end on buying drinks, etc. I couldn't have been more surprised if he'd accused me of stealing bar glasses. I got mad as hell, which of course was true to character and did no good, and didn't try to make a defense because, as I told him, I knew in my own mind he was full of shit, and let it go at that.

But it's a hell of a thing to have the guy think that at all; it's even worse because he seems to hold things against me from the time of the crossing. Hells bells. If I'd been sober today I wouldn't have known whether to laugh or cry, because that's the first time in my life I've been faced with a thing like that.

Brodie bases his accusation on what he seems to think is my unwillingness to spend my own money and, too, my apparent willingness to spend his. He said, and I quote, that isolated examples were chickenshit, but put together and viewed collectively they weren't. He said he was embarrassed, he said a lot of things but it's all a bit hazy.

So I stand accused of being stingy.

Which, at 1:00 o'clock in the morning and while I'm sober, I think is something I'd better examine and "discuss" with myself. Brodie must have had some justification—he did. In the matter of spending his money, I've borrowed from him with the best intentions in the world of paying him back—and haven't paid him. That is pure oversight. In the matter of buying drinks, I'm confused. I have let people buy the drinks and have, as far as I know, tried to pay for them as often as the next guy. But I differ from Brodie in that I will not argue with people on who buys. I hate all the fluff and spouting: let me get these—no it's my turn—here I have it right here—please let me—and so on ad nauseam. My policy is offer to pay and then if the other guy just must spend his money I don't engage him in a contest of generosity. If he wants to buy 'em, I let him; if he wants me to buy 'em, I'm glad to. At least I've never consciously shied from paying for anything just to hang onto my money. If Helen knew I'd been called tightfisted, she'd laugh like hell—and Dad, after all his lectures on thrift, would have a fit. But no matter. The problem now is to unhang this thing from over my head; which is going to be extremely difficult because anything I do now will be interpreted the wrong way. It isn't that I want to show Brodie he was mistaken—I don't want to shower money all over the place with the idea of proving I'm just a misunderstood philanthropist. God knows this is the only place in the Pacific money is worth a damn and a man would be subnormal not to throw it away as everybody does, but I intend sticking with my policy and to hell with Brodie's ideas on the matter.[23] I'm actually hurt—naturally—that he feels the way he does, but I feel he's wrong, I told him so, and that's as far as I'll go with it. Damn, this is a new thing with me and frankly I'd rather have been accused of a lot of other things than that. It's a distasteful business.

Brodie and I are certainly a funny pair to be kicking around together all the time. Some of the things he does annoy the hell out of me and I'm sure it's vice versa. We get mad at each other and don't say anything which is something Helen and I—and I think wisely—agreed at the beginning never to do. It's better to get it off the chest.

But Brodie and I keep quite until such times as today. The first vocal disagreement we had was on Button when we were drinking and he said, "Aren't you the little tin god!" I immediately, as Jackson says, became unhappy. Today was the second case. I imagine there will be others, but it's to our credit I think that under combat strain two high strung characters managed to keep their grievances to themselves.

One of Brodie's habits that particularly gripes me is his manner of doing my thinking for me—not exactly that, but of passing judgment on how I feel about things. He's wrong more often than he's right, which is the only thing I don't like about it and he will not allow any other idea to enter his head. The fact that he is extremely candid is good, but the fact that he makes mistakes in judging what goes on in my own mind sometimes riles me.

The biggest effort I ever made in my life to keep from telling somebody off was on the Canal and again at Noumea. I had to almost physically force myself to keep my mouth shut and the only reason I didn't pop off was because it would have been little of me to mention it. It regarded Brodie's story of our first day on the front. He told it on the Canal, wrote it to Spence in a letter which I happened to notice with a glance, and spread it on thick to Hall and Palla, et al. I got so mad that time I had to leave the room to keep quite, and yet he left me with almost nothing to say in defense.

His story was this: "We were on the trail with snipers in the woods, and Mack kept chopping my arms off to get in front of me. I couldn't figure why, until somebody told me that was the hot spot—the last man. Mack kept chopping my arms off." Truth of the matter was, and why Brodie refuses to recall it, that I was on the hot spot—consciously on it—the whole time but once when an infantry rifleman came up behind me and I went in front of Brodie who had his hands full. Fact is, the "somebody" who told him the last man was on the spot was me. That was one day up there I felt very moral, because in my own heart I was actually trying to look out for Brodie if I possibly could because the guy gets so out of the world he can't look after himself. He and I separated up there and I went wandering around all over hell looking for him—which I wouldn't do again, knowing better now—because I thought he might have wandered into a fire lane.

But his laughing recollection, badly distorted, of my jumping in front of him when I purposely stayed behind the silly bastard two-thirds of the way up there made me so damned mad I couldn't see. Aside from the fact it's a very badly chosen commentary on me personally, it's twice as bad in my mind because it's just the reverse of what I really intended. I was boiling when I first heard from Gene, I think, that he'd told that tale. But I couldn't say anything because to call him a liar or to make any sort of denial at all would have been chickenshit in the extreme and it wouldn't have done the slightest good, because B. had told it often enough to make any change in his mind completely out of the question. It was an effort, also for the same reason, that every time I tell the story of our first sniper shot I tell of stepping behind the peep and then being shamefaced by what the hysterical medico said, but have carefully avoided mentioning the fact that when that shot was fired, Brodie ducked backwards and busted his ass on the ground in the sitting position. One of my strongest impressions that day was of the look on his face when he raised back up. He was scared. So was I, but two minutes later I felt myself getting mad—which is something I'm frankly damned proud of—and I threw a shell into the chamber and started up the trail (last man). It was an effort, after I heard Brodie's version, to omit that little scene, but the truth was that his reaction then was purely reflex and he recovered instantly. The look on his face told me that he was scared, but I didn't need a mirror to tell my own expression of emotion at the moment. I remember walking away from that peep and taking deep breaths so my heart would go down where it belonged. I wasn't afraid of the next shot— it was the first one that snowed me. I had the same feeling 30 seconds after I dipped running boards with a car head on at home once.

So now I've gotten the whole small, smelly business out of my system.

Such a discourse as this always leaves me relieved and at the same time feeling a little unwholesome. It's now three and I've been drinking beer and writing for two hours—venting my spleen, to be corny about it, and generally getting my pettiness out for an airing. This kind of stuff I get perverted pleasure out of, which is the best excuse in the world for a diary. If I talked as I write in here sometimes it would be terrific. I know that in me there are some peculiar strains—a psychoanalyst would have a field day with me if I told him the honest truth, but I guess there must be things deep inside a man that only God ever really knows of.

The "rest leave" in Auckland is a case. I don't seem to be able to extract the full pleasure from it. To say I'm not enjoying myself would be inaccurate— I'm having a hell of a time. I'm doing two things to the limit—eating and drinking. But I'm still frustrated. There is something screwy with me sexually, or else I have a latent moral instinct that takes some funny twists. I came down here with a completely open mind on women—I was going to let my conscience be my guide. So I ran smack into this Valarie business which almost made me vomit. Now I find myself in my usual state—with an eye for the gals but without any great energy to chase 'em down. Next there was Kay. There is a pushover if I ever ran into one. She came up to the room, drank beer, and I pawed and crawled around on her to a disgusting degree—and wasn't a damned bit enthusiastic about it. Sexually I was excited, but mentally I was almost indifferent. She wanted to go to the Peter Pan and I didn't. She left; I went to the Pan alone and ran into her, brazened my way through with some kind of explanation, because I didn't comprehend that women go stag to night clubs and I didn't expect to see her there. Anyway, she impressed me like an American two bit whore or a cross between that and a charity girl prick teaser. But it seemed so easy, I can't get it out of my head that she should be had just on general principles. So today I told her to come up to the room for some drinks; she accepted. I got drunk in the meantime and didn't particularly give a damn whether she came or not. She didn't—she was in one of the crewmen's rooms. So I went looking for her, didn't find her—it wouldn't have made any difference if I had—and came back to my room to pass out on the bed. The episode of Kay is finis. I quit.

Right now I don't know what I want. The little blonde across the way is a cute kid, so I threw out a line there which may pan out later. She isn't the easy type by her looks, and I honestly believe I's rather go to the show with her, or somebody like her, than to fool with Kay or somebody like her. But I don't know. Here I am back from the barren Solomons to get my fill of women, wine and whiskey, and I fiddle around. Brodie is smart. His gal said at the beginning she'd take care of him for the full 14 days and she wasn't fooling. She surely is.

When I get back to the islands and read this over I'll cuss myself as a stupid sonafabitch, naturally, but here I'm all fogged up. For one thing my marriage vows snow me. I get conscience-stricken. But is the sin any less in the mind than in the physical participation? The only time in my life I have ever been sexually happy was in New York. Marriage is more than sex, of course, but there I found what I wanted, basically. Here my desires, when stimulated, are no less but the other circumstances are so damned different it takes all the kick out of it. For another thing I'm afraid of disease. The worst two weeks I ever spent in my life—emotionally—was the time just before I got married when I thought I had blundered into a dose of syphilis. God—what agony. And another thing is the fact that at least anything here would be a hit and run business—crawl on and crawl off—unless I shacked up with some gal who had every emotion in the book, and the likelihood of that is too small for consideration.

I don't like a situation like that, never did. My idea of sex, before the act, differs from the rabbit habit. During the act me and the rabbits are right together; after the act, sleep—always sleep. So what have we? Frustration, and—now—the start of a beery glow. Hell, I'm certainly not satisfied, but I don't know what to do about it.

I've got a streak of exhibitionism in me a yard wide—not the flaunting, public-gaze kind, thank gosh—but the type that asserts itself at odd times in privacy. Reversing the situation, I have a streak of Peeping Tom . . . . . which saw its heyday the first month in N.Y. I don't get excited over watching a woman undress, but a sort of mild fascination, which might be a little akin to the way I feel about wanting to be in the know on things—to experience something no one else knows about or is aware of; or to watch anybody when they're not aware of being watched. I stalk around in my room or lay on the bed balls naked, perfectly aware that girls across the way are watching. If I had any modesty at all I'd cover up, but I don't.

I don't give a damn if they look—which is an exact reverse of my way of thinking under any other conditions. I once insulted some nice people by refusing point blank to go in swimming at the Shelton because I didn't want to look like a killdee to two girls. But here I fool around like a month old baby and listen to a bunch of factory girls giggle and don't give a hoot in hell. And last night I watched some gal, stripped, for five or ten minutes, with a mild sort of excitement, but much more of a casual interest. It might best be described as a horse fancier watching a thoroughbred, because my motto has always been the old gag about women: like elephants, like to look at them, hate to own one. I love to "own" the one I have, but that doesn't change the first part. As Fred Davis so beautifully put it: "I got married, but I didn't die."

So now I've spent most of the night making myself a confirmed bastard with erotic tendencies which can be traced back to the time I was five years old if I cared to go into those lonely days from which, I think, stemmed whatever there is in me self-centered, self-conscious, and sensitive. Childhood is a funny thing—I'm glad I can remember so much of mine because maybe I'll know from it the best ways to guide my own when the time comes. I hope so.

Tonight is the first time I've really felt like writing in a couple of weeks, and for the first time in my life I've bared on paper some of the things that mill around inside me. There are such things, I'm sure, inside everybody—I remember hearing Rev. Umbach, a guy who knew human nature, make that observation when I was just a kid. I don't know how well I or anybody else keep them hidden, but there must come moments in all lives in which every detail at one time or another comes out. For a newspaperman I have a remarkably poor perception of such things in others, and I'm not enough the student of psychology to understand them in myself.

One thing I understand: that I was never happier in my life than when I was with my wife, whose name I don't feel right in associating with this bilge, and that before we were married and since I left her in N.Y., I have been unbalanced and frustrated. On Guadalcanal and on 43rd St. I found stabilization—complete abstinence—complete knowledge.

Friday, February 26. No change.

Allan Jackson and 'Enry 'Awkins got in.

Saturday, February 27. Of all the drunken orgies I ever was mixed up in, last night's binge put on by the 31st crewmen at Glendowie was the worst. Oh, I got stinking—and, worse, acted like the world's worst heel to top it off. I passed out mentally about the time we left the club—which must have been around 2:30—but unfortunately didn't pass out physically. From reports I gather I was a bit obnoxious to Mickey and his girl Betty, because I wouldn't get out of the cab—wouldn't do anything. That I don't remember and consequently regret it, but don't blame myself for it. But I do remember and do blame myself for wolfing Mickey's girl. Jeepers, what a thing that was. Betty is as cute-looking a little rascal as I ever saw, so I got the idea of dancing with her. I remember having seen one of the other boys kiss her, so I got that idea myself. I did—several times. She's one of those girls that always hit me a certain way—one of the very few—I just wanted to hold her, like a golden-headed child, and do nothing else. At least there was nothing carnal about it, and I'm under the impression my feelings along that line are shared by several of the crew. She just has a face that does that to people, and I think my desire for absolute tenderness toward somebody—anybody—was at that moment stronger than any other emotion. Anyway Mickey didn't like it, and I certainly don't blame him. I'm damned I wouldn't have. I apologized this morning, rather feebly, but I do feel like an ass.

Brodie and I had toast and coffee with a girl named Yana this afternoon.

She's Dutch and looks like the perfect double of Ann Rutherford; she's a 21-year-old globe trotter, been everywhere. Interesting character, in more ways that one. But the prize today was Brodie's Gay—my God, what a woman!

Sunday, February 28. Last night it was the same thing again, except I didn't get so drunk. This time it was at a beauty salon, and a N.Z. leftenant played the piano, everybody drank and sang and paired off with a girl. There were extra women for the stags. I really enjoyed myself—hooked up with some slim little cat named—of all things—Daisy. Kept it clean.

Betty was there and Nap was in my shoes. He had her away from Mickey (he takes a beating) and was doing the usual mugging. I found her alone once and the conversation went something like this:

"Hello, Mack, you've hardly spoken to me all evening."

"I owe you an apology last night."

"But why?"

"I was drunk. Don't remember anything at all after we left. I understand I was pretty awful after we left."

"I don't remember."

"Oh."

"Do you remember before we left?"

"Some. I apologize."

"But all you did was gather me in your arms and kiss me."

"I'm sorry."

"But—why?"

"Oh."

Now what the hell does a man do in a case like that? She acted like she liked it. Well, maybe she did—but I quit. No more of that stuff for me, because, for one reason, Mickey was getting madder and madder. I saw him watching us, and I haven't a leg to stand on.

I finally got Daisy home, and caught a ride back to the hotel to find Brodie troubled about his girl, Gay, a truly professional woman who hooked onto him. "A coat of armor of girdles," moaned B. She wants him out at her beach house. He doesn't like the idea.

N.Z. women—bless 'em—are just out of this world.

"Got to Get on the Ball"

Monday, March 1. This is now reaching epic proportions, like nothing I've ever seen or heard of before. I am not now kidding when I say that we're going to have to go north to get a rest.

Now there is one Freda Forno (I call her Kate for short) who was originally Bainter's woman and got around to me because Jerry was whipped down. I know how he felt. That girl, who is really not bad looking, turned me every way but loose. She knows tricks in the art of oscillation that I never heard of. Ooof.

Last night another party, but strictly nothing to drink and consequently not lively. I came into it half-high, with Daisy, and took her home without firing a shot.

Today was the usual rat race, drunk on brandy before lunch. Saw Bob Cromie, looking the wrath of God after two weeks of malaria. Had dinner at the grill with him but hardly remember it.

Somewhere in the maze of hangovers and debauchery, I've forgotten to mention Harry Belgrade, whom I snowed under but beautifully. It was Friday that we finally got together. Harry is still a T-model corporal and is disgusted with his present station in life; he's been accepted for OCS, AC administration. Good.

Then, yesterday, I had a session at the bar with Charlie Palloica, and gave him a snow job, too. It is impossible for me to talk down here as if Guadalcanal were really nothing at all—I have to put some allure to it—despite my sworn oath not to pop off. I think Harry and Charlie expected as much, and I didn't disappoint them. I have given them the usual line—the garden variety of combat stories—which I neither know nor care whether they believe or not. But I did get a little perturbed at Charlie's companion, a naval ensign, who tried to tell me about Cactus without being there himself. I reserve the right to at least speak with preeminence in a case like that.

Tuesday, March 2. Today I got my watch back with a new spring. Within two hours the thing quit running. I give up. Still no word from the office on that $75. What the hell goes on? It's getting to the point where I need that money, and no fooling. Yesterday afternoon's Auckland *Sun* carried a story quoting a Marine combat reporter which I would have sworn was a pickup of my Story of a Battle. But it had everything reversed and I got all hot and bothered with the idea that somehow my art had been prostituted. Talked to Dowling who calmed me down by telling me something I didn't know: that Ned Burman had done a similar story on an identical thing that happened with the 2nd Marines. That's the price a man pays for being an egoist. I felt like a fool. Delivered Jackson's letter to his girl, Miss Beveridge, who is a nice piece of baggage but somewhat on the snooty side. She deplores Auckland's reputation as a Pickup Paradise (which I made no gallant effort to refute) but I think it was partly due to the fact a sailor had just tried to find out who she was as she waited outside the hotel for me. She is very nice; I should say definitely Jackson's speed, and somewhat the type I'd like if we were going to be here awhile.

But on rest leave, there's no time for that. Last night and tonight there was Freda. Bainter shoved off last night and left her to me, which was all right because I'm not proud, nor ambitious either, as regards women here. Thus far the only real result has been an increased laundry bill and a couple of lessons in how to make love, and there I sit at the foot of a master. Last night I was just coming off a drunk, and tonight we went to a double feature, but she took me home and turned on the heat. Somehow, I can't really enjoy it.

Wednesday, March 3. I'm writing this while half stewed, but I want to put it down on paper just for the record to show that the men who are called heros in the states are the same as other men, but differ from the average in that they will do things and have done things that are beyond the vale of average human tendencies. I saw a picture entitled *One of Our Aircraft is Missing*, a British film, which showed the crew of a bomber riding calmly thru a hell of flak—anti-aircraft—without changing expression. Well and good. I would have been scared, but many men wouldn't, perhaps. The RAF may be different, but by God I doubt it. And therein lies my story of the moment.

I know a boy named Knapp, an engineer on a B-17. He's been in combat since the Battle of Midway in July. We were in a cab the other night, going to a party, Knapp, who has been pretty drunk most of the time, said out of the clear sky: "You know, boys, I must be getting yellow—I don't want to go back up there." I said, "Nobody wants to go back." Knapp came back. "Yeah, I guess not. At first I wanted to get into it . . . . . but now . . . . . Goddamit I don't want to go back." Knapp is a kid—a small kid—and his crew thinks he's the best engineer on a Flying Fortress aloft. He has the Air Medal, the Silver Star, and, I think, the DFC.

A few moments ago I talked to Bob Gordon, of the same crew. I like Bob very much—he's a swell boy—has the same decorations as Knapp—25 combat operations in the Solomons. There is something about the whole crew, Knapp, Bob, Danny, Grigher, Joe, Jerry—the whole gang—that makes me proud to be an American. But Bob spoke at the bar: "God I hate to go back. At first I didn't mind—I wanted to get into it, loved it up there—but when you get down here, where you can live again, you . . . . . you don't want to go back. I figure there are other guys who can do my job—I've had enough."

So what? So these men—the boys we're going to fly with—are heroes in every sense—any sense—but they're fed up. I know.

Thursday, March 4. We leave tomorrow morning, and of course I got drunk this afternoon, but now—waiting for my watch as usual—I've sobered. It was possibly my last afternoon binge on Auckland.

But the trouble with me—and I'm sure of the answer—is that I'm love sick—I want my wife. I know it because something hit me a moment ago that made me realize it: I saw a kid sergeant and his girl—both of them dark eyed, clean-cut and nice—sitting in the lobby. The girl was sitting down and the sergeant—he wasn't over 21—was on the arm of the chair with his arm around her. Their heads were together—they were just staring into space. It hit me like a ton of brick—one of those funny things that can happen to a man. I knew then and there what was wrong with me—it's simply that I seek the love I once knew and that there is no substitute for it. Helen is the only one in the world. I have told her that before—just talking—but now I know it's so. This interlude here is a substitute—I can't accept it. It's no good. I always knew it wasn't the answer; there is only one real answer and that is the happiness we'll know when this is over. I'll wait. The Battle of Auckland is a faux-pas, a mistake for me—a phoney. I should have gotten drunk and stayed that way; I almost did. Freda has called today; I won't call back. Belgrade wants a farewell drink—I'm glad.

Sometimes I think I must be a complete nut—a pure dope. Yesterday I was drunk and poured out my life story to Brodie—things I never put into words before in my life. Why did I, drunk or sober? Last night I was with Freda: I pretended enthusiasm, but my heart wasn't in it—I just fooled around to keep the spirit, as it were. What point in that? Why?

I think I really want to go back . . . . . to clean myself.

Wednesday, March 10. We missed leaving on the 5th, but got away the next morning following, too early to allow us to spend much of the $84 per diem we each drew. Imagine getting paid extra for being in Auckland!

So now we're back in New Cal, back at Barnes, waiting.

We returned to find mail that had been held—4 letters from Helen, 2 from Dad, several from the office. We also found the March 5 issue of *Yank*, and when we looked at it both of us almost exploded. They had a layout of Brodie's work with a little box which proclaimed "these drawings done under fire"— and damned if two of them weren't done at Button. The rest were such a poor selection of Brodie's stuff he had actually done under fire that it just stunned the guy—it really did. And it sort of stunned me, too—the stupidity of the whole mess. It stank! And the thing that got me was the way they handled my "Story of a Battle"—they gave it page one all right, but they headed it "Jap Trap" (typical) and then butchered it down to a half page run over to a column. They lost the flavor of it—missed the point—generally fucked up beautifully. I was furious. Both Brodie and I have written letters expressing ourselves on the thing in no uncertain terms—it was my first personal flare-up and I didn't kid them. They just played the thing with their feet. And of all the stories I've done, that was the only one I really thought they'd make something really nice out of. Damn! What a let-down. I wrote it to be cut, but I didn't write it to have all the guts neatly penciled out. I'd like to be on that copy desk. And while I realize there's no point in crying over spilt milk, I can't understand what they're doing back there. A couple of my stories they've gone overboard on, when I didn't think we rated as much space as we got, and then on this—my best effort— they practically murder it. Hells bells![1]

We have already put in for orders to start us on our tour, planning to stop awhile at Button and do what we can on the air corps. I am looking forward to flying with the gang we met in Auckland.[2]

Our orders originally were to take us to Efate, Santo, Fiji, Tongatabu and Bora Bora. In requesting travel orders I included Hawaii—for practical reasons—but Lt. Sanford called me in today and told me it would be impossible to authorize transportation to either Tonga or Bora Bora. That was a disappointment because I'd certainly looked forward to getting to those particular places. I figure if there is such as a true South Sea setup, it must be there. But the Lt. said we have no troops at all there now, and that there is no air transport available. He did say, however, that if we could hitchhike there it would be okay. We'll see. Dammit, I wanna go to Tahiti. The orders should be out in a couple of days and we plan leaving Monday at the latest.

Saturday, March 13. Orders came out today authorizing travel to Roses and Button only. We have to go there, finish our work, come back here for new orders before hitting Fiji or Samoa or Pearl. Reason: no direct connection from Button to Fantan. We plan leaving Tuesday.

Saw Joe Melton today at the PX, with a scrapbook. Seems his mother writes him she's hearing from people she never knew before and Joe's getting all sorts of clippings. The AP picked the story up—Dad sent a *Journal* copy. Hall says Joe was going around Tontouta autographing copies of the paper. Sometimes I wonder . . . . .

Dad's most recent letter stated that Mr. Bangs had told Mr. McCoy that he had "taken me when I didn't know a newspaper from an airplane, and made a newspaperman out of me." That guy becomes more obnoxious every time I hear of him. Jeepers. He is to the *Daily Star* what Col. Shope is to the PRO, even tho both have been nice as hell to me. They're the same type men exactly—big operators.[3]

Received Spence's March 2 letter on March 10. Can't get over it. Said typewriter, camera both on way. If typewriter wasn't crated, I'll never see it. Spence said couldn't use artillery story, but would appreciate artillery under fire. Well, I tried.

Also received Feb. 3 issue *Yank* with "They don't Smile When the Bn moves Up." Printed in full my first story from the Canal, a color piece on the front as I saw it—and illustrated it with Brodie's sketch from Button of a boy taking a piss. Of all the dumb bastards![4] That's the second time they've goofed off on us. Brodie is really low—in one respect they're almost ruining his reputation. He felt so bad about that "under fire" thing that, he told me later, he felt like resigning. It was enough to make a man wonder what the hell he breaks his neck for if this kind of stuff is to be the result. But we both want to get back to work—the sooner the better, damn 'em.

Thursday, March 18. We arrived at Efate yesterday morning before noon, and were taken in hand by a Lt. Zucker, the newly-arrived PRO who once worked in Washington with Walter Kerns.[5] Zucker set us up in a quonset hut behind headquarters in Vila, and then drove us around some during the afternoon. There isn't much here. But the food is good, so far.

Efate itself is one of those places where troops are stationed for the security of the island, and hardly a man here except those in the hospital, has seen action or anything remotely resembling it. Naturally, they're not in very good spirits; but even so they seem to be taking it pretty well. Most of the men I've talked to, white and colored, have been here about a year. The island is a pretty nice layout, much the same as Santo. The field is about three or four miles from town and the road ran thru typical tropical country—big banyan trees and heavy underbrush. I understand men are scattered at outposts all over the place—and just sit there. There is a Negro infantry outfit from Benning here and they do the same old stuff. Talking to a couple of men, I got the impression they were more or less just rotting and wanted to change scenery. Worst deal I've heard so far was the 198th C.A., I think, who were 13 mos. on Bora Bora and were ordered to leave. They all thought they were going back to the States, of course, but instead wound up over here. I understand they liked B-B pretty well. SCAT and an interceptor squadron is about all the AC there is. The strip is practically deserted. It rains a helluva lot here, apparently, but it isn't terribly hot.

Vila is a town strictly from Jack London's *South Sea Tales*. Its one main street runs parallel to the shore and the stores are right out of this world—you almost expect to stumble over a diving helmet when you walk in the door. Actually, I think they're better stocked than those at Noumea. There are Tonkinese here, natives from this island and from Santo, and actually a very few troops, comparatively. Down on the wharf we watched jellyfish and a school of brilliantly colored tropical minnows swimming around. I'm not certain, but I think the natives are bigger and better developed than those of Santo, but the women are the same huge black critters with their bright sack-like dresses and big bare feet. As a town, Vila offers nothing a soldier wants. I noticed in one of the shops some ladies slippers "made in Japan" and I saw a Japanese poster on another wall. Most of the advertising is dated American or Australian, but the news bulletins and official notices are in French. I understand there were once 800 white French and British here, but certainly aren't that many now. There is a company of native troops garrisoned just below headquarters; we watched them do close order drill under white officers yesterday. Brodie tried to draw one of the native women 'smorning—he had a prepared speech in French— but she wouldn't pose. I think she had the idea Brodie wanted to make her. There isn't a paved street here and the houses are all that peculiar style of French lattice-work in wood or stucco. There's a place called Don's Hamburghers, but we only tested their ice cream. The PX here is darn well stocked, more variety than in Noumea, and the RC has a nice library, but nothing else. I don't see much.

Haven't been around this headquarters bunch long enough to know any but a Sgt. Sullivan, but at mess they impressed me as being the usual headquarters type guys—bright guys who sling wise-cracks a lot. (Am and have been listening to a Kay Kyser Kollage of Musical Knowledge, just going off the air at 2:00 p.m.—I think it's a direct shortwave broadcast of his Wednesday nite show.). These Hq guys may be somewhat subdued, but they're still pretty much on the ball to have been cooped up here as long as they have. Eleven months in this place would drive me crazy, or pump all the life out of me anyway. They kid constantly with a couple of Australian boys who've been ordered home after only seven months in the "tropics." The Australians certainly live up to their rep of being able to take it or dish it out—particularly in one instance where they just laughed at a very raw crack about the "Royal Australian Navy." One said to the other: "Laugh, George, that was a Yankee joke."

This Lt. Zucker is a nice kid, who has been over about a month. He told me something I certainly didn't know—that he went to Benning to get commissioned as PRO officer and that was the War Dept's way of putting trained PRO men in the field. Didn't know it was possible—he said he ran no risk of being shanghaied into a platoon leader's job. News to me.

Colorful as this place is, I'm damned if I know what to do here. The place is a secret base anyway and according to Col. L'Abbe, the G-2,[6] he won't stand for too much detail, so I'm sort of up a tree. But we'll find something. I'm planning a color story which I can guarantee 'em won't say much.

Sunday, March 21. Don't feel any too brilliant at the moment, being in a condition which borders on the hung-over. Had a wonderful trip yesterday and came back loaded down with things people gave me, including a bottle of gin which Brodie and I killed between us last night. Brodie had the misfortune to get sick and I remember wanting to climb a palm tree, and, failing that, to walk thru a mile and a half of jungle to a lagoon so we could go swimming. Glad I passed out before I got started on that. I find my drinking is getting progressively worse—not the drinking, but the damn fool things I can think of under the influence.

Flew over in a Cub to Quoin Hill yesterday morning to look around the 44th Fighter Sqdrn. Was surprised it the same outfit I did a story on at the Canal. Three of the men mentioned in that story—Capt. Johnson, Ray Morrissey and Mike Carter are now MIA. That gave me a shock—it is the first time I've known men who later got it. Was particularly sorry about Mike—he was certainly my idea of the symbol of the Air Corps: he was an "eyes on the sky" boy if ever there was one. Hope the office has used the story.[7]

Spent most of the day with a boy named Rocky who treated me like a king.[8] He showed me the whole layout, took me to a native village, paddled me around in an outrigger canoe over the most beautiful coral bed I ever hope to see, bought me souvenirs and bananas off the natives, and gave me two stories. I think I saw a true South Sea setup yesterday. He introduced me to a French plantation owner—M. Dupuey—and wanted me to go with him across to another island to meet the family—the mother and daughter (15)—but like a fool I didn't go. Rocky says they are wonderful people, who insist that every soldier must be wined and dined in their home.

The native village was small and clean, with flowers all over, and big Melanesian women washing clothes while the few men either planed down the hulls of a couple of long-long boats, or slept in the cook-shacks. They spoke Pidgin-English very well—but seem to be lazy as all hell. The planter, who's been here 30 years and who looks like Patrick J. Hurley,[9] says when he first came they were all right but with the arrival of soldiers they aren't worth much. Too much easy money now. They don't do much of anything except laundry— their gardens of bananas and lime and papaya are just jungle-cluttered patches which they "harvest" when they feel like it. There is no pearl diving here, or anywhere except at one spot on Malakula. I enjoyed the experiences yesterday as much as any since we came across. Even flying in the Cub across some of the most exotic mountainland I've ever seen was a thrill. From the air the surrounding islands are beautiful—almost theatrical—and Efate is so small you can see the ocean on both sides from 2000 feet.

Rocky said the sqdrn was going to be moved to Vila at one time and the men, who like where they are, raised so much hell about it that the whole thing was called off. And this is the only place in the islands where enlisted men can get something to drink—and they have all they want.

Monday, March 22. While I don't seem to be able to turn out a line of copy fit to read—have down a color story and discarded it—there are so many things here I want to get down that it might be best just to outline them and try, from these notes, to put together a composite picture of Efate. I'm very much afraid of getting my wires crossed—but this is definitely the most delightful island we've seen yet. In the first place, it is beautiful here: from our hillside we look down on the bay where coral turns the water green and in the harbor it is blue and gets bluer out to sea. The climate, tho somewhat moist, is delightful—it rained our first two days here but since then has been generally fair. I can look out over the harbor now, with the morning sun on it, and it is beautiful—the sea, first blue, then green; then a white strip of sand; then green trees that cover a hill which slides a steep slope almost to the sea itself. This is a landlocked bay—almost a lagoon—and the houses on shore are bright in the sun with their tin roofs, red or green, breaking in with harsher colors on nature's spray of pastel shades. I'm not being poetic—this is magnificent. But even more magnificent was the night last night. Brodie and Charlie and I went to a band concert down the hill in a palm grove. There was a full moon, and as the evening wore on it rose higher, silhouetting the palm fronds and high-lighting them with spots of light that glistened like onyx. Flying foxes on lazy wings wheeled thru the trees, seeming almost to keep time to the music with the beat of their wings. We were under a battery of strong lights and yet there were no mosquitos. I leaned against a palm tree and let the music play over me like strong breakers on the beach. And, too, there was a French girl who persisted in pulling her dress six inches above nice knees—she was slim & dark, with almond eyes. That was the complete touch. After the concert I tried to work, but couldn't. The moon was high and on both sides of our hill it bathed the water and the trees were tall and rustling in a light breeze. Stars, huge, shiny things, sparkled in a sky that was a deep vibrant blue—bat blue. I hated to go to sleep. I stood outside and drank in the splendor of the night and smelled the light, soft smells of the trees and marveled that there were no mosquitos to mar the most perfect South Sea island setting I've ever seen. I'm a romantist at heart, but on every island but this one my experiences have been less than romantic. Perhaps I've gone completely whacky in my interpretation of Efate, but I speak only of the natural attributes of the place—not of the man-made things—but I an only human in that the fact that I saw a woman and can get something to drink has its influence. Men who have been here for 11 months are not so well satisfied; others, including Charlie, who have just come in from Bora-Bora think the place is terrible. As for the town and the people—not much. Picturesque as it is, I can see that for any of us it offers nothing at all. Unless a man makes the most of the things at hand here he would not like it at all after a short time because, close as it is to the Solomons, hardly a man on this island has seen combat. That makes a tremendous difference—I was told, and can see that they don't think they're doing much in the war; at least they feel that down inside, altho they know very well that it is vital that they should be here. Some have told me they'd much rather get a crack at some action, and I think they were sincere. I'm sure that only when they go to New Cal or Santo or the Canal will they be able to appreciate Efate. It's always that way tho, you can't tell a man he's living among the best—he has to have it proven to him. This, in the true sense, is a place where men can make what they want to of it—if they choose to be miserable, they will be; if not, they can enjoy a unique sort of existence in this area.

The town of Vila isn't much. There is one main street, unpaved and either muddy or dusty, that runs along the shore line. A couple of the larger stores are fairly well stocked, but some of their merchandise must have been on the shelves for twenty years. I noticed the ad posters—American, Australian, and once, Japanese in English, which are all in the '30s or before. Some cheap novels had illustrations with costumes of the people dating them somewhere in the middle '20s. The larger stores, as in Noumea, are general merchandise affairs; they sell a variety of stuff, practically none of which could be of any possible use to a soldier. The PX here is surprisingly well stocked—better than Noumea, I think. The smaller stores are largely owned by Tonts and are small and narrow and cluttered. There is one hamburgher joint, however, which does a booming business. Pretty good burghers.

Wednesday, March 24. Yesterday I did a typical trick. In the morning I was writing Helen and trying to get some work done; my mouth was so raw and I felt so all around lousy that I decided to take a couple of snifters of brandy. Except for two drinks, I killed the half pint—straight. So I felt better. Went down at noon for lunch at Francois' and after that I decided to bum a ride across to the other island. I was pretty tight, I guess, but I walked across the top of the hill and down to the beach on the other side where there were a lot of outriggers. Finally found a native who would loan me a paddle and, having taken off my shirt & cap, I rolled up my pants and shoved off. Got a couple of hundred yards out and the damn boat turned over—the outrigger smacked me across the nose and my shoes and socks went down in about 30 feet of water. I slipped off my pants and started to swim the boat back in; a native paddled out & helped me. There was no trouble. I told him I had no clothes on and there were native women on the beach but he said "They no care," so I didn't either. Came ashore naked as a jay-bird.

Got my pants back on, gave the native the only bill I had (which unfortunately was $10—but I felt I should give him something) and with my shirttail out and barefooted I came back to this side. Got some coral cuts on my feet. Guess I must have looked like a ship wrecked sailor. Went thru town okay, but half way up the hill a lieutenant snagged me. "What outfit, sergeant?" I told him. "Got any proof?" I hadn't, on me. "Where are you stationed?" Told him was just passing thru. "Well where are you staying?" I told him. "Let's go up there." Then I explained to him what had happened. I'm sure he didn't believe me and I think at that moment he must have thought I was a mighty suspicious character. He made me mad and in the office where the boys identified me he said, "Well, you have to admit he does look funny." I flared up then, but conservatively. Lt. Zucker got me a new pair of shoes, The whole thing was unfortunate, more so because, with salt water in my eyes, I must have looked much drunker than I actually was.

Then last night there was a party at the NHDF. Brodie and I killed the other pint of brandy and there was beer there. We had a hell of a time singing and I danced twice with some French gal who weighed an easy 210. Among those present was Ollie—Oliver Stephens—who was the guide for Martin and Osa Johnson when they were in this area. I think their book centered on Malakula.[10] The Australians—one a little sergeant-major in the NDF—sang a lot of service songs, which is certainly something I admire those boys for—their songs are the kind men sing, they're funny or crazy or full of pride—not only that, but the Aussies sing just for the joy of it and they know the words to more of our own songs than most of us do ourselves. I found the same things in N.Z. The party broke up at ten o'clock, but everybody had fun—clean fun. There were a lot of native troops, who finally sang some of their songs and one danced for us. Their songs are almost chants but have a definite rhythm and harmony. They sound almost like hymns. The boy who danced did so with his whole body, arms and legs working. He danced in a half crouch as I've seen them do in pictures.

I have been terribly lazy here and half-hearted in the work I have done. It has nothing to do with the raw deal we got from the office, but to be merely an inclination on my part to let things slide. I hate to be this way. The last story I did was six weeks ago and I feel thoroughly ashamed of myself, and even more mad at myself because I haven't done the SCAT thing yet. I'm almost sorry we came here—it would have been much better if we'd gone on to Santo and stopped here on our way back. As it is now I don't particularly care when we leave or what we do while we're here. Brodie isn't having a great deal of success with his drawing either—we've both laid off entirely too long. I wanted to get back in groove again, but now I'm writing this partly to talk myself out of my lethargy. It's no good to become indifferent.

There is a great deal of color in this place and yet I can't get it down on paper. There must be a couple of good personality stories and yet I can't get at them. As for the military stuff, it's all censorable. I've got to get on the ball.

Friday, March 26. Yesterday morning I found a certain return to normal, getting the story on Rocky written and turning it in together with the color stories, neither of which are any masterpieces.[11] Had my teeth looked at again and hitchhiked to the hospital on the outskirts of town to have a prescription filled at the pharmacy. When I finally got there they told me I'd have to have my own bottle, so I tore up the paper and walked out. The hell with it.

It has rained steadily for three days and yesterday afternoon I was horny as hell, so to try to drive out the condition I spent my time drawing the worst kind of pornographic pictures I could think of. They were awful, but it worked.

Last night we saw *Take a Letter, Darling* which was as good as the first time we saw it in Auckland. The boys liked it for its smart line of chatter. It was a smoothie on the dialogue, all right.

Hope to get one more story on the 198th CA band today and call it quits. Brodie's drawing the Col.—command performance. Maybe we can get some rum tonight.

In the tropics when it rains the cloud gods turn the nozzles on and go away for the weekend. As far as eye can see, westward to the ocean and eastward across the lagoon to the hills, the rain comes down from a sky that is dull gray, unbroken and unrelenting. The horizon's diffuse with the gray of the clouds and the gray of the rains and over all the earth it seems there must be nothing but a gray curtain which is moist to the touch.

And on the land the rain comes together, trickling down from the roofs and from the soggy trees, and each drop joins each other drop to go look for lower ground. Not finding it, the rain remains on its spot of ground where rain before it has fallen and after it will fall again. The grass and the trees and the rich ground of the jungle becomes full of it and the air thru which the rain comes down takes on the qualities of the rain and brings the moisture where rain itself could never reach. There is no escape from it in the tropics; man and every living thing bows to the cloud gods because, with rain in the life-giving air and rain on the blankets and under the collar and on the paper and inside the cellophane and beneath and over and around the house and in the house, man must live with the rain.

Outside the houses the rain comes down and on the ground it becomes mud which travels on with each thing that passes its way. The rain never stops moving, because it is in the mud and with the mud—it made the sticky, dirty mud—and when no more rain comes to join it and keep it alive—for rain feeds on itself—it will move again, this time out of the mud, back into the air thru which it fell and then back to the gray palace of the cloud gods who will send it out on its journey again. The rain is never still.

And when the rain falls in its steady beat, man goes on, not comfortably nor jubilant in his work, but he goes on subdued because he is impressed with the omnipotence of the gods of rain. He goes on because he has work to do and because the gods are merciful if omnipotent and will suffer him to go on, but not comfortably in the tropics. And man and the animals are alike—the rain in its legion of millions subdues all.

But man has an answer to the gods because he is so made that the rain soothes him. He listens to the rain above his head and around him and his brain becomes a million rain drops and his eyes seek a lower level, and his head and his arms and his legs. And he passes into oblivion. Who has won—men or the gods of rain?

Monday, March 29. Two days ago—on the 27th—we came back to Button. Stayed Saturday night at the SCAT transient barracks, where we split two bottles of rum with a bunch of guys and had rather a nice time. There was only one fight; somehow I wasn't involved, altho I got up to watch.

Yesterday we moved over to the 5th Bomb Hq. I regretted the move, but perhaps it's not so bad because it offers working space at night; but the chow—such as I've eaten—has been pretty awful. I walked over to the 31st Bomb area and then on to Force Hq where I discovered George & Shorty still intact.[12] I learned a number of things.

Today I went back to Force and spent most of the day there, accomplishing, among other things, the feat of listening to Major Curran shoot the bull for a couple of hours before giving me the story of the 172nd. That is a story I think will have possibilities.

My gums have been bothering me so much and I've had such miserable luck in getting them treated that I've gotten to the point my nerves are on edge. It's like having a slow burn that refuses to go away. Had them treated in Noumea and then again at Vila. Now I can't locate a dentist here and the damn things are getting me irritated good & proper. I don't want to do anything until I've gotten this trouble over with once and for all. Three days steady would do it.

Among the things I learned was that Jerry Bainter has made a water landing and is now back in Auckland as a reward. Knapp and the boys are due back from the Canal in a couple of days, but I think Bob Gordon is here, sick in quarters. From George I learned that the 172nd has been shifted to Cactus and that Gen. Rose is probably island CG at the Russells.[13] George and Shorty, who treated us like kings, hope to join him there shortly. The new one star, Gen. Lockwood from Tonga, doesn't seem to be to their personal liking too much. I gave all the laundry I had to Geo this afternoon; his Malakula boys will do it for me. Nice break.

The pettiness of the service got me this morning talking to Major C., who is a good guy but a snow artist if ever there was one. It was this way: he was talking about a man in Efate who sat in his office there, took credit for organizing the coast watcher setup and received decoration for it. He could mean only Col. L'Abbe. At Villa, I was indoctrinated with the organization of the C-Ws by that outfit down there—Capt. Garrison told me all about how they had— and still do—controlled the thing. Curran says they take his reports and screw them up—it's all confusing to me—but Curran was big about it: "I didn't come out here to win any medals," he said, magnanimously. I think he must be capable, but he certainly loves himself—and yet—I like him. I guess somebody has to talk for him, so he does it himself. He has magnificent ego.[14]

I talked with—but did not meet—a Marine Captain in Curran's office today who was CO of A Co of Carlson's Raiders on the Makin Island deal last August. He said some interesting things, chiefly that until they got back to Pearl Harbor they were ashamed of themselves. "Hell, we thought it was a blotch on the service until the reception met us." I asked him why and he said that the raid didn't come off according to schedule and was pretty fucked up on account of landing thru a terrible surf. He said when they came back in on the sub he expected to be shunned by society, but instead they were met by ship after ship with bands playing and sailors in whites lined on the rails, cheering. Admirals carried the first stretcher cases ashore. The Capt., a helluva nice fel- low—young & clean-looking—is now on the staff of Col. Roosevelt's new outfit here. I'd like to meet the Col., but there's not a damn reason in the world why I should—none that I can think of, anyway.[15]

Saw a March 12 issue of the paper today with a nice layout on the New Guinea deal and a little piece by Al which was nicely done. Note Kahn & Neville now commissioned and will write no more for the paper. What's the score? Also have to hand it to *Life*—pix in March 1 issue of Lunga log we used for laundry. That Morse is really, as Shorty says, a jitterbug.[16]

But the crowning incident, and the most complex, was the Tourville business. Lt. Tourville has a wife—nee Margaret Hawkins or Hochins—who is a Tazewell girl. She either knows or knows of, Helen. She wrote the Lt. that I was in the area; he replied that I'd been thru his APO (708) in December. Somewhere figures in a guy named Pete who works in the Tazewell PO. He's related to somebody. Small world. At first I thought the guy was crazy—"Are you Mack on *Yank*?" "Yessir." "Well, I'm adamn, let me shake your hand!" Then he explained.[17]

The SCAT story looks up—they have nurses aboard.

This air corps deal begins to get screwier—the 31st—our bunch—is op- erating now and then the 23rd goes up. But they're going before I will be finished here so Brodie may go on up and leave me here until I can wind this up. So my whole plan of living with the crew before & during the operational action, goes into a cocked hat. So what—it was just an idea. We'll do the best we can. But I'm damned if I do anything until my gums are well—they're driving me nuts.

There is certainly one helluva lot going on here—this place is a bee-hive—but most of the hustle seems to be Navy. The Big E is in, but that means nothing. Troopships pulling out for the States with the last of the 11th Bomb. Good. Nobody ever deserved to go home more than they.

Tuesday, March 30. Have just had my gums treated with a blue solution of some kind and my mouth looks like a fox's rump in polk berry time. Brodie has gone somewhere to see about something, so I'm just sitting. In times like this I yearn for a typewriter, because I could do a story while I'm waiting to get a chance to use one. I never thought of it until this moment, but I'm going to have a helluva time on Cactus in that respect. I was lucky the first time that Bob or Bill would loan me theirs.

I'm a little confused with the situation here, altho Brodie seems to be making progress nicely. I want to do the 172nd story first—should be doing it right now. Then I want to work SCAT: I'm going to do a story on SCAT come hell or high water. I've fiddled around long enough on that—am disgusted with myself. With those two out of the way, I can devote my attention to the air, but this isn't the place to do it. My idea of covering bombers has been and is to get as close to the planes and the men who fly them as possible—here we can't do either one very well. To reach even the planes on the ground—which are just planes with men working on them (doing things I never heard of)—I have to walk at least a mile. And when I get there I'm about as well off as a fly in a bowl of soup—I don't know the score and don't speak the ground crew's language. I'm going to have to learn—but Cactus is the better place.

Am certainly a creature of inertia—when I get started I'm fine, but when I'm stopped I'm hell to get started again.

Hope to get some work done today.

"Time Out for
an Air Battle"

Thursday, April 1. Got off the story on the 172nd, altho Major Fuller raised some question on censorship. I couldn't argue with him, altho I don't think there was anything censorable in it at all.[1]

Spent yesterday, last night and most of today with George and drank so much coffee that my nerves are jumping. At least, I hope it's the coffee. George has been really a prince. I went over yesterday & asked to take a shower. Sure—soap and towel. Came back, he had laid out a complete clean wardrobe which he insisted I wear until all my clothes were washed and pressed. Got dressed and found he'd even had one of his native boys shine my shoes! Ate lunch and dinner yesterday with his gang, breakfast and lunch today. We went to show last night, came back and George put up a cot for me, with a comforter and a sheet, no less. Stopped to see Mr. Harris—Burns Philp man—who knows more about what goes on on this island—knows more people—than anybody I've seen.[2] John Stephens—Ollie's brother—was there.

Brodie left yesterday morning for Cactus, breaking up our team for the first time since we met in New York. I'll join him up there in three or four days—as soon as I clean up SCAT here. Just thought of a catch line to use in connection with the nurses who fly the planes—SCAT Cats—only I don't think the ANC would appreciate it. Aren't I cute? Like the sign on the officers' mess at force headquarters: "Hutset Quonset." Hope to get all the material I need on the SCAT thing tomorrow so I can get the hell the thing written and get out of here. Two solid months on one story is long enough to get material for a novel—and this story is going to be far short of sensational. I'm going to have to play the nurses—dammit—because the combat angle is now too old. But maybe the girlies will make it.

By chowtime tonight, all the boys from the 31st were back—Knapp,

126

Danny, Ginther—those three especially because of their beards. Danny looked like a 13th portrait of Christ and Ginther, handsome anyway, looked like some captain in the court of Elizabeth. And were they proud of their record up there—three missions at least. They successfully covered for the TBFs laying mines at Kahili and nobody lost anything. However, Knapp's ship was blown to hell by Charlie, who dropped one alongside the plane which was loaded with eight 500-pounders. Knapp said there was a hole 40 feet wide & 30 feet deep— that was all. Charlie had been getting luckier—he tore up the mess hall and some stuff and the boys in the outfit had some close ones. They lost one man. I certainly regret not having gotten here in time to go up and fly with those guys—they're really nice people. I understand everything is looking up for them now: they're supposed to go to Fiji for a month to break in some new men, come back and hit Cactus once more and then go back to the States, with possibly another Auckland trip to boot. As foreign as aviation is to me, techni- cally, I think I could have done some good work by that gang, with their help. As it is, I'm following Brodie and will probably work with whatever crew he happens to be with. That's okay with me.

I have a feeling—justifiable or not—that AC are an extremely clannish bunch of people, but at the same time they seem to be generally a strictly intelligent bunch. Their intelligence is more alive than some types—line sol- diers, say—and less alive than the average headquarters bunch. The desk sol- dier, if he is alive at all (and all of them aren't), has a mind that sparkles by comparison—but he's usually bright, whereas the line soldier may be just as intelligent but not so sparkling. The line soldier doesn't have much reason to be sparkling. These AC boys, what I've seen of them, are somewhere in between.

My impression of the 5th Bomb boys is that they are clannish, being AC, and doubly so, being Regular Army.[3] They've spent time at Hickam—years there before they saw combat. And it burns them up to see selectees ride over them to the ratings. But that is true of every soldier, no matter what his com- ponent, who has more service that the next guy. At Vila the Signal boys pissed and moaned to high heaven because the replacements for their outfit were all non-coms when they arrived from the States. I don't blame them, but at the same time the men who go thru technical schools expect to get something out of it. It's just one of those things. This business of promoting men just because they're going overseas is not such a hot idea.

The 5th men have their officer woes, too, but less than the average sol- diers, I believe. The whole soldier-officer dissention centers not on "business relationships" so much as on privileges enjoyed by the officers and not by the soldiers. If men & officers worked together and then, off duty, enjoyed the same privileges, there wouldn't be much trouble. I hear the word "morale" used here and at Efate, mostly kidding, but more than on the Canal, where everybody was on the same status. But where there are parties for officers, dates with nurses for officers, whiskey for officers—there is bound to be reaction. Personally, I get the urge for bars three times a day at chow when I wash a mess kit, sweat out a line, take what I can get to eat, while I see the officers eat like gentlemen. Some of the boys say the officers eat better than we do, but I rather doubt it—the food's just presented to them better. That is a small thing, but it has its effect—on me, anyway. Of course there is the dreaded word "responsibility"—but sometimes I wonder about that. They say that when you become an officer the fun's over. I wonder about that, too—I think both of those things are in the individual's mind.

I, personally, have no reason to complain, But it would be against my nature—and against human nature, I think—not to want something better. The question is, could I better myself by becoming an officer? To have my job and be an officer or the equivalent at the same time would be the answer. To leave the job to become an officer would not be. In other words, as always, I'd like to have my cake and eat it too. The office's plan to give us special ratings comparable to civilian correspondents is of course the nearest possible solution, but apparently that has been buried in the Washington cemetery, at least temporarily. I know Brodie has ideas of becoming an officer and I think he would make a good one, but how he plans doing it and continuing his drawing is something neither he nor I have figured out. I think his immediate plan is to learn all he can about the Army—maneuver himself into a position where he has military confidence in himself—and then start looking for a chance. It doesn't do me any good to see all those people going back to OCS, or to read that Breger and Kahn and good buddy Neville are now officers and off the paper. I think that instead of being off the paper they are probably all connected with it in some way other than in actual writing. Under combat conditions I wouldn't give two hoots in hell whether I was an officer or not—truth is, if I were back in the line I'd rather be a non-com simply because, now, I don't think I'm qualified to be a platoon leader. If I couldn't be a really good leader I wouldn't want to be one at all, because there are enough lousy officers in the Army as it is. I'm not being noble about that, either: I just don't think that as I am now I'd make a good line officer. With plenty of re-education on the tactics & techniques of infantry, plus re-understanding of the "command psychology" I might; otherwise, no.

In combat it doesn't make much difference—the barriers are down and the officer differs from the man only inasmuch as the officer is supposed to be the better soldier and the enlisted man expects him to prove it—or at least prove he's just as good. That the average officer does or does not prove it is beside the point here. If he doesn't prove it chances are he'll still be an officer, tho not a good one. A really good junior officer is a precious thing in an outfit.

But outside of combat in the hierarchy of the Army, people are either officers or enlisted men. One or the other. Both have their advantages and both have their drawbacks. They both have their responsibilities. I look at it this way—if a man is a good enlisted man the chances are he will make a correspondingly good officer. I don't think the average soldier who has a decent education and who has a decent American background is going to make a poor officer just because there have been limitations set on the height he can reach as of now. I know of some tech sergeants who wouldn't make a good corporal and I also know some majors who wouldn't make good tech sergeants. Yet they hold their rank all right and the only difference is that one is of the privileged class and the other isn't. Granted that neither incompetents should be allowed to retain their ratings, the fact is they do retain them and who is the better situated—the major, of course. He is an officer. An officer is somebody. I have long since ceased to regard officers as any special work of the Lord, and I respect a good officer for exactly what he should be and is: a superior person. But the average officer as an individual is just like anybody else—like any enlisted man who has the same qualifications. There is very little difference in intelligence or anything else. The big difference: the officer is the fellow who sits down front, because he can.

Friday, April 2. Spent this morning with George, for lunch ate the steak he saved for me. Gave me old campaign hat once owned by Gen. Rose—something I'd rather have than sun helmet two to one. To SCAT this afternoon where spent three or four hours, at last successfully, getting Capt. Jarbel to tell me about the early days of SCAT on the Canal. Talked to Marine tech sgt. who says things on Russell are hot as hell—bombing, shelling, strafing. A Gen. Baker in command there—never heard of him. Lt. Gerkin at SCAT unusually nice for some reason—took me over for coffee. Funny: Curran says he wasn't worth a damn and today he told me Curran wasn't worth a damn. Curran no longer G-3, shifted to CT. Shake-up? Show tonight. Lupino in *The Hard Way*. Enjoyed it. Short was song fest of Army Navy Marine tunes. Boys sang swell, but the thing ended with Marine Hymn and Air Corps song wasn't included at all, whole outfit booed, yelled. Two new crews came in while we at show—snow jobs started at once. The veteran 5th office forces wasted no time. New men were at Canton when Japs bombed there last week—didn't know that. Best scuttlebutt yesterday was story of riot at Fiji when MPs called 182nd boys "USO soldiers." That must have been good.[4] Have worked most of the night on SCAT story—it now almost 4:00 a.m.—but think piece actually pretty fair. Hope to get out of here Monday at the latest. May have transportation trouble.

Saturday, April 3. Got the SCAT story off thru Major Fuller.[5] Nothing new; spent most of the day with George. To PX for talk with Major Seasholes, but found him too busy with flower business. Asked for *Yank*, was told they all sold out. Flowers for Easter & Mother's Day thru PX is a good thing, if it works. I ordered some for Helen couple of days ago, and sent money order for orchids to Blackstock couple of weeks ago, so she should get something out of it.

At 5th tonight Johnson said over 200 replacements came in this afternoon. I was surprised when he said that just about brought the outfit back up to strength.

Heard also that the coast watcher reported men safe who were lost in February—also a Navy man who went down back in August! What a story that would be—maybe I'll be lucky enough to blunder into it. Talked to a Marine Sgt. yesterday, but forgot to mention his statement that one of raiding planes was a Heinkel. Interesting, if true.[6]

Understand L & M companies 182nd still on Canal. Boy at QM talking about transferring back into outfit, since he feels no ratings are coming his way. Ratings—how those stripes figure into a man's life here. If he gets a promotion, he starts working on another one—because there is always somebody less deserving who is higher than he. If he doesn't get it, he pisses and moans. It's one thing to say a rating means nothing—another to prove it. Notable case is little "Donald Duck"—three years RA and still bucking for Pfc.—and cheerfully. That's one thing I liked about my old outfit: when a man got another stripe, the rest of the gang didn't cut his throat; generally they let him do it himself. USAFISPA is a stripes hungary bunch.

Monday, April 5. Arrived back on Cactus via SCAT about 8:30 a.m., four hours and 15 minutes out of Button. Mud knee deep after hard rain yesterday and last night. Finally got set up in the 31st Bomb area, only to learn we may move in a few days. This best camp spot I've seen on Cactus, except very muddy.

Brodie has malaria. Walked into [hospital][7] to find him looking like somebody had drained his crankcase. He came down the day after he got here, that is, Thursday. Altho he is getting well, the quinine treatment has just about floored him. He should be okay in another three or four days, but right now he's mighty shaky on his pins.

While I haven't been anywhere at all today, Brodie tells me the whole gang we know here has scattered: Frommell is in Button on the *Curtiss*—Givens at OCS—Burchfield with the American, supposedly. That leaves only Beaton and he's sweating out transportation for OCS. Brodie says he saw Walter Stewart; says he is a right guy. Want to see him for old-times sake.

No strikes or searches out of here yet.

My getting up here today was strictly a high-pressure job. Found out after the show last night that the ride I thought I had on a 17 didn't pan. Called SCAT and then got Major Concannon out of bed at 10:30 to get my travel certificate signed. Then stayed up all night to catch the 3:30 plane which left at 4:15.[8]

Tried to sleep this afternoon but was suddenly possessed with the idea that I should write a short story. So I almost got one finished. Another reason for wishing I had a typewriter. Have never tried fiction, but would like to take a crack at it just for fun and if I could get lucky and sell a couple it would mean a little extra in the bank. I think the market would be wide open for some stuff that I could base on incidents from here. I don't know—if I could get ambitious I might be able to work something up.

Tuesday, April 6. Have slept the whole day long. Got up too late for coffee this morning, so walked up the beach almost to the Tenaru for my constitutional; after chow went back to sleep and woke up for chow again. Had planned going up to Corps. All I accomplished was a shave and wash up. What a life.

Had an alert about 2:00 o'clock this morning, but it didn't pan. There was something up, but it didn't come in. I understand there are night fighters here now and that one of them got a bomber about 30 miles out earlier in the evening.

Brodie still not feeling so hot.

Still nothing going on here. Apparently we walked into another shake up situation—everybody is either going to move or thinks he should. Nothing has happened yet, but all the talk is Koli Point or off the island. I wish to hell we'd have gotten up here a month ago instead of now—when the 31st combat crews were here—but maybe we can salvage something. I feel a little lost.

There seems to be quite a rivalry between the 23rd & 31st boys, at least, among the ground crews. Chippy, our fight fan from Brooklyn, is in ordnance and he's pe-toibed over the fact that the 31st has had to do all the work. He's a strong squadron partisan.[9]

The AC has a way with itself at that. Sign on their latrine: "31st thunderpit—Capacity 6 Pfc's."

The way my head is aching at the moment, I wouldn't be surprised if I come up even with Brodie ere long. The percentages on malaria are about to catch up, perhaps.

Am still struck with the idea of a few short stories. Read yesterday's effort again, and while it's not one of the ten best, I do think there are possibilities.

Wednesday, April 7. The condition is red—anticipation of some 100 Bogies coming down. Seems like everything we've got is in the air. This should be a dilly, if they get in.

Last night we had a pretty fair raid, about 45 minutes. A bunch of the boys were over on the mat watching *Wake Island*. Just as the Japs were about to bomb Pearl Harbor in the picture, the audience looked up and saw a Jap in the lights overhead. They broke up the picture. Three flares were dropped and the guys said they were pretty worried because there is no shelter on the mat. I felt pretty much at home in the foxhole listening to the ack-ack, but we didn't have any warning and I took shoes with me in my hand. Another alert later didn't pan.

Went up to XIV Corps this morning and saw a few of the old gang—a very few. Saw Beaton, Ackley, Col. Brown, Timboe, Aldrich and a couple of others—all that are left now that the American has pulled out to Fiji. And apparently all the old gang are trying like hell to get moving. Timboe has started on his 7th month here and so has Beaton, of course. That's long enough, certainly.

At the moment everything is out trying to spot aircraft. Indications are they may be after our convoy which just pulled out loaded, I think, with the 182nd. It would be tragic if those guys got hit.[10]

But back to Corps. Met Major Walter Stewart and we had a nostalgic conversation on the Jackson-Betsy football game, plus name-swapping on newspapermen. Walter is an okay guy, but, like Brodie, I somehow got the impression he is a major and I am a sergeant. Perhaps that's not justified. I don't know yet. At least I'm not picking a fight with anybody, especially since the guy is from my home state.[11]

The men up north haven't been rescued yet. I'm sweating.

The personnel of Corps headquarters were at Brownwood, Texas, and of the few I talked to I got the impression they are typically higher headquarters men who have known each other under better conditions. The reference to the Canal as a Godforsaken place went so far—as the story goes—that the Chaplain put out some Easter greeting cards with the quotation: "He is risen; he is not here." I saw a notice on the bill board recalling them, so I suppose the cards actually went out.

Time out for an air battle—they just had a dandy over Tulagi . . . . . and it's not over yet, The AA just opened again and a limb fell on the roof. More fun. But the air battle—we couldn't see much, except a heck of a lot of AA from Tulagi, then bomb splashes, then a column of gray smoke (they must have hit something) then I glimpsed a speck going down & saw it hit the water, then a spot of fire going down, two columns of black smoke between Savo & Tulagi. But it was all too far away. Planes overhead were all ours, I think, sort of playing secondary defense. Anyway, it was better than a $1.50 seat at the movies. I'm interested in getting the score. Odd shots are still being fired here and there so it may not be over yet, but the weather is closing in so I don't guess anybody will be able to see very much.

One interesting fact I got today is that the Tenaru River as the Marines called it, isn't the Tenaru at all, but the Ilu, or "Alligator Creek." The Tenaru is further up by Corps Hq. When the Marines fought the "Battle of the Tenaru," their maps showed the rivers' names swapped about. But Hell's Point on the Ilu (now) is just the designation of an Army ammo dump. It should have been the battle of the Ilu, but to the Marines and to Dick Tregaskis I don't suppose that made a helluva lot of difference. Anyway, it wasn't such a terrible place to fight a battle—at least the visibility is good there, between the palms, and the underbrush is about waist high or less. A cub outfit is bivouacked there now.[12]

Apparently the war isn't over yet. Our AA just let go another burst and a patrol of F4Fs is still sniffing around up there. Maybe they did bring 100 planes over.

Three planes of the 23rd struck Kahili last night and they say they had a helluva time—made one initial pass and nothing happened, came back a second time and 12 search lights converged on them at once. They were blinded. Two of the ships had motor trouble, one badly. These crates have been flying so long they're ready to come apart, and I imagine there are a few B-17s still patrolling the coastline back in the States. Somehow I can't see why these people should fly patched-together airplanes.

Saw George Doling today—we took a bath in the Tenaru—and he's a woebegone character. Practically all his buddies have left him and his immediate superior is based in Noumea, leaving him practically the only Australian within 500 miles. He's ready to pull out, but sees no hope. Timboe has papers in for his return to the States. Beaton is sweating a transfer or OCS.

Saw the Chinese boys rescued from the Japs. They still haven't fully recovered from the starvation they experienced. They're acting as bat boys for the officers, getting their orders from a Chinese-speaking man in the outfit; I understand they speak no English.

Wrote Helen a brief note, telling her I'm back. There wasn't much news I could tell her; that would be interesting anyway.

So this is my third day back on Cactus and I haven't done anything, nor do I have anything particular in mind. I'm still not enthused about bomb missions—particularly at night—and I haven't as yet even seen the proper people who could authorize a flight for me. I've been waiting to get the score here and so far it's still nothing to nothing. But I do feel better being back where something is going on. I want to get over to Tulagi, and up to Russell Island; but I came up here to do AC and that at the moment is the important thing.

Thursday, April 8. Five ships on strike last night; men came back 'smorning and at chow went into their session. It seems that there are new navigators aboard—I've heard a lot of talk about navigation in the last couple of days—and that they aren't trained for over-water flight. Last night one ship started for Kahili and wound up near Buka. It was so dark nobody could see anything, so they don't know exactly what the hell they hit. Twenty-four SBDs went along and the first 17 dropped flares. I think everybody got rid of their bomb loads, however, either at Kahili or somewhere else on the line.

Scuttlebutt score on yesterday's scramble was 26-7, but we lost at least a tanker at Tulagi. I don't know how such things get around but the tale last night was of a Jap who cut in on our frequency with: "You American bastard." Some-body answered, "I'll get you, you yellow son of a bitch," and the Jap is supposed to have said, "Don't worry, I'll be back tonight." We had two alerts last night, but nothing happened.

Funny thing yesterday—when the news of the Japs reached here, every-body ran down to the beach with every kind of armament they could carry—rifles, pistols, tommies, BARs—in the hope of getting in a lucky shot if the Bogies came in low. Beau Geste,[13] anyway.

I understand all missions scheduled for the squadron are night missions—damn. I don't see much percentage there at all, but I guess I'll go along once or twice, anyway.

After talking to Lt. Thom, however, I'm not so sure.[14] He suggests some ground crew stuff—which is like pulling teeth—and promised me a ride on the first day flight. He says the two night flights have been bitches—impossible, even for the crew. Doesn't think they'll get any better until there's a moon—and I know how it is in the moonlight. So what the hell?

Went over to the mat, crawled all over a 17, found out there is a differ-ence between a line chief and a crew chief and some other kind of chief (my ignorance is abysmal), was shown how bombs are loaded, what makes them tick, and numerous other odds and ends. Met a lieutenant from New York who knows some boys from around home.[15] Listened to a line chief as he met trouble after trouble—no oxygen here; where's your prop expert?—hell, if we have to put that on we might as well fly the plane—what have we got specialists for? Where do we get this? Twenty-six miles up the road? Hell, send for a new engine—this one's shot. How about that horizontal stabilizer? Is 405 still out of commission? Jesus Christ, do you think I'm supposed to shit an airplane for you? Fix it! So the problem of maintenance here is somewhat complicated. If I can get the hang of it—as I think I can by listening at B-17 engineering for awhile—I think that will be my first story.

Met Berton Burns' Uneager Beavers this afternoon—a bunch of guys whom I'd seen before in Auckland, but never got to know.[16] I think this crew—discovered by Brodie—will be the bunch to operate with. They've certainly got the life. Another boy was one who came over to Oahu on the *Noordam* with Miller & Bushemi. He wants to get some pix Bush took because one of the three crews on that boat went down over Shortland.

The Beavers' crew chief is a boy named Sidler who impresses me as being a right character. I am invited to fly a mission with them some time.

This afternoon's scuttlebutt is of a general screwing up of planes as every-body had them figured. Seems the 72nd is back and that other crews, already relieved, are coming back. To hit the Jap task force?

And some men from the States arrived. How these guys look down on them—"USO soldiers—look at those shoulder patches!" (They wear the AC eagle yet).[17]

Tonight after chow a small group collected around a Special Services record player to listen to "Mr. Five by Five" and other, older numbers. I was impressed by the bunch—all of them boys who have considerable service overseas and a helluva lot of combat experience. They were certainly a far cry from the well-groomed, glamorized air corps people I used to envy back in the States. They were muddy, standing in mud, with grease from the planes on them—some of them in shorts, underwear, fatigues, unshaven, etc. The AAF out here, while it isn't in bad shape compared with some of the ground outfits, still doesn't live the life of luxury. As somebody said a few days ago, this is not a gentleman's war. I wonder if any war is.

I was also impressed with the pilots—how young those guys are. Most of the combat officers look like a bunch of kids. For instance the operations officer, a Capt. Conradi, doesn't look much older than I am, but he does look as tho he has seen a lot.[18] I don't know whether I'm right or not, but a couple of wrinkles around his eyes make me think his mother would be surprised to see how her boy has changed. I more or less expect to find kid fighter pilots, but for B-17s I expected some of them to be past their freshman year in college. I think the average in the 11th Bomb are a little older—altho Majors Edmundson and Lucas were no venerable old characters. Speaking of young officers, I hear Lee Cagwin is now a major. Met a Polish kid out of the 35th, and his conception of the number of casualties in his outfit was amazing. I doubt there were that many American soldiers killed on this island. Read Major Kynett's resume of the Guadalcanal campaign; his estimation of Jap casualties was 40,000—which in my opinion and Major Timboe's is high. It certainly is, unless our artillery raised hell in the rear areas.

The B-17 engineering tent has a little platform on the center pole. On it is a snaggle-toothed Jap skull, with a helmet at a rakish angle. On the helmet is painted, "Made in Tokyo."

Friday, April 9. And still the talk is of leaving, going somewhere—Auckland, Fiji, the States. The talk is in proportion to the time men have spent here: the ground crews have been here since December, without a break; the combat crews, like the ships they fly, are veterans—Midway, the Coral Sea, etc. I noticed a memorandum on the bill board at Corps to the effect that the policy of relieving men after four months on Cactus has been rescinded. Damn few outfits got relief in four months.

The old cry in the Pacific is "Golden Gate in '48." I know a rookie in Vila who took stock in Halsey's prediction. His phrase was: "Santa Fe in '43."

Heard a new expression at chow 'smorning. A boy said, "Pass the sidearms." He got sugar and milk.

This place is absolutely alive with rumors, so much so, that for the first time overseas, I'm beginning to get tired of hearing people talk about going home. I don't want to get that bug myself—yet—so I don't want to listen to it. It's like mass hysteria, involving people who otherwise wouldn't be involved at all in the mental agony of home-sickness.

Spent most of the day on the mat, looking over the "Sad Sack" and trying to get an angle for a story. At B-17 engineering still no dice. It's like trying to do a feature on garage mechanics, much as I hate to say it. I've got to at least inject some sort of feature angle into it. I still want to shoot the bull with the line chief. If I can get him to give me a snow job, it will be a story.

Was going to try to get on a search tomorrow, but the Beavers are going on strike to Kahili tonight so Brodie & I are going with them. Takeoff at midnight.

Rumor is that 90 Bogies are coming in, and if they get here the boys will be singing, as I heard a boy on the beach this evening: "I've got those Foxhole Blues . . . . . oh Lordy, Lordy, Lordy, got those Foxhole Blo oooo es."

Saturday, April 10. Brodie and I have slept most of the day, having gone on a mission last night. It was quite an experience but, as on the Munda raid before, of little practical value to either of us. Both of us got what we needed for mood, but the story value isn't much except as I will try to set down here.

Actually, the mission was a miserable failure—the third such out of three times at bat for the 23rd here. We couldn't find the target: Kahili. We were over Bougainville and got a little AA over Munda on the way home, but our 14 300-pounders made the round trip with us. We had a new navigator, and I think we were lost from the time we cleared the island until we got back this morning.[19] It was 6':10." That gives me 14 hours combat flight. Henderson the bombardier was sweating out the takeoff and as he said he was watching the trees with one eye and the air speed indicator with the other. We go off at 1:30; it was close. Since the "Sad Sack" is still out of commission we flew "The Skipper"—veteran of Midway. It really wasn't the navigator's fault alone that we got the DFO on this one—we were the lead ship of a 6-plane flight and none of the other navigators called his hand on the course at all. They stuck with us and at 22,500 we couldn't see anything because of overcast. Capt. Burns went down twice, but we couldn't get in.

It was Brodie's first night flight and my first in which we expected to meet heavy ack-ack, bombing in formation. We wore oxygen masks of course, from 12,000 on, and put on the leather high altitude flying suits—which are really something. Together with the Mae Wests, we had on more junk than a vaudeville comedian. Naturally, I found I had to relieve myself and not being able to get to the relief tube in the bomb bay I devised what I thought was a nice trick. I used my canteen cover, filling it half full, and then held onto it for a long time, waiting to drop it when we got over the target. I finally had to pour it down the john, dammit.

Takeoff time was moved back to 12:30. Everybody gathered at Operations where there was hot coffee. Sidler had his cowboy bell and was kidding; Debby and Rogers and I shot the breeze. There was tension under the foolishness. I had sweated out the flight on my bunk, lying here in the dark, thinking, Occasionally Brodie & I would say something to each other, but not much. When I got with the boys the tension began to ebb away and on takeoff I felt swell, absolutely unconcerned. But I sweated on my bunk. Unpleasant things flashed across my mind and I would think of something else; but the unpleasant things came back.

At Operations we talked of many things. Operations was jammed with men, clustered in tight little groups, drinking coffee. The air was hot with men and cigarette smoke made it close. Operations is a wall tent with a single light bulb. There are four desks and a map board.

A staff sergeant with a shoulder patch edged in.

"This your first flight?"

"Yeah."

"You an observer?"

"Yeah, and I never saw an anti-aircraft burst except in the movies."

"Well, just count the search lights and try to spot the AA guns."

"I know. How do you think it will be up there tonight?"

"What doya mean?"

"Well, this is my first combat mission. I don't give a damn, y'understand—but I just wondered how you think it will be."

"You'll see anti-aircraft tonight. Tomorrow you'll be a hardened veteran. Hardened anyway."

Debby coached me about oxygen. We kept up some kind of conversation, but that wasn't hard because "Buck" Rogers sitting across the table, his cap brim up, streamed wise cracks. He talked of his private public bar a block from his home. He said he was going to lease a seat at the bar and just put a relief tube in, so he wouldn't ever have to leave.

The weather report came in. Bad over the target area, but not too bad. People came in for coffee and went back outside.

Then it was time to go. Pilots collected crews and a safari of flashlights single file, reached from Operations to the motor pool. Men stepped ankle-deep in mud and cursed. Two crews apiece to a truck and the little convoy, blackout lights on, moved to the mat. A quarter moon was low in the west, just above thunderheads which flashed at intervals with white lightning. Somebody found the Big Dipper. "The damn thing's upside down." I said to Debby, "Did you say 'Frisco Bay by the first of May'?" He laughed. "Nope. Make mine 'Chi by the fourth of July.'" We found the plane. Henderson Field was dark and lonesome. Watches were synchronized at 11:33.

Capt. Burns called the crew together. He's tall & slim with a red face. The men think he's the squadron's best pilot; the officers all call him Tex.

"Two B-24s will drop 50 flares each. We will make one one minute & 15 second bombing run; if we do not get our bombs off, we will make another run. We are the lead ship of the leading element."

The co-pilot, a captain with a bristling mustache, talked weather with Tex. The navigator, a chunky kid, didn't say much. Sidler began to wise off:

"Cap'n, ever time we get over that target, I keep seeing that Golden Gate Bridge. Sure does look good, too."

"Hell, I've been in the Pacific so long I'm gettin' attached to these damn islands. Two years over here, but a lot of that was in Oahu. Damn nice place, Hawaii."

"But it wasn't so good for enlisted men, Tex," the co-pilot said.

Tex defended himself: "Well, there were women and whiskey."

"Waikiki in 43, boy," Sid said. "I'm sweating this one out tonight. They've really got the AA up there. I know."

"What is this—for my benefit?" the navigator said.

"Don't you think you could sort of get us lost, lieutenant," Sid laughed. "Say head for Fiji or someplace?"

"This is going to be an easy mission," Tex said soberly. "One of the easiest we've had, if it goes right."

"I sweat 'em all out," somebody said. "We'd better just make one run on that target, Henderson."

Tech-Sgt. Henderson chuckled. "A couple of pilots already told me if I miss tonight I'm a private tomorrow."

Everybody laughed, even Tex.

"We can't miss," Henderson said. Flatly.

It was 12:10. Tex looked at his watch.

"Let's go."

Little Weaver the tail gunner patted the ground affectionately and said, "See you in the morning." He climbed into the fuselage. As an afterthought he added, "I hope."

We got aboard and with flashlights counted out the flight clothes, picked the Mae Wests, checked the oxygen masks, selected our earphones for the interphones. Frankly, I was—and had been—sweating out Charlie. I would have hated like hell to get caught out there with no shelter at all. I was watching the sky out of all windows.

The motors turned over and warmed until takeoff less a couple of minutes. Around the field, five other 17s revved up. The field lights, outlining the mat, were on.

Averbeck crawled into the ball turret. The 22-year-old 'Beck had said: "Every time I get into that thing it takes me back 22 years."[20]

Before takeoff, the Uneager Beavers are happy-go-lucky. In the ship, they're serious people, each with something definite to do. I envy them that— a job to do.

We rolled to the mat, pivoted and without slowing down, took off with the lights flashing by.

We rendezvoused and headed for Kahili.

Night flight in formation is a weird and beautiful thing. On a 17 there is a white light on the vertical stabilizer and blue lights on the cowling and looking from the waist windows the horizontal stabilizers glow pale purple, an incandescent plane in space. The motors roar so loud that speech is impractical and in the dark a man feels himself to be a solitary unit, connected to the rest of the world only by an interphone which occasionally blares sounds like the amplified double talk of a ham burlesquer. The super-chargers of the engines trail a veil of light and sometimes the props shimmer in a light which comes from I know not where. To right & left are the wing ships. Theirs is a gaudy splendor in a night of soft starlight and darkness on the sea & islands. The sea is dark, but the islands are darker and their outline is plain—surprisingly so. In a bank, the horizon becomes utterly lost and stars seem suddenly to have fallen into the sea. The wing planes shift, now up, now down, close in & far out. Two red lights on the left wing, green on the right, with the white light on the stabilizer as the apex of the triangle. Close up the dim blue lights on the fuselage add their faint touch, giving body to the triangle. The wing planes slide off in a glide, as a plate is scooted along a counter, and the motion is so effortless it seems to be the changing of props in a magic lantern show. A thunderhead is hit dead ahead and the ship lifts with a physical, elevator-like surge and then the world closed down to the wing tips where red and green lights glow mistily and the exhaust, already a veil, becomes a paler cashmere which streams back and spends itself in its own rush forward. A flashlight from within beams out the window and catches the millions of tiny drops which dance hysterically past in the slip stream. And then the plane breaks free of the shroud and becomes alive again, the flight almost clear the cloud, gathers itself together again as men do when they come out of a dense wood into a field. To the right are the seven stars of the Dipper, to the left the black nebulae of the Milky Way. The course is West to Kahili.

At dawn, rosy and white and blue, we were headed East into the rising sun. From the bombardier's seat in the nose, the ocean slid by like a blue and white towel on a roller rack. In the early light, the element looked fresh and clean even in its muddy paint and oil covered motors. But inside each ship were men with cramped bodies and tousled hair, sticky skin and tired sleepy eyes. "Shut your eyes, boy, or you'll bleed to death." We were tail heavy and everything was moved forward to the radio compartment, ammo boxes first. Weaver and Debby and I looked out the radio-gun hatch and the slip stream beat our hair so that the ends of it hit our foreheads like a thousand tiny lashes.

We approached the island from the NW, and I was stunned by the beauty of it. I don't think I've seen a prettier landscape for the air. We came in somewhere around Maravovo or Kimimbo, rounded Esperance and buzzed down past Tassafaronga, Kokumbona, Pt. Cruz, Lunga and circled in to a landing.

In the dawn light Guadalcanal was green and gray and purple; the mountains inland were cloud-caped and the hills were a dark green for the jungle and a soft green or gray for the cleared spaces, the palm groves were a green, too, but they looked blocked in, row on row, perfectly straight, bisected by the main road from Lunga landing. The sun hit the land with long, strong rays and while the shadows gave an emphasis to heights and depth I knew what I was seeing was an outright lie. From the air a man gets an exalted, utterly false, impression of the ground. But I found long ago that the beauty of the Canal comes out, like the female malarial mosquito, only at sunset and dawn.

We were tired and the Beavers were out of sorts. The mission had been unsuccessful and worse—it would be blamed on us, the lead ship. But, the boys said, at least we tried. We landed first. "So they think this bombing is glamorous," said Debby. "That's a crock of shit."[21]

Sunday, April 11. This afternoon the story I've been sweating out finally fell in my lap. But only a part of it. Three of the men—Capt. Tom Classen, pilot, Lt. Balfour Gibson, bombardier, and Lt. Bob Dorwart, navigator—who were shot down Feb. 9, came back. The rest—the co-pilot and five enlisted men— are still on the Carteret Islands.[22] With the three who came down was Delmar Wiley, shot down in a TBF off the *Saratoga* on August 24![23]

Tonight they told me their story—one of the most amazing I've heard. Their buddies in the 72nd had long since placed a memorial for them at Button.[24] And the three of them gained weight.

There are two complications: first, the rest of the crew remains to be rescued; second, their tale is shot thru with references to the natives and to the coast watchers—both of which are strictly taboo in censorship. Truth is, if it hadn't been for the natives and the radio at the coast watchers' station on Choiseul, the whole outfit would still be in the middle of Jap territory, or dead.[25]

On the Carterets they split up two men to an island, with Gibson on the smallest one alone. He and a native man were the only males there—the rest were women. Gibson said if a man went blind and lost his memory, he might try something but his nose would change his mind. Classen said the natives told him a Jap (who crash landed after the Tulagi raid Wednesday) asked for a woman the first thing after they picked him up. The Jap was shot later as he tried to get away after he saw our men, but with that beginning he had two strikes on him anyway. Classen said that the natives are very finicky about their women. He said they found a German named Peter there—had been there for years and knew only that some kind of war is on—that he had tried to buy a woman and the natives wouldn't sell. Seems he executed a rape job there once and they didn't like it. Wiley told Peter we are at war with Germany; he didn't know anything except that his supply ship doesn't come in any more. Classen said he speaks no English, nor any German either—only Rabaul Pidgin English and some of the native tongue. The question was raised as to whether he should be taken off the island for precautionary reasons. They all agreed he couldn't get along with white men anymore and that, since he has no place to go, it would be better to leave him there. They don't believe he'd want to leave, anyway. I was a little awed to be present when men casually determined whether another man should or should not be brought back from absolute oblivion.[26]

Classen said the natives are pro-American to a great degree—considering us as their superior because we are white and considering the Japs on a par with or below themselves. Gibson laughed when he said they called the crew "Master." Dorwart explained they meant "white man."[27]

One note: they said they found Wiley teaching school and that all the kids cried when he left. One of the crew has taken over his professorship now. Gibson said the native missionary had taught them how to count to 199 and that Wiley was teaching them from 199 to 1000.

They brought out a lot of stuff as to the habits and skill of the natives which would be good but I can't use it. The native chief, to gain prestige apparently, insisted that he be allowed to drink water from a canteen, which he did with a wry face. They rarely drank water at all, preferring coconut milk. They have some kind of concoction made of coral growth which is a cure-all if ever there was one. The stuff, after it is dried in the sun and heated, becomes a white powder, vile smelling, which they use to caulk boats, as a medicine for open cuts, and even as a component for an intoxicant which gives them a hangover.[28] They have feasts, get drunk, and then starve to death until the next feast day.

Classen, in telling of their first attempt to get off the Carterets in a canoe, said the four of them finally argued the natives into repairing a decrepit old outrigger which they loaded with rations for their trip. He said they were going to try to make it alone but when they started out everybody in the village, including the women, wanted to go along. The men got three or four miles out and capsized the canoe, on which they have my sympathy.[29]

Before their second attempt three Jap planes came over and one landed on the lagoon, taxied around looking the island over and then took off again. Classen had every one of the natives armed and was praying the Japs would come ashore so he could get their airplane. He's never flown a float plane but he said he was desperate enough to try anything. But the incident scared the natives. Classen said that after their first unfortunate attempt they wanted a native to come along to handle the outrigger. He said the natives helped them load the boat, put up the sail, and when they shoved off nobody made a move to join them this time. The natives just said goodbye and stayed ashore. The men sailed over to another island, where there were four white men—who or why I didn't get—and were kicked off because of shortage of food.[30] Finally, Gibson talked the man on his island into building them an outrigger. He made them a 35-footer, doubly reinforced the outrigger and wove the sail from palm leaves. He was a master shipbuilder, they said, because the extra braces he put on saved the boat in a storm off Shortland. I'm pretty sure they said he sailed with them all the way down—they brought a native down from Choiseul, I know. Naturally, they want to reward him. They were in hellish danger twice of being spotted by Jap aircraft because once two patrol planes flew over and again 15 planes went past. They figure that if they were spotted the Japs thought them only other Japs on an inter-island trip but I doubt it because they almost certainly would have gone down for a look. They were smart in keeping the prow of the canoe turned always toward the Japs, presenting the smallest possible visible target.[31] Classen reckoned if the Japs ever found out about it, "they'd be kicking their asses all over Bougainville." They never saw an American plane the whole time they were there, until the PBY picked them up at the rendezvous point yesterday.

They all had foot trouble—coral infection. Classen & most of the others were barefoot from the time the plane went down. All had recovered from wounds.

They talked of the coast watchers, two men of the RAN, who have a dangerous job that will be a wonderful story when the war is over—but not before. Classen, who is 24 and doesn't look a day older, was highly indignant that they make only about $60 a month. That seems incredible to me, but the British don't pay very well. Their record up there is nine Americans saved and nine Japs shot. Dorwart was laughing about a Jap pilot who made a water landing there and brought ashore a parachute and a battery—"just what he needed in the bush." The Australians use the battery now to light their station.[32]

The three of them seem to be in perfect health except for their feet. They look good, well-nourished and of course all as happy as any three people could be. Gibson still has his beard, but Classen is clean shaven and even got a crew haircut from Dorwart. They will go to Button tomorrow & then, I hope, to the States.

Monday, April 12. I am, in the vernacular of the Army, highly pissed off. Brodie, having suffered a relapse, has been taken to the 20th Station Hospital to sweat out his second case of Malaria. We decided today to leave Guadalcanal as soon as he recovers.

At Corps this morning, found waiting for us the March 26 and April 9 copies of the paper from the office. One of them contained a story on Chaplain Smith, with pix, which I did for PRO back in November. Neither had any of Brodie's stuff. But one did have Miller's story on the Kiwis, with pix by Bush—a nice layout—and another had a two page spread on medical evacuation in Hawaii. That was enough for me.[33]

Had another talk with the survivors this morning and since Brodie is sick I was sweating out pix. Went over to see Major Stewart to enlist his aid in getting a cameraman and he has access to absolutely nothing in that respect. But he came over and we re-hashed the story with Classen. I learned from Dorwart that a marine c.c. named Growder took some excellent shots,[34] so the major and I went to Wing to see about getting prints. I was amazed to see how well set up those people are—beautiful set up they have, with 8 men, including two officers who write, a field artist who says he did four pages for *Yank*, a combat correspondent, two still cameramen and two movie cameramen. They have lights, typewriters, etc. And they play to the home-town trade, with always an eye for crashing the big time. Lt. Mathieu who knows Bill Richardson, indicates they are turning out plenty of stuff and I certainly don't doubt it.

I hate to admit I'm licked—and I'm not yet—but the way things are I'm beginning to wonder what the hell I'm doing here. I can piss and moan till hell won't have me—and I think that's just what I'll do so I can look back later and say "you poor thing." I've counted the stories I've done—21—and out of that many I know of only 6 that have been printed. And out of more than 50 drawings by Brodie they have printed only about 12. If I thought we were doing lousy work it would be different, and it would be just as different if the office thought so and said as much—but all the mail we get from Spence indicates he is pleased. Then why in hell don't they use the stuff? Why do they take up two pages with a layout on card tricks—in two issues—and why do they print sheer crap like the Chaplain Smith thing when there are stories of combat—and better—sketches of combat? They have some swell stuff from North Africa by Pete Paris and Slim Aarons and a nice little piece from Dave. Those, I think, are what the book should have in abundance—not so much eye wash. But that is merely my opinion and it is tempered by the knowledge that we must have humor & plenty of it. What gets me is the medical evacuation thing in Hawaii. As a picture story it's beautiful—for a civilian magazine it would be swell—but my contention is that we should feature what we *do* and *have done* in combat, and not what we are going to do. I think Bush did a wonderful job of coverage but I'll just be damned if I can see that much importance in the thing.

The answer to a great deal of these mysteries is to me very simple: a camera, or better, a cameraman. I defend Brodie's work before I do my own, but a camera to me would be like another pair of arms or something. Today was typical: to get a picture I had to go hunting for somebody who, if I found them, might be kind enough to do me the favor of taking, developing & printing some work for me. It is one hell of a note. Being 50% pictures, the book has to have art, and some stories just won't stand up without it. I've gone into that before, however.

Another thing is the typewriter. The situation here is that we can't work at night and no typewriters are available during the day.

A third thing at the moment is just plain me. I've got this rescue thing in the refrigerator, with no idea when the rest of it can be written. They may pick those men up by sub and if they do the story is up the creek right there. Our flight the other night netted nothing and, with the antics the office is pulling, I can't see that further flights would be worthwhile. The ground situation remains stubbornly sterile, but I'm still trying. I may just go hog wild and try to turn in all the crap I can put my hands on: one thing I have in mind might be fair at that.

Anyway I am, for the first time, just plain disgusted. It's like starving in the midst of plenty—like whoever it was who couldn't reach the grapes. When Brodie is well, we're leaving here and I'm not going to do a damn thing but sit on my ass until I get equipped to do a job. I'm tired of this crap.

But my troubles are microscopic in comparison with those of the poor 23rd Bomb. Last night they pulled their first even remotely successful mission—dusk raid on Kahili again—and lost two ships. Every plane was out searching for them this morning and they were both located. One crew has been brought in; two of the men were killed in the water landing. The bombardier had a broken back and died in the raft; the engineer's neck was broken, they think, and they couldn't get him free of the bomb bays before she sank. The second crew is somewhere off the Russell Islands, with all intact—they think.[35]

It is absolutely a crying shame that these men should have to fly airplanes which should have been scrapped months ago. If there are as many B-17s in the States as I think there are, then it isn't a shame—it's murder. That's a strong statement but I've seen too much not to believe it. Rogers' ship last night, for example, came within an ace of crashing. They threw out everything that wasn't nailed down—guns, ammo, radio equipment—in order to keep it in the air. Another ship piled up when it came in from search this afternoon: something snapped as it set down. This is getting rugged.

Continuing the story from the Carterets, Dorwart said today Wiley had taught the native kids to sing "One little, two little, three little Indians" and altho their counting wasn't consistently accurate they sang like demons. He also taught something else along that line—"Shortnin' Bread"—or something, so they caroled like a bunch of canaries.

They're trying to get their native back home. And I hope a Cat goes up after the rest of the crew.

Tuesday, April 13. Took a deep breath and turned out my first copy on the island—a stinking little ditty about the peculiar names around here. If I were a clever writer it might have gone, but every time I try to get funny in a story it's pretty pathetic. This was more or less a test—I want to see what they do with it, if anything.[36]

Spent most of the day at Corps. Saw Brodie this morning and he looks like a sick kid. The cure must be worse than the disease in malaria.

Talked to Capt. Burden today and he gave me some interesting dope on prisoners. His estimation of their number—about 1000—does not exclude the termites captured here in the beginning. He thinks probably 200-300 soldiers were captured, but he has no way of checking the Marine total. In relating an experience he had a few days after the Horse's Neck, he said a Jap he was bringing back kept begging to be shot. The Capt., who speaks the language like a native, said the Jap went like this: "Shoot me here, please . . . . . why are you bringing me way down here to shoot me? Shoot me now—you're going to kill me anyway . . . . . (they came to a Jap foxhole). Here's a nice hole—shoot me here—I can fall in here and it will be easy to bury me." It is obvious, the Captain said, that every Jap firmly believed he would be shot if captured. Their officers must have given them that idea—and I imagine we strengthened it—so an antidote was the PA broadcasts. The Captain said—and I substantiated it later—that 75% of the prisoners taken by the Army were captured in the two places where he broadcast to them for surrender. Which certainly proves you can talk to a Jap, after all. That's useful information.

Walter Stewart and I had a little bitch to pitch which I suppose was inevitable after we saw the Marine layout. The major, by himself with no camera and as he says "a battered typewriter" (he talks journalese), wonders how he is expected to cover the Solomons. It's a good question. One thing is certain: he has the field almost to himself, now anyway.

Beaton begins his seventh month of service on Cactus. Six months ago today the 164th—first Army outfit on the island—landed, and got shelled. Certainly a lot has happened since then.

Had a peculiar thing happen this morning. I was told the censor, Lt. Weeks, wanted to see me so I thought I'd said too much in a letter. He began rather embarrassedly with "I know this is none of my business, but . . . . . " then went on to explain that he had read my letter to Helen in which I explained I was stymied on stories here. He seemed unwilling to believe that I could be with "the most famous bomb group in the Army, except the 19th" and not be able to get a story out of it. So he wanted to help me. He's a swell kid—a Virginian—and altho his initial statement was exactly right I almost have to agree with him that my attitude here is ridiculous. I feel like a fool, and at the same time I have not yet seen a story here which in any way increased my heart beat; the Carteret thing is the exception, of course. Was talking to the Beavers last night and they agreed to taking me with them on a search—which is a story one way or the other. Faulk—Bushemi's friend—wanted to know why the hell I wanted to tag along when the planes are going to pieces. He has the $64 question there. But the funniest incident of the day was Major Stewart's sudden recollection of his crossing in February. He said they stopped in Fiji and that a *Yank* correspondent, whom he didn't know was aboard, was put off the boat with a bad dose of the clap. That one really snows me. If true, I wonder who in hell it was. The ship came direct from the States, so the guy must have been unlucky in San Francisco. I notice we have a correspondent in Fiji, but didn't recognize the name at all.

Stewart knows Jim Burchard very well, having covered a regatta with him at Poughkeepsie at which place Jim had quite an experience with a lady with weak kidneys; quite a story.

The second crew which went down was brought in today—a little banged up but otherwise okay. Had a talk with Major Glober, a very nice sort of guy.[37] Burns' co-pilot came up and pitched a terrific bitch about having to stay on here as an exec. officer when the other men with six month's combat are leaving. Glober, I think, was somewhat embarrassed because of a conversation we'd just had on "what an officer should be." Hell, I don't blame the guy for yelling—I'd yell too in his place.

Story of the night was told by Lt. Bralley about Col. Blakey's driver.[38] They were driving thru a blackout and the colonel wanted the lights on. "Turn off those fuckin' lights," yelled an MP. The driver said nothing. They drove a little farther and another MP yelled "Turn off those fuckin' lights!" The driver got mad. "I can't turn off the fuckin' lights—I got the fuckin' colonel with me."

The officers are singing "One Ball Riley" and "The Eyes of Texas," etc. Forget yesterday & tomorrow—tonight we live.

Wednesday, April 14. Tulagi put up a beautiful ack-ack barrage last night—hundreds of tracers which slid up and over toward us, brilliant orange-red, twisting and arcing—and we watched it closely for some results on their target, but Charlie is hard to hit. An AA display is a nice thing to watch when it's 20 miles away.

Nothing accomplished except a start on the ground crew story. Talked to Lupin and Bralley and Flanagan today and got what will have to do for material, because between them they are my only source of reliable information.[39]

Saw Brodie, who looks much better. Also saw a boy we knew on the *Tryon*—out of the 214th. He's now blind in one eye and is going back to the States. Don't know how it happened.[40]

Walked over to the cemetery this afternoon. The last time I saw it was in January and it has become much larger; a new plot, almost as large as the first, is full. Apparently some of the men were exhumed in the hills and brought back. I wish every person back home could walk between those crosses, see the names and read the inscriptions. All the outfits I was with were represented there and some of the markers placed at the heads of the mounds are classics of feeling, of comradeship, of simple soldiery. The 132nd and some others made concrete blocks, with mess kits cemented into them and names, dates and a few words scratched on them. On them all was "Killed in Action" or "Died in Line of Duty." The Marine air people used props and at one grave, the glass cowling of an F4F. The soldiers had helmets (one perforated by shrapnel) rifle stocks, bayonets, crosses cemented in by .45 caliber bullets. The Jewish boys had Hebrew Stars and there were rosaries on many crosses. But one or two hit me—their buddies had placed snapshots of the boys on their markers. They were all just grinning kids with garrison caps tilted on the back of their heads.

One thing noticeable was the Catholic & Jewish symbols—the pictures of the Virgin, the little metal pieces, the Latin inscriptions, the Stars—and on the Protestant graves the conventional memoria, plus personal tributes which were so simple and sincere that they have to be seen for what they are there to be appreciated. Nobody walks in there and speaks except in lowered voice. I suppose that is convention, but I think it is also sheer respect born of understanding. I noticed a lot of inscriptions, "Killed in Action on Hill 27." One was Ervin Bickwermert the corporal whose last words were "Hold that Hill." I felt like uncovering at his grave, and I did.[41] There is nothing particularly morbid about that place, with the faded palm fronds still over some of the mounds, and almost all of them decorated in some way by the men who fought here, but I couldn't help remember Rickenbacker's statement in *Life* that he "wouldn't give the life of one American boy for the whole damned island." There were more than 50 graves marked "Unidentified."

For the first time on Guadalcanal, I saw native women today—three of them over near the native labor camp, wearing dresses—not Mother Hubbards—and looking almost slim in comparison with all the other native women I've seen. One carrying a child which, so help me, was blond & white. Might have been an albino. There were a bunch of other brats, but they were black.

Hope to get my ground crew story off tomorrow. Flanagan was very definite in his curiosity over why the combat crews should fight for six months and go home when the ground grippers worked for six months under combat conditions and kept on working. People certainly have their troubles—I don't guess the Army would be worth much if they didn't. But I'd like to find out.

At 10:45, sitting in a truck and writing by flashlight, I'm continuing because I'm between the devil and the deep blue sea, quite literally. In our tent, Chippy and party are raising merry hell after killing three gallons of raisin' jack; in the next tent Sam and a bunch of the boys are playing records which brought

back to me such poignant memories that I couldn't listen any more. I believe
the best way to get over nostalgia is not ever to get it.

> *Tell the U.S. Marines and the fighting Philippines*
> *And the boys at Manila Bay*
> *That the Air Corps' comin', with their big bombers hummin'*
> *And we'll fight all the harder*
> *When we think of Pearl Harbor*
> *And we'll make those yellow bastards pay*

They just sang that version of "Old Gray Bonnet"; first time I'd ever heard it.
Those guys can't sing sober and even with a guitar they can't sing drunk. But
they sure are trying.

Over in the other tent, Glenn Miller plays "Sunrise Serenade" and all the
tunes that remind me of that 250 mile round trip to Knoxville; Sammy Kaye
plays "Miss You" which puts me back with Helen in the Paramount in New
York; Frank Munn sings, which reminds me of *Prelude in C Sharp Minor* that
night; Dennis Day sings "This is Worth Fighting For" which is a memory of
Broadway and Helen—there's no use torturing myself, so I'm out here writing.
Funny thing about these recordings—they include plugs and all: "the next time
you buy Coca Cola, think of . . . " or "So go to your drugstore and ask for Sal
Hepatica by name . . . ." We all laughed. These songs fascinate me, yet they're
poison to me.

Had a funny thing happen, walking over to the mat 'smorning. Heard an
explosion not far away and looked over to see a boy ducking as something went
off. I paused to watch and he tossed another hand grenade over into the field
about 50 yards from me. It exploded and something said "Linmmng!" over my
head. I walked on. It takes all kinds, I guess, and he'd run out of play things
anyway.

Thursday, April 15. At chow saw the Beavers—Burns's Buzzers—ready at
Operations. Debby invited me along so I gave up a steak supper to toss incen-
diaries on Kahili. Sounds fascinating, but we didn't go. Flanagan met us at the
plane to say the mission had been called off, presumably because of bad weather.
Everybody grinned, said "That was close" or "They're just trying to scare us—
and they did." We went back to camp and I had steak for supper.

Was asked if I wanted to go on search tomorrow morning at 5:30—
turned it down. That's too early, and it won't do me any good to go up with a
strange crew. Ten hours in the air with ten guys I never saw before—this is a
new crew flying— is something I want no part of.

One thing I found out about our thwarted mission tonight is that when
I just jump aboard and we're ready to go it's much better than waiting three or
four hours. I was asked tonight—for the third or fourth time—why I wanted to
come along at this particular time. Which is why I like to just git up and git—

without having the opportunity to think about water landings, et al. I had no worries this time—felt good. I hate to sweat 'em out.

Got the ground crew story down in longhand, but haven't typed it out or polished it up any. Re-read my copy since start of this trip and frankly felt like packing up and going back to the bush. They smell—but maybe it was just my mood today, I hope.

Didn't get over to see Brodie, but took pad & pencil down to the beach to write my story far from the sounds of Italian voices. I'm surrounded by Wops in the tent here. Got a sunburn this afternoon. I can feel it simmering now.

The boys in the area have new fad: slingshots. They've been shooting at the evening birds in the palms.

A gang is on the record player again—the little one which was torn up by shrapnel a couple of weeks ago. An item for the Tokyo Gazette or something would be that when that bomb hit it broke the record which was on the turntable. On one side of the platter was "Remember Pearl Harbor," on the other "We've got to Slap the Dirty Little Jap." Frankly, I can't think of a record I'd rather had broken. Even as seldom as I hear that crap over here, it turns my stomach every time.

Forgot to mention yesterday that I saw a memo on Stewart's desk from COMGENSOPAC directing that the ban be lifted on air travel by correspondents. They certainly took their time doing it. Sherman told me a month and a half ago that the lid had been put down only for reason that all air space was needed—or so they thought—during the "emergency" back in February.

Typed the ground crew story and it smells only mildly—but still smells. The office must think I've gone bushwackey out here or something.[42]

Understood tonight from all and sundry that it is a Group order not to allow any more passengers. "It makes the rafts too crowded," they grinned. Well, I don't know exactly what to do about that, but I haven't bothered them too much anyway.

Capt. Burns is taking a skeleton crew for some practice bombing in the morning so I can tag along on that. I believe the ban is only on strike missions, because the search offer was still open and my answer was still the same. They get up at 3:45.

I wrote the boss a very crisp letter. The first one was full of alibis, and I tore it up. If there's nothing going on that's all there is to it, so I'm not alibiing. I'm not satisfied with what I've done—yet—period.

Friday, April 16. Went over to see Brodie this morning and was startled to learn that yesterday—the day I missed—he broke out in a rash and the doc diagnosed it as allergic eruption due to quinine. He said that such a thing— which is extremely rare—may mean the end of tropical service for Brodie. He explained that the allergy might not be present the next time malaria developed, if such should happen, but then again it might and since Brodie has had malaria twice now it might be dangerous because quinine could not then be used in treatment. He was positive that the rash was not merely manifestation of dengue—which would have been bad enough at that. Brodie is much better today and since he got off quinine yesterday the spots have almost disappeared.

But the real morale-builder was the arrival of a personal letter from Spence dated February 18 which set us straight on what the office had intended and, I presume, has done with Brodie's work. I have never read a nicer letter, and it was written before the arrival of our screaming bitches to the office on the March 5 layout. Spence, who agreed with us on every point, said, "you will be sick when you see it, but no sicker than I was." Which indicates that, as we thought, he was away from the office at the time. He also said, "for my money you and M.M. are the hot team of the war, etc . . . ." I'm glad everything has been straightened out about that thing, because, try as I would, I couldn't get it out of my head that the office didn't know what it was doing. I could make a case of their inconsistency by pointing to the three pages devoted to the Battle of Savo, written in New York and a straight interview piece on the Navy, compared with the treatment of my battle story. But I'm tired of whining about that. It still galls me, but Spence's letter ironed out a lot of things that for both of us were badly in need of ironing. Also received April 16 copy of paper today, with my story on George and Trouville. And—I almost fainted—my poem. Quick Watson my cape—I'm a poet now. Me's the bard.

Apparently I am destined not to fly on a strike mission with this outfit. Have just put away my pistol and laid aside my canteen after Capt. Burns— who at first said okay—told me that it is Major Wanderer's[43] orders that there will be no more passengers after what happened the other night. So that is that; I had thought and had been told that perhaps an exception would be made in my case, but I see now that when nine men's lives are in jeopardy there are no exceptions. This, then, puts the lid down—definitely. I can imagine that, since the major insisted that the order be enforced, it also includes searches. I can swap over to the B-24s but I don't think it would do any good and I don't like the idea at all. Just another problem in the life of a GI war correspondent. I'll have to look around for something; perhaps I will go over to the 307th, don't know yet. Even the little practice bombing this morning didn't work out—I got crowded off by extra bombardiers.

Spent this afternoon toning up my tan and memorizing for the second time in six years—"The Shooting of Dan McGrew." What a life—but such a day—even if I did get off a story—makes me feel like hell. Might as well be in Noumea. Perish the thought.

Debnekoff went with me to see Brodie 'smorning and when we walked over to Corps Spangler ran Deb off (no shirt) and bawled me out (wool shirt). "This is a Corps Hq," said Spang. "We're not fighting a war here." Oh, Cactus, thou hast lost thy charm, The whole thing was so ridiculous I didn't even get mad—it was funny.

At the hospital a psychoneurotic case gave me a poem. The poor guy is crazy as a hat—his hands tremble and in a way he's like a little child. The poem . . . . . The boy has been knocked out of a gun pit four times. He's in the 214th AA.

A palm frond crashes down. All over the cries: "Timber!"

When I write most in here is when I have the least to do. Just now I walked thru the palm groves to the edge of the field, retraced my steps to the beach; I experienced a Guadalcanal sunset—one of these magnificent things that seems to be peculiar to this latitude. It's so easy to see the evening come down across the mountains, then walk a few hundred yards and watch it across the sea. Perhaps it's even more stirring to me because, in either setting the sun sinks across historic space and the light lingers longest over the targets for to-night. The flight of six 17s buzzed us on their way out tonight—exactly at 5:30—and they too were magnificent in their own way. Perhaps I'm only feel-ing mellow and even somewhat bored, but there are times, floating instants in some cases, when I feel an immense pride in all this—to be here and be a part of it, however insignificant & unnecessary. When the Forts went over I felt it. I wish I were capable of setting down the philosophy and the psychology of the people who fight this war. I wish I could explain how it is that men complain and balk and curse and howl, and yet how they do the things expected of them insofar as it's humanly possible, and never, never, call attention to the fact that, underneath that veneer of biting language, there is the courage to do almost anything. I wish that I could make it understood that when a man says, "the hell with this—I want to go home" or "This mission and one more and we get out of this hole" he doesn't mean that he would quit before he is supposed to, that he would back down. I have never heard of a man refusing to go up, even in ships which they fully expect to conk out on them, yet they have a right to if they like. I wish I could reconcile the griping with the courage so that people who didn't know would understand. But I have a feeling that there are many, being human themselves, who could not understand that the men out here are human, too. I'm afraid that they would expect the many to be like those few who keep their opinions to themselves and who are thus, apparently, men of less fear. They are not. But fear—what the hell it is—I know but don't know.

I am not sure fear, as such, exists among these people. The air is their element and the pilots, in particular because they are the men who control, seem to take to it with great confidence. The men who fly, but who do not have control, are also in their element but their confidence is not in them-selves—rather in the men up forward. It is one thing to say "I can fly" and quite another to say "I believe he can fly"—no matter how strong that belief. I think that must be a joy of pursuit flight—the pilot is responsible for himself alone and has confidence in himself and his ship, as a single unit. That isn't true of bombardment. Two men fly the ship—in their hands is the responsibility for all. The other seven men look to them for the one thing which, after all, is the vital essential: flight. The navigator is responsible for guiding the direction of flight; the bombardier for the military success; the radio for contact; the gunners for protection. They all look to the pilot for the first thing, which is flight itself. Debby said today he didn't like 24s, said they "make me nervous." Henderson chuckles at the close ones, chuckles at the risks but is aware of them. Averbeck is the subtle kidder, but I don't think I've heard him say anything about risks except to joke about AA once—he has two Zeros to his credit. Weaver thinks of the chances and makes off-hand, rapid fire remarks which are not so funny themselves but are the way he says them. I've never heard a word from Schmidt, one way or the other.

-0-

We just had a half hour raid. They hit a gas dump about a quarter-mile away; those bombs coming down sounded closer. Made a beautiful, bulbous fire, but made me mad just to look at it—the bastards. A million bucks of octane gone—Pfft!

But the raid wasn't so bad as sharing the foxhole with my Italian neighbors. I can no more blame a man for being bomb happy than I can blame him for his face, but I can sure keep away from him. In anticipation of another raid momentarily I've prepared our house shelter here which I'll occupy by myself. I'd rather do that than listen to those boys. They didn't bother me this time and I just want to make sure they don't.

Saturday, April 17. Got a story on the 101st Medico band today, but ran into a vicious circle of people who want to have a finger in it. Had trouble getting past histories of boys in name bands because the conductor wanted credit to all or none. Which is where most people, including myself, make the mistake of viewing "news" and "credit" as one and the same thing. I wonder why all bandmasters are such crotchety old characters—I don't think I ever knew one who didn't have a streak of it in him somewhere.

Last night's strike was a big success. Tex & Mac sang all the way home, according to Deb. Ole Miss Out Me.

Charlie dropped four in Brodie's back pocket last night. They hit behind the Corps mess shack. Brodie gets out Monday. Apparently Charlie was all over the lot last night. He hit beyond the Lunga, killing some mules. Everybody around here is fixing up foxholes. I've seen that happen before.

Sort of half hearted about this band story, altho it should be good stuff for Newt, because Terry said there were a couple of other bands that really caught hell—the 164th—for example, but of course I was too dumb and too wrapped up in combat to think about them while the outfit was still here.

The Lunga and its environs is a changed place. The field of grass has seeded, so that the whole meadow looks white. The original bridge is out and a pontoon affair serves traffic which comes in behind our log and goes by the MAN Power House, on the other side.

Brodie's doc—from N Orleans—was telling the story of an Army officer who was brought in dog drunk the other night. The poor guy was really crocked—breathing two times a minute. He'd had a fight with two Marines before he finally passed out. The doc said while they were working over him the guy came to a second and muttered: "I'd rather have a sister in a whorehouse than a brother in the goddam Marines."

A chance remark by Fats next door tipped me off to the fact that the rest of Classen's crew came back today, so I got the rest of the story which I've certainly been sweating out—and it is a dilly. Now, if only the Marines Corps will come thru with pictures I'll have a story which I think should make worthwhile this otherwise unproductive junket.

The boys gave me some dope on the officers which was worth remembering: they fairly worship Classen—"sweatin' out the captain was the worst thing of all"—and the co-pilot Ruiz they didn't get along with at all. After much beating about the bush Martin came right out and said that "You can put him down as a prick." He pulled rank on them. And Dorwart was their boy. "He's a delicate-looking little guy, but he's got guts. Nothing bothers him. He's all the time making cracks about something and half the time you can't tell whether he's eatin' your ass out or kiddin' you."

Martin told this incident about Classen. After they had fought this terrific battle and it was obvious to everybody that they'd have to make a water-landing, Classen came back thru the ship and, taking down his pants, said: "This is one time I can take a shit without having to clean the toilet bowl. Where's some paper?" Ten minutes later they went down.

Hunt said: "I'd already shit."[44]

Classen impressed me as being a hell of a swell person and the boys say he can really fly an airplane. They credit him with saving all their lives because, even as badly as the plane was shot up, he made it stand on its ear when the Zeros made their favorite head-on passes. Martin claims that because Classen is eager they've been shot up more than anybody—three times they've brought their ships back in pieces.

The plane they were flying in February had been Gen. Harmon's personal plane just turned over to the 72nd. It had a pair of puckered lips and arched eyebrows painted on the nose—"like a Honolulu whore." Its name: "My Lovin' Dove."[45]

Palm Sunday, April 18. Got off my story on the band and it took me some-thing like 2½ hours to do 2½ pages. I just couldn't get moving with it.[46]

Took several swallows of Guadalcanal air, marched myself out to the hos-pital and got a Kahn test. Results Tuesday. I can stand just so much and then I've got to know the answer. The Lord must have fitted me up with an imagination that will surely drive me nuts if my conscience can't. It seems that the most intense mental agony I have ever experienced has been on the one subject: venereal. In my mind I can't find any good reason in the world why I should be diseased, but in my heart I know there is a reason—just one—and since we were in Roses I have been tormented. I found that I was tightening up—that this suppressed tension was telling on my nerves. Little muscles in my body twitch and I know that I can't take it. I went thru exactly this same thing once before and I swore that never again would I give myself cause for such a thing. It's my own fault—I should have been stronger.

Brodie gets out tomorrow. He wants to leave at once and I certainly don't blame him.

At Corps today read excerpts of translations from a Jap diary. The guy landed here around Nov. 14 and was scared to death from before the time he got off the boat. He repeated time & again: "The people at home would never understand." He certainly had a hellish time. The best line was his description of Guadalcanal, "Hell's Front Line."

The blond draftsman at Corps, from the 164th, certainly set up a con-vincing case against flight pay. He said a combat crewman in the hospital bragged of 19 strikes. "How long were you over the target?" "An hour." "Then you've had 19 hours of exposure to enemy fire in two months. My outfit was con-stantly exposed to it for 30 days." Any way you take it, that's a good argument. But—after all—there is no place to duck in a plane.

Getting back to that Jap's diary. The translator said he was a truck driver, but there was no name. The guy came in on that convoy which we pounded to pieces and he was bombed and strafed dizzy. There was no rice and after the third day here he & his outfit were wobbly. We shelled hell out of them. The Jap kept saying, "Really, I am miserable." He had to make trips up to the front and told of seeing "defeated remnants:" and in the same breath he said, "I pray that the day shall soon come when we shall conquer." And then he got malaria. He seemed to think that inevitable. Two or three times he said, "I can not describe it by tongue or brush." He heard he would be relieved around the first of the year and he was sweating it out. The constant pounding had him groggy—even hysterical in his writing. "I too am going mad . . . .all people are the same." From early December until the last of the month he didn't write because of his illness but when he did resume things were no better. Then: "Jan. 1, 1943—New Year's Day—I can think of nothing but my homeland . . . .I can write no more."

And that was all. There was no clue as to how he died. Guadalcanal for him was "hell's front line" and he went over the top. I think this campaign must have had some effect on the Japanese soldier—at least he must realize that there is such a thing in war as defeat. The Jap gave a hint as to their psychology once while he was very sick. He said: "I cannot die here like this." I think that he didn't so much fear death as he disliked the idea of dying of sickness or starvation rather than in battle. He seemed absolutely dumbfounded that he and his buddies were taking such a licking. "If the Imperial Army told of this to the people at home they would never understand—no matter how many times they were told."

Really, that boy didn't like this place or anything about it. I wouldn't have either, in his place.

I'm writing now by moonlight—the condition is still red and has been for the last two hours. The Bogies made three or four passes and must have started a small fire somewhere. This has been the noisiest air raid I know of—not so much from the bombs and ack-ack, but the officers started singing early in the evening and are still out in the moonlight singing like a bunch of high school kids after a ball game. They didn't stop, except to yell like hell when the AA came close enough. I watched the ack-ack a couple of times—it's like watching a championship game of horseshoes except that the stake moves around. Right now, irate enlisted personnel are yelling insults over toward the singing—"Shut up, you goddam USO soldiers." Three or four men howl like dogs. The singing goes right on, regardless. They've sung everything I can think of and I think—I hope—they've about exhausted their repertoire.[47]

I see firing over at Tulagi. Charlie's back. They're really throwing it up, tracers and everything but the kitchen stove. (Ten minutes later). Charlie just left—the bastard let one go close enough to jar my teeth together and knock dirt off the side of my foxhole. Lazzle, zizzle—whoom! this may be one of those all-nighters: it's a beautiful bombers' moon. It's now 10:30. The songbirds are hushed.

11:45—Charlie's been over twice again. The AA outfits must be panting. Lights again over channel; they're coming in from all directions, apparently. Tulagi again. Something still buzzing out there—may be P-70. 12:00. I hear a Bogy, for sure. Lights on, off. I hear two planes, plus one truck, plus Chippy arguing as usual. The people in those two tents are just like New York taxi drivers—argue incessantly and never get anywhere with it. They just raise their blood pressure. All clear 12:10—area comes alive again. Everybody cheers.

Just for the hell of it, and because I don't believe the Japs are going to waste such a beautiful night as this, I'm going to keep on writing awhile. It isn't often I can work at night at all, much less attempt a play-by-play of a bombing. It was such a night as this at Roses this time last month that gave me such a kick—moonlight on the palm fronds. Strangely that seems much longer than a month ago, whereas when we got back here I felt as tho we had been gone only a little while.

The apparent anti-climax of the all clear following my description of hearing planes is one of the things that contributes to the true "sweating out" of a raid. That I heard planes I am positive, and that one was a Jap I am equally sure. What they do up there and where they go is part of the game—like "heavy, heavy hangs over your head." I can imagine the Jap must have ventured in for a last look to see if he started anything. When he left the time before he must have been too busy to notice—he was getting ack-ack from here, from Tulagi and from a ship in the channel. The ship sent up tracers, apparently 20mm, which looked like fireworks—the higher they got the slower they went and they reminded me of a pole vaulter straining to gain another inch; then they gave it up and started down, their brilliance gone. I don't think you can ever see tracers after they've lost their velocity. It's 12:30.

Charlie finally came in again at 4:10, dropped four and left by 4:30. It is possible that he was shot down in flames by night fighters; I never saw a flare make the light that we saw. There is still a question—the light had a magnesium quality, at that.

Monday, April 19. Brodie is back, and I was certainly glad to see the guy. As close as we two have been, it left a gap with me. He has good reason to want to steer shy of the malarial area for some time—until his resistance is built up again at least. He lost some weight, I think. The hospital, he has said several times, is surprisingly well-equipped and the personnel efficient, but he said they practically starved him. He ate like a horse tonight.

Went over to Marine Wing today to check on pictures of the rescued men but found that, of course, everything has already been sent thru channels. I'll get the office to pick them up from Marine PRO in Washington. Met Growder, the combat correspondent.

Didn't accomplish much today, except to square away my stuff and wash a few clothes.

Picked up a boy from the 27th now stationed on Tulagi. I still haven't gotten over to that place.

Didn't mention yesterday the masterpiece a boy in G-2 turned out. A script, it has to do with Eddie Ackley and, knowing him, I laughed until I cried. The thing was called, "A Day in G-2—Or My Goodness, my Goodness, my Goodness!" Lt. Ackley is really a swell fellow, but he has the mannerisms of a Hollywood version of the filthy rich, complete with all the expressions, language, temperament.

I see the smoke from my cigarette streaming straight up like a blue-gray ribbon in the weeds. It can be delightfully calm here sometimes, but very rarely. There is always the sound of motors & men. But now the birds have the stage to themselves.

Tuesday [Wednesday], April 21. Drove up to Carney Field today, past lush meadows beyond the Nalimbu River, past men playing baseball on a skinned diamond while others watched them from parked vehicles. The road is good and I breezed along in a borrowed jeep, feeling more at home in my surroundings than I've felt in a long, long time. The meadows and the clumps of river trees and the mountains in the background reminded me strangely of home.

Carney Field—named for a Navy captain commanding Seabees, whose death is a chapter almost unbelievable—is a thousand percent improvement over Henderson.[48] The 307th is based there, and the 6th Night Fighter Sqdrn. The P-70s are a sleek looking airplane, but the ground crew wouldn't let me nose around them. When I asked how many in a crew, the boy didn't answer; I was glad to see that he didn't.[49]

Brodie and I had intended leaving in the morning, but SCAT has a bunch of priority ones, and altho we were placed on the passenger list for Col. Allen's B-17, Capt. Conradi said tonight that they had decided to take only a couple of medical patients. Brodie, in the meantime, is working overtime to get enough sketches for a panel on bombardment. I can see that he is torn between a desire to work and a desire to get out of danger of malaria. His health is the more important. I'll try to get another story off.

The Kahn test was negative.

Debnekoff was up tonight for a bull session as we waited on Charley, who, for some reason, didn't take advantage of the full moon. There was an alert, but no raid.

Deb, for all his sweat talk, is an Eager Beaver and I think a damn smart boy. He gave me info on the Beavers.

Wednesday [Thursday], April 22. At Corps this morning found the April 23 issue, which gave us a swell double truck on the Kokumbona story. I am, frankly, quite proud of it and I think Brodie is much better pleased in the presentation of his work. Except in that one instance the office has given us wonderful breaks on almost all our stuff and I feel confident that if Spence had been there at the time that would never have happened. I was frankly amazed that they used the story at all because I wrote it three months ago almost to the day.

SCAT advises us they can take us Friday. I'm glad we're not rushing out of here at that because there are always loose ends.

I think that Brodie, in the last three days, has accomplished enough to make our trip worthwhile. That boy has worked like a dog. As frustrated as I've been, I believe the missing men story will make up for a lot. But still and all, it's been pretty poor. I tried to get something on Major Stevenson's combat intelligence school, which I thought would make a good training note, but was told I couldn't touch it. I don't see why, but Col. Brown said no. Saw Col. Crawford again today—for the first time this trip—he is one of the most genteel people I've known. He and Stevenson are two damn good men.

Got ahold of a portable for the afternoon, and really enjoyed myself—working out the first five pages of the missing men story. Also toyed with possible leads on what I think will be an unusual treatment: the story of an unsuccessful bomb mission. People don't do those things; I want to try it.

Tonight I went down to the beach to watch an orange-red moon crawl over the tops of the low rim of palms at Koli Point. He was a lop-sided fellow and his wizened face seemed to leer as he looked over the trees, peering down his nose at Guadalcanal. But across the water was a straight band of orange reflection which rippled as the slow land swells moved shoreward and fought against themselves to climb the beach. In the other direction, a single star stood at the apex of a filmy cloud formation which gave the illusion of a comet arrested in full flight. Savo and Florida blended into black clouds that hugged the horizon. Crouching on the beach, looking first up and then down, I imagined that again the Japanese Imperial Marines were marching in formation down the sandspit to die gallantly—if absolutely ridiculously—in the face of our machine gun and canister fire. I thought of one of the first stories I read from Guadalcanal, of the Marine sergeant who lay for hours waiting until a Jap on the beach moved—and then shot him. I could feel something of the tension he must have felt. I let my mind roam and a shiver went up my back. The beach and the sea were deserted and utterly still—we had just had an alert and then the all clear. There was little to suggest that the island was not as it was six-eight months ago: that actually, in the palm grove 150 yards away, men were waiting to see a Damon Runyan movie. I caught the acrid smell of gunpowder, real or imagined, and the sand itself smelled wet and warm. The lop-sided moon slid upward into a cloud, I crossed the barbed-wire entanglements and walked thru the palms to my tent. The movie's on.

8:20—We just had another raid, signaled by firing at Tulagi. As at the time before, men left the movie and headed for home in a hurry. This time, the minute the Klaxon ground out all clear, everybody sprinted back to the movies to claim their favorite spot. If anything, they went back faster than they left. "I'm going to see that damned show if it takes all night." It may do it.

9:00—It is a trick to understand Runyanese under the best conditions, quite another to understand it when TBFs and SBDs are drowning out the dialogue. It's also a trick to keep one eye on the screen, another on Tulagi, and at the same time watch a search light position. But men would go to a movie, regardless. I once saw Pride of the Yankees at the 101st Medics, in January, when the firing on 155s was so loud it smothered the sound and so close that with each round fired the screen buckled as tho someone had hit it in the pit of its stomach.

Coming back from Corps at noon, I found a steak dinner waiting for me—complete with onions, French fries, catsup, bread, fruit cocktail. Yesterday it was hamburger, served on order. Sammy Cirena, the Italian kid next door, is one of those people who actually love to cook and enjoy watching others eat more than they enjoy eating themselves. He forces food on us, as if we needed forcing. Sammy, from Rochester, N.Y., is to my mind unquestionably the best guy in the bunch, for several reasons. He argues like the rest, but briefly. Having once cooked for 5,000 guys, he gave it up for ordnance because he couldn't devote the attention he wanted to each individual dish. Here he gets the food on a sack-job setup from the kitchen.

Thursday, April 23 [22]. This is actually the *22nd;* I find that I skipped the 20th.

Finished the missing man piece, which I think will make a good story, even among all such pieces that are common around here—if the censor doesn't tear it apart.

Spent most of this morning bulling with the Beavers, who are certainly a study in personalities at war. I want to do a story on them but damned if I think I can do them justice. I'm certainly going to try. Debnekoff asked Henderson for a cigarette. Rosy gave him a slow grin, dug painfully into his pocket for the pack, and drawled:"If I ever raise another kid like you I'm going to teach him to steal." There is something about that outfit which is almost a symphony in humanity to me—they clash violently and yet they blend together in a perfect harmony. It's hard to describe.

Deb was up to the tent again tonight and we talked long of many things—the range of conversation from *Il Trovatore* and *Carmen* to the prices of exclusive whores. Deb, who studied pre-med, played bass fiddle in Chicago's All-Jewish Orchestra. Rosy studied pre-law. Sid lacked six months to finish New Mexico Military. Beck, who has five Zeros to his credit, wants to fly fighters. Smitty finally loosened up, and Gums beat merrily along about USO soldiers.

Tonight's monologue by me was an account of my arrival on the paper, from beginning to now. Deb asked for it, and so did Sammy the other day. I let 'em have it. For some obscure reason I think both of them were sincerely interested; looks like I've found a home here. Deb & I shook hands—"Take it easy . . . . . ""Luck to you ole boy." The fleeting friendships in this man's Army make the whole thing rich & worthwhile.[50]

Friday, April 23. Aboard SCAT, Tontouta bound. Take off 7:10.

I felt quite differently about leaving Cactus this morning, for several different reasons. I didn't mind leaving but at the same time I wasn't really anxious because I felt very much at home there—more so than at any time since we left the States. There was just the right combination of freedom and excitement; except for the incident at Corps we felt as free as soldiers can possibly feel—and to me that is worth a great deal. At the same time, regardless of personal reactions, I don't have the feeling of "professional satisfaction" that I had before. Considering the handicaps I suppose we did as well as we could—I at least tried, and Brodie sprinted to produce after he left the hospital—but I personally didn't do what I came up to do at all. You cannot do bomb stories if they won't let you on the plane, and it was our luck to hit a wrong night when we did go aboard. If I do any more bombardment, it's going to be in the daylight where I can see something—regardless of whether or not I know the men in the crew. They pay off on what you produce in this business, but I wonder if they give you an E for effort. Four stories in three weeks, regardless of how little was going on, is no bright and shining record—and only one of those was really worth something. I'm sweating out the tools of my trade—their arrival will certainly narrow the margin for excuses.

Saturday, April 24. Arrived yesterday at Tontouta, 5' 41" out of Cactus. Took us three hours to get to Noumea and back to Barnes. We set ourselves up in rather exalted style (for me anyway).

There was more mail than I'd dreamed of, some of it dating back to November—but still no typewriter and no camera. Helen is getting along swell and seemed to pass over the Auckland deal with complete lack of imagination. Dad struggles to give me news. Had a letter from Crockett, two from Harvey and an odd assortment of other stuff, including Helen's two packages and the lighter. News from home that gave me a shock: death of Harry Nave; report that Ben Franklin and Louie Kinch are MIA. I'm going to check on Louie—I don't believe it.

A bunch of stuff from the office—two swell letters from Spence, one explaining the March 5 thing. That Spence is a master of diplomacy. Also found the March 19 issue on sale here with the four page spread and cover by Brodie. Marvelous. Actually there is so much stuff to be attended to that I don't know where to begin; I'm going to dig into it. I'll be up to my neck for a week, at least. It certainly is a kick to come back and get all this stuff but it sure snows me under. First people we ran into here—in the dark and by sheer accident— were Brown, Stone and Baker, the Marine interpreters from the old days at Cactus. We had a reunion.

Brodie got an offer from *Cosmopolitan* and I got one from Cecil Brown Publishing Company. Could be. Brodie got a note of thanks from Gen. Harmon for the portrait. Both of us have been getting a bit of publicity in our home areas. *Yank* ran Brodie's pix which Allan Jackson made on the Canal, together with the worst line of sheer snow I've ever read. We both laughed like hell.[51]

The missing men story is ready to go. I typed it up today. I think our position is undergoing change.

Sunday, April 25. Easter Sunday and I slept until 11:00 a.m. after working until 2:50 last night. I really intended going to church today: don't like to miss Easter.

Worked this afternoon at Shope's office, clearing the missing men story without a cut[52] and getting off a piece by Zucker on a glass eater at Roses. Shope wanted a memorandum on the PRO setup as I saw it, with especial emphasis on the Marine setup at Cactus; he was sick when I told him about it. I complied. It does seem stupid for the Army to buck Marine competition with the meager equipment & personnel it has and this is one instance in which I think there is justification for howling about inadequate facilities. I find myself much more in harmony with Shope this time because the guy at least is worried about shortcomings and I can see that the office is beginning to hit its stride as a working unit, on New Cal, at least.

Wrote long letters to Helen and Dad tonight—including the suggestion that if the baby is a girl she be named Dian. I'm in love with that name. Had intended writing Spence in re plans & promotions but will hold fire until I do a little more thinking on the matter. This will require tact, but I think Brodie and I should have some idea as to office policy. Patience!

I don't want to give him the idea we're bucking for anything—so that he'll begin to keep an undue eye on us—but at the same time I want to get over the idea that we're both open to a change in the situation. A change in our travel orders received in the batch of mail, takes our per diem from us—which is once an order meant to help us came a cropper. I feel like burning the damned things.

Brodie and I have had brief conversations on what we want to do, since it is obvious to us that we have reached a point in our assignment here beyond which we feel there should be some change in status. Under our present setup— after we have seen Fiji and Samoa—I can see no future for us as effective correspondents; that is, of course, unless something breaks—and I have an increasing suspicion that nothing is going to happen around here for awhile unless the Japs try something. I may be wrong.

Two things I know positively: Brodie wants a first-three-grade rating, and he would like to get out of this area to seek greener pastures. I personally don't mind the tropics, but I sure as hell would like to see more of the world and I'd like to go somewhere where there's a touch of civilization for a change. I'm fed up with this island stuff. I want to make the rest of this tour and then I'm ready to go elsewhere, or back to the States—or both. But I don't want to go to the States and then come back out to the same place. Maybe I don't know how well off we are, but I'm willing to find out.

For my part, I'd like a commission—outright or otherwise—but only in connection with the paper. I feel that, with 2½ years service, I'm qualified for one, and I don't like to feel that all avenues of advancement are closed to me on this job. If I had to choose between a commission and the paper, I'd take the paper hands down. If I could choose between writing for the paper as an enlisted man and being in some creative capacity on the paper as an officer, I'd take the latter, hands down. I love my job, but I want to be an officer just on general principles. In other words, I want to have my cake & eat it too. I don't think my attitude is particularly wise and in a pinch I might reverse my decision, but I've experienced a growing desire for some time in that respect—augmented constantly by my buddies turning up as captains and guys on the paper deserting to the *Stars and Stripes* as officers. I don't want to let my ambition run me into the ground, but I feel justified in my desire to add something new here and there. Nine months a corporal and 13 months a buck sergeant is no brilliant advance. My friends now officers in line outfits deserved every promotion they got because, in their field, they worked for them. I'm an infantryman, but I don't think I'd set the world on fire as an infantry officer because that is no longer my field. If I wanted it that badly, I believe I could wind up as a flunky in an S-2 outfit somewhere. I don't want the bars that much.

Spence said something about a "big job" for us. I've no idea what he means—but I want to hear from him on a few things. It's 12:45. Bed.

Monday, April 26. Answered Curtis Brown, stalling for time, and the Bank of New South Wales, yelling for my $75 which I don't expect to get. Prepared cards itemizing the stuff I have to do—which is considerable. Wrote up the message for Gen. Harmon to sign—tried to get Jackson lined up for some publicity shots—will do. Wrote a long letter to Spence in compliance with request to relate personal experiences in combat. I gave him a snow job in one breath and begged him not to publish it in the next. I don't think it smart to wave our own flags, but I figured that if they are set to give snow jobs they might as well get it straight rather than screw up as was done in Brodie's case. Poor old Brodie—he takes a beating. Sent him my Horse's Neck pictures which I certainly hope get thru. Also wrote suggestions as to our anniversary play—the principle one being that we print a map with pictures of all correspondents superimposed. Another that we explain the whole setup in plain English and let it go at that—very simply and without patting our backs.

Checked the Service Club and was told by Miss Guthman that the RC can let me know about Helen within a couple of days. Swell.

Hall tried to get me a typewriter, but the red tape thickens. He has to see a Colonel or somebody.

Seven correspondents in Shope's office this afternoon for handouts on the missing men. What a helluva way to pick over a sweet story.

I've been constantly busy since we got back and so has Brodie. It really feels good to dig in and produce something in black & white. There's still plenty of work to do yet—catching up on office requests. Okay.

Thursday, April 29. Have worked almost constantly since our return, trying to comply with office requests in time for them to use it. Did a long song and dance in answer to questions on how combat has changed the Army. It was all amateur commentary and before I got started I found that I couldn't really put down in black & white the things I thought at first I could. Got Major Bollard to look it over. His idea is that nothing has changed—that perfecting of training has been the important thing. I guess if everybody carried out to perfection everything he had been taught to do in combat, there wouldn't have been any trouble. I sensed in the Major's conversation a reluctance to admit that any of the Army's established ideas were bad, and that it was necessary to make changes. Young as he is, I got the impression of his being set in his ways—none too willing to accept something new. Perhaps he was only being cautious—not willing to act on anything until it had been definitely proven, and perhaps he is right. It doesn't pay to jump too quickly, but at the same time a man has to keep up with the times.

Got the required quotes by passing out typed cards at the RC—and never felt so foolish in my life. Had an idea for setting up a message center for the paper at the service club; worked on it tonight. Have given up the idea of publicity pictures. Asked the PRO to help me out but we haven't been able to get together and they are under no obligation to do me favors at the expense of their own work. I still think they'll do it, but I'm in no position to rush them. Perhaps before they get to it, it will be too late. The Harmon letter is still out, but hope it will be returned in time to reach the office before deadline. Am moving all the stuff I have to them tomorrow.[53]

Saw Classen and his boys today, all ensnared in correspondents, red tape and delay. There is a move to get them into a bond-selling campaign in the States which I think—and sincerely hope—will fall thru. These guys deserve a break, not a crap detail. What price glory? They're already disgusted. And I've lost out on my exclusive story, dammit.[54]

Took a rainy afternoon off two days ago and spent hours with an encyclopedia, making notes of theory in psychoanalysis, etc. That was an idea I hit on at Cactus and, seeing a chance to read up a little, I did. The principles of Freud, Adler and such people intrigue me. Helluva time to think about that.

Friday, April 30. Worked all night, going to bed at 7:00 this morning, but finally got off the material for the anniversary issue. I'm still short the Harmon letter and the publicity shots, however. Slept all day.

Wrote Spence a long letter in which I finally broached the subject of promotion and possibility of commission, and asked him to give us the office policy on term of service in this theatre. I will certainly look forward to his answer, but I'll bet he gives us the runaround; in which case I will interpret it as a way of telling us that we're stuck here.

Became WD Correspondent 574 today with the arrival of a BPR press card and a shiny new C brassard. So that is our "special correspondent rating." Helluva lot of good it will do—I wouldn't wear the arm band and there's nobody to show the card to.[55] Brodie didn't get anything at all in that respect; he says he thinks he has an explanation for it—which I'll be interested in hearing.

A letter from John was encouraging and beautifully written. That boy is certainly a smooth man with the English language. His first letter was almost a masterpiece. Dad wrote that the town was full of uniforms; it's just long enough after Christmas for everybody to have put in for another furlough.

If I get up enough nerve to brazen thru with this Message Center thing, then I'll just about have exhausted myself here. I don't think we'll have much trouble getting out of here again, but this time I don't greatly look forward to it. I've lost the impetus, momentarily. Will just have to wait until I get good and bored again, which won't take long.

Right now I'd like to pull a good drunk. When Brodie finishes I think we will.

"So Ends a Chapter
of My Life"

Monday, May 3. Jackson, Brodie and I left Noumea this morning for the trip up island. Tonight we are situated in a modern little room, exactly like something we'd expect to find in an auto court at home—but certainly nothing like we expected to find more than 100 miles north of "civilization" in New Caledonia. The name of the place is Houailou. For lunch we stopped at Bourail. We passed some of the most beautiful scenery I can ever imagine, and there were times when I completely forgot where we were and thought of it all as an excursion in the States. It seemed so because as we drove we all saw things that reminded us of home. The road was like the one to Asheville. We followed a little river for miles, and it was beautiful—the banks green and the water perfectly clear, with cattle grazing alongside. Crossing the mountains there was some wonderful scenery—mountains and the sea . . . . . the Coral Sea.

This hotel at Houailou is out of the world. It's run by a Frenchman and his half-caste wife—the Burzon's—and the accommodations are good. We couldn't get anything to drink except vin rouge, which is all right but I had too much of it and got sick after oysters for dinner. The dining salon is in the basement and its decorations are wooden tribal totems, etc.

Too much of the grape too quickly really knocked me for a loop. Oooh, what a head.

Tuesday, May 4. Another day of beautiful scenery, and natives. We passed a village where there was a stone church in ruins; we stopped for pictures and the place swarmed with kids. At another place there was a detachment of Kiwi's—only five or six—and we got pictures of a big-breasted native girl carrying a load of grass. The way the natives jump to get in the picture is something. We got a late start from Houailou and were very late getting to Touho where Ma-

165

dame Le Bec had waited lunch on us. There is the place—clean home, big grassy yard, the sea only a few yards away. There were two women and two men—one husband & wife—one brother & sister, I think—but they certainly live well. Simply and quietly, but well. The meal was served by a half-caste Javanese girl who would peek in the door to see if we had finished each course. We crossed nine ferries between Houailou and Hienghene. They're primitive but effective—strictly cable & manpower. Coming to Hienghene we passed some volcanic formations which are the wildest, weirdest, most unbelievable things I've ever seen. They were huge and black and jagged, with caves in them and birds or bats flying around. We're going back for pictures.

We are at the Hotel Terminus—Hienghene is the end of the road. This place is another of those exotic, unexpected stopovers I never would have believed was here. It's run by a Mme. Courte, who has a blonde daughter, which makes the joint even more interesting.[1]

Saturday, May 8. The news from Africa today was great—Tunis & Bizerte— and the way it spread over camp and downtown was amazing. I heard it first at Barnes, went directly to town, heard it there, came back to Barnes for chow and got the confirmation. The "Barnes Scoop" is getting out an extra.

Have some catching up to do. We got back from the five-day trip yesterday afternoon. I had mail from Helen and—from all people in the world—Jean Oxford. Worked until 4:00 o'clock this morning—letters to Dad, to Helen, to Miller in Oahu, to John Bloomer whose address finally came thru Helen's letter, and to La Oxford, who wrote suspiciously like a little girl who might not be having the time of her life as an Army wife.[2]

Have spent most of the day trying to solve a riddle which as yet remains as much of a mystery as it was six days ago. I got a cable signed Somerwell addressed to me saying "have him submit story 831st Signal Service Company's action exploits. Illustrating same have him obtain pictures." I've checked with a Lt. Jones in the Signal Office here and he tells me the 831st has seen no action whatsoever. Talked to one of the boys in the outfit and he tells me the 831st has been activated only a couple of months. I've tried and tried to contact Capt. Brett, the CO, to at least get an inkling of what the hell it's all about. I'm certainly in the dark at the moment—I just don't get it.

Fired about 100 rounds of ammunition today and am now convinced that I'm, if anything, an even worse shot than I was two years ago. I might as well throw the gun at the target. Brodie, on the other hand, has the making of a crack shot—maybe I should have given the gun to him instead of vice versa.

A mimeo letter from the office mentioned the Guadalcanal screwball name story and passed on word from 1st Sgt. Jeffcoat of Hood.

There's a dance tonight . . . . . for GIs, in the mess hall.

Went to the dance but couldn't get enthused at all—once a wall flower always a wall flower, I guess. Danced with one plump little Frenchie who had BO, then gave it up entirely. It was a good dance, considering, tho. This ain't the Waldorf.[3]

Tenembaugh tells me now that the $7.50 which I drew a couple of days ago will be all I'll get until next month. Because one word was on the wrong line my quarters allowance for two months was redlined, so I'm damned near broke. The trip cost only $12 apiece, but I still ain't in clover.

Made the overtures today on the proposed trip to Oahu. Am still somewhat confused as to what would be the best policy—to go straight there and hit Samoa & Fiji coming back, or vice versa. Then too, if we leave in the near future, we will miss answers from the office on several important things. Joe is signing the mimeo sheet again, indicating Spence is out of town, and from what Spence said about "rumors" re himself I have a hunch he may be in Oahu, or somewhere in the area.

Lt. Lambert told me something interesting today—that a boat ships from New Zealand to Tonga, Tongareva and Bora-Bora, making the round trip in about 34 days. That little excursion fascinates me. I think, with luck, we could get in on it and it's certainly the only way we will be able to reach those places. Air transportation is definitely out. But I don't want to figure on that at all until this junket comes off. It's already taken us six months to hit five of the seven places we were supposed to hit in six week's time under the original idea.

Am already starting to sweat out mail re B's illness.

Sunday, May 9. After checking every known source with negative results, I came to the conclusion that the 831st story was impossible, and wrote the office accordingly. Too bad my first assignment by radiogram didn't pan—the old 831st has broken up and scattered.[4]

Talked with Col. Sherman who said he'd set the wheels on new travel orders, but again, it appears we may not get to travel as we at first intended: may have to go directly to Pearl and come back without stopping over at the other places.

Another letter from Oxford, padding for the first, and a little more reserved.

Was in Bassett's office and noticed photo of Press in the jeep—me with my eyes closed again.[5] Which reminds me that in talking to Brockhurst the other day I learned that the entire gang is either in the States or in another area. Brock himself has since gone to Australia, I was told today. The Press here raids Shope's office for handouts—they keep a file of incoming stuff, and some of it isn't bad.

Picked up our *Yank* insignia from the madame who embroidered them for us; they were, as I had feared, a little out of line.

I am amazed at the length of time required for me to do anything. Today, except for a final absolute check on the 831st, I did exactly nothing. Yet it took me all day and it's now 1:00 a.m. What I do with my time is a mystery—down past Anse Vata to see a girl in a 2-piece bathing suit, to town twice, in and out of Shope's office, to the Service Club for coffee, back to camp, in and out of G-2 and drafting, chow, *Fleet's In* at the Seabee's, bull session with the boys in combat, coffee. I work harder doing nothing than most people doing an honest day's work.

Monday, May 10. Sometimes the train of events in a day become as theatrical and melodramatic as any suspense-artist could create in a novel.

This morning I woke up with a feeling unlike anything I can remember experiencing before. I had, I firmly believe, a premonition of something about to happen. I shook it off, mentally kidding myself, and then things started adding:

In G-2 sat Father Gehring, the Navy chaplain whom everybody admired on the Canal. We exchanged greetings and I asked him what he intended doing. His reply: "I'm going back north." To Cactus again? "No, further than that." Between the lines I sensed something in either of his remarks. Father Gehring said nothing directly, but spoke as tho he believed I knew something which, in fact, I didn't know at all. I wondered.

At chow I cornered Hall—what's the score? "Well, we're not just going to sit. There are plans. The APO is already set up." I couldn't get anything more, but it was a definite lead. I noticed a large-scale, remarkably complete map on the wall in the Colonel's office. It hadn't been there before.

This afternoon I asked Jackson. He told me what he knew—what he had heard for the first time today. "We are going into New Georgia. Outfits have been alerted for a week now. The Marines and Seabees, and then the Army. Soon—probably this week or next."[6]

This afternoon I saw Marines with full equipment in trucks. A Marine on the street yelled as one passed by: "Where are you going—back to the States?" A kid in the truck hollered back, above the traffic's noise, "Hell No!"

So now the picture changes. I have talked to Brodie. My information is far too incomplete to make a definite decision at this time, but is it too incomplete to make a decision on the Hawaiian trip? If the orders come thru within a few days, shall we go to Oahu and trust to luck we can get back for the Army's initial part in the show? Or just what is to be our course of action? I don't know—yet—and until I learn more, and from some source which can be called accurate, I won't know. Emotionally, I'm equally undecided. I don't stomach another fight in the islands and yet if there is to be a fight there is where we should be. There is no evading that simple fact.

Just what this amounts to I don't know—wish I did. When it will happen, the order of battle, the force are things I don't know and almost don't want to know. I'm not even sure that any of my information is accurate, to what degree its accuracy extends. Tonight I heard something of another thing entirely, but it may have been a deliberate evasion. The Col., when I asked about orders, gave no hint that now would be a poor time to leave. But would he have given me such an inkling even if he could?

But the situation at least indicates something in the wind. I am puzzled, first, that everything should come out today, and, second, that information on such a thing should be floating around at all. I assume that as a newspaperman there are people who automatically take me into their confidence, but I can't help wondering how many more there are like me. I hope—very few. I'm going to be listening very carefully for slips which would indicate the extent of this thing. I don't think it is all just another rumor—and yet there's something screwy.

Which brings me to another point: Brodie is not hipped on the T.H. deal and has never been—tho why I don't understand. I don't think he ever really understood my reasons for wanting to go in the first place, but I explained to him today that a personal contact with the office there would be helpful to us both. If it were merely a matter of getting back to civilization, I'd go back to Auckland. Honolulu, altho I'd like to see the place, is not my idea of a liberty town—and we don't want or need liberty anyway. I have counted on the Oahu thing as a pointer for a number of things affecting our futures. I have looked upon it—after all this messing around—as a fresh starting point. I still do.

At this moment I feel like going thru with the trip come hell or high water up north. That sentiment is subject to change without notice.

In the event we do go north again, I must go as an independent unit and I must have the stuff to work with. I'll get it before I leave, if I have to steal, because I'm damned if I'm going to try to cover combat without a typewriter & a camera. Experience at a place already set up to some extent has proven how difficult the job is; on virgin ground it would be almost impossible—almost not worth the effort to me.

I have entertained hopes of getting out of this area altogether. I don't know whether to go on entertaining them or not—it's rather foolish if we get going again soon. I have thought of perhaps moving to another front, seeing another kind of war; now the whole business begins to cloud up. The dear old Army—it never changes. Well, it certainly didn't get a cherry, anyway.

Tuesday, May 11. One year ago today two bewildered boys—Hay and I—walked out of the elevator on the fourth floor of the Bartholomew building, turned right, and saw the quiet lettering on the door: "YANK-The Army Newspaper." We entered an area of glass cubicles, white walls, hollow sounds. We reported to Hartzell Spence, a "newly-minted captain." We saw the city room, bare and deserted except for one table, one typewriter, and one chair. The phones were on the floor.

One year ago I began to see new horizons. I left the Infantry, but took it with me in my heart.

The first six months on the paper in New York are now vague and unreal and dramatic—as much so then as now. The next six months have been recorded in here. To try to analyze either period would be impossible. They have combined to form the most exciting, the most valuable, the most varied year of my life.

I have learned much, and yet I have so much to learn. I have learned from the men I worked with—from Bill Richardson, a new approach to writing; from Al Hine, a zest for things; from Bob Neville, a respect for truth and a great admiration for knowledge; from Hargrove, a sort of simplicity; from Art Weithas & Ralph Stein, a respect for craftsmanship; from Ed Cunningham, ruggedness in outlook; from Pete Paris and Harry Brown, cynicism to a certain degree; from Tom Long, the svelteness of a tinsel world, but a fascinating one. I say that I have learned from these: more accurately, they have demonstrated each of these various things to me. At least, from these boys, I have a better understanding of some things.

Memories of the year are vivid and varied. I recall intense emotions—pleasure, pain, hope, fear, confidence, disconsolence, frustration, realization. Over all, I feel a certain pride—a real pride—in having contributed, however little, to the success of a new and tremendous undertaking.

Wrote Spence a letter. To anybody else in the Army I'd consider it a raw example of AKing, but not in this case.

Got two letters from Helen today, but seem to have missed the one in between. She says my mail has been taking some funny twists, too.

Went downtown with Summers to try to work out a camera idea of mine and, as usual, got nowhere. I'm not blaming Chilton D., but I still wish to hell I could shoot my own stuff.

Did two editorials, one of which is fair. When a man is reduced to taking pictures of eating houses, passing out questionnaires, and writing editorials—he's in pretty bad shape. It just comes to me that with the closing of the main PX, it might be a good idea to check on distribution here again. This was *Yank's* garden spot in the Pacific—I hope it still is. It also comes to me that Harmon never did sign that damned letter. I wonder if the Col. explained to him why it was wanted?

The pressure of yesterday's subject is more or less off. I think it was so much malarkey, but we can't afford to overlook anything like that. Brodie and I made tentative plans on our course of action if the thing does go thru, then cornered Hall and talked to him like a Dutch uncle. We frankly asked him, and he told us his opinions based on the stuff that crosses his desk every day. He can't see it. With such odds and ends and explanations as he gave us, neither can I. Still, we have to be sure.

Brodie has drawn up four alternatives, three of which I had considered. The fourth I hadn't—that he go on the beachhead and let me know in Honolulu when to come in. I wonder if he thinks I'm scared? I'm not yet, but I might be. But that doesn't mean a thing. What the hell?—I always am.

Thursday, May 13. Letter from Helen today enclosing a page from the *Spinnerette* pictures of Harry Nave, Ben Franklin, and Bob Davis. They were swell reproductions—of three swell-looking kids who died in the air.

I wrote an editorial tonight based on their deaths. It isn't much and I don't know whether they'll use it. It is a pitifully weak thing, by comparison. Anything is weak compared to the sacrifice of men who die that others may live. Harry would snort at that—he died trying to learn to fly. Ben and Bob would snort at it too—they died trying to get an airplane from one place to another & back again. Pretty insignificant as individual incidents—they weren't killed while defending the prostrate body of a friend in danger. No girl at home can say she is in more danger of being raped by a venereal Jap because Bob Davis got lost off Australia last July. But she is.[7]

O hell—what's the use? There isn't much I can say that wouldn't be melodramatic. The more said, the more inconsequential it all becomes, the more shallow. In war, men die. The others go on fighting, or doing whatever is their job. Perhaps in the knowledge of these deaths the others fight, or work, harder. I think so—I hope so.

Letter from Spence today. In words he said nothing extraordinary except for me to use my own judgment about Brodie. In tone he said quite a lot; between the lines he indicated that we will be in this area for some time to come. I had expected that, but I am not at all resigned to it. When he answers my last letter I will have something concrete to act on. I'm not at all sure that it will make much difference what he says.

I'm beginning to get restless. Sweating out orders.

Slept until two o'clock yesterday afternoon, having stayed up all night. Was awakened by the boys taking down the tent, so got up; we had the thing halfway down before I was wide awake. Worked until after dark on the floor, which is as sad a sack as I've ever seen. But it's a floor. Worked most of the morning on finishing touches. With all the building going on around here, this headquarters should move within the month.

Shope left yesterday for the northland. Understand Lloyd Douglas and his movie outfit arrived today. Interesting. Hall got me a new field jacket today—the only one I ever had that fits me. Paradoxically, like all the others it is a 38.

Sgt. Becker, God's gift to the U.S. Army, came into the office tonight wondering whether Brodie is given to temper. It developed B had stood all of Becker possible and almost thru the gentlemen out on his ear. My only regret is that he didn't mash his mouth while he was at it. Becker is one of the very, very few people on this side of the Pacific whom I think is a Grade-A prick.   ·

Had a letter today from Aunt Nina, dear old soul—she took up a page and a half telling me about her victory garden. But the letter had one major result—it precipitated my answering her, writing Evelyn, and also Ned Burman. Aunt Nina sent a clipping on Jim Hurlbut which I forwarded Ned.[8]

Outside of the three editorials and the start of that pix layout on the hash houses, I haven't done a damned thing here. And I really should try to work over New Cal for story possibilities again. I seem to have the idea that this place is not newsworthy, whereas I'll bet there are some neat little pieces here if I'd just go nosing. Am beginning to feel terribly self-conscious, having been around for three weeks and exhibited absolutely no excuse for my room & board. And it's bad publicity for the paper to be seen loafing around.

Friday, May 14. A radiogram arrived this morning, ordering Brodie back to the States. At first he said flatly "No!" but then we talked it over and he decided to go. It is a break, and he would be a fool not to take advantage of it. His initial objection was returning under the circumstances; he doesn't want to take advantage of an illness and possible further illness under certain conditions, both of which actually are somewhat remote.

But, he decided (with my insistence) the advantages of the change far override the "medium" thru which it is effected. He will be of much more value to the paper because he will be more productive in another area where a change in background, costume, and equipment are different. He never for an instant considers remaining in the States once he gets there—he will ask another combat assignment immediately—possibly Africa, or England. He suggested, too, that it may be for the best that we divorce ourselves since neither of us has been necessary to the other's work. Brodie is much more of a free lancer in his work than as half of a team, not to say that we haven't dovetailed at every possible opportunity.

Altho we have spoken tentatively of a few things regards the split-up, there remains a hell of a lot of ideas and suggestions I want to work out before he leaves.[9]

I have spoken to Lt. Sanford, who tells me the orders on the Oahu trip are approved, but of course they can be amended. He said that with the Colonel's approval he can get Brodie back by air. This Lt. Goof or Goff in the office doesn't seem to like that idea much—"Why, generals have to sweat out boats." Nuts.

Well, this is the change of status I had an idea about. But it wasn't quite as I had expected it would be.

Tonight the full realization of our breaking up has not hit me. To be over here without Brodie is going to be damned hard to get used to. We have depended on each other's presence so often in so many strange places that the prospect of being all by myself is none too joyful. To have one close friend among a thousand strangers is enough for me—but to have him is something I consider almost essential. Brodie doesn't—and won't—know that his leaving is going to hurt me like hell; but in the light of his better opportunity such a thing is of no importance whatsoever. In the infantry, I felt that to leave the outfit and the close comradeship of my friends would be the worst thing that could happen to me. But I learned differently. A man can get used to anything in a matter of time. In one respect our breaking up may mean either more or less freedom of movement and action for me; that statement is certainly intangible and the idea itself is intangible, because Brodie's presence definitely has never had any effect on my goings & comings. Of course his leaving will make a big difference in things personally, but from the standpoint of production I don't see why it should, particularly.

Immediately the question is who Spence will send to replace him. My guess is Bushemi. If so, fine. But to tell the truth I'd like to knock around a couple of places by myself for awhile just to see what it's like. In combat, tho, I'd want somebody and want them damned badly. I know that Brodie is going to welcome breaking free. He is a lone wolf in his work and will undoubtedly work better by himself because he can time his work as he pleases. I had never thought of it in that respect before, but it must be that he would much prefer to be his own boss, to do what he alone thinks best, when and how he pleases. He wasn't dependent on me for support, and vice versa, so in that respect the new arrangement will probably be greatly to his advantage.

To me Brodie is one of the most vivid characters I've ever known. To analyze him would be difficult, because he is a complex personality—at once simple and at the same time profound.

In a good many instances he has acted as a balance for me. He is one of those people whose character is such that it can be counted on as a reserve in cases where something extra is needed. He has, in a good many instances, exercised a terrific influence on me—but just how I can't yet tell.

Brodie is something of a paradox to me—I have never quite been able to wrap all the loose ends of him up and get a neat package. Something always sticks out. He is extremely pleasant and easy to get along with, and yet there are things about him which I have grown to accept, but never fully. His consideration for other people's rights & feelings is truly admirable.

He has a driving energy, a great capacity for work. He rarely does anything in true moderation. Like me, he smokes too much. He is a creature of impulse—he suddenly gets an idea that he wants to do something, whatever it is, and he doesn't relax until he does it.

He is an independent thinker and one of the most candid persons I have ever known. His frankness is cold and impersonal and he likes to have a reason for doing things. Yet sometimes I don't understand his reasoning. He has one characteristic that occasionally gives a mild and none-too-pleasant shock to casual acquaintances: under circumstances of congenial conversation or relaxation he comes out with a biting little footnote to something someone has said or done. I've seen their faces suddenly chill and then Brodie laughs, kidding them out of it. They always relax at that smile.

Brodie plays as hard as he works—he plays to win. He is hard-headed to a degree, once having come to a decision or set an objective he keeps a straight line on it. He has something of the Prussian in him, deep inside, and I recognize in him a great many of the things I knew so well in Hammer back home.[10]

He is the type person who will succeed. He won't let himself fail.

Brodie's mind is as complex as the rest of him. When he concentrates, he does so with every bit of his energy, forgetting everything else. Get a fact or a statement firmly implanted in his head and it's almost impossible to get it out. He has a beautiful one-track mind in that he assembles things according to one plan of logic and it is difficult to encroach upon that plan to even the slightest degree. To talk to him sometimes, I would almost have believed him dumb, yet he is brilliant in many respects. Mentally, he is comparable to a person who chews each bite of food carefully and slowly and swallows it only when it is masticated to the utmost; he will choke on anything else.

In his work he has a profound singleness of purpose. I have never seen anything sway him from it. On the Canal he seemed indifferent to anything that did not have to do with his further education on combat or the Army or art. He is a passionate learner. As I look back on it, I see that his reaction to danger or discomfort was also in direct proportion to his work. Regardless of what confronted him, he merely expressed annoyance if it bothered him to such an extent that it affected his work. Bugs, malaria, air raids, bullets—they were all the same to him if, because of them, his fullest capacity could not be reached.

I have spoken of him as if to Brodie the world centers on Brodie. Nothing could be further wrong. To Brodie the world centers on art and things related to art. In a great many ways Brodie is an introvert, yet his understanding of people amazes me. He tears them down by psychoanalysis as a chemist tears down to its basic components some complicated emulsion. Brodie is, therefore, one of the most understanding people I know. He has a keen perception, a calculating mind, a steady hand and an equally steady eye. When something enters his ken he misses nothing; when it doesn't, he misses all. Everything to him is a bright light or in the deepest shadow, beyond the pale of his comprehension.

Knowing him is a privilege and a great experience.

He has a high moral instinct, one of the few persons I've ever known who is dedicated to doing right as he sees the right. His ambition in life is to become a true artist and I am convinced that he will come as close to achieving that ambition as is possible to his makeup.

Brodie is using the Army as a property for the testing of Brodie the man, and the student. He never misses the opportunity of learning something which he thinks he should know, and it has done him a great deal of good to put up with some of the things which he has experienced. It is self-discipline for him. I am sure that the Army must have changed him, but I don't know to what degree.

Brodie has a terrific ego, which he bends over backwards to hide. Generally, he does an excellent job of concealment but the little things sometimes are the only ones which give positive indication of the existence of an ego at all.

During the six months we have lived and worked together—as closely as two people can, and under as wide a range of circumstances—I have grown to like Brodie a great deal. I admire him as a person, envy him some of his characteristics, respect his judgment on a number of things.

My feeling has grown out of competition, for almost since the day we left New York both of us have engaged in a duel of personalities. Each of us has tried to prove ourself superior to the other—not openly or vulgarly or bluntly— but in a subtle way which conveys to the other the knowledge of a point gained or lost. It has been a stimulating contest; I don't think either of us would admit a major defeat.

In Brodie I have recognized a great deal of myself—in some respects we are a great deal alike and in others as different as daylight and dark.

When two people have known each as intimately as he and I, it is difficult to sum up the experience in words. Probably each of us has left his mark on the other which we will bear the rest of our lives.

Sunday, May 16. I've been in something of a fog for three days, but the situation as it exists tonight is:

I leave at 6:00 a.m. for Tontouta to catch the shuttle to PDG. Brodie doesn't leave until tomorrow afternoon on the same thing. I think there is every likelihood that we will leave on the same plane from PDG. If we don't it will be one of those freak tricks the Army sometimes plays, tricks that are ironic & pathetic at the same time.

Our intention of course was to go to Oahu together. Once things had been definitely established regarding Brodie and it was learned that, contrary to Goof, the people here "prefer" air transport for returning personnel, I got to work on my own orders. They came out yesterday and Brodie's came out today. Everybody here knows we want to go up together but we still leave here at separate times and, being unfamiliar with the ATS setup, I don't know what to expect. It seems a little silly that I should precede Brodie by, say, six or eight hours, all along the line.

True to form, everything here has been with the best possible official cooperation. Sanford couldn't have been nicer. One of the biggest reasons he has done so much for us is that he is returning, thru his offices, the favors Brodie has done in sketching the General, etc. All those things tie in.

We are all packed and ready to shove. Brodie, limited to 55 pounds luggage, has given away a mass of stuff; he sold some of his art supplies to Dick and Brodney. I am still trying to get my pay situation straightened out; got entries made in my pay book which I hope allow me to draw quarters for March & April in Honolulu. To be on the safe side, I hit Brodie up for $50. Even so, my spending will be limited.

Brodie has been busy taking messages and promising to see or call people for boys when he gets back. He is not, by any means, enthused over going back. He's pinning his hopes on assignment to another front. I know exactly how he feels.

My orders read to Fiji, Aitutaki, and Pearl. Why they gave me Aitutaki in place of Samoa, which I requested, is something which Sanford explained to me but which I still don't understand. The Cook Islands seem to me a long way out of the way.

My itinerary will be in reverse; I'm going to Pearl first and hit the other places on the way back. This is necessary to give me the best possible avenue for return in case something breaks. I don't want to get caught at some out of the way station should things suddenly explode. I hope there won't be any question with the ATS people there. If there is, I'm hooked: my hope is that Brodie, Bushemi, Miller and myself can get together in Oahu to discuss things. If I have to go to the other places first it will screw everything. I believe Spence will send me Bushemi: I hope to catch him in Hawaii before he leaves. If there's a delay, I may not . . . . . and the confusion will be terrific. I'm taking a chance even leaving here, in a way, and if something upsets my plans it's going to be a rugged deal. But there's no use borrowing trouble—I think it should go smoothly.

We agreed that Brodie would return this diary to Spence to be placed in the office safe. Then we talked to Hall who said there was a chance that somebody would shortstop it somewhere along the line but that if it was returned by officer courier there was no possibility of any mixup. I don't want to take any sort of chance—when this leaves my possession I want to be damned sure it will get back to the office to be put in safekeeping.

Had lunch with Jackson and Weiss today and Bob is brooding again—this time because he is applying for a commission altho he hates the thought of becoming an officer. Bob, as Brodie so neatly put it, is an emotional infant. He certainly has terrific complexes and in a way is an intellectual snob. Yet he can be the most likeable of persons.

Saw the big-eared, be-speckled little purser Thomson today, so the *Tjisadane* must be in again. Six months since I saw him.

Local news is that hereafter MacArthur will command operations involving our joint forces. The talk is that the Navy has been supplanted as king bee in this area. The boys think now they can get all the beer and Coke that the Navy's had heretofore.

At Bassett's office yesterday saw Henry Keyes, who said "Oh, hello," rather more cordially than usual. Couple of other interesting things: a periscope shot shows Fiji—a beautiful thing. If that's released in the States it's picture of the week. Also a mid-April copy of *Time* showing the gang on Cactus, with Col. Brown, his back to the camera, sitting on a gas can. Half my face and legs are in the cut—I damned near had my picture in *Time*, anyway.[11]

Jackson has contact prints of all the up-island stuff: I picked out about a half dozen for Brodie. Bob says a complete set will be upcoming sometime later.

Talking to Tenembaugh today, I realized that something must be done about this double allotment. He's going to write Washington and have them stop it and he says they will notify Helen how much we owe the government. That amount should make a dent in our bankroll, which was beginning to get really healthy, comparatively.

Strange coincidence in the editorial asking for a war song. Weiss read it, then pulled out of the file a story by Jack Mahon, INS, which he'd done on the 5th. We both had said almost exactly the same thing.

Last night Brodie and I pulled a bender in honor of everything. Australian rum—$10. I got pretty looping but managed to remain sensible I believe. Eventually got sick, of course, and today had butterflies. You never realize how much a canteen cup will hold. Anyway, it was fun.

Brodie, as a parting gift, gave me his hunting knife which I appreciated one helluva lot. I cleaned up my Jap bayonet, so he can take it back to New York.

Tuesday, May 18. Plaines des Gaiacs—PDG—is the hub of ATC in the South Pacific. Thru Operations here passes a steady stream of people who are all Short Snorters—going from and coming to Amberley, Nandi, Hickam and Hamilton. Here the men of two theatres, and the USO soldiers from the States, mingle as they wait for planes.

This is our first time at PDG and I am struck by a number of things: the deep red clay of the runway by the sea; the absence of mosquitos; the Red Cross service club built of native material—a remarkable thing and a Godsend to boys stationed in this isolated spot; the mess which costs us $1.25 a day; the flow of men who hit here and are gone.

We got in yesterday, flying up from Tontouta in 45 minutes. The transient barracks are the same Australian built tin affairs as there, but overall PDG is far and away a "better 'ole." Brodie calls it a summer resort. If I had to take a GI desk job anywhere in Melanesia, I'd take it here; sooner or later I believe I'd see half the people I know in the Army.

But, as always, the boys stationed here aren't too crazy about it. We've seen two boys who came over with us on the boat, here now in a weather outfit, and both of them have their complaints—one of his officers and the other of the mess. Our transient mess, which is said to be good because we pay for it and we buy it, bears the sign: "Abandon hope ye who enter here." It isn't that bad.

Radios at night pick up dance bands and symphony orchestras. The *Honolulu Advertiser* comes in on the plane a day or two late; the weekly mags get in a week old. *Yank*, bought thru the Noumea PX, apparently, is still too far behind. But the guys read it.

The conversation now is between a USO tech sergeant and some boys of the 23rd. One of the old boys just made a break by referring to new crews as "USO soldiers." The T/Sgt said "Who's that?" and then, "Oh." Somebody snickered, embarrassed. The USO boy talks of unrationed cigarettes costing $1.30, of trying four months to buy a Ronson lighter.

Joining in, I've talked for 45 minutes with the boy whose face was split on a water landing the night the 23rd lost two planes. We talked generally of many things, specifically of sweating out air raids, of Burns' crew—Sidler, Averbeck, Schmitty et al, of shipping at Shortland and night missions over Bougainville. It's strange how, in the presence of the uninitiated, men who have seen combat cling together. This boy—I haven't gotten his name—is going back to the States for reassignment after seven months. He and a part of his crew received the Silver Star yesterday. "A general pinned it on . . . . . I stood there shakin' . . . . . people staring at your face . . . . . I wish he'd just handed it to me and said, Here, that's good." He already has the DSC, the Purple Heart and the Air Medal with cluster. We knew a lot of the same people, the same planes, the same situations. Strange that, as many as there were on the Canal, there seem to be so few once we have left the place.

I talked to a Lt. yesterday who told me Knapp and the boys are now in Fiji but will go back to the Canal. The boy tonight says Sidler and the gang are at Button. He also said Burns had made a crash landing, ending up in the water. I can just see Sidler & Henderson and Deb—they'd been sweating out a water landing, and damn near made it; or something worse. I'm glad they're out of it for awhile—they deserve a break.[12]

Today I noticed the 23rd boys with their decorations pinned on. They looked, but didn't act or talk, like "heroes"—just like ordinary guys who were damned glad to be on their way home and at the same time a little sad at the parting—as men so strangely are. I know what those men have done, I know that they deserve every bit of credit anybody can give them. I am proud to have known the men they know and to have been with them, even for a little while.

But there is one thing that sticks in my craw. What does the infantry get for its service on the line? A campaign ribbon, no promotions, no extra pay, no return to the States. The Air Medal is for 100 hours combat flight. Air Corps men get 50% flying pay, plus 20% overseas pay. That amounts to money. If the AC gets a medal for 100 hours combat, what does the infantry get for 28-32 days of constant combat—constant strain—constantly being under fire—consistently living under the worst conditions, eating the worst food, sleeping when and where they have the chance? Nothing. There is no Ground Medal. There is no extra money for carrying a pack and a rifle, altho four hours of flight for AC men means 50% more a month. There is no justice in that. There should be extra money for men who do the actual fighting—regular money for the men who "fight" by doing any one of the million other things in this Army except shooting a gun and being shot at.

I certainly don't hold that flight pay should be discontinued, or that the Air Medal should not be given. I do hold that the man who sits on his ass at a desk should not draw as much money for it as the man who undergoes the most extreme form of earthly hell. If there is a difference at all, that difference should extend to all who fight.

Thursday, May 20. Aboard an LB 30 out of Fiji. We got in yesterday afternoon after 4½ hrs from PDG, crammed into the bomb bay of a converted B-
24. The ride was okay but we couldn't see anything and now, heading out over
the northern Fijis I can look thru a tiny slit in the bomb bay door and catch a
glimpse of the land. Takeoff was at 0600.

Brodie and I went into Nandi yesterday afternoon and walked the 4½
miles back last night just to enjoy the moonlight. The climate was swell.

Nandi is a tiny place, its one street running perhaps a couple of blocks.
On both sides of the street are shops run by Indians, selling souvenirs of shells,
pictures, and, mainly, necklaces and bracelets allegedly made of silver. The Hindus will tell you that certain pieces were made in India, while others they make
themselves in the shop. Each one has his own anvil and sits cross-legged on the
floor, working. Their prices for the silver run from seven to $15 or $20. Brodie,
suddenly become souvenir conscious, bought seven strings of shell beads and
one bracelet which cost him $9.

The Hindus, which impressed me by the absolute blackness of their hair
and eyes and by the striking features of the be-turbaned old men, are the trad-
ers of the town. The two cafes where it's possible to get meals are both owned
by Chinese but apparently run by Hindus. Nandi is much the same as any other
island town, but I got the impression that it is a little cleaner, perhaps because of
the tennis court—grassed—in the middle of town.

But in the couple of hours we were there, I got a hell of a kick out of the
place. Coming into town on a truck, we saw a native girl by the river do a Sally
Rand with her lava-lava, taking it off and re-wrapping it so she could walk into
deeper water. After months of Mother Hubbards I was amazed to see a native
thigh. The women don't wear the Hubbards, but effect a distinctly novel appearance by a blouse and a long wrap-around skirt which they wrap extremely
tight; the costume looks good because the gals are not all 200-pounders—most
of them are pleasantly plump but some are built along our lines. The men, who
offer a deep "Boola" in greeting, are big bastards: like the Caledonians in phy-
sique but with more refined features.

Our major experience was meeting Tina, the girl who works in the
Chinaman's dimly lit cafe. Tina is a Fijian glammer girl—she wore a blue print
dress, low cut, and white anklets with oxfords. She speaks English perfectly
with a soft, semi-Southern accent. We didn't know at first whether she could
understand us, but there was no more question after we heard her crooning: "I
Don't want to Walk without You, Baby." When she had brought our food—a
good dinner of ham and eggs and coffee—she sat down with us and ate Chinese food with chop sticks. We talked. I noticed she had a beautiful set of teeth.
She told us that she loved parties and native dances. "There's a dance tonight—
I'd love to take you boys but the MPs would cause trouble." She explained
troops aren't allowed into the villages because there had been trouble over the

women. Sometimes they danced American dances: they play the guitar and mandolin, but when I asked if they had drums she smiled and said no, as much as to say you dumb dope.

She said she liked the conga and the rumba, a fact which floored Brodie who is a Latin from San Francisco right up to the hilt. Tina said yes, she liked to have a good time and dance and drink with the officers. She'd been out last night.

Tina said she had four girl friends who had worked with her, but they were all in the hospital now. Naturally we asked their trouble. "Oh," said Tina, "they've just been having too much of a good time."

She said there'd been a wonderful party last week—eight officers and eight girls. "Oh, there was plenty to drink—there was even champagne—and we had the best time. We were all a little drunk and sang and did the hula. One girl was very drunk—oh, she was drunk—she called to the lieutenant: 'Jimmy, come and take my dress off.'" I trust the lieutenant remained a gentleman.

Tina was as sophisticated a gal as I've seen in a long time. In her own way I think she has it all over the average smart set Stateside because her sophistication was based on a pure simplicity. When she had nothing to say, she was silent; when she talked to us, what she said made sense. That she was a sexy piece by the cut of her made that much more interesting. That she looked and smelled clean was a relief from the run of the mill in the islands. I imagine she's well shacked up.

She served us seconds on coffee. Brodie asked me if it was GI or not. Before I could answer, Tina said: "No, it isn't—it's British. We used to serve GI coffee, tho. Boys come in here every morning for coffee, lots of them." I could see why, after that stinking French stuff . . . . . and I was beginning to marvel at Tina's store of Americana.

We shook hands as we left. Altho, from the conversation with her boss in our presence, I think she was toying around with the idea of showing us around if we had asked her. But we didn't.

We went out the back door into the light of a full Fijian moon and walked thru town & to the airport beyond. There are some strange & fascinating places in the world.

Wednesday, May 19. We took off from Fiji on Thursday morning and landed in Samoa on Wednesday afternoon, something like five hours flying time—but across the International Date Line. We were in Tutuila about an hour, just long enough to eat and take off again for—I think—Canton. There is one thing about this trip that I don't like at all; there are 12 of us here in the bomb bay, with our luggage, and we can't see a damned thing. There are no windows except in the main compartment aft where the officers are.

The field we hit is about ten miles from Pago and we were all displeased that we weren't stopping over night so we could see the place. My first

Polynesian island and I didn't see a native—except four in a boat a long way off, altho not too far to see that one wore a flower in her hair.

The chow was terrific. We ate at first-three-graders table in the Marine mess, with two mess men waiting on us hand and foot—with plates and silver-ware and paper napkins. All of us—especially the 23rd combat crew—were snowed under. We asked for coffee and at first were told there was none, but later a mess man came in with a pot reheated from breakfast. Such service none of us could hardly swallow in one sitting.

Samoa to me looks exactly like Button, with the dispersal fingers running back into vine covered tropical trees. The runway is a beauty. It had been raining when we got in and the clouds were low and misty on the mountains which rose tall and rugged almost out of the sea. I noticed a thin waterfall which seemed to come down an almost incredible distance from high up on a mountainside. I'd like to have seen that in the morning sunlight.

-0-

We missed the Uneager Beavers at Nandi last night. They're pulling searches by day and benders by night, apparently.

Friday, May 21. Brodie is gone.

That is the first sentence of this notation from Oahu. Brodie and I raised our hands, grinning, in half salutes this afternoon at 5:15 p.m. We said, "So long, fellow—luck." And that was all. We stood on a street corner with Miller & Bushemi who, in all fairness, could scarcely understand why we preferred that our farewell be short and simple and nonchalant. Neither of us would have had it any other way.

As I write, half tight, at 6:45 on my bunk at Moana Seaside Cottages (or bungalows)—and Miller & Bushemi have just come in demanding to know where I returned and why—I have no sensations except to put something, anything, on paper.

As casually as we departed a few minutes ago, Brodie and I are no longer together. He is still at Hickam Field, still on the island, but now we are five miles apart and we might just as well be 1500 or 2000 or 5000 because I have, until the war is over, seen him for the last time.[13]

So ends a chapter of my life.

Brodie and I got in yesterday morning, having flown all night from Can-ton. We arrived at Hickam Field, Hanger # 9, at 9:30—having seen exactly nothing since we left PDG because we were cooped up—12 of us, including Eddie White—in the bomb bay—and promptly were put through Customs. I was, internally, resigned to having this diary taken from me and knew well that I had no defense; but I had put it in my navigation kit which I did not present to the inspectors. They looked at my B-4 bag, saw my orders in my wallet, asked me if I carried any uncensored letters, and let me go. As I was one of the last I decided to slip he diary into the navigational kit, which I did, and nobody saw me. I was just lucky, absolutely. I was sure they'd ask me questions which would force me to lie, but they didn't—not that it would have made any difference. I was scared from the time we heard of the shakedown, at Canton, until we were past the Customs' tables, but after that—okay, so what?

I had a helluva time locating M & B. Brodie & I were separated (altho I am not actually drunk I find I have made more mistakes in penmanship than ever before, in these two pages). Finally I contacted someone who knew where they were, hitched a ride with a Jap who took me right to their front door. He gave me a running commentary on Honolulu as we passed thru town and would take no money when I got out of the car (apparently because I had told him I had come from the South). Anyway, Bushemi & I went back to Hickam, found Brodie and brought him back to Waikiki. Miller was there shortly after and we had a swell reunion—dinner and then a shit session until we fell asleep.

Today we did nothing except settle Brodie's mind on the time of his departure; car driver got us a quart of Cream of Kentucky, and—split six ways—we drank it. Bushemi engineered some pictures at Waikiki, with the Royal Hawaiian in the background, but they are just tourist stuff—strictly from nothing.

We—Brodie & I—became separated and had only a moment to wish each other luck. He went off to Hickam and I went with M & B to an OWI friend of theirs—and from there I came, rather unceremoniously (as is my unfortunate custom) to here. When I am the least bit tight—as I am at the moment—I have no scruples whatsoever about getting up and leaving. I did just that. It's extremely impolite—but effective.

The four of us have, in this short time, talked over a number of things, come to a decision on none. I spoke privately to Brodie on what he should tell Spence but it was unnecessary because he & I know how each other feel, exactly. He will talk to Spence exactly as I would and any doubt I may have had in that respect was dispelled by his conversation with Miller & Bushemi. I know positively, now, what he will say Stateside.

The papers today are full of the Tokyo news break that Yamamoto is dead—killed in the air in the South Pacific. It is possible that I have the only exclusive story on that—something I got on the return trip from Cactus and have been sitting on ever since. Rex Barber—the man who shot him down— came down on the plane with us—and slept the whole way.[14]

Sunday, May 23. Honolulu, up to dinner this evening, has appeared to me thru a mist of semi- or complete intoxication. Last night, after trying without effect for hours, I really got stinking. It was a pleasure.

This evening Ira Wolfert and (Capt) Maurice Evans were over for a long bull session which was spiked with Ira's talk of his experiences—an account which sounded like the wildest sort of fantasy, but which I have no reason whatsoever to doubt.

I met Ira yesterday when John & I went up to his apartment. We were together—amid an afternoon of drinking, dinner, then a party with a maze of people woven thruout—until late last night.

I succeeded in making an ass of myself when, as the drinking progressed, I produced my Jap tooth to be shown to an admiring audience. The "oh" and "ah" was going smoothly and I, like a fool, was enjoying it (what a phoney) until Ira said—"That's no human tooth." I got pissed off. "The hell it ain't—I pulled it out of the skull myself." Ira said flatly—"It ain't human." I got mad. "By god, I don't like to be called a liar to my face." Ira laughed. "Better that way than behind your back." That shut me up. I'd been taking straight shots of bourbon in an effort to get an edge on, and by then I was beginning to succeed. Ira laughed and left, but I still sulked, like a little boy. What a sophomore! The curse of an aching ego.[15]

Anyway, there was no reopening of the wound today and I kicked myself for getting involved at all. Someday I'll learn.

It's after 3:00 a.m., and since I can't sleep perhaps I can write. I came here to get a line on several things and have thus far achieved exactly nothing. But my information has been this:

a. *Yank* is to be printed here, but there are complications. Miller is sweating out Spence's arrival from the Mainland.
b. Miller promises to look around for a typewriter.
c. Both boys want to see some action.
d. Bushemi tells me he wants to go back with me but I can see he is torn between two desires.
e. Neither is bothered by officer woes, which is as it should be. Reasons are obvious.
f. This entire set up is shot full of the old fluff stuff. There is intrigue and biting conversation.
g. The liquor situation is not good, but I complain not; the women—altho this is a land of slacks & play suits—are to be seen and that's about all. So be it.

Generally, I'm enjoying myself here but for a steady diet—I think not. There are a number of advantages to this situation—the first and foremost being that here is, at least, civilization. I like my comforts and this offers them despite restrictions and the terrific criticisms I've heard of the place. There are people worth knowing, things worth doing—but the cost of living is terrific.

The disadvantages are legion: As I knew it would be the place is alive with blasé characters who know all about the war: there are cynics and the experts and the little people who snipe and belittle. I despise such an atmosphere. As a field for material, the place is barren comparatively. I don't envy Merle his jog here in that respect and, with knowledge of the condition, I admire him for the work he has done. If the paper is to be printed here there will be a great deal involved—which I want no part of. The censorship is rugged. The presence of people muscling in—or trying to—is in evidence. The whole thing, from a standpoint of strict newspaper opportunity—is far inferior to my own area. This is my first impression because I have seen nothing but Hickam, Shafter, and Honolulu. From the standpoint of a comfortable existence, surrounded by the luxury of varying degrees of wine, women, song and culture, it offers everything whereas my area offers nothing. I was amazed when Bushemi said he hadn't eaten GI chow in six months—mon Dieu!

I am thankful that I did not come directly here from Cactus—if I had I would already, in four days, have been so disgusted I'd have been miserable. The contrast would have been too great, I'm afraid.

I've been to two or three houses—friends of the boys—and been treated royally. Friday night to Vic & Olive for movies and a sample of the much cussed but very good island gin. Yesterday afternoon with Ira & friends at the _____ [16] and last night to Jerry Luker's, later ending in the apartment of a bag-eyed bag named Kelly who is dumber than most females and uglier than almost all. She had us in for a final drink. Today back to Vic's where I met Larry McManus—a nice guy—and some more drinks. Olive, who was somewhat high and wore no bra underneath her lounging pajamas, is a swell hostess but I hated hitting Vic's preciously rationed firewater. I'm afraid these people would not understand how I feel relaxing with a drink among pleasant people and I'm damned sure they wouldn't understand how I feel about bare white breasts flaunted in front of my face. Tonight there was dinner at the Moana with Ira & Capt. Evans.

As a tourist, my impression of Honolulu and such are not very strong, probably because I didn't come here to see Hawaii. Waikiki Beach, which is a couple of hundred yards away, is just another sand strip which barely finds room to crowd in between the sea and the hotels. The breakers are its redeeming feature; as a beach, purely, Anse Vata is just as good or better. The installations and the female scenery are of course the big difference. Diamond Head is pretty, but nothing to rave about. It's sort of puny, comparatively.

Honolulu, as a town, is not much—but any town looks good to me. I've seen very little of it, and it's smaller than I thought it would be. The residential districts are garden-like, but the homes are flimsily-built. The weather (altho it is raining now) has been wonderful. The Royal Hawaiian is a gaudy thing, taken over by the Navy. It is across the street to the right; across and to the left is The Moana, still a civilian establishment—and high on food. There must be 500 MPs around the streets; there's a saluting jag on now. Everybody looks so well laundered, with their ties tight & belt buckles shined; the gas mask-helmet business was called off the day we got here, praise the Lord.[17]

The boys probably think I'm a first class bastard, a moral degenerate and a husband untrue because of my attitude toward the sight of white women who speak English, wear thin rayon playsuits, slacks, halters, swim suits, etc., etc. I have explained that when I was married I didn't die and that for almost seven months the sight of a civilian broad, looking & acting like Americans, has been denied me. I don't want to own one—I'm still a guy who doesn't turn away his eyes if the view is pleasant.

Two or three things here have impressed me—the amazing number of Japs. I had expected a mob of service people and a reasonable number of slant-eyes. But it almost seems that the civilian Japs outnumber us; of course that's ridiculous. but still I haven't been at the same place with as many Nippos before in my life, not even on Cactus. Another thing is the blackout, which goes into effect at 8:00 o'clock, absolutely choking the life out of the town. Blackout curtains; people who get excited if a light shows thru an open door. Naturally, it all seems silly as hell to me—but apparently no sillier than to everybody else here. Curfew at 10:00 clears the streets. Still, if that's the way it is there's nothing I can do about it, so what the hell? Thirdly, my overall impression is one of kindness toward the whole business: I like it—the boys' rooms are comfortable, we have breakfast at the drugstore, dinner so far at the hotel. The atmosphere there is somewhat pathetic—everybody is trying so hard to be snotty and sophisticated and having such a hell of a time doing it. Same way on the beach—it's hard to be filthy-richly relaxed with barbed-wire against your back. Seaside Cottages are a group of apartments scattered about a green lawn which makes me want to lie down and roll on it. I haven't seen a movie yet but I notice long ques in front of theatres and I'm in no mood to sweat out a long line here. My only experience in a bar (open 10 to 2:00) was a few minutes in the South Sea. Same old stuff, only costlier and perhaps, noisier. I've thought of Mary Moore: this is not her Hawaii, I'm afraid.

I wired Helen today—25 word night letter—which should have been delivered by noon today. Hope she answers. It seems like a month since I wrote her, but actually it's been just over a week. I'm going to have to catch up on my correspondence—especially at this time.

Miller wired Forsberg per instructions that Brodie & I had arrived so there will probably be something from him. I'm hoping against hope that Spence will arrive while I'm here. I certainly would like to see that guy, but I gather he's been "on his way" out here for six months now.

-0-

Meeting Ira Wolfert was a pleasure. The guy—a chubby, pleasant person—is, as McManus so aptly said, "making nothing but money out of this war." I've read neither of his books nor his novel, but he seems to be the Name Literarily in the Pacific—he & Dick. Ira isn't too much impressed by it all, at least not obviously. He's a marvelous story teller—a snow artist from way on back.

Maurice Evans was the bigger surprise. Billed as the Shakespearean hoity-toity boy, the Captain tonight seemed the most democratic guy imaginable. Except for his accent, he's plain as hell. He looks less like an actor than most people. And—I don't think he was merely being nice.

Also met Art Cohen, fresh from the States on a New Guinea assignment after years as a West Coast sports writer. His stories of fight people & the rassling racket are out of the world. The *Time* mag man drank with us, too—a mild little guy I've seen somewhere before, but I can't remember where or when.[18]

Tuesday, May 25. Last night Ira called, inviting us to sit in on a party at Bob Trumbull's place. There we met Paul Sample, a huge man with a blond mustache and a huge swelling on the back of his right—his painting hand—the result of a fall in the blackout. Trumbull, a soft-spoken blond, is finishing a second book—"Silversides."[19] Bob's wife, I'll bet, wears the pants in that family. Bushemi, coming in late from the darkroom, brought blow-ups of shots he'd made of Ira & Capt. Evans. The closeups of Ira were a sweet job—Ira autographed one to us for Hohn's gallery-on-the-walls here.

I confided with Ira last night, telling him part of the things I'd heard below and asking him to give me the low down on what he knew here. He said he thought it was so much crap, based on the information he had. Which shows you how it goes—who knows? Ira himself is sweating transportation south & thence to China. I've just been reading his book and came across a reference to Mario Sesso—a captain who came up with us on the plane: little things like that give me a mild kick sometimes.[20]

Became a Short Snorter last night. Strange that on all the times Brodie & I have been on planes on over-water flights, I remember only once that that nebulous organization received new members. Stranger still that I should "enroll" in a neat apartment at Waikiki.[21]

Went up to Pali today—beautiful view & windy. I've been in Hawaii only five days and yet it seems like a month. I have accomplished nothing concrete as far as business is concerned. I wish to hell would hear from office. I feel like an odd thumb around here.

Rounding up a few odds and ends which were overlooked somewhere in the alcohol week:

Alan Gould, Associated Press big shot, told Miller he liked my stuff and promised me a job after the war. Hope I have better luck than that last time the AP at home made me an offer on the day I left for camp.

Saw Russell Cordell on the street. I couldn't remember his name and vice versa at the time—had even forgotten that he joined the navy just after he got his discharge in September of '41. He was feeling no pain and said he had been in the Solomons.

Bought a pair of civvy slippers; the first clerk told me he had none with buckles and then John's friend Jay talked to another clerk, told him I'd "lost my gear" and he brought out what I wanted. Speak-easy stuff. Ten bucks—ouch— and I now have six pairs of shoes.

Helen answered my wire this morning, says all's well. Damn—I must write that girl . . . . . what kind of husband am I? If it wasn't so damn much trouble getting censors to see them, I'd send night letters every few days while I'm here. May anyway.

Pictures One-Shot made of Brodie & I were okay, except the one with me laughing. I have one of the most unattractive grins I've ever seen—face like a top studded with mare's teeth. Brodie always looks three times worse—physically—than he does in actuality.

Tried briefly & futilely to do a little work but can't settle down for a minute. This time there's nothing wrong but—just me. New copies of the paper have story of the *Coolidge* with a nice spread—lousy rewrite on the lead, tho, and advance story-plug on water landing. That just about clears me.

Wednesday, May 26. Bought this Parker 5t today for $13.75 and after writing this one line I'm beginning to regret it. Also purchased Freud's *Introduction to Psychoanalysis* for $1.50. Am now down to four bucks out of $55—a complete mystery to me.

To Schofield this morning for an abortive attempt to do a story on something or other. Driving past a PX I spotted Tony Pierce who used to be top kick of "C" company. Stopped and talked to him, exercising my best military courtesy, since Tony long since got his OCS commission. I'm afraid I can't understand why some people become second lieutenants and pricks simultaneously.

Ira left last night. Bon voyage.

Letter from the office says George made a landing on Attu. Nice business.[22] Also that paper got Classen pix in Washington.

Larry up tonight with Lt. Steve Fischer, B-24 navigator just up from Cactus. Ex-*Chronicle* man. Bull session. We searched ourselves for some possibility of getting drinking liquid, but couldn't do the trick. Civilians & officers are the boys here, but, poor things, only a quart a week.

Past Pearl Harbor and thru Wheeler Field today. Pearl too far away to observe, but Wheeler still looks a little chewed up here and there.

Conversation tonight was on the Negro situation. It was me against the world; I wish I could give concrete reasons to back up my ideas which are a cross between the liberal attitude and the old hide-bound Southern way of thinking. But every time I talk I get my tongue twisted—which makes it only worse.

Friday, May 28. Yesterday afternoon finally came to grips with the people who operate the *MidPacifican*, supposedly our competition here. I was interrupted in the middle of trying to do a story on the Zero Hour, so said to hell with it and went out with this guy—Grossenbecker—to meet the gang. Miller joined us later. It was throughout, the maddest afternoon I spent in some time. I still don't see what the argument is all about here and I don't want to—and didn't—get mixed up in the squabble. The *Pacifican*, as I see it, is just another ambitious GI newspaper having its trouble and calling out its reserves of rank on the island. What the hell? It's staff was feeling entirely too sorry for themselves to suit me.[23]

Finally wrote Helen and Dad—I feel like a horrible heel for having allowed myself to wait so long.

I think this trip here is going to do me a lot of good, psychologically. Altho we are pressing our demands that the office tell us something—anything at all—I feel that I'm going to be almost glad to get the hell back to people whose main concern is fighting a war. It amazes me that I hear so little of combat here—everybody seems to think of everything else but that.

Saturday, May 29. I'm feeling low—bored, lonesome, disgusted. Miller & Bushemi are off somewhere at separate places and I'm by myself for the first time, I suppose, among thousands of people who seem to be doing all right, judging from the sounds of merriment. Oh, am I sorry for myself! And what a laugh that is.

I guess I just can't stand civilization—both here and in Auckland I've felt the same thing, a sort of frustration which is almost harder to bear than being lost among 50,000 soldiers in some ridiculous place like Noumea. How I despise that place and yet how much more it offers than some of the others.

I suppose the only kind of comfort I really want is that kind which I can share with Helen. I don't get the full effect of this place or any place like it without her—it was the same way in New York until she came there. I can have a certain amount of fun, but the real pleasure—the full enjoyment—is lacking.

Just at the moment I'm utterly unhappy—and it makes me mad to admit it. My only reason for unhappiness is within myself—I'm just too damn hard to please.

There are things that I could do, and I've started two stories, finished neither of them. Something always interferes.

I could start drinking at ten o'clock in the morning and by two I wouldn't care whether they stopped selling drinks. But that's no solution to anything.

I've felt guilty each time we've had drinks in private homes—as tho I was eating someone else's food. Last night, during a brief stay at Charlie O'Brien's, I writhed in the chair.

I haven't said fifty words to a girl since I got here. That's partly because talking to women here isn't the simplest thing in the world and partly because I just don't want to get involved. That old "I do—I don't" business again.

First and foremost, I wish to hell the office would come thru. We understood that Charlie—so he said last night—received a wire that a captain is coming out right away. That undoubtedly means Spence isn't—damn it. He is the guy I want to see.

Anyway, this is at least the inner self—this writing—and I feel better than when I started a few minutes ago. I suppose there is method in this madness.

Monday, May 31. On the veranda of the Moana, ran into Capt. Purnell, the Texas fighter pilot whom I saw first on Cactus and again in Auckland. He was with the captain whose portrait Brodie did at Tontouta in early December. We were delighted seeing each other, and Purnell sold me four fifths of burgundy which is cooling in a bucket of ice. We went up to Purnell's room, Steve along, and talked of the usual things. Purnell wants 30 days rest and then combat duty again, this time in China. He says he wants to be turned loose and allowed to get there as best he can; he described his idea of the "ideal life of the fighter pilot" as being one in which he could fly a few missions with one sqdrn and then move on to another—"see the world on the Army's pay." The Capt. has 220 hours combat flying in the Solomons, 18 months in the South Pacific. He's sweating out transportation home. He said he's been recommended for the Silver Star as a result of that action in which he, a P-38 pilot, took up a P-40 for the first time, and shot down two Zeros.[24]

Finished the editorial yesterday and got off a letter to Helen.

Nothing about Honolulu gives me a lift any more, and I'm beginning to be entirely too satisfied to lie around and do nothing.

Still no word from the office. What the hell is the score on this deal, anyway?

"I Got That Old Feeling"

Tuesday, June 1. The conversation in the outer room is politics, about which I know nothing and care less.

Steve and I carried thru on the idea I've had for several days—to start at ten in the morning and drink until there was no more. Even at that, I didn't get drunk.

We spent most of the day with Fred Purnell and Williams who for hours talked combat aviation. Not since I've hit Honolulu have I so much enjoyed myself.[1]

There are things here which I don't like particularly, but today brought me back into the fold—among people who regard this war as the most important thing in their lives, who eat and sleep and live combat. It is one concrete thing among so much stuff around here that is pure crap. To drink and talk is good for what ails me—or rather to drink and listen. To listen to Purnell, and to be included . . . . . "You remember that day . . . ?"

Bushemi developed the pictures he'd taken a few nights ago; they turned out swell and he made up two prints of each which I'll send home.

I'm hooked to talking to some guys at Schofield tomorrow night—that should be good.

It amazes me that I can spend so much money in this place. I'll be broke in a few days and with practically no money coming in even if I draw what amounts to two months pay. So what?

Wednesday, June 2. A batch of office mail to the boys said absolutely nothing of interest to me, except of course their reference to a Capt. Balthrope who should arrive in a few days.[2] I sat down to compose my first letter to Spence in almost a month, and now have decided to tear it up. In it I sang the blues, which sounds a little too off key. I'll bide my time awhile. McCarthy remarked on my request to lay off the snow jobs—which makes the second time a crack of his has hit me the wrong way.

June 11 issue of the book has the missing men story with some nice pictures and two pages of type. They did well by that yarn. But now I have no backlog whatsoever—everything except a couple of not-too-good features has been used. I'm going to have to get back in the saddle.

Met Charlie McMurtry 'smorning. He told me AP had picked up "several" of my stories; I know of only two.[3]

Went out to Schofield tonight to talk to guys in the rear echelon of the 27th Division. Altho they said it was an interesting hour and a quarter, I felt like a dope. Most interesting was the question-and-answer session: the boys wanted to know the usual things—was there close-in fighting, equipment on the lines, communications, supply, snipers, knee-mortars, fanaticism, etc.

An officer carried on the Guadalcanal discussion after I quit, speaking from memory of some of the things told him in a lecture by Gen. somebody or other who was supposed to have been somebody's chief of staff. I thought he meant Seabury, but apparently he didn't. However, it was obvious that the general had made some pretty gross remarks about the Navy. That is my idea of how not to carry on a war.

If my experiences overseas had all been on a par with those of the last two weeks, this diary would be a waste of time. I don't know any other reason for making entries now other than merely to keep myself in the habit . . . . .

Get up, eat, talk, eat, try to find something to drink, talk, listen, go to bed. What the hell is this?

My letter to Spence today contained a paragraph "Since leaving Guadalcanal the second time I think I've been completely frustrated—the same sort of frustration I felt when I asked for assignment overseas—when it seemed I was merely banging my head against a wall and getting nowhere . . . . . " All of which is more or less true, but hardly the thing to be writing the boss—he could only either tell me it was TS or give me a pat on the head and a phoney pep talk. I tore the letter up.

Actually, I think I must have some type of persecution complex—as if I were being condemned to the islands which I sincerely regard as damn poor places in which a man can exist. I don't like the idea of going back down there and at the same time I feel like an ass being here. I see pictures of Tunisia and know that it is tough there; I see pictures from the Aleutians and shiver at the thought of being stuck up there. Then what the hell is wrong? Nothing at all—it's very simple: the boy who talked himself into combat assignment is beginning to turn cold on the deal, and at the same time he can't see himself doing a lot of other things on the paper. I suppose to be recalled to NY for awhile would make me happy, but I undoubtedly would be screaming for something else within a few months. It is disgusting not to know even one's own mind. I don't.

Saturday, June 5. This thing is reaching a head—I either want something to do or I want to get the hell out of here. This place is driving me nuts.

By "something to do" I mean I'd like to get a line on the printing, like to talk to this captain if and when he ever gets here, find out if there is anything I can do, and act accordingly.

For some 15 days I've been doing exactly nothing. I can see less and less reason for my being here. The office knows I'm here and obviously if they had anything to tell me they would already have notified me. Apparently they haven't. I'm sweating out word from Brodie, also from Helen, and from Dad.

It amazes me that I haven't heard a peep from NY. Apparently they are making no plans to replace Brodie, or, if they are, perhaps they have entrusted the information with Capt. Balthrope.

I don't know what I should do—remain here until I hear from Helen, go back south and get back to work with the AC, fool around with the printing if and when it gets started, or just go to Fiji and sit in the absence of Haworth who is back Stateside for hospitalization.

I feel so utterly useless here now. And yet, if I were south, I don't think I'd feel any better about it. I felt useless down there when I left.

Wednesday, June 9. Letter from Helen arrived two days ago—all's well—and from Dad yesterday—ditto. Sent Helen a third cable today, hoping to make up for an absence of letters. I started writing her Wednesday, minutes after her letter arrived, and finally finished three pages tonight. This place is a madhouse.

I got paid Friday—$118.00—after 4½ hours of trying to find the right finance office. Paid Miller back the $50 I had borrowed from him and now (I can hardly believe it) I have $20 left. Money just disappears in this place. Maybe I can collect my per diem in a couple of days.

To Hickam this morning with the boys on an aerial gunner story; was suddenly and strongly hit by the desire to go thru the five-week course. It would do me a world of good and if I could possibly work it I might do it. The office would more than likely raise hell—but I figure they're going to start yelling pretty soon anyway.

Have made up my mind to stay here until the Helen-and-the-baby news comes thru. I want to know all about it immediately and call her. Dad says he likes his new apartment, which is sweet music to my ears.

I'm afraid there's bad news about Bobbie Hilton; good news of Louie, I hope.[4] Dad didn't give me any details—mixed up mail somewhere.

Tuesday, June 15. Perhaps I should catch up chronologically:
On Friday, the 11th, Capt. Chuck Balthrope arrived.
On Saturday, the 12th, I felt my first flush of malaria.

On Sunday, the 13th, I went to the hospital.

The captain made a terrific impression on us—he has one of the most forceful, and likable, personalities I've ever encountered. We hadn't known him an hour before we felt we were old buddies. He's that kind of guy.

He was at work on the paper even before he saw us, having talked to Col. Whatley who is the SS officer and the man with the fuzzy nuts in re publications, GI.[5]

He and the boys were in this morning and the score is still 0-0, but accomplishments so far amount to this: we will probably print at the *Advertiser* which offers the best deal, including office space. When such will get underway is not yet known; just how entangled with the *MidPacifican* we will be—who knows? We will probably not do more than print the mats as we receive them from New York, at first; we will gradually inject as much local stuff as possible.

Just what my position is here I don't know. The captain said he wanted me to stick around for awhile but the office probably won't like that idea. I think, if it came to brass tacks, I could ask for a permanent assignment here and probably get it. Somehow, if this set up functions as it should, I think that would be a good deal. But I don't know.

To catch up on other things: subsequent letters from Helen and Dad contained the news that Alvin Pierce was KIA in North Africa after winning the Silver Star;[6] that Louie, instead of being MIA, was awarded the Air Medal; that Bobbie Hilton is MIA. I wrote Charlie. Also that Dad is well situated in an apartment near Helen; two letters from Helen didn't say much new, except that Scottie seems to be becoming a fixture in the house.

Merle said that he would pick up the portable today; we wheedled it out of the QM people last week. Praise the Lord!

A budding friendship may have sprung up between the boys and a certain Thelma Alemeda and her gray haired chaperon Vickie, who say they are coming up for a visit. They all had a date last night.

Vic and Olive Scherenborg were over the other night and we were set for a pleasant evening until Groppenbecker blundered in, drunk. The bastard, besides crashing the party, drank most of our gin. What a guy.[7] Bushemi got a picture of me scraping paint off Olive's toe nails—with a sheath knife—which I don't think Helen would appreciate unless she knew Olive.

Sgt. Skidmore, a "friend" of Chuck's, called on Miller recently, engaged him in a drinking bout and snowed him under with tales of his journalistic ability, his intimacy with the captain, and his (Skidmore's) plans for the future of *Yank* in Hawaii which he expected to join in the near future. The evening ended with Miller stroking him across the mouth with a closed fist.

At the moment I am ensconced in a private room in Ward 2-B of Kam Hospital, formerly a swank school taken over by the Army a couple of years ago. The place is high on a mountain overlooking Honolulu, Diamond Head to the left, Pearl Harbor to the right and the Aloha Tower down stage center. They call it Shangri-la, which is an apt description—I've never seen a GI hospital quite like it.[8]

My line of reasoning that Oahu would be among the better places to have malaria proved nicely correct. I guess I was as sure I would have this stuff as Helen is of having her baby. But I picked a damn poor time—just when the captain got in, and when Helen may deliver any day. I wanted to be ready to wire her and call her almost immediately.

One thing, after 2½ days, appears obvious—I have a mild case. It started off typically: I had to leave the table at the Moana Saturday night, had a slight chill followed by a terrific fever and Sunday morning was as weak as a kitten and sore all over. Entered the hospital at noon.

Felt fine until last night when I had my first real chill—lasted three or four hours. But this morning my temperature was back to normal and the doc says he thinks that will be all there are of them. I hope so.

After spending 24 days in one of the joints last year—slight case of concussion—I don't want to take up any sort of permanent residence like that this time.

Anderson, the boy in the next room, was on the Canal one night. He's been here three months with the stuff, damn near died with it twice.

Wednesday, June 16. These few days of hospitalization have given me my first opportunity for honest concentration since I've hit this Rock. It hasn't handed me a decision to my problems, yet—but it is helping.

A sick cameraman has been dropping in for talks and he made one statement which expressed itself in my mind very well. "I've always wanted to be a positive character," he said, "to make a decision and stick with it." So far in my life I've been that sort of person, more or less—at least I've been able to consider my opportunities and/or my desires and outline some plan of action. But damn if I seem able to do it any more, the best reason probably being that the "opportunities" presented so far are mainly in my own mind and otherwise nonexistent as far as I know.

It's time I tried to put down in black and white the things that are chewing at me—if I can—and to outline some plan of action—if I can.

1. I think what I really want is a brief spell from bouncing around doing nothing, or more particularly, a spell from doing nothing. I'd like to dig into something and work at it with a visible goal to be attained and possibly even a time limit in which to attain it; a deadline on a daily hasn't its only value in meeting composing and circulation requirements. But what I'm saying I want is regimentation, authority over me, assignment? No! To wilfully submit to that is jeopardizing the

precious attribute of this job—its freedom, even in the Army. Then what the hell do I want? I'm not quite sure, but it's a combination of things which add up to concreteness—work to be done, satisfaction in doing it, and satisfaction in having done it. In a sense I've had those things all along—see a story, work on it, see it in print. But the intervals between stories destroy the brief illusion of concrete accomplishment, especially amid surroundings in which so much actually is being accomplished. In those intervals I've felt lost.

2. My attitude toward combat now is about the same as it always has been. It fascinates me and scares me at the same time, like women watching a street fight. I haven't seen but very little fighting, by lots of comparisons, and by other comparisons I've seen a lot more than some people ever will. I've seen just enough to know what it is; in about the same ratio as an acquaintance of a few meetings is to an old friend. I haven't made up my mind whether to cultivate that acquaintance, or to drop him. I'm inclined to cultivate him. Perhaps it might help if he wore a different suit on occasion.

3. Even my attitude toward civilization clouds. I want it, I suppose, because I didn't like the raw bareness of the islands. And yet I've bought a bar of candy in New Caledonia that gave me more pleasure than any purchase I've made here: I felt I was getting more. I've found here in the hospital that not being able to squander doesn't make for any loss of sleep—I'm used to it. I suppose what I mean by "civilization" is really a home in which I can share things with Helen. I get just as lonesome for her as down there, and more. And I get just as bored here as there, almost. Everything becomes commonplace. When they do, I usually move on.

So what?

So I've got to make up my mind in the very near future whether I will go back to New Caledonia with anything but a "frown on my face and a curse in my heart" or whether I'll try to stay here and get my fill of—what?

I'm beginning to see which way the wind blows, but the decision is reserved.

Saturday, June 19. I'm so full of "good reading" that I feel that to live the real life, the full life, the true life, I'll have to go out and get a good lay immediately; otherwise, according to some 16 playwrights, 93 authors, and Ludwig Bemelmans, I'll be relegated to that limbo of the life insignificant. Having read some of the better plays of the last 20 years, plus an anthology of "last works" of a variety of people, I'm impressed with the whore on the American scene. I'm not being a backhanded moralist—I've just become aware of the tremendous crutch that is sex. I suppose they didn't have anything else to write about or that sex, being the only thing remaining in the world that people don't drag out into fresh air, offered the last frontier of realism. I welcome the day when people say "fuck!" in polite and mixed company; then, and only then, perhaps the cream of American literati will get their blood pressure down from that high point it has reached while they try to say it without saying it. Some of them, when the bars finally come down, won't be able to write a word. Hemingway: "Obscenity in the milk . . . . . " If Steinbeck can say Grandpa was full of piss and vinegar why can't Hemingway say "shit in the milk . . . . . " and let it go at that. Two books on sex strain so hard to say plainly, fuck, that you want to scratch out the paragraphs and write it in the margins to ease the authors' pain.

A Texan moved in with Andy today after hitting a Negro this morning when the Negro called him a son of a bitch. The Texas kid was so mad he sat on his bed and cried like a baby.

"I'll kill that nigger sonuvabitch, so help me God I'll kill him."

He was still all puckered up, snarling and sulking, hours later. He developed a persecution complex immediately, based on the fact that he was damn near moved over to the prison ward.

"Just because I'm a rebel, by God. If I'd been a goddam Yankee they'd give me a medal. No black bastard is going to call my mother that. I'll kill the sonuvabitch. You've heard of a Texans' temper, aintcha—well, I got one of the worst, I don't take no sonuvabitch from no man—red white black or yeller—in fun or not. An' I don't care whether they got stars or bars, I'll tell 'em."

All of which is a point in the Negro problem which the average Yankee either doesn't realize or doesn't understand or chooses to ignore: a Southerner's pride, something he is born with and nurses along as he grows older. To me pride is a virtue and it makes up for a lot of other things or at least helps ease them over. When it comes to Yankees quite a lot of Southerners put up a front to cover what amounts to an inferiority complex, or an active defense against a tangible or intangible expression of superiority. In turn, there are Southerners who exert a reverse complex against the Negro; in other words, if a Negro rises against a white man the white's sense of superiority—inborn in him—is outraged—his pride suffers in the knowledge that a nigger disagrees. The Southern attitude toward the Negro, in some areas and in a good many respects, is ingrained in him as deeply as is his attitude toward taking a piss in public. If a man sees a bum taking a piss on the sidewalk in the presence of his wife the man is outraged. If a Negro rises against the Southerner, or seeks to rise against him, the Southerner is outraged, he's furious and his fury is regulated by his pride.

This Texas kid had too much pride. His attitude toward the Negro, and his temper, both were regulated by that pride. Pride in a Southerner is something quite apart from pride in other people. There should be a word for it.

All of which doesn't matter.

Saw Bob Miller's by-line tonight, from somewhere in Arizona. So Uncle Robert is on a Stateside beat.

Hit Parade tonight had No. One as "Coming in on a Wing and Prayer." Down south they sang "there's a burlesque theatre where the boys all go to see queenie the cutie of the burlesque show—she's as fresh and as wholesome as the flowers in May and she hopes to retire to the farm someday . . . . . " Or else, "One Ball Riley (Here comes the Goddam Son of a bitch)."

It seems possible that Tin Pan Alley is making a noble effort to write a war song. I wish 'em luck.

A tall thin boy with long sideburns walked in tonight, said hello—I'm from Betsy town. I didn't recognize him. He was Bob Sneed who used to drive a Checker Cab, been in the Army 10 months, over here eight. Been bad sick, stomach ulcers, operation, wired his Dad a preacher that he wasn't expected to live, laid in recovery ward 34 days and couldn't move an arm, said worst case they'd ever had.

Well we talked. He told me about people. Two—Siney Grindstaff & Bounce Carter—are here, so are several others from home. Being as he used to drive a cab he knows every street and house number in town, told me Dad lives two houses from Helen instead of one. Also said Bill Whitson and Earl Marshall are still at Jackson, which amazed me.

We talked about the Country Kitchen and Fritz Brandt's and the Hitching Post that burned down. Showed me a lot of pictures of people and I tried to recognize the backgrounds but couldn't. Couldn't think of the name of Valley Forge, which convinces me that when other things—so new and different—crowd your mind some of the old familiar things are liable to be temporarily lost in the shuffle.

It was good to hear the old names and discuss people, even a lot of those I'd heard of but didn't know very well. Even better, it was good to sit back and listen to the Mother Tongue—the queer inflections of speech which could only come from home.

The news for three days has been of the big fight over the Canal when the Japs brought down 120 planes, hit from three directions and got hell knocked out of them. First reports were 77 planes, later raised to 94. We lost six. That was Wednesday.

Read a story by George Jones this morning describing the thing and I got that old feeling. All I could see was the air over Cactus that day the Japs hit Tulagi—and feel again the intense excitement on the ground.[9]

Since I've been in the hospital I've caught myself living over again the days down there, seeing everything as clearly in my mind as I ever saw it with my eyes—the men on the front—pale, bearded, big-eyed, their fatigues no longer green but an indefinite mud color—the boys in the rear—wearing shorts,

burnt beautifully by the sun, trick beards, rumors of going home, bitching—
the combat crews who somehow could carry the jauntiness of the Air Force
even to the mud floors and the palm groves.

Looking back I realize even more now than I did then—and I was aware
of it then—that the friends a man makes in a place like that are the one thing
that makes such an existence what it is: not too bad then and pleasant to remember.

So, at the age of 23, I am in danger of becoming a war veteran who, like
the pathetic characters of my boyhood, lived too much in the memory of
things. All of which is silly. At the time I saw no glory, no grand life in the works
on Guadalcanal. I felt myself a part of something historic, but there was no
glamour in it. Why should there be now? I'm nuts.

Wednesday, June 23. Caught snatches of a radio interview with Joe Foss and
his wife. Couldn't get it all, but listening several rooms away I heard Joe falter
and blush verbally thru several minutes of smooth questioning by a suave announcer. The wife, as ill at ease as Joe, followed in the same channel.

I saw Joe only once on Cactus but he impressed me as the sort of person
who must go thru hell for patriotic publicity. On the Canal he was in his
element—wearing a black baseball cap, fatigue pants and a T shirt. He was full
of life, just on his way for a scramble. He jumped into the jeep full of fliers, put
his foot on the running board—pardon—the fender, turned and waved. Bob
Cromie, who almost idolized him, was working up a story. Joe at that time had
passed Capt. Smith but he didn't have his 26 planes at the moment, as I recall.
Bob had one favorite quote from Joe. I don't remember exactly how it went
but they were discussing fighter tactics and Joe replied, "A lot of crazy people
live around here."

Also saw a newsreel in which Joe made a speech, obviously in torment.
Crucified—the price of becoming a hero. At least, tho, Joe is the real goods.
He is not a *Liberty* mag phoney.[10]

Bill Hipple is in town and a story quoted him as saying "Tired of the
States—want to get back into action." Crap—the draft board probably made
him much more weary. I don't blame him for getting the hell out.

Story on *Yank* and the boys in the *Advertiser* 'smorning.[11]

-0-

There is no point in my going into my tension here—I'm almost nuts—
no word from Helen, none from the office—nothing. And they keep me in this
goddam hospital as if I were actually ill. I'm beginning to tighten up to the
point where, if something doesn't happen soon, I will be sick. Wrote Helen a
long letter yesterday, explaining everything the best I could.

Sunday, June 27. No word from Helen, but a letter yesterday said today would probably be it.

Said she had a letter from Brodie who told her I was to be recalled. I doubt that, but a letter from Forsberg referred to "replacement for you," and a cable yesterday said I am to remain here "until further notice."

I'm not worrying about it.

Monday, June 28. Yesterday afternoon Bushemi brought in Vic and a folder of mail from Jackson—now T/Sgt. Jackson—which contained all the information I could ever desire. Briefly, I was told:

1. That I am to be recalled.
2. That I'm under consideration for promotion to tech.
3. That I have an offer to do a book.

All this, plus $75 from the Bank of New South Wales. It's wonderful news.

But there is one hitch. The circulation of *Yank* in the Pacific is going to be a terrific job and I am in a position to be of a great deal of help here for awhile. I'm not crazy about the idea of hanging around here too long, but it seems that I should stay here and help get things set up. That will mean, I hope, a junket into the islands again and a chance to see a couple of places I still haven't reached in the area.

The office was very complimentary, which I appreciated. They plan pulling back four of us; Spence indicated that I might work out of New York for a time and then go overseas again. Could be.

At any rate, things seem to be breaking right down the alley. I'm still a little numb.

No word from Helen, but letter yesterday said she knew I was in hospital—Dad, fearing detection, told her.

"The Army of the Pacific"

Friday, July 2. I got out of the hospital on Wednesday, the 30th, and an hour after I got to the office I learned about Rendova and Munda. Now I don't know what to do—I should be there.[1]

Wednesday night we killed a quart of bourbon and last night, without intending to, I got mixed up with rye. Had dinner with Bill Hipple, looking like a million dollars again after having gained back 25 pounds in the States. Bill and I talked of people and places and I realized that, compared to him, I hadn't been anywhere in the Pacific.

Leaving Bill I ran into Allan Lacy from home. We got drunk on his whiskey at the Moana. He's a 2nd Lt, FA.

Still no word from Helen. I'm beginning to get worried.

This thing down South has me down.

Saturday, July 3. Letter from Helen that she is all right but sweating it out (on the 28th). Still no word.

At the moment I'm in a hellish mood—I wish I'd never come up here, because I've been screwed since I set foot on this rock. In the first place I feel like hell, physically, and look the same. In the second place I feel like hell mentally and as a result am practically tongue-tied. People I've met since Wednesday must think I'm a complete dope; I'm not even articulate.

I've played everything with my feet—didn't miss a trick: left my area wide open and a new offensive starts, got myself into the position in which, having been told I was to go home, it will be twice as hard to go back; shot off my mouth and overestimated my damned importance in asking Spence to let me "stay here and help out." What I'd like to do—upon word from Helen—is to get on a plane and go South, or else get a direct order from the office calling me to N.Y.

The thing that galls me is being away from the area at a time like this: I feel like a fool. Everything is straight up in the air.[2]

Balthrope won't let me leave until he hears from the office, I don't want to leave until I hear from Helen, and the office is bound to want New Ga. covered, regardless of when I should go home. I'm not dope enough to want to tear back down there when I might be all but set to leave for the Mainland— and yet I'm a newspaperman enough to not want to miss out down there. It's a helluva thing to be South Pacific correspondent and be in a dump like this at a time like this—I feel like a guy caught off third base.

And I screwed up on this P.E. deal: I don't want it—not now. I either want to go home under orders, or South under orders. Golden Boy sure got his ears pinned back: " . . . obviously in a position to be of help here . . . ." Balls!

The mental strain of everything happening at once is tough, coming on top of sweating out the Captain, sweating out the hospital, sweating out Helen. I feel as tho I've aged five years since May 20. And drinking to kill tension is definitely not the answer. I've got to settle down—this business is strictly no good.

Monday, July 5. Cable from Spence to Miller. "Advise M that baby boy born dead this morning. Helens physical and mental condition excellent."

I have cabled Helen.

Tuesday, July 6. Cabled flowers; wrote Helen. FD refused payment $148 per diem. Broke.[3]

Saturday, July 10. I have been numb since Monday, and unwell—for the first time in my life—purely as a result of nerves and attending elements since before I left the hospital. This trip has been a fiasco. Apparently many of the things which could have gone wrong, have gone wrong.

But there is a brighter side, even in this mess. I think I am now a tech sergeant. Orders have come thru for my return to the area where, according to a letter from Brodie, I am to await my replacement.

Above everything else I want to go home to Helen, but a return to work will help a little. I should be home in a couple of months or so, anyway.

Miller & Bushemi are waiting on transportation now and I am to follow them a week later, meeting John in Fiji, and we will go back to Noumea. It seems silly to go all the way back to New Cal without getting up to Munda. John is rarin' to get started and I'll welcome some kind of return to normalcy.

I'm absolutely of no use whatsoever here—not worth a damn for anything. This is not my kind of work, not my territory and not my element. The hell with it.

The stillbirth news came by cable from the office to Miller who opened it, left the room for ten minutes to talk to the Captain, invited me to "have a cup of coffee" and then, when I said, "give me the cable," gave it to me. I had caught a glimpse of a couple of words when he opened it.

My feeling is—and was instantly—for Helen alone. There can be no grief for a child who never knew conscious life. Helen, who wrote such happy letters and thruout pregnancy looked forward so eagerly to having a child, must be miserable, so heart-broken, that she may take time to recover. That is the thing I dread for her, and pray that she won't be affected inordinately by it. I feel so helpless here because there seems so little I can do, and everything I can think of seems so small. I want to be with her. I don't know how this has hit her—whether she can take it in her stride, or whether she can't—she's such a tender person. She has a terrific capacity for sympathy, and she's sensitive. This is a terrible thing for her—something which she didn't deserve. I don't suppose it could possibly be a question of "deserving" a tragedy—it's one of those things that happen. But Helen—why should she have it happen to her? No one could have "deserved" it less than she.

My personal sense of loss is not so strong and has become no more or less with the full realization of what has happened. That is a heartless, brutal thing to say, but it is true. I wanted a child and if the boy had been born alive we would have been very happy. But a child now faces every sort of uncertain future. I am sorry he won't have a chance to live it out, come what may, but Helen and I are young and perhaps we can have another—when we may be able to see ahead farther than we can now, when we can give him a normal life right from the start.[4]

I hope Helen will take it well, and I think she will. She's an intelligent girl, but she must need me now to help her. It's been my fault that she's had everything tough, and now I'm not even around to help her absorb the shock. I wonder how she feels?[5]

Tuesday, July 13. Miller and Bushemi left tonight.

Friday, July 16. Cable from Helen on 14th saying she is "steadily improving" then a letter form her dated the 3rd, saying how anxious she was. Letter from Dad today, dated 5th gave the details and said Helen was in good shape. Nihill moved in this afternoon.

Saturday, July 17. I'll probably shove off Monday.

Monday, July 19. Take off tomorrow morning at 5:30.

I'm going to leave this record here with Capt. Balthrope because I'm afraid to try to run it thru customs inspectors again.

I hate to do it.

Here is contained an account of the past eight and one-half months, a period which I shall never forget. I want to remember every minute of it, with only a few exceptions.

I do not feel that this record is in any way complete. In reading it I find gaps which should have been filled by, not so much of my personal trials, but by more of the lives of the hundreds of people in the islands with whom I came in contact.

It is too self-centered.

This record will be continued in a loose-leaf notebook on—I hope—a typewriter.[6]

As I understand it I am to go to New Caledonia and wait for a replacement. I may do that, and I may go to New Georgia instead. As of today we still haven't taken Munda.

I need to get back to writing and, even more, I need a refresher course on the islands. Honolulu, in two months, has deadened too much of me toward the men down there—not deadened, but temporarily made me forget things which so many people have never realized, never known. I have seen just how little civilians and soldiers alike understand . . . . . so many things.

It is wrong to say they are not conscious of war—they are—but they are not aware of war as a man in combat is aware of it. They are unable to feel as he feels, so deeply.

It is foolish to act as seer, to button-hole people and say, "why are you so wrapped up in your own little world when . . . . . " because I have been wrapped in my little world thruout the pages of this book. It seems to be an unfortunate ingredient of human nature.

Perhaps I can in some way, however, present to the people the case of the Army of the Pacific.

This is the diary of Sgt.
Marion M. (Mack) Morriss 20456209
Correspondent on the staff of
Yank—The Army Weekly
New York City

NOTES

Introduction

1. Two typed copies and a carbon of the story, dated 21 July 1941 and called by the Public Relations Office, "How the Soldier Reacted to President Roosevelt's Speech," are among the manuscripts, letters, notebooks, and diaries Morriss left at his death and which are now in the possession of his widow, Helen Morriss Wildasin, Elizabethton, Tennessee. Hereafter, this collection will be cited as Morriss Papers. The song "I'll Be Back in a Year, Little Darlin'" was written by Ben Shelhamer Jr., Claude Heritier, and Russ Hull in 1941 and recorded by the Prairie Ramblers. (I am indebted to Ronnie Pugh of the Country Music Foundation, Nashville, for this information.) For the politics of the situation in which Morriss found himself, see Robert Bruce Sligh, *The National Guard and National Defense: The Mobilization of the Guard in World War II* (New York: Praeger, 1992); for the army's predicament in the face of the growing world crisis, Forrest C. Pogue, *George C. Marshall: Ordeal and Hope* (New York: Viking Press, 1965); for the logistical problems, Marvin A. Kriedberg and Melton G. Henry, *History of Military Mobilization in the United States Army, 1775-1945* (Westport, Conn.: Greenwood Press, 1975), 541-694; and for the mood of the nation as war approached, Robert Ketchum, *The Borrowed Years: America on the Way to War, 1938-1941* (New York: Random House, 1989).

2. Mack Morriss to B.H. Morriss, 23 November 1941, Morriss Papers. As could be expected, the one and one half million men in uniform were disappointed to learn that they would not be going home. There was much griping. One soldier was quoted as saying, "To hell with Roosevelt and Marshall and the Army and especially this goddam hole and the Germans and the Russians and the British. I want to get the hell out of this hole." *Life,* 18 Aug. 1941. But the mass desertions some feared, or professed to fear, and symbolized by the word *OHIO*—Over the Hill in October—scrawled on latrine walls, never occurred.

3. Morriss typed out his thoughts on three consecutive days, beginning at 4:15 P.M., 7 Dec. and ending Tuesday morning, 9 Dec. 1941. The quotation is from the first entry, which is dated 7 Dec., but which was actually written the following morning. In the first entry he was "trembling with excitement," in the second, sitting in the lobby of the Wade Hamilton Hotel in Columbia listening to FDR's call for war in a speech that he thought

would "be recorded in history, would be written about, spoken about for centuries and generations to come," and in the third more sober assessment, asking with others, "Where's that Navy we were always thanking God for?" Multiple copies of these manuscripts are in the Morriss Papers.

4. Mack Morriss to B.H. Morriss, 20 Oct. 1941, Morriss Papers. Helen Davis worked at the *Elizabethton Star* (where Morriss had been editor in the summer of 1940), doubling as social page editor and bookkeeper. Their relationship started out in a casual fashion but began to turn serious by the Christmas of 1940. They were married 21 Dec. 1941.

5. Mack Morriss to B.H. Morriss, 4 Apr. 1942, Morriss Papers. Erskine Hawkins was playing the Negro dance at the City Auditorium in Columbia. In that era of segregation, the whites went only to sit in the stands and watch the dancers or to listen to the music. Morriss and his friends were drinking and had had a scuffle with some "college boys" prior to the incident. MPs arrived on the scene quickly, and since no disciplinary action was taken against Morriss, it would seem that the police officer overreacted. By that time there was little love lost between the town and the camp. J.W. "Bill" Arbuckle, who was at Fort Jackson from 1940 to 1942, wrote that "the 'open arms' welcome with which many people greeted our arrival soon wore pretty thin, with resentment growing among civilian and military." *A Front Seat in Hell* (Johnson City, Tenn.: Overmountain Press, 1991), 33.

6. Mack Morriss to Helen Morriss, 8 and 12 May 1942, Morriss Papers. His statement in Ralph's is in Ward Morehouse, "Broadway after Dark," *New York Sun,* 4 June 1942. A description of the *Yank* offices at the time of start up, sparsely furnished with confiscated enemy alien property, is in "Yank for the Yanks: New Army Paper Gets Going and Starts Drawing Soldier Staffers from the Ranks," *Newsweek,* 18 May 1942. A number of the men originally sent up from the ranks failed to make the grade and were returned to their previous duty. Both John Hay and Ed Cunningham became *Yank* staffers.

7. "An Army Newspaper: Report of Special Committee of the Joint Army and Navy Advisory Committee on Welfare and Recreation," 23 Feb. 1942, Record Group 407, National Archives. The committee was chaired by Egbert White, a *Stars and Stripes* correspondent in World War I and afterward an executive of the New York advertising firm of Batten, Barton, Durstin and Osborn. White was the man most responsible for the creation of *Yank* and was its first executive officer.

8. Telephone conversation with Robert M. White, II, 31 May 1994.

9. B.H. Morriss to Mack Morriss, 18 Oct. 1942. A nearly complete run of *Yank* makes up part of the Morriss Papers. The easiest access to the paper today is *Yank, the Army Weekly, 1942-1945,* 4 vols. (New York: Arno Press, 1967). The orders for the redeployment story are in Lt. Col. Jack Weeks to Lt. Col. Charles Holt, 29 May 1945, Morriss Papers. Weeks was the last executive officer at *Yank* and was responsible along with C.H.E. Stubblefield for compiling what amounted to be the after action report in "History of Army Information Branch, Information and Education Division, War Department" (No. 2.3.13), Center of Military History, Washington, D.C.

10. Mack Morriss, Handwritten Manuscript (no title), 6 pp., 16 Sept. 1960, Morriss Papers.

11. Prior to World War I, Carter County, which was largely rural, contributed no less than three companies to the 3rd Infantry Regiment, Tennessee National Guard. With the outbreak of war in 1917, the 3rd Regiment became the 117th Regiment, 30th Infantry Division, in the reorganization brought on by mobilization. The 30th Division went into battle in July 1918 and in the Somme offensive in late September, led the assault that broke the Hindenburg Line. Elmer A. Murphy and Robert S. Thomas, *The Thirtieth Division in the World War* (Lepanto, Ark.: Old Hickory, 1936). By the time the Government Printing Office published American Battle Monuments Commission, *30th Division: Summary of Operations in*

the World War in 1944, the 30th Division was once more driving east, this time toward the old German imperial city of Aachen. Called by Allied correspondents "Work Horse of the Western Front," and by the Germans, "Roosevelt's SS," the 30th is widely held to be the premier infantry division to fight on the Western Front. Robert L. Hewitt, *Work Horse of the Western Front: The Story of the 30th Infantry Division* (Washington, D.C.: Infantry Journal Press, 1946). Morriss caught up with his old unit on 16 Sept. 1944, the fourth anniversary of the call-up of the Guard, near Maastricht and found a few Carter Countians still in "A" Company. His story, "My Old Outfit," *Yank*, 1 Dec. 1944, was reprinted in the *Star* back home and in *Liberty*, 28 July 1945. In addition to the above, I am also indebted to Dan W. Crowe for material he provided and his insight into the military tradition of Carter County. Crowe, who has a number of works on the area to his credit, knew Morriss personally and regarded him as both a friend and a teacher.

12. Ira Wolfert, "The Army's Magazine Reflects a Vivid Picture of the War," *PM*, 29 Apr. 1945, a review of the first *Yank* anthology, *The Best from Yank, the Army Weekly* (New York: E.P. Dutton, 1945). Two years later in a review of the second anthology to be published, *Yank: The GI Story of the War* (New York: Duell, Sloan and Pearce, 1947), William Hogan wrote in "The Story of Yank and the GIs," *San Francisco Chronicle*, 18 May 1947, that "*Yank* writers were working for probably the most critical audience in the world. They had to be accurate; they had to know what they were talking about." He concluded that "the most impressive writing seems to have been done by Walter Bernstein, in his accounts from the Mediterranean, by Mack Morriss, from Germany, and Ralph G. Martin, from North Africa, Sicily, and the Western Front."

13. Mack Morriss, typed manuscript (no title), 2 pp., 22 Aug., with handwritten addenda, 3 pp., 25 and 30 Aug., 1973, Morriss Papers.

14. Mack Morriss to Helen Morriss, 18 Jan. 1945, Morriss Papers.

15. Biographical information and Morriss's comment on the novel are in Mack Morriss, handwritten manuscript (no title, no date, but probably written in 1973 for use in his obituary), 4 pp., Morriss Papers. As this work was getting under way, Marc Thompson, a graduate student in English, elected to write his thesis on *The Proving Ground*. For this, see Marc A. Thompson, "From Old Field to the Minefield: The Call of the World in *The Proving Ground*, A Tennessee WWII Novel by Mack Morriss" (masters thesis, East Tennessee State University, 1989). I am endebted to Marc for helping me collect, sort, and copy the Morriss documents and papers.

16. The quotations are from "Remembering Mack Morriss," *Elizabethton Star*, 23 Feb. 1986. Cleo Reed, manager of Radio Station WBEJ, has given me access to historical documents at the station and has helped me in my understanding of this period of Morriss's life. Edward G. Speer, a graduate student engaged in Carter County research on an unrelated subject, has helped me with the minutes of the meetings of the Board of Commissioners, City of Elizabethton, Elizabethton City Hall. I have also used with profit Frank Merritt, *Later History of Carter County, 1865-1980* (Elizabethton: privately published, 1986). Morriss's comment on writing is in Mack Morriss to Ralph G. Martin, no date but probably written in the summer of 1972. The letter is handwritten and corrected, which leads me to think it was typed and sent. On the other hand, there is the possibility it was not. In any case, it was in response to Martin's suggestion that he do a biography of Billy Graham or perhaps write a historical novel about the Tennessee frontier. Morriss's letter and Martin's correspondence are in the Morriss Papers.

17. From 1944 to 1959, Morriss's stories, articles, and reviews appeared in *Mademoiselle, McCall's, Life, Collier's, Cosmopolitan, Holiday, Saturday Review,* and *True*. Of these, the best known was a short fiction piece about mountain justice called "Courtesy of the Road,"

which was translated into several languages and reprinted in the Alfred Hitchcock anthology, *Stories My Mother Never Told Me* (New York: Random House, 1963), 229-33.

18. Herbert Mitgang, "Tennessee G.I.," *New York Times Book Review,* 22 July 1951.

19. Paul Fussell was himself a combat veteran of World War II and won international acclaim for his work on World War I, *The Great War and Modern Memory* (New York: Oxford University Press, 1975). His *Wartime: Understanding and Behavior in the Second World War* (New York: Oxford Univ. Press, 1989), however, met with a less than enthusiastic reception from the literary establishment. The quotation from Morriss is in *The Proving Ground* (New York: Duell, Sloan and Pearce, 1951), 2-3. Morriss wrote the novel under the title "The Gullible" and changed it at the suggestion of his editor.

20. James Jones to Mack Morriss, 12 Nov. 1957, Morriss Papers. Jones had just finished *Some Came Running,* for which, two months later, he would be hit with a flood of abuse. Frank MacShane, *Into Eternity: The Life of James Jones, American Writer* (Boston: Houghton Mifflin, 1985), 162-68. To date I have not been able to locate the letter Morriss wrote Jones, but the circumstances prompting him to write it seem to have been his great admiration for Jones as a writer on the one hand, and, more personally, a conversation Jones had with Brodie some time before in which Morriss's own novel was discussed on the other. Had I had the opportunity to talk with Morriss about the two works, I would have been especially interested in his reaction to the Appalachian character that figures so prominently in both—Prewitt from Harlan County, Kentucky, in *From Here to Eternity* and Witt from Breathitt County in *The Thin Red Line* (in *Whistle* published after both Jones and Morriss were dead, he is Prell from West Virginia). Reading Morriss's copy of *The Thin Red Line,* I was struck by the character Witt. I was born and raised in Laurel County in the foothills of the Kentucky Cumberlands, and my father was born and raised in Harlan County. Never before—or after (except perhaps in the stories of Gurney Norman)—have I seen my own people portrayed so accurately and honestly. I wondered how Jones could have pegged us so exactly, and as it turned out so did others. One of these, Professor Loyal Jones of Berea College, shared his work with me, a manuscript now published as "James Jones' Appalachian Soldier in His World War II Trilogy," *Journal of the Appalachian Studies Association,* Vol. 3 (1991), 152-65, as well as his notes taken from telephone interviews with men who had served with Jones in "F" Company, 27th Infantry. The real Appalachian soldier who was the model for the three character was Robert Lee Stewart of Letcher County, Kentucky.

21. The quotation is from Wolfert's review, cited in note 12 above. The incident itself is described in detail in the 23 May 1943 entry in the diary.

22. Morriss was referring to New York and the so-called "Home Front" in general when he wrote out his thoughts while waiting for his final travel orders to be cut. "I am tired," he wrote, "of the fake patriotism of the War Bond cuties, of the intellectual sophistication, of the bad movies and stinking radio plugs." Mack Morriss, typed manuscript (no title), 3 pp., 24 Oct. 1942, and beginning, "I was told today that we are 'on call.'" Three copies in Morriss Papers.

Yank also had had its share of troubles in the early months, the main one being that having billed itself as the fighting man's paper, there was very little action as yet to cover. The correspondents had to be content with "getting ready to fight" stuff that while a poor second to the real thing, was better than nothing. The frustration spilled over into print in the 19 Aug. issue when managing editor Bill Richardson wrote an editorial called "To Whom It May Concern," asking "When in God's Name Do We Fight?" Syndicated columnist Henry McLemore sneered at the *Yank* men for fighting from a "Foxhole in Gotham" (*Baltimore News-Post,* 1 Sept. 1942), but the sarcasm was wasted on editors throughout the country who agreed that wanting to fight was laudable. A significant segment of the press came to

Yank's defense—"*Yank* Goes Overseas," *Parade*, 29 Aug. 1942; Leonard Safir, "*Yank the Army Weekly*," *New York Mirror*, 28 Sept. 1942, and James T. Howard, "*Yank the Army Newspaper* Is Bawdy and Bold ... A Robust Journal Written by and for Men Only," *PM*, 30 Oct. 1942—and the War Department chose to put a humorous face on the episode. At the same time, however, and seemingly not known at the New York office, the editorial staff had made a powerful enemy in Hollywood as a result of a column called "Hollywood in Wartime." The offending columns had satirized Louis B. Mayer and Mickey Rooney in particular and the movie industry's contribution to the war effort in general. (This episode can be found in RG 407, NA, in particular in Gen. F.H. Osborn, director, Special Services, to Fred W. Beetson, executive vice-president, Association of Motion Picture Producers, 9 Sept. 1942.) The upshot was that Richardson and White lost their jobs—both transferred to London to set up the first overseas edition. Franklin S. Forsberg replaced White as executive officer and Joe McCarthy replaced Richardson as managing editor. Both men held these positions for most of the war.

23. Howard Brodie to Mack Morriss, 15 May and 26 July 1975, Morriss Papers. In the 15 May letter, Brodie wrote that he had "got a partial copy of Jones's manuscript, in which he mentions my South Pacific sketches (your name is mentioned ...'with *Yank* writer named Mack Morriss.' It's limited to that in this Pacific section since it's an art book)." The book in question is James Jones, *WWII: A Chronicle of Soldiering* (New York: Grosset and Dunlap, 1975), published that following October. (Art Weithas did the graphics for this work.) Brodie went on to quote from the manuscript: "Brodie and Morriss were on Guadalcanal the same time my outfit was ... what Brodie called the 'Horse's Neck' was in fact what we called the 'Horse's Head' and got its name from the fact that the whole complex of hills was named the 'Galloping Horse' by some bright young staff officer because that is what it looked like in an aerial photo" (*WWII*, 57-58). In fact, Brodie and Morriss were not with Jones's outfit, the 27th Infantry, which took the Galloping Horse, but rather were with the 35th Infantry on a neighboring complex called the Sea Horse, which also had a "neck" and a "head." The mistake arose out of the twin facts that Brodie's sketches obviously portrayed 25th Division infantrymen (both the 27th and the 35th Regiments belonged to the 25th) and that one of the sketches had been labeled "from the Horse's Neck front." The reference to the diary is in Mack Morriss, handwritten notes (no title, no date), 3 pp., in the possession of his son, LCDR David M. Morriss, Washington, D.C.

24. In the order of publication, the books mentioned in the text are Richard Tregaskis, *Guadalcanal Diary* (New York: Random House, 1943); John Hersey, *Into the Valley* (New York: Alfred A. Knopf, 1943); Samuel Eliot Morison, *The Struggle for Guadalcanal, August 1942-February 1943* (Boston: Little, Brown, 1949); James Jones, *From Here to Eternity* (New York: Charles Scribner's Sons, 1951); James Jones, *The Thin Red Line* (New York: Charles Scribner's Sons, 1962); Samuel B. Griffith, II, *The Battle for Guadalcanal* (Philadelphia: J.B. Lippincott, 1963); Thomas G. Miller, *The Cactus Air Force* (New York: Harper and Row, 1969); and James Jones, *Whistle* (New York: Delacorte Press, 1978). The most comprehensive history to date is Richard B. Frank, *Guadalcanal* (New York: Random House, 1990), which makes more use of Japanese sources than previous works. Norman Mailer's opinion is in *Cannibals and Christians* (New York: Dial Press, 1966), 112. Given the relationship between Jones and Mailer, the latter's statement might equally be interpreted as compliment or slur.

25. De Witt Gilpin, associate editor, *Salute*, to Mack Morriss, 24 July 1947, and Mack Morriss to De Witt Gilpin, 29 July 1947, Morriss Papers. Gilpin had covered the European theater for *Yank* during the last months of the war. *Salute* was one of many magazines started up after the war, and it billed itself as "Produced by former editors and writers for *Yank* and *Stars and Stripes*."

Morriss was not alone in feeling that the "Army got the short end of the publicity thing." James Jones recalled his feelings when the 19 Mar. 1943 issue of *Yank* found its way into the hospital ward where he and others from his unit were recovering from wounds and injuries suffered on Guadalcanal in the January fighting. On the cover was a Brodie sketch of a 25th Division infantryman—readily identifiable because of the two blue birds tattooed on his breasts—and the caption, "Last Days at Guadalcanal." "We all saw the word *Guadalcanal* often enough—always attached to something about the Marines," Jones wrote. What attracted the men in his ward to this particular issue were the Brodie Sketches. "We kept poring over them until someone put them away," Jones continued. "We were astonished. Somebody *had* understood. We *did* exist after all. And in the next days we would get them out and pore over them again and again, there in the wilderness of the suburbs of Auckland, New Zealand. *WWII*, 58.

26. Morriss, Notes. The entry he had made on his birthday, 11 Nov. 1942— ". . . no son of mine will ever lift a gun if I can help it . . ."—caused him to scribble:

> quote "no boy of mine. . . ."
> my gen. will do better.
> if anything, worse
> you become pro, not fodder.

At the time he wrote this, his only son, David, had just begun his first year at the United States Naval Academy, and Morriss was as proud of him as any father could possibly be. These notes in fact were included in a long letter he wrote David, 16 Sept. 1975, the thirty fifth anniversary of his going into service and the last anniversary he would keep. Letter is in the possession of LCDR David M. Morriss, Washington, D.C.

27. Mack Morriss died 18 Feb. 1976. Newspapers across the state and the nation noted his passing and tended to emphasize his role in local government and community service. The quotation is from the *New York Times*, 20 Feb. 1976.

"Going Overseas"

1. The records indicate that in addition to Morriss's ship, *Tjisadane*, the transports *Mormacsea*, *Cape Flattery*, *Pennant*, and *Klippfontein*, escorted by light cruiser *Honolulu* and destroyer *Crosby*, an old four stacker built in 1919, sailed from San Francisco 3 Nov. Routing and Convoy Files, PW 2157, Tenth Fleet Records, Naval Historical Center, Washington Navy Yard.

2. The play is on the word *Danlay*, but just what Morriss meant is uncertain.

3. Howard Brodie has already been introduced in the Introduction to this work. He will appear many, many times in the pages to follow.

4. Boni was en route to the Southwest Pacific Area to cover the fighting in New Guinea; Morriss and Brodie were going to the South Pacific Area, which included Guadalcanal. Boni was later wounded at Nassau Bay in July 1943 for which he received the Purple Heart. See, Robert W. Desmond, *Tides of War: World News Reporting, 1931-1945* (Iowa City: University of Iowa Press, 1984), 248-50. For the theater divisions in the Pacific, see John Miller, Jr., *Cartwheel: The Reduction of Rabaul* (Washington, D.C.: Center of Military History, 1959), 2-3. Longitude 159 east, which splits the Solomon chain, divided the two theaters.

5. *Tjisadane* had been built in Amsterdam in 1931 and was listed at 9,288 gross tons.

Like the other Dutch ships making up the convoy, she had been part of the *Koninklijke Paktevaart Maatshappij,* or K.P.M. Line, that operated in the Dutch East Indies before the war. The ships were able to escape the Japanese invasion forces and make port in Australia and India, where they and their crews were placed under charter to the British Ministry of Transport. This agency in turn allocated them to the U.S. Army. For this, see Samuel Milner, *Victory in Papua* (Washington, D.C.: Office of Military History, 1957), 26. *Tjisadana* served throughout the war, was slightly damaged in May 1945 off Ie Island in the Ryukyu Islands one month after Ernie Pyle was killed on Ie, and was returned to the Netherlands Ministry of Shipping in 1946. Roland W. Charles, *Troopships of World War II* (Washington, D.C.: Army Transportation Association, 1947), 305.

6. Boni was picking up and reporting the news of the Battle of the Santa Cruz Islands, the second and, as it turned out, the last carrier engagement of the Guadalcanal campaign, fought 26 Oct. 1942. The United States lost carrier *Hornet* and could only claim damage to the Japanese fleet. Add to this that by a stroke of bad timing the Navy only got around to reporting the loss of carrier *Wasp,* 15 Sept. 1942, on 27 Oct. (just as the news of the Santa Cruz engagement began coming in) and it is easy to see why the news was a bit confusing, especially the American claims of victory. In addition to Morison, *The Struggle for Guadalcanal,* see Eric Hammel, *Guadalcanal: The Carrier Battles* (New York: Crown, 1987).

7. Escort carrier *Altamaha,* loaded with seventy-four planes and fifty-odd tons of aircraft parts, and transports *President Monroe* and *Weltevreden,* carrying over three thousand officers and men of the Second Marine Division, made up the San Diego element of convoy PW 2157. Routing and Convoy files, Tenth Fleet Records, Naval Historical Center, Washington Navy Yard.

8. The "Betsy Flasher" was the Elizabethton High School newspaper, which was printed in the *Star.* Miss Olive Allen, an English teacher, was the sponsor, and her advice to the student journalists was simple: "Don't just put trashy things in there. Make it good. People on the outside are going to read it." Interview with Miss Olive Allen, 19 July 1992, tape in my possession. In 1964 while Miss Allen was home on furlough from the mission field in Southeast Asia, Morriss broadcast a tribute to her over WBEJ in which he said that "she was one of those teachers of whom, I suppose, it can be said that they do in fact make a life-long impression on their student . . . . beyond that, a life-long influence." Mack Morriss, typed manuscript (no title, radio broadcast), 1 p., dated Sept. 1964, Morriss Papers.

9. *Yank* men got accustomed to being accused of having "a racket." Barrett McGurn, who covered the fighting in the northern Solomons, was hit in the face and chest by shrapnel from a Japanese knee mortar shell on Bougainville and, after the medics cleaned him up somewhat, he made it back to the walking wounded station. Marines there gave him a cup of coffee and one of them asked: "Are you from *Yank?*" "Yes," McGurn replied. "Gee, what a racket," the Marine said. Fifty years later, McGurn wryly commented that maybe *Yank* was a racket—up to a point. "What other soldier—from general on down—could have given himself a week of R & R in New Zealand!" Barrett McGurn to Ronnie Day, 3 Feb. 1994.

10. Morriss's reference is to an article, "Fighting Dirty," *Yank,* 1 July 1942. The lieutenant (who was not named in the story) is shown using hand-to-hand combat techniques on an "enemy" soldier wearing a Japanese uniform.

11. The nurses were from the 39th Army General Hospital and in all there were 119 of them on board. See, Denys Bevan, *United States Forces in New Zealand, 1942-1945* (Alexandra, N.Z.: Macpherson, 1992), 184-89.

12. This parenthetical entry was made later, probably at the time that the news of the invasion reached the ship, which seems to have been 9 Nov. There are three more similar additions, all made during the voyage. That of 12 Nov. refers to the "Second Battle of Guadalcanal, Sea," known officially as the Battle of Guadalcanal; that of 13 Nov. refers to the

Rickenbacker rescue; and that of 30 November refers to the "Battle of Lunga Pt." which came to bear the official name of the Battle of Tassafaronga Point.

13. Eddie Rickenbacker was on his way to the South Pacific war zones on a fact-finding mission for Secretary of War Henry L. Stimson when his B-17 missed Canton Island through a navigational error and went down at sea. Although the mission was secret, the plane's last distress mission with Rickenbacker's signature was picked up, and the news media quickly turned the story into a national drama. After twenty-one days at sea in open rafts, during which one of the men died, the others were rescued. Rickenbacker continued on his mission, visiting both New Guinea and Guadalcanal. By March 1943 his story, Edward V. Rickenbacker, *Seven Came Through: Rickenbacker's Full Story* (New York: Doubleday, Doran, 1943), was in the book stalls. With the war going on, of course, Rickenbacker could not and did not tell the full story, especially the rebuke from Stimson he personally delivered to General Douglas MacArthur. For this and the rest of Rickenbacker's involvement in the war, see Finis Farr, *Rickenbacker's Luck: An American Life* (Boston: Houghton Mifflin, 1979).

14. The naval Battle of Guadalcanal, 11-15 Nov. 1942, was the turning point of the campaign and has extensive coverage in Morison, *The Struggle for Guadalcanal* and Frank, *Guadalcanal*. The history of one ship that participated in the engagement, battleship *Washington,* is in Ivan Musicant, *Battleship at War: The Epic of the USS Washington* (New York: Harcourt Brace Jovanovich, 1986).

15. The convoy split up at Point Yoke, latitude 19°-21' south, longitude 168°-07' west (due south of Samoa and almost due east of Fiji). Destroyer *Farragut* came out from Fiji to escort *Altamaha* to the New Hebrides. *Mormacsea* headed for Fiji. *Cape Flattery, Pennant,* and *Klippfontein* sailed for Noumea, New Caledonia, with *Crosby* and *Honolulu. President Monroe* and *Weltevreden* turned toward Wellington, New Zealand, with the contingent of Marines. *Tjisadana* sailed on alone for Auckland. Routing and Convoy Files, Tenth Fleet, Naval Historical Center, Washington Navy Yard.

16. Morriss somehow managed to hang on to a copy of the fourth number of the "Salt Water Taffy," 21 Nov. 1942, which contained the Brodie sketches. Given the talent on board, the "Taffy" was a rather sophisticated publication as ships' papers go. For this number, Boni did a news roundup and included a discussion of the censorship in effect in the war zone. Morriss did an article on *Yank.* There was an article on what to expect in New Zealand and some cartoons. And, of course, the Brodie sketches, one of which portrayed a soldier gazing over the rail as the rest of the convoy turned away leaving *Tjisadana* alone in the South Pacific.

17. Robert Neville and Merle Miller were both on the staff of *Yank.* Neville was an experienced journalist and had worked for the *New York Times, New York Herald-Tribune, Time,* and *PM.* He had covered both the Sino-Japanese war in China and the Spanish Civil War and was in Warsaw when the European war broke out in 1939. Miller, who was the same age as Morriss, had worked for a year for the *Philadelphia Record* and had gone to Honolulu with *Yank* photographer, John Bushemi, at the same time Morriss and Brodie had shipped out. Mack Morriss to B.H. Morriss, 28 Oct. 1942, Morriss Papers.

18. Brooks Gifford, a California attorney before the war, had replaced Markey as public relations officer in New Zealand in November 1942. Markey, a writer and producer who had been married to actresses Joan Bennett and Hedy Lamar, moved on with headquarters to Noumea. Bevan, *United States Forces in New Zealand,* 278.

Code names were often used by both the men and their families back home. Poppy was the code name for New Caledonia (APO 502). White Poppy was the capital city of Noumea. Other code names Morriss used are:

Button—Espiritu Santo, New Hebrides Islands, APO 708 (often the plural, Buttons, is used just as Santo is often referred to as Santos).

Cactus—Guadalcanal, APO 709
Fantan—Fiji, APO 913
Roses—Efate, New Hebrides, APO 932

19. *Tryon,* named for James R.Tryon, Civil War naval physician and later chief of the
Bureau of Medicine and Surgery and surgeon general, was built at Oakland, California, in
1941. She was acquired by the navy in 1942 and used as a transport evacuation ship throughout the Solomons campaign, carrying casualties back to Suva, Noumea, Wellington,
Auckland, and Brisbane and fresh troops up to the combat areas. Later, *Tryon* served as an
attack transport evacuation ship and took part in the landings in the Marianas, Palaus, and
Philippines, delivering assault troops to the landing areas, then embarking casualties as a
hospital ship.After the war, she was converted to an army transport and renamed *Sgt. Charles
E. Mower* and under that name served first in the army and then again in the navy until struck
from the list in 1960. James L. Mooney, ed., *Dictionary of American Fighting Ships* (Washington, D.C.: Naval Historical Center, 1981), 7:319-20.

20.The orders were either retrieved or copies found.Travel orders authorized Morriss
and Brodie to travel by aircraft, vessel, or rail and set the per diem allowance for food and
quarters. Operating orders directed them to report to the Headquarters, Commanding General (Maj. Gen. Millard F. Harmon), USAFISPA, in Auckland (as it turned out, HQ, CG,
USAFISPA had moved to Noumea, New Caledonia) and detailed their instructions.These
fell into two main categories: (1) they were to work with the Army Exchange Service to help
with the distribution of *Yank* and report on sales and promotion of the paper to the New York
office; and (2) they were on their own initiative to secure the news and feature material
suitable for *Yank.* It was this freedom of action that was the envy of every enlisted man in the
service. Paragraph 6 said in part: "It is hoped that the Commanding General will make it
possible for you to forward eye-witness accounts of air combat by permitting you to join task
forces engaged on combat missions. When permitted to join such task forces, you will be
armed and perform any combat duties assigned to you. *Yank* is a paper for fighting men and
wants, above all, fighting stories."The cover letter to the Commanding General stressed the
same need for freedom of movement and action. "It is particularly requested," the third
paragraph stated, "that Sergeant Morriss and Private Brodie be given the maximum freedom
of movement; that they be free from military duty other than that connected with their
particular mission; and that they be given opportunity to be present in combat action when-
ever possible. *Yank* wants fighting news." Headquarters Detachment Special Services Division, 205 E. 42nd St., New York City, N.Y., Travel Orders Number 167 and Operating
Orders, 12 Oct. 1942 and Franklin S. Forsberg, Acting Officer in charge, *Yank,* to Commanding General, USAFISPA, 13 Oct. 1942, Morriss Papers.

21.John Graham Dowling was the son of actor Eddie Dowling and comedienne Ray
Dooley. He had been with the *Sun* (later the *Sun-Times*) since its founding in 1941 and spent
the entire war covering the Pacific areas. Dowling wrote one of the most famous war songs
of World War II, "I Wanted Wings," a typed copy of which is among the Morriss Papers. See,
obituary (he was killed in a plane crash in Paraguay) in *Time,* 27 June 1955. Francis L.
McCarthy (Morriss has him as Frank) covered both Guadalcanal and later the New Georgia
campaign.

22.The carrier was *Enterprise,* the battleship was *Washington.*

23.This is one of the few times that shipboard scuttlebutt can be checked for accuracy,
and the palm tree story comes up short.The fact was that after grappling with the problem of
war claims in the Solomons, the British in the end decided against compensation. Small
planters like the one whose plantation ended up under the immense airfield at Munda Point
in the New Georgia Group were ruined while Lever Brothers simply wrote off its destroyed

property. Memorandum of Resident Commissioner, British Solomon Islands Protectorate on Proposals for Settlement of Claims of War Damage, 31 Jan. 1945, BSIP 1/III F9/74, Pt. 1, Solomon Islands National Archives (hereafter cited as SINA), and Judith A. Bennett, *Wealth of the Solomons: A History of a Pacific Archipelago* (Honolulu: Univ. of Hawaii Press, 1987), 303.

24. Another tall tale. According to Gary Wills, *Reagan's America: Innocents at Home* (Garden City: Doubleday, 1987), 114, Reagan made one short trip in a small plane in bad weather in 1937 and never got back in a plane for nearly three decades.

25. The story could be apocryphal. It is not the type that would be found in official records or that would find its way into the histories. The 164th Infantry, a North Dakota National Guard unit, was a part of the Americal Division (formed in New Caledonia in May 1942 out of American units stationed there and thus the name *Ameri-cal*) and was the first Army infantry unit to see action on Guadalcanal. The 164th landed on Guadalcanal, 13 Oct. 1942, just in time to undergo the naval bombardment by Japanese battleships during the night of 14 Oct. and to fight with the Marines in defense of Henderson Field during the Japanese counteroffensive that began a few days later. See, Francis D. Cronin, *Under the Southern Cross: The Saga of the Americal Division* (Washington, D.C.: Combat Forces Press, 1951), 28-29, 51-60.

26. William A. Wellman's Paramount production of *Beau Geste,* starring Gary Cooper, was released in the summer of 1939. See, *New York Times,* 3 Aug. 1939.

27. Fought shortly before midnight, 30 Nov. 1942, this surface action—as it turned out, the last in the Guadalcanal campaign—is known officially as the Battle of Tassafaronga and pitted Japanese destroyers against American cruisers. Of the four United States heavy cruisers engaged, three were heavily damaged and one, *Northampton,* was sunk. (*Northampton's* ordeal was portrayed in Herman Wouk's *War and Remembrance* (Boston: Little, Brown, 1978), which was made into a television miniseries). Morriss probably did not know this at the time, but *Honolulu,* the escort for the convoy and the only light cruiser engaged at Tassafaronga, came through unscathed as a result of some fancy ship handling.

28. Lt. Col. Lawrence C. Sherman and Capt. Homer T. Freeman.

29. A few months before the outbreak of the Pacific War in 1941, the Australian journalist, Wilfred G. Burchett, published a book that became required reading for the Allies, *Pacific Treasure Island: New Caledonia* (Philadelphia: David McKay, 4th ed. 1944), in which he referred to the island as the "Malta of the South Seas," the key to the defense of Australia (p. 216). As it turned out, the Burchett analogy was an apt one. When France fell in June 1940, the French high commissioner in Noumea declared for the Vichy government. But the resident commissioner of the New Hebrides to the north declared for the Free French and deposed him in September. The Free French victory in New Caledonia precluded the island being given over to the Japanese as was to be the case in Indo-China. A week after Pearl Harbor, the Free French government made the island available to the United States for use as a base and it was from New Caledonia that the Americans launched their attack on the Solomons. In addition to Burchett, see the works of Sir Harry Luke, British Governor of Fiji and High Commissioner for the Western Pacific, who was involved in the events of 1940: *From a South Seas Dairy, 1938-1942* (London: Nicholson and Watson, 1945); *Cities and Men: An Autobiography* (London: Geoffrey Bles, 1954), 3:112-45; and *Islands of the South Pacific* (London: George G. Harrap, 1962).

"Christmas Day on Cactus"

1. Helen made it a habit to write the date a letter arrived on the envelope, and so we know that she received the 1 Dec. letter on 9 Dec. The only other letter Morriss had been able to post since leaving San Francisco, the V-Mail written on board *Tjisadane* 18 Nov., did in fact make it home (he had expressed doubts that it would), but not until 24 Dec. Actually, Helen's first confirmation that Morriss and Brodie had arrived at their destination came a day before the first letter arrived. Greta Jones, secretary at the *Yank* offices in New York, telegraphed Helen 8 Dec. that "Mother Arrived Safely Brothers New Address," but gave the APO as 715, which was New Zealand. So the 1 Dec. letter was the first to alert her to the fact that he had gone elsewhere. Mack Morriss to Helen Morriss, 18 Nov. & 1 Dec. 1942, Greta Jones to Helen Morriss, 8 Dec. 1942, Mack Morriss to B.H. Morriss, 1 Dec. 1942, Morriss Papers.

2. IAC is an abbreviation for I Army Corps. Morriss served with the Public Relations Office of I Corps during the Carolina Maneuvers, 25 Sept.-1 Dec. 1941.

3. Morriss wrote *Yank* Editor, Captain Hartzell Spence, that "Freeman is a swell guy who understands our situation, and it was he who fixed everything up for us to operate with all the freedom we could possibly have as enlisted men." Mack Morriss to Hartzell Spence, 4 Dec. 1942, Joe McCarthy Papers, Yank Collection, U.S. Military History Institute, Carlisle Barracks (cited henceforth as McCarthy Papers). McCarthy, managing editor of *Yank* for most of the war, saved correspondence and the like for a book he planned to write about the paper. As it turned out, he wrote or edited a half dozen books over his career as a highly successful writer, including his autobiography, *Days and Nights at Costello's* (Boston: Little, Brown, 1980), but never got around to writing the book about *Yank*. After his death, Art Weithas who had been with *Yank* from the beginning, first as Art Director in New York and then as a combat artist in the Pacific, began work on his own book, *Close to Glory: the Untold Stories of WWII by the GIs Who Saw and Reported the War—Yank Magazine Correspondents* (Austin, Tex.: Eakin Press, 1991), and found the black footlocker of papers at Mrs. McCarthy's residence. For a number of years, Weithas has been helping me with my work and had made all of the papers in the footlocker that related to Morriss available to me. In 1993, in a ceremony at the Pentagon on the occasion the 50th Anniversary Commemoration of *Yank*, the papers were presented to the U.S. Army.

4. James Bassett served most of the war on Admiral William F. Halsey's staff and after the war set two of his novels in the South Pacific. The best known, *Harm's Way* (Cleveland: World, 1962), was the basis for Otto Preminger's *In Harm's Way* (Paramount, 1965), which boasted an all-star cast that included John Wayne, Patricia Neal, Kirk Douglas, and Henry Fonda. For a review of the book, see *New York Times Book Review,* 25 Nov. 1962; for a review of the movie, see *New York Times,* 2 Apr. 1965.

5. Sgt. Renaldo Palla was in the PRO section, G-2, HQ, USAFISPA.

6. Heavy cruisers *Vincennes, Astoria, Quincy,* and *Canberra* (Royal Australian Navy) were all sunk on the night of 9 Aug. 1942 in the Battle of Savo Island, the first naval engagement of the Guadalcanal campaign and a disastrous American defeat. The latest work on this battle and one that goes far in setting the record straight is Denis and Peggy Warner, *Disaster in the Pacific: New Light on the Battle of Savo Island* (Annapolis: Naval Institute Press, 1992).

7. The Pacific Hotel (which more recently has housed the South Pacific Commission) overlooks Anse Vata Beach, listed in the guides today as topless. The architecture is reminiscent of the old French style found in New Orleans. Early in the war, the Pacific Hotel served first as General Harmon's headquarters, then as Gen. Alexander Patch's, the commander at the time of the Americal Division. As American installations expanded at nearby Camp

Barnes, the Pacific Hotel was converted into an officers' club. A duo-tone reproduction of a painting by Sgt. Robert A. Laessig is in Benjamin E. Lippincott, *From Fiji through the Philippines with the Thirteenth Air Force* (San Angelo, Tex.: Newsfoto, 1948), 16.

8. Morriss met Sgt. Robby Robertson on board the *Tryon* en route to Noumea. Robertson, referred to in the diary as "Robby," was also a photographer and assigned to PRO, HQ, USAFISPA.

9. "Resisters" was omitted and the space left blank in the diary, but in the story Morriss wrote about Melton, "Meet the Sergeant from Guadalcanal," *Yank*, 13 Jan. 1943, the tale is repeated word for word with resisters in the proper place. Melton had just returned from Guadalcanal, and to celebrate he threw the party that Morriss describes. The party, described as lasting three days, and his ability as a talker, "the talkingest man who ever entered the Army," got him two paragraphs in the official records kept by the unit. Historical Narrative, Hq 347th Fighter Group Two Engine, 7 June 1944, GP-347-Hi (FTR), Oct. 1942-31 Dec. 1943, in USAF Collection, Air Force Historical Research Agency, Maxwell Air Force Base (hereafter cited as AFHRA).

10. Kenneth Markel, Vaughn, and Lloyd Dorsey were all members of the ground maintenance crew of the 67th Fighter Squadron. An undated page from a notebook in the Morriss Papers has a sketch of a propeller with the notations "power unit" and "vacuum" and two groups of four dots carefully arranged. This is probably Morriss's attempt to understand what it was Dorsey had done to the propeller.

11. Elements of the 67th Fighter Squadron flew into the newly finished Henderson Field on Guadalcanal, 22 Aug. 1942, arriving the day after the first Japanese counterattack had been repulsed at the Battle of the Tenaru River (actually the Ilu River) and two days after the first American air units, Marine squadrons, VMF 223 (fighter), and VMSB 232 (dive bomber), had arrived. Thus the 67th was a charter member of what came to be called the Cactus Air Force. In addition to Miller, *The Cactus Air Force*, cited previously in the introduction, see Robert Lawrence Ferguson, *Guadalcanal, the Island of Fire: Reflections of the 347th Fighter Group* (Blue Ridge Summit, Pa.: Aero, 1987). The standard work on Marine aviation is Robert Sherrod, *History of Marine Corps Aviation in World War II* (Washington: Combat Forces Press, 1952), and the official Army Air Force history is Wesley Frank Craven and James Lea Cate, *The Pacific: Guadalcanal to Saipan, August 1942 to July 1944*, Vol. 4 of *The Army Air Forces in World War II*, (Chicago: University of Chicago Press, 1950).

12. The American Volunteer Group (AVG), more popularly known as the Flying Tigers, was disbanded shortly after the United States officially entered the war. Morriss left nothing to indicate that he followed up on the story and the particulars are so vague that I have not been able to verify the "at gunpoint charge." But, it could have happened. Gregory "Pappy" Boyington wrote in his memoir, *Baa Baa Black Sheep* (New York: G.P. Putnam's Sons, 1958), 115, that General Claire Chennault had recommended that he be drafted against his wishes into the Tenth Air Force.

13. John R. Crockett was a close friend of Morriss's and had gone into service with the 117th at Fort Jackson. He later left the unit and became a commissioned officer in the 302nd Infantry. John R. Crockett to Mack Morriss, 1 May 1944, Morriss Papers.

14. Morriss was referring to the fact that Neville left *Yank*, evidently at Eisenhower's request. He ended up with *Stars and Stripes*, replacing Egbert White, the director of the Mediterranean editions (the same Egbert White who had helped found *Yank*), when the latter was fired in a dispute over censorship. For this, see *New York Times*, 28 July 1944.

15. The turf war was mainly over who controlled Brodie's stuff. As Morriss wrote Spence, "Everybody here, including a general commanding and two or three different official outlets for Army publicity, has taken an immediate and very great liking to Brodie's stuff. They think it's wonderful, which it certainly is. And there's the rub. Under our setup—and

they have us by the well-known testicles—the PRO has moved in on Brodie with just too much rank to ignore." Mack Morriss to Hartzell Spence, 11 Dec. 1942, McCarthy Papers.

16. Months later, the piece on Chaplain William R. Smith of Smith's Grove, Kentucky, "All the Boys Call This Chaplain a 'Good Joe,'" *Yank,* 26 Mar. 1943, appeared under the byline Yank Field Correspondent.

17. The two pilots who put on the air show at Tontouta were from the 68th Fighter Squadron. Joe Lynch, a graduate of Georgia Tech in aeronautical engineering, had the reputation of being a daring pilot and, while he survived the war, was killed near the end testing the new jet fighter, the F-100, for North American Aviation Company. Paul Hansen, who also had a reputation as a daring pilot and who also survived the war, was called Ace by his mates because they were sure that he had wrecked at least five or six planes. Interview with William K. Hart, Sr., 31 May 1994.

18. Bill Hart was also a member of the 68th Fighter Squadron. He had started flying as a youth in Johnson City, Tennessee in a glider towed by a Model T Ford and was so determined to get into the Air Corps that he had the local congressman, Carroll Reese, intercede for him when the medical examiners objected to his having a permanent dental bridge. Interview with William K. Hart, Sr., 31 May 1994.

19. Morriss had grown up with Robert Lee Davis, and Bill Hart had known him in flying school at Kelly Field. Davis was in a bomb outfit as the copilot of a B-26 bomber in the Southwest Pacific Area, where in May INS correspondent Pat Robinson flew a mission with his crew. The story was reprinted in the local newspaper as "Correspondent Aloft with Co-Pilot Davis," *Elizabethton Star,* 5-7 May 1942. Morriss was at *Yank* in July 1942 when his father wrote that "Mrs. Davis was notified yesterday that Robert Lee had been missing in action since the 14th." B.H. Morriss to Mack Morriss, 26 July 1942, Morriss Papers. By the time he was reported MIA, Davis was flying transports in the 22nd Transport Squadron. The 24 Oct. 1942 Elizabethton-Bristol High School football game was dedicated to Davis, and the newspaper offered the prayer that he "may still be alive somewhere in the vast expanse of the islands of the Pacific." Davis was one of the first of Morriss's boyhood friends to be killed in the war.

20. In a letter to Spence, Morriss gave Leslie R. Shope's rank as lieutenant colonel.

21. The *Coolidge,* carrying the 172nd Infantry and 103rd Field Artillery, 43rd Division, struck mines in Segond Channel off Luganville, Espiritu Santo (then called the New Hebrides, now Vanuatu) 26 Oct. 1942 and sank. Only two lives were lost, but all the equipment and supplies (including the entire reserve supply of quinine sulfate) was. See, Arthur J. King, M.D., *Vignettes of the South Pacific: The Lighter Side of World War II* (Cincinnati: privately printed, 1991), 47-56. Today, the wreck is a well-known diving attraction. See, David Doubilet, "Wreck of the *Coolidge,*" *National Geographic,* April 1988.

22. Morriss was not alone in playing the good Samaritan to the 172nd. Edgar N. Jaynes, who was 172nd Adjutant, told me that the military personnel ashore "all looked forward to our landing so they could steal from us, a rooky outfit. The reverse happened. No matter what we needed some GI would find it for us." Edgar N. Jaynes to Ronnie Day, 30 June 1993.

23. Al Hine was on his way to the Middle East. He served there as a *Yank* correspondent for the next two years before returning to the New York office and becoming overseas editor. For a decade or more following the end of the war, Morriss and Hine maintained a sporadic correspondence, some of which is in the Morriss Papers.

24. Three of the four pieces appeared in *Yank.* The first was the Melton story already mentioned, the second was the alert story published in *Yank,* 20 Jan. 1943, as "P.S. Nothing Ever Happens Here Except an Air Raid Every Day or So," and the third, the "color," a substantial piece with sketches by Brodie, was published as "With the USAFISPA," *Yank,* 27

Jan. 1943. For obvious reasons, a B-17 crash was not the type of story the paper wanted to run this early in the war.

25. Gen. William I. Rose had brought the first detachment of American troops to Espiritu Santo in May 1942. An account of the initial reconnaissance is in Ritchie Garrison, *Task Force 9156 and the III Island Command: A Story of a South Pacific Advanced Base During World War II, Efate, New Hebrides* (Waban, Mass.: privately printed, 1983), 87-92. The standard work on naval construction is Bureau of Yards and Docks, *Building the Navy's Bases in World War II: History of the Bureau of Yards and Docks and the Civil Engineer Corps, 1940-1946,* 2 vols. (Washington, D.C.: Government Printing Office, 1947).

26. The 26th, 42nd, 98th, and 431st squadrons of the 11th bomb Group (H) arrived in the South Pacific in July 1942, and on the last day of the month, the group commander, Col. LaVerne G. "Blondie" Saunders, led a flight of nine B-17Es to strike targets at Lunga Point, Guadalcanal, opening the assault on that island. In addition to Miller, *Cactus Air Force,* and Craven and Cate, *Army Air Forces in World War II*—both previously mentioned—see Clive Howard and Joe Whitley, *One Damned Island after Another* (Chapel Hill: University of North Carolina Press, 1947), a history of the 7th Air Force to which the 11th Group returned following the Guadalcanal campaign, and 11th Bomb Group Association (H), *Grey Geese Calling: Pacific Air War History of the 11th bombardment Group (H), 1940-1945* (n.p. privately printed by the 11th Bomb Group Association, 1981).

27. The editors back in New York must have agreed with Morriss, for neither piece was published. A number of manuscripts from this period have survived and are in the Morriss Papers. In this case, however, neither did. A sketch Brodie did of the Japanese prisoners showed up much later in "Sketches from the South Pacific," *Yank,* 23 July 1943.

28. All three men were from the 11th Bomb Group. Col. Laverne G. "Blondie" Saunders was the group's commanding officer and something of a legend in the South Pacific. He was soon to be promoted to general. Maj. James V. Edmundson and Capt. Walter Y. Lucas were both pilots.

29. The story was among those in "Yanks at Home and Abroad," *Yank,* 9 Sept. 1942. Morriss wrote Spence that he felt foolish seeing that the incident had happened in the New Hebrides rather than New Guinea (as he had written in the piece) and had felt even more foolish when he had talked to the Negro soldier, who had received the Soldiers Medal and got the real story. Mack Morriss to Hartzell Spence, 31 Dec. 1942, McCarthy Papers.

30. Morriss spent several days at Fort Hood (then Camp Hood) in September 1942 and wrote an article called "Tank Destroyers," which was published in the 7 Oct. 1942 issue of *Yank.*

31. Atabrine was the drug of choice for the suppressive treatment of malaria during World War II. A yellow dye, it is excreted slowly. The effect is cumulative and produces a yellow discoloration of the skin. The recommended treatment was 1½ grains daily or 15 grains weekly. Among the troops in tropical areas, rumors abounded as to the serious side effects of the drug, the most common one being that it caused impotence. As a result, officers had to enforce the taking of the drug. For this and other aspects of tropical medicine during the war, see Thomas T. Mackie, George W. Hunter, III, and C. Brooke Worth, *A Manual of Tropical Medicine* (Philadelphia: W.B. Saunders, 1945).

32. From the direction given for Henderson Field, Morriss was sitting on the ridge just west of the field. He was facing in the direction of Lunga Point (now spelled Lungga on the maps), and the Lunga River would be to his left. Fighter No. 2 was just across the river at Kokum. Brodie provided me with both a description and a sketch of a map of the area. "Mack and I were in a pyramidal tent (with a couple of other enlisted men, one a Navyman) on the jungle covered ridge of that hillock; the 'Cave' was on the cliffside-bank opposite to Henderson, of that hillock. Spreading out below the sharp 40' cliff-bank was a field with

large clumps, 6 to 7,' of huge grass (I'm vaguely associating swordlike) or bushes. . . . I recall them vividly because a crazed cow startled me running past one, and I thought the field would be no place to die with dignity being trampled to death by a lone cow on Guadalcanal. On the far side of the field were distant coconut palms and, I believe, tents going to the beach around Lunga Point. Looking out from that 'Cave' to the palm grove and tents, the Lunga river was a considerable distance to the left unseen behind low jungle growth." Howard Brodie to Ronnie Day, 13 May 1991.

33. By the time Morriss and Brodie arrived on Guadalcanal the last week of December, the situation had tilted heavily in favor of the American forces. From August to November, Japanese forces had made four major attempts to retake Henderson Field—all had ended in disaster. The remaining Japanese troops on the island were dug in to the west of Henderson Field with the line running from the coast up to the hills behind Point Cruz. These forces were in fact stranded and disease and starvation were rampant. (I have it on good authority that there was at least one case of cannibalism.) The Americans, on the other hand, now had three full divisions on the island—Americal, 25th, and 2nd Marines—and were preparing to take the offensive against a foe defending well-prepared positions on some of the most difficult terrain encountered in the war. With the Japanese Imperial Command's decision to withdraw from Guadalcanal at the end of December, the defending units were literally committed to fight to the death. The result was that in terms of casualties among the ground forces, the attacking American forces lost in little over a month almost as many men as fell during the three months of defending the Henderson Field perimeter. The major difference, however, was that the 1st Marines suffered most of the casualties defending the airfield while those that resulted from driving the Japanese from the island were spread among three divisions. Frank, *Guadalcanal*, 598-618.

34. Morriss got a pretty thorough tour of the front as it existed in late December 1942. The road that impressed him as the worst he had ever seen led up to the northeast slope of Mount Austen and had just been named Wright Road in honor of Lt. Col. William C. Wright, commander of the 3rd Battalion, 132nd Infantry, who was killed 19 December when the reconnaissance party he was leading ran into hidden Japanese positions. Although it was not known at the time, 3rd battalion was coming up against the strongest Japanese position in the hills west of Henderson Field, the "Gifu," and in the attack that morning of 26 December, five men had been killed and twelve wounded. Sometime later, Morriss did a pencil sketch (which is in the Morriss Papers) of the jeep coming down Wright Road with a GI holding the wounded soldier and the dead soldier covered and on a litter strapped to the rear. From where he stood, Morriss could see much of the area in which the naval struggle for the island had occurred. Savo, a volcanic island jutting out of the sea at the western entrance to Sealark Channel (now called Ironbottom Sound), lent its name to the first night surface action fought in the campaign, 9 Aug. 1942, in which three American and one Australian heavy cruisers were sunk. Cape Esperance, which is clearly visible from Morriss's vantage point although he did not mention it, appears just to the left of Savo and stands as a sentinel at the northwest tip of the island of Guadalcanal. It lent its name to the night surface battle of 11 Oct. which went in favor of the United States Navy. The transports Morriss saw were beached at Tassafaronga Point and were relics of the Japanese defeat in the mid-November naval and air Battle of Guadalcanal. Before the month was over, Tassafaronga had lent its name to the last major surface action fought, that of 30 Nov. Going back down to the Mataniko River (the name of which Morriss could not spell), he saw the tanks (nine in all had made the attack) that had been destroyed 23 Oct. trying to cross the sand bar at the mouth in the third Japanese attempt to retake Henderson Field. The details of the military action for 26 Dec. is taken from the official account, John Miller, Jr., *Guadalcanal: The First Offensive* (Washington, D.C.: Historical Division, Department of the Army, 1949), 245-46;

those of the Japanese attempt to send tanks across the sandbar at the mouth of the Mataniko River in October come from John L. Zimmerman, *The Guadalcanal Campaign* (Washington, D.C.: Historical Division, U.S. Marine Corps, 1949), 114-16.

35. Henry W. "Harry" Keyes, *Daily Express*.

36. Robert Miller, a UP correspondent and a member of the Guadalcanal Press Club in December 1942, had been on the island longest.

37. Carney L. Givens listed in General Orders No. 67, Headquarters, Americal Division, 31 Dec. 1943 as a master sergeant in the Headquarters Company, Americal Division. The list is of men included in the Presidential Citation of Americal Division who "served in actual combat with the 1st Marine Division, Reinforced, on Guadalcanal at any time during the period 7 Aug. 1942 to 9 Dec. 1942. (I am indebted to Dave Myers for sending me a copy of this document, the original of which is in the National Archives). Morriss's friendship with Givens may explain why so much of the scuttlebutt he picked up turned out to be correct.

38. Hathaway, who had led Company "A" of the Tennessee National Guard into federal service in September 1940, served in the States during the war, rising to the rank of lieutenant colonel. After the war, he returned to Elizabethton and the Barnes-Boring Hardware Store, which he and other members of his family had bought in 1935, and ran it until two days before his death at age eighty seven in the autumn of 1981. "The Colonel . . . the last from the old school," *Elizabethton Star,* 20 Nov. 1981.

39. Morriss must have hitched a ride with VP-12, the Black Cat squadron operating from Henderson in late December, but Richard C. Knott, *Black Cat Raiders of WWII* (Annapolis: Nautical & Aviation, 1981), 86-92, does not mention a mission for 29 Dec. and I have been unable to find any documents relating to it in the archives at the Navy Yard. Morriss's piece on the mission was not published and the manuscript did not survive. The only other mention of the incident was in a confidential report to Spence. "When I went on the PBY raid we had a couple of bursts of ack ack from a 20mm, but I was on the other side of the plane and didn't see it at all," Morriss wrote. "Nevertheless I was scared when a plane zoomed by us as we came over the target; I thought it was a Jap night fighter for a minute but it was one of our own ships. I just caught a glimpse of it against the moon as it went past so I jumped at a conclusion which happily wasn't right." Mack Morriss to Hartzell Spence, 31 Dec. 1942, McCarthy Papers.

40. Col. John M. Arthur's 2nd Marines had been a part of the initial assault force in August 1942 and were not relieved and evacuated to New Zealand until the end of January 1943.

41. William Hipple was a correspondent for the Associated Press at the time of the Guadalcanal campaign. (Later in the war he switched to *Newsweek*.) As so often happened when Morriss sent in a piece he "half-way hoped never saw print," it did—in this instance as "Marine Saga on Guadalcanal; Japs Ain't Supermen, They're Dopes," *Yank,* 26 Feb. 1943.

"Whatta Racket"

1. Since Christmas Day, the 1st and 3rd Battalions of the Americal Division's 132nd Infantry, an Illinois National Guard unit, had been stopped in the advance along the northern slope of Mt. Austin (commonly called the Grassy Knoll) west of Henderson Field by strong Japanese defenses. The 132nd, in fact, was up against the strongest enemy defensive position on the island, the "Gifu," situated between Hills 30 and 31 to the north and Hill 27

to the south and named by the elements of the Japanese 38th Division holding it after a prefecture in central Honshu west of Tokyo. To break the stalemate, the 2nd Battalion, which had been on the beach, was brought up, and the regimental commander, Col. LeRoy E. Nelson, a National Guard officer, was relieved by Lt. Col. Alexander George, a West Pointer. (George had led a reconnaissance battalion on New Caledonia equipped with jeeps, which at the time were also called peeps.) On the morning of 2 Jan, the 2nd Battalion quickly occupied Hill 27, which flanked the Gifu to the south and which had not been included in the Japanese defensive perimeter. Extremely heavy fighting occurred from around 11:00 a.m., 2 Jan. until dawn of 3 Jan. as the Japanese attempted unsuccessfully to retake the hill. I am indebted to the late Wayne M. Douglas (Lt. Col. USA, ret) for my understanding of the action on Hill 27. Colonel Douglas, then a sergeant, assumed command of 1st Platoon, Company E, one of the units that bore the full brunt of the Japanese counterattacks during the fighting of 2-3 Jan., for which he was awarded the Bronze and Silver Stars and a Battle-field Commission. Interviews with Col. Wayne M. Douglas, 25 and 30 June 1992, tapes of which are in my possession along with notes and sketches of the positions on Hill 27. An-other eyewitness account and one that shows the importance of the extremely accurate artillery fire placed on the hill that night is John F. Casey Jr., "An Artillery Forward Observer on Guadalcanal, *Field Artillery Journal,* August 1943, 563-68. Also see, in addition to Miller, *Guadalcanal* and Frank, *Guadalcanal* (both previously cited), the personal account in John B. George, *Shots Fired in Anger* (Plantersville, S.C.: Small Arms Technical Publishing, 1947), 104-28. George, who later was with Merrill's Marauders in Burma, was an expert rifleman and an authority on firearms. Half of the work is a technical description of the small arms used on Guadalcanal.

The Jackson mentioned in this passage was Sgt. Roberts Jackson, who was assigned to the PRO section, HQ, USAFISPA. Since INP photographer Allan Jackson arrived back at Guadalcanal in early January, there is on occasion some confusion as to which Jackson Morriss meant when he simply wrote "Jackson." Keep it in mind that Roberts Jackson was an en-listed man while Allan Jackson was a civilian war correspondent, the context of the passage will usually make clear the identity.

2. In the diary, Morriss left out one *g* in spelling Diggory, which I have corrected. Brodie remembers Venn from the *San Francisco Chronicle* but does not remember the depart-ment the latter worked in. He also remembered that "somewhere, somehow, he did tell me that Diggory Venn was a character in a novel and not his real name, still, he used it on the *Chronicle* and I assume he enlisted in the Corps under that name." Howard Brodie to Ronnie Day, 9 Mar. 1992. A quick check showed Brodie's memory to be correct. Diggory Venn is a character in Thomas Hardy's *Return of the Native.*

3. The wounded man who was the center of the story was Arthur L. Hatfield. But *Yank* never ran the piece. Years later, Morriss put a note with the original manuscript in which he wrote: "This was my first story from Guadalcanal. It was not published; I don't know why—I thought it was a pretty good piece but needed editing. I played John Wayne going up, was terrified when I got there, helped carry this casualty back down." Morriss Papers. The reason the story was not run is probably because, early in the war, the media shied away from stories and photographs of wounded and dead GIs. This changed as the war turned victorious; in fact, Morriss later did a piece, "Battalion Aid," *Yank,* 10 Dec. 1944, during the Siegfried Line campaign, which opened with the description of a GI with his arm blown off.

Robert Cromie was a war correspondent for the *Chicago Tribune.*

4. Morriss replied to his wife's letter, stating that he always tried to write each Thurs-day. Mack Morriss to Helen Morriss, 7 Jan. 1942, Morriss Papers.

5. Col. Douglas H. Gillette. Morriss was perhaps a little unfair in his appraisal. In an

interview at Fort Shafter, Hawaii, Gillette was quite articulate in describing the bravery of the engineers under fire. Robert Trumbull, "Japs Reported Losing Taste for Jungle War," *Honolulu Advertiser,* 24 Aug. 1943.

6. The 35th Infantry was relieving the 132nd on Hill 27 and moving into position to attack the complex of hills known as the Sea Horse west of the Gifu, and this is probably what Morriss referred to as a minor push.

7. Thirteen PTs intercepted nine Japanese destroyers in the night action of 10 Jan. 1943. But no vessels were lost by either side. See, Robert J. Bulkley, Jr., *At Close quarters: PT Boats in the United States Navy* (Washington, D.C.: Naval History Division, 1962), 101-2.

8. Morriss never sent in the piece on the kid and no manuscript has survived. He did submit the artillery story, but it was not used. Mack Morriss to Hartzell Spence, 12 Feb. 1943, McCarthy Papers. "We are not using the Artillery story because I am afraid the artillerymen would think we were getting excited about something which after all is old stuff to them," Spence replied. "With that single exception, your work has been very handsome." Hartzell Spence to Mack Morriss, 2 Mar. 1943, McCarthy Papers.

9. Bob Brumby was an INS (International News Service) correspondent. A sketch Morriss did of Brumby relaxing and smoking his pipe is in the Morriss Papers.

10. The correspondents referred to themselves as the Guadalcanal Press Club, and their billet on the ridge near headquarters was called Cactus Heights. Brodie's tent was known as the Artists & Writers Club and the full address given inside a notebook Morriss kept was Cactus Heights, Bomb Alley, Guadalcanal, Solomons. Morriss Papers.

11. Lt. Col. Stuart F. Crawford, then as Morriss stated, Division G-2, but in the New Georgia campaign back in command of his old unit, 8th Field Artillery Battalion.

12. This incident is related in Robert C. Muehrcke, *Orchids in the Mud: Personal Accounts of Veterans of the 132nd Infantry Regiment, 1941-1945* (Chicago: 132nd Infantry Association, 1985), 145, which reports that the "kid," an unnamed infantryman from "E" Co., 132nd Infantry, went out to get a wounded Japanese captain's sword. When the latter grabbed him, he became hysterical and hacked his head off. He gave the sword to Father Francis Gorman to hold for him and was hospitalized for battle psychosis. The sword in question is in the Americal Division Museum, Fort Devens, Mass.

13. Father Frederic P. Gehring, a navy chaplain, did not mention this incident in the book he wrote describing some of his adventures on Guadalcanal (and some previous ones in China prior to the entry of the United States into the war), *A Child of Miracles: The Story of Patsy Li* (New York: Funk & Wagnalls, 1962). Gehring was with the troops on Guadalcanal from the beginning to the end, and when he left in February 1943 after the island had been secured, the Guadalcanal Press Club awarded him the D.F.C.—"Distinguished Friendship Cross."   .

14. Some three thousand Solomon Islanders worked in the Labor Corps during the campaign as laborers and carriers. The latter was particularly strenuous and dangerous. In 1988 I was fortunate to be able to talk with a former carrier, Arial Mare, Honiara, Guadalcanal, and he later wrote me his reminiscences. A former worker at the Gold Ridge mine, Mare described the work as the most tiring he had ever done, but added that it built muscle. Once he was nearly killed by a bomb, and before the campaign was over, he had been wounded. Arial Mare to Ronnie Day, 28 May 1989. An additional danger was being mistaken for the enemy, and after an incident in December 1942 in which three islanders were killed and two wounded, the authorities recommended that the natives not wear shoes or clothing that could result in mistaken identity. Memorandum, Resident commissioner to District Officer, Guadalcanal, 8 Jan. 1943, BSIP 5/I F1/4, SINA.

15. The action on 15 Jan. that would be the subject of Morriss's story was the capture of Hill 44 (which along with Hill 43 made up the complex known as the Sea Horse) by the

35th Infantry, 25th Division. The Sea Horse was just west of the Gifu strongpoint, and its capture pocketed the Japanese defenders in the latter. See, Melvin C. Westhall, *Lightning Forward: A History of the 25th Infantry Division (Tropic Lightning), 1941-1978* (n.p.: 25th Inf. Division Association, 1978), 19-25.

16. The Mataniko River operation in which Morriss took part was known as the "Pusha Maru." Both American and captured Japanese boats were used to ferry supplies up the river and to bring wounded back down to near the mouth where they could be transferred to jeeps for the trip to the hospital.

17. Captain John M. Burden broadcast the surrender appeal to the Japanese troops surrounded in the Gifu in the early evening of 15 Jan. and repeated it the following two mornings without significant result. A complete transcript of Burden's appeal is in Morriss Papers. Miller, *Guadalcanal*, 298-99, reports that five emaciated prisoners were taken.

18. Commander first of the Americal Division and then of XIV Corps on Guadalcanal. For his role, see William K. Wyant, *Sandy Patch: A Biography of Lt. Gen. Alexander M. Patch* (New York: Praeger, 1991), 59-69.

19. The original manuscript of "Story of Battle" has not survived, which is unfortunate because as will be seen later, Morriss was very unhappy with what the editors did to the story in New York, including changing the title to "Jap-Trap." William H. Schumacher, who was in command of the mortar platoon placing the fire on the Japanese positions and who figured prominently in Morriss's story, found only one error in it. Morriss had listed Capt. Leland G. Cagwin as company commander when in fact he was the battalion S-3. The commander of "K" Company was Capt. Joe L. Payne. Maj. Gen. USA (ret) L.G. Cagwin to Ronnie Day, 23 July 1994. Schumacher added an interesting piece of information I had never before encountered: at the time of the fighting on the Sea Horse an earthquake occurred which the men thought was a time-on-target artillery concentration into the Gifu strongpoint. Lt. Col. USA (ret) William H. Schumacher to Ronnie Day, 11 Dec. 1992 & 4 June 1993.

20. Seventeen of the short pieces Morriss did for PRO have survived. All but one are press releases about 132nd infantrymen decorated for bravery during the Hill 27 action. Of these, some had been killed in action and most of the remainder had been wounded. The lone exception was a humorous piece on a captain who got entangled in his tent when the air raid warning sounded. Morriss Papers.

21. *Curtiss* was a large seaplane tender anchored in Segond Channel, Espiritu Santo, and used as a PBY tender and as headquarters for Land-Based Air, South Pacific Force.

22. This could have been Brig. Gen. Louis E. Woods (who has made it into at least one other document as "Wood"), Commander, Air Solomons (COMAIRSOLS) until Dec. 1942.

23. Sgt. Edwin J. "Ned" Burman was a member of the original Marine combat correspondent group that took part in the invasion of Guadalcanal. In the diary, Morriss spelled the name "Burnham," but in a list of names that has survived he had the name correctly spelled.

24. "Gen. Vandergrift Writes His Wife," *Life*, 16 Nov. 1942.

25. The rumors were correct. Kokumbona, just west of Point Cruz, had been the center of Japanese activity on the island. It fell easily to troops of the 27th Infantry on the same day that the last resistance in the Gifu ended.

26. J. Norman Lodge was a veteran Associated Press correspondent who had covered the outbreak of the war in Europe; John A. Brockhurst was a News of the Day newsreel cameraman.

27. Morriss's editorial note to his own entry.

28. Morriss sent the poem, "Can We Go Back?" and it was published in the section

called, "The Poets Cornered," *Yank,* 16 Apr. 1942. Morriss was not a poet—enough said.

29. Morriss wrote his father that "for a long time I couldn't get him to remember our playing ball together as kids. Then he did." He went on to ask his father to get in touch with Bullock's family because they did not know where he was. Mack Morriss to B.H. Morriss, 12 Feb. 1943, Morriss Papers. Bullock was in "B" Co., 27th Infantry, 25th Division, one of the units that had participated in the capture of Kokumbona. He remembers the encounter with Morriss and attributes his failure to recognize him to the strain he had been under. Bullock fought on with the 27th Infantry through New Georgia and into the Philippines where he was wounded in the heavy fighting at Balete Pass. He was awarded the Bronze Star and the Purple Heart. Interview with Walter Bullock, 11 Apr. 1994.

30. Morriss called the story, "Push," and as he wrote Spence in New York, it was strictly an after-the-battle-piece—the "result of shooting the bull with men who had just been relieved." Mack Morriss to Hartzell Spence, 12 Feb. 1943, McCarthy Papers. The editors in New York, however, ran it as " 'C' Company at Kokumbona," *Yank,* 23 Apr. 1943, which was a bit misleading. "C" Co., the unit that was the subject of the story, had indeed led the assault over the hills behind Kokumbona but had not participated in the capture of the village itself. The story was dramatized on "Voice of the Army," Blue Network, 11 June 1943.

31. Col. Parker M. Reeve was commanding officer of 65th Engineer Battalion. Morriss spelled his name Reese in the text.

32. Col. Everett E. Brown who after Col. Robert B. McClure was promoted to brigadier general and made assistant division commander of the 25th Division, took over the 35th Infantry and served as the regiment's commander during the New Georgia campaign. The evidence for this identification rests with the statement in the diary later on that Brown was Burden's superior and General Cagwin was able to ascertain that this was indeed the case at the 1994 25th Infantry Division Reunion in Sacramento, California. Maj. Gen. (ret) L.G. Cagwin to Ronnie Day, 10 Aug. 1994.

33. There is the possibility that this was Col. William D. Long, Americal Division.

34. Capt. John W. Mitchell, 339th Fighter Squadron, was the P-38 pilot who shot down the Japanese plane. His kill that morning was his eight confirmed; in April he would plan and lead the mission that shot down Adm. Isoroku Yamamoto, commander of the Japanese Combined Fleet and the architect of the attack on Pearl Harbor. Morriss described the event in more detail in a story called "Fighter Breed," which *Yank* did not publish. Manuscript is in Morriss Papers.

35. Morriss called the story "Fire in the Hole" and took as his theme the engineers working under fire. The editors, however, chose not to run it. Manuscript is in Morriss Papers.

36. Brodie's sketch of the jeep running over the Japanese corpse appeared in the collection making up "Last Days at Guadalcanal," *Yank,* 19 Mar. 1943. This was the piece that so pleased James Jones and the other wounded men from the 25th Division. It was also run in the *San Francisco Chronicle,* 28 Mar. 1943. Brodie, it might be noted, has sketched more violence probably than any man alive. He covered World War II, the Korean War, and Vietnam; he sketched the execution by firing squad of a German infiltrator on the western front, an execution in the gas chamber at San Quentin, and an execution in the electric chair at Starke, Florida.

37. "Condition Red," was never published. The manuscript is in Morriss Papers.

38. In a notebook Morriss carried with him at the time of the Hill 44 fighting, he listed the 35th's chaplain as Father T.P. Finnegan. One chaplain with long service on Guadalcanal published an account that provides a good description of what it was like for men of the cloth. See, W. Wyeth Willard, *The Leathernecks Come Through* (New York: Fleming H. Revell, 1944).

39. Lt. Col. William J. Mullen Jr. was commander of 3rd Battalion, 35th Infantry at the time Morriss and Brodie witnessed the fighting on the Sea Horse.

40. Captain Orloff Bowen mentioned in Morriss's story, " 'C' Company at Kokumbona," as "CO of the first outfit into Kokumbona," was most likely commanding officer of "B" Company. He was a West Pointer, and before he was killed in action on Bougainville in January 1944, he had been awarded three Silver Stars and a Purple Heart. L.G. Cagwin to Ronnie Day, 23 July 1994.

41. J. Lawton Collins was commander of the 25th Infantry Division on Guadalcanal and later on New Georgia. In 1944, Morriss interviewed Collins, then commander of VII Corps on the Western Front, on the respective merits of the Japanese and the Germans. "2-Front Fighter," *Yank*, 10 Nov. 1944. See also, J. Lawton Collins, *Lightning Joe: An Autobiography* (Baton Rouge: Louisiana State University Press, 1979).

42. Morriss's analysis is similar to that found in the interviews conducted with officers, especially in regard to leadership. Brig. Gen. John R. Hodge, assistant commander, 25th Division, put his finger on one very real problem when he told an interviewer: "Jungle warfare is a young man's game and unless a man is already in excellent physical condition or is capable of attaining himself into good fighting form, he should never be allowed to go to the front. Officers and enlisted men who are old in age, whose endurance is limited, should never have been sent out with fighting units." VII AF: Report on "Activities in South Pacific Area," 27 Jan. 1943 by Frank O. Brown, Maj. A.C. (740.306-4), USAF Collection, AFHRA.

43. The National Guard versus Regular Army was, as Morriss indicates, a touchy issue. The operations report of the 35th Infantry was openly critical of the 132nd Infantry. Summarizing the final action at the Gifu strongpoint, the report stated that "with all due respect to the regiment the 2nd Battalion relieved, their information of the size and positions of the enemy were meager and their maps of the area inaccurate. This should teach us not always to trust implicitly all information from other units." Operations Report, 25th Infantry Division, NA, Suitland Branch.

"I'd Write Hallelujah"

1. Hilton and Wilson had both gone into service with Morriss when the 117th Infantry had been called up in 1940.

2. Nine B-17s of the 72nd Squadron, 5th Bomb Group, flew the mission to the Shortlands to strike enemy shipping there. Fifteen to twenty five Zeros intercepted and as Morriss had heard, three bombers were shot down, identified as the Hensley, Hall, and Haux crews. Narrative of 72nd Squadron History (SQ-Bomb-72-Hi), 18 Feb. 1918-28 Feb. 1944, in USAF Collection, AFHRA.

Pvt. James R. Beaton is listed as member of Service Company, 164th Infantry.

3. *DeHaven*, the destroyer sunk off Savo, was part of a force that had transported troops around Cape Esperance and landed them at Verahue Beach on the western end of Guadalcanal in the hope of trapping the Japanese. Morison, *Struggle for Guadalcanal*, 364-66.

4. As mentioned previously, Miller and Bushemi were stationed in Honolulu. On their trip to Noumea, they did a story with photographs, "The Kiwi from New Zealand," *Yank*, 9 Apr. 1943.

5. Mike McCoy, a photographer/naturalist living in Honiara whose *Reptiles of the Solomon Islands* (Papua, New Guinea: Wau Ecology Institute, 1980) is the best guide to the subject, is certain that the snakes Morriss tangled with were the Brown Tree Snake, *Boiga*

irregularis. Mike McCoy to Ronnie Day, 15 Apr. 1991. The Brown Tree Snake is a rear-fanged colubrid (not elapid as is the case of the highly venomous snakes of Australia and New Guinea such as the Taipan) and while venomous is not considered a threat to adult humans. Before the war, the range of the Brown Tree Snake was New Guinea and the adjacent archipelagos, the Solomons, and Australia. During the war, however, the snake hitched a ride (from Manus Island, it is thought) to Guam where it has now put bird life in jeopardy, caused millions of dollars of losses in the power industry by causing power failures and has been identified as the source of near fatal snakebites in infants. The federal government has now joined the fight, but so far the snakes are winning. See, Mike McCoy, "Fighting the Snakes," *Islands Business,* April 1991, and Jim Carlton, "It's Man vs. Snake in Guam: For Now, Bet on the Snake," *Wall Street Journal,* 12 Dec. 1991.

6. The 147th Infantry Regiment was originally a part of the 37th Infantry Division, Ohio National Guard, and entered federal service with that division, 15 Oct. 1940. (For the history of the 37th Division, see Stanley A. Frankel, *The 37th Infantry Division in World War II* (Washington, D.C.: Infantry Journal Press, 1948). In early 1942, however, the 1st and 3rd Battalions of the 147th and the 134th Field Artillery were detached from the 37th and formed into the 147th Regimental Combat Team (the 2nd Battalion was not reunited with the 147th until early 1943) and sailed for the South Pacific in April 1942 as part of Task Force 0051. By the end of November, the 147th (less the 2nd Battalion) was on Guadalcanal, serving first as part of the perimeter defense at Koli Point and then committed to action in the XIV Corps offensive in late January. From 30 Jan. to 5 Feb., the 147th was involved in heavy fighting in the attempt to cross the Bonegi River which empties into the sound at Tassafaronga Point. Later, the 147th took part in the occupation of Emirau Island, northwest of Kavieng, New Ireland and saw its final action on Iwo Jima in March 1945. William Marshal Chaney, a Kentuckian transplanted to Ohio before the war and presently national secretary of the Guadalcanal Campaign Veterans, was with the 147th from 1940 to 1944 and took part in the fighting at the Bonegi River. He has provided me with a copy of his personal account, "Ah! Yes. 'We Remember,'" parts of which have recently been published as "147th Infantry Dogfaces on the 'Canal,'" *Guadalcanal Echoes,* October-November 1994, as well as additional material on both the 147th and the 14th Seabees. Largely as a result of Chaney's contribution, Wayne Rasnick, a graduate student in history has completed his study, "Orphan Regiment: A History of the 147th Infantry Regiment from Camp Shelby to Guadalcanal, 1940-1943" (masters thesis, East Tennessee State University, 1995). In the course of Rasnick's study, I was able to study the complete file on the 147th at Guadalcanal, RG94, INRG 147-0.1, 5, NA, Suitland Branch.

7. Allan Jackson, like Brodie, came from the San Francisco Bay area and since both were interested in snow skiing, they formed the Guadalcanal Ski Club. Brodie drew a cartoon of the event which Jackson kept among his mementos of the war, but cannot now locate. Allan Jackson to Ronnie Day, 26 Oct. 1991. After Guadalcanal, Jackson covered the New Georgia campaign and was on the light cruiser *Helena* when she went down in the Battle of Kula Gulf. Later, he covered the European theater and took one of the most famous photographs of the war there, the meeting of the Americans and the Russians at Torgau on the Elbe River—the Link-Up. The cut in the *London News-Chronicle,* 28 Apr. 1945, hailed it as "A picture the world will never forget." Morriss seems to have taken out a bit of his own frustration at "bomb nerves" in this entry. In one of the letters Jackson sent back to the *Oakland Post-Enquirer* (his old newspaper, which ran the letters as a series), he wrote about the bombing that "When the malaria and dysentery got me, I just lay in my bunk and let them 'whump' and be damned to 'em. I was too tired to drag myself through the mud and slime to the dug-out." Quoted in Jack Price, "Allan Jackson Writes of Life on Guadalcanal," *Editor & Publisher,* 29 May 1943. Like the men who fought on the ground and in the air at

Guadalcanal, Allan Jackson has made a huge contribution to this work, providing me with details of the civilian combat correspondents, allowing me to use rare photographs in his possession, and inviting me to his home on Santa Rosa Island, Pensacola Beach, to spend a weekend talking about Guadalcanal.

8. Herbert C. Merillat, public relations officer with the 1st Marine Division for the duration of the division's fight for the island (and author of the first history based on the official record, *The Island: A History of the First Marine Division on Guadalcanal, August 7- December 9, 1942* [Boston: Houghton Mifflin, 1944]), is as good an authority as any on the civilian correspondents who covered the first four months of the campaign.

"I'm sorry to see Bob go," he wrote in September as Miller rotated out. "He's a good reporter and a cheery, pleasant chap. But he was beginning to get on our nerves, and his brassiness and lectures on strategy infuriated some of the staff." *Guadalcanal Remembered* (New York: Dodd, Mead, 1982), 147. While working in the archives at Maxwell AFB, I came across a document that called to mind immediately Merillat's remark. I had in my hand, preserved for all posterity, VII AF: Lecture by Robert Miller at Off. Club Hickam Fld, 4 Nov. 42 on Solomons. USAF Collection, 740.309-1, AFHRA.

9. The scuttlebutt was remarkably accurate. On 5 Feb., a lone bomber flying reconnaissance and at the extreme limit of its range, reported Japanese carriers, battleships, cruisers and destroyers moving south from Truk. Halsey prepared for a major engagement; the rumors Morriss heard of American carriers at Tulagi stemmed from this move. James E. Merrill, *A Sailor's Admiral: A Biography of William F. Halsey* (New York: Thomas Y. Crowell, 1976), 82.

10. A word here is unintelligible. It could be Nisei, but Brodie does not recall meeting any Japanese-American soldiers on Guadalcanal. Howard Brodie to Ronnie Day, 2 Mar. 1992.

11. In the diary, Morriss clearly has Col. Timbell, but in the list of names that has survived for this period, he has it as Col. Timboe. This was no doubt Col. Arthur G. Timboe of Headquarters Company, 2nd Battalion, 164th Infantry.

12. Sometimes referred to as Southern Cross Air Transport, but SCAT officially stood for South Pacific Combat Air Transport Command. During that month of February 1943, the 13th Troop Carrier Squadron, flying C-47s from Tontouta Air Base, New Caledonia, and with personnel and critical supplies first priority, logged 88,205 nautical miles and carried 594,300 pounds of cargo. Squadron history is in Robert C. Duffey, Capt. A.C., to CG, I Troop Carrier Command, Stout Field, Indianapolis, Service Factors for Consideration in Connection with Troop Carrier Command Training Directive, 30 Apr. 1943, USAF Collection, AFHRA.

13. Morriss was referring to his friend, Ed Cunningham, whose "Jinx Flight," *Yank*, 20 Jan. 1943, had as its angle the series of accidents that forced a B-24 bomber down, but ended with the recovery of the crew. Cunningham himself had survived a B-24 crash in the South American jungles on his way out to the China-Burma-India theater in July 1942 and wrote the story of that incident, "Ten against the Jungle," *Yank*, 12 Aug. 1942.

14. Fighter #1 was southeast of Henderson and west of the Tenaru River.

15. The Japanese had evacuated their remaining troops—13,000 is the number usually given. It was a brilliant feat, by anyone's reckoning, and led to criticism of Patch and the Army for letting enemy troops escape to fight again another day. Patch's biographer quotes a letter the general wrote his wife in March 1943 to the effect that during the offensive, he had received a "long series of urgent messages from Higher Command—in fact, very high— warning us to be prepared for *defense* against a major enemy attack." Quoted in Wyant, *Sandy Patch*, 73. Patch continued the offensive, but Morriss's account of the first week of February bears strong witness to the tension and uncertainty as to enemy intentions that prevailed at headquarters on Guadalcanal.

16. Morriss sent the story in under the title "Too Much Guts." The editors ran it as "The Colonel and His Top Kick: Both Were Tough but One Was Lucky," *Yank,* 16 Apr. 1943. The original title was more appropriate, for George was somewhat of a legend in the South Pacific. In New Caledonia, while known for being the "peep troop man, he also acquired fame of a sort among the University of Pennsylvania physicians serving as the 52nd Evacuation Hospital on New Caledonia for disregarding the warning of a doctor and eating his fill of Bancoulier tree nuts, a nut the natives used (and only *one* sufficed) as a laxative. He had to be hospitalized for diarrhea so severe some of the doctors thought he had a rare and unknown tropical disease. When he took over command of the 132nd at the Hill 27 fight, he made his appearance on the front wearing shorts and carrying an '03 Springfield rifle. To demonstrate to his men that their fear of snipers was misplaced, he walked along the line standing up so that the Japanese could shoot at him. The Japanese fired away—and all missed. · George liked to say that he was the "best goddamn pistol shot in the army," and those who saw him shoot agreed. As a result, when he wounded himself accidently with his .45, rumor on Guadalcanal hinted that it had been done deliberately so that he could get off the island now that it was secured and get into action again somewhere else. The material on George and the Bancoulier nuts comes from King, *Vignettes,* 45-46; the demonstration at the front is in Muehrcke, *Orchids in the Mud,* 131-33.

17. Morriss was listed as one of the contributors when the article, "Malaria: It's as Dangerous as the Axis," *Yank,* 16 July 1943, appeared. This was one of the educational pieces the paper ran, and it tried to lay to rest the fear that one's skin would be permanently yellow from taking atabrine.

18. Camp Barnes, near Noumea.

19. Morriss may have meant E. Astley Hawkins, the Reuters correspondent.

20. Morriss obviously did not meet the beautiful young women—all from Noumea—who posed for *Yank* photographer Dillon Ferris. See, "How Do You Like American Soldiers?" *Yank,* 5 May 1944. Ferris covered the Bougainville campaign along with correspondent Barrett McGurn and artist Robert Greenhalgh.

21. The piece was a double-spread of photographs, "Guadalcanal Battleground," *Yank,* 20 Jan. 1943.

22. Bevan, *United States Forces in New Zealand,* 127, describes Peter Pan as a ballroom. In the diary, de luxe is such an awful scrawl that I could make no sense of it. Denys Bevin, however, recognized the word immediately as the popular way at the time of describing something a bit beyond the ordinary. E. Denys Bevin to Ronnie Day, 20 Apr. 1995.

23. Morriss stuck with being careful about spending money for the rest of his life. He tended to keep careful records of what he spent and many of these itemized accounts have survived among his papers.

"Got to Get on the Ball"

1. Morriss lost no time in letting New York know that he and Brodie thought the piece stank. "Usually on things like this I get madder as I go along, so bear with me," he wrote Spence. It was fair warning. One tightly packed page blasted the editorial staff for what had been done to Brodie's piece, followed by a page and a half listing their sins in regard to his article. Mack Morriss to Hartzell Spence, 6 Mar. 1943, McCarthy Papers. On the other hand, "Jap Trap," *Yank,* 5 Mar. 1943, does not appear to be quite the disaster Brodie and Morriss thought it to be.

2. I have been unable to identify further the Knapp crew.

3. M.S. Bangs was owner and publisher of the *Elizabethton Daily Star* at the time Morriss was editor.

4. The sign, which read, "Short Horn Stand Close," should have made clear to all what the GI was doing. Mack Morriss, "They Don't Joke on Guadalcanal when a Battalion Moves Up," *Yank,* 3 Feb. 1943.

5. Lt. Carl Zucker, III Island Command public relations officer.

6. Col. Norris M. L'Abbe, is listed as executive officer in a photograph taken at Efate, December 1944, in Garrison, *Task Force 9156 and III Island Command,* 95.

7. "Fighter Breed" was not published. The manuscript cited previously, is in the Morriss Papers.

8. Sgt. Walter A. Przewrocki, squadron electrician. As Morriss relates later, he did a story on Przewrocki called, "Rocky," but it was not published. The spin Morriss put on the story was the chicken farm that Przewrocki operated. The manuscript, dated 25 Mar. 1943, is in Morriss Papers.

9. Patrick J. Hurley, secretary of war under Herbert Hoover, was taking a training refresher during the Carolina Maneuvers of 1941 where Morriss got to know him. "I guess he is the first 'celebrity' I've ever known anywhere near intimately," Morriss wrote his father. Hurley did not get the military command he had hoped for when war came; instead, he became Roosevelt's personal envoy going on missions to the Southwest Pacific, Russia, the Middle East, and China. Either going or returning from Russia in late 1942, he ran into Al Hine in Iran and sent Morriss greetings, which were conveyed through the mimeographed news letter the office in New York sent out to the men in the field. Mack Morriss to B.H. Morriss, 17 Nov. 1942 and 12 Mar. 1943, Morriss Papers. Details of Hurley's career come from Russell D. Buhite, *Patrick J. Hurley and American Foreign Policy* (Ithaca: Cornell University Press, 1973).

10. Martin and Osa Johnson visited Malakulu Island, a large island between Efate and Espiritu Santo, in 1919 hoping to photograph an actual cannibal feast (which they succeeded in doing). Martin wrote a book about this adventure, *Cannibal-Land: Adventures with a Camera in the New Hebrides* (Boston: Houghton Mifflin, 1922), and after he was killed in a plane crash, Osa wrote two—*I Married Adventure* (Philadelphia: J.B. Lippincott, 1940) and *Bride in the Solomons* (Boston: Houghton Mifflin, 1944, in which the New Hebrides story was included. In these, a Stephens (no first name given) is mentioned, described as half English, half Samoan.

11. None of the color pieces were published, and the manuscripts have not survived. On the other hand, it is highly probable that some of the sketches Brodie did at this time were part of his "Sketches from the South Pacific," *Yank,* 23 July 1943.

12. George Maynard. He and "Shorty" appear on a list Morriss compiled 15 Dec. 1942 under the heading Santo. List is in Morriss Papers.

13. In late February, the 103rd and 167th Infantry Regiments of the 43rd Division had occupied the Russell Islands, which lay 35 miles northwest of Cape Esperance, Guadalcanal. Shortly thereafter, the 172nd, the remaining regiment of the 43rd, moved from Santo to Guadalcanal. In early July 1943, the 43rd would launch the assault against Munda Field on New Georgia in the central Solomons.

14. Captain Garrison is no doubt Ritchie Garrison whose book, *Task Force 9156 and III Island Command,* has been cited previously. Colonel Curran remains unidentified. The Coast Watcher network mentioned here was separate from the Solomon Island network that played such an important role in the Guadalcanal campaign. The New Hebrides (since independence in 1980 called Vanuatu) are make up of eighty-two islands, of which the largest are Espiritu Santo, Malakula, Efate, Erromango, Ambrym, Tanna, Penecost,

Epi, Aoba, Vanua Lava, Santa Maria, and Maewo. During the late nineteenth century, when the British and the French were dividing up the area, the New Hebrides were organized into a joint Anglo-French Condominium with what amounted to two govern-ments. When war came to the South Pacific, the condominium, with the help of the Royal Austrialian Navy, organized a coast watcher network modeled on that in the Solomons, and when the Americans arrived, they took it over and, as Morriss's sources said, ran it from Efate. For this see, Garrison, *Task Force 9156*, 42-56. Efate shared intelli-gence with the Solomon Islands network and there is some correspondence between L'Abbe and the resident commissioner in the Solomons, W.S. Marchant, in the file on Coast Watching, BSIP 5/I F 1/7, SINA.

15. The 2nd Raider Battalion under the command of Lt. Col. Evans S. Carlson and with Maj. James Roosevelt as executive carried out the raid on Makin, 16-18 Aug. 1942. Samuel Eliot Morison, *Coral Sea, Midway and Submarine Actions, May 1942-August 1942* (Boston: Little, Brown, 1954), devotes chapter 11 to this operation.

16. Dave Richardson, "There's No Front Line in New Guinea," and Al Hine, "First G.I. Report from Iran: It's Cold, Expensive and Strange," *Yank*, 12 Mar. 1943. E.J. Kahn and Robert Neville were the two *Yank* staffers commissioned. As mentioned previously, Neville went to *Stars and Stripes*. Ralph Morse took the picture of the Lunga log at the time Morriss and Brodie were on Guadalcanal, and Morriss had helped with the cutlines for it and some other photographs. Mack Morriss to B.H. Morriss, 30 Mar. 1943, Morriss Papers.

17. Helen Morriss stayed with relatives in Tazewell, Virginia, during some of the time that Morriss was in the Pacific, but does not recall the incident mentioned here. Her parents, Beverly H. Davis and Alta Mae Van Dyke Davis were from nearby Buchanan County and moved to Elizabethton around 1925 because of the job opportunities at the large rayon plants opening up there. On the other hand, Mrs. Tourville also visited her relatives in Tazewell during the war. A marriage certificate in the Tazewell County Clerk's Office records that Bernard J. Tourville, Fort Washington, Maryland, and Margaret Whitley, maiden name Hawkins, Arlington, Virginia, were married 27 June 1942. The ceremony took place at the home of her brother in Tazewell. At the time, Margaret Hawkins was working in the Depart-ment of Interior, Washington, D.C., but she too, visited her relatives in Tazewell at least once. *Clinch Valley News*, 27 Aug. 1943.

"Time out for an Air Battle"

1. Published as "A Story of American Courage," *Yank*, 28 May 1943.

2. Burns Philp was a Sydney-based trading company that did business in the South Pacific region.

3. The 5th Bomb Group (H), 13th Air Force, was made up of the 23rd, 31st, 72nd, and 394th Squadrons. The only published history of the 5th of which I am aware is *The Story of the Fifth Bombardment Group (Heavy)* (n.p.: Hillsborough House, 1946). The records of the 5th for this period are not as complete as one would wish. I have relied on History of the 5th Bombardment Group (H), 19 May 1918-31 Dec. 1943 and Benjamin E. Lippincott, et al., Activation History of the XIII Bomber Command, 13 Jan. 1943 to 1 Jan. 1944, 752.01-1, USAF Collection, AFHRA.

4. My sources, who shall at their wish remain unnamed, said that the fight was be-tween men from the 164th and men from the 182nd. The cause was a grudge that went back to Guadalcanal, where a unit of the 182nd supposedly lost some weapons to the Japanese,

which were later used against the 164th. An even more serious confrontation occurred between the 132nd and a black quartermaster battalion later the same year in Fiji.

5. *Yank* did not run the story. The manuscript is in Morriss Papers.

6. Reports of German involvement in the Pacific—both personnel and equipment—began with Pearl Harbor and continued—at least during the first two years of the war. John B. Lundstrom, *The First Team and the Guadalcanal Campaign: Naval Fighter Combat from August to November 1942* (Annapolis: Naval Institute Press, 1994), 139, 143, relates two instances of enemy planes being identified as Me-109s in the Battle of the Eastern Solomons.

7. Morriss left out hospital in the diary. I put it in so as not to break unnecessarily the flow of the narrative.

8. Maj. John F. Concannon is listed as adjutant general, 403rd Troop Carrier Group in a 11 Nov. 1943 Report on Activities of the 403rd Troop Carrier Command for Commanding General, I Troop Carrier Command, Stout Field, Indianapolis, USAF Collection, AFHRA.

9. The 31st served as the host squadron at this time on Guadalcanal and the 31st Ordnance Section serviced the flight echelons of the 23rd, 72nd, and 394th as each rotated into Guadalcanal for two to three weeks and then returning again to a rear area, flying search missions at Fiji and other bases, going on rest leave to Auckland or undergoing transition training in B-24 aircraft which were replacing the B-17 in the South Pacific. So the 31st Ordnance along with the rest of the ground personnel enjoyed no respite from the very hard work of maintaining and arming the planes. Lt. Col. (ret) Walter S. Bralley to Ronnie Day, 2 Apr. 1992. As will be seen later, Colonel Bralley, then a lieutenant, was ordnance officer of the 31st.

10. The convoy was carrying the American's 132nd Infantry, the unit that had captured Hill 27. Wayne Douglas, then a sergeant, was on board the *President Jackson* off Lunga Point when the raid began. He remembered that he "walked to the rail to see if he could swim to shore," and was relieved when he "figured he could swim it." Interview with Ronnie Day, 19 Apr. 1991. In the end, none of the troopships were hit.

11. The Elizabethton High School team won the state championship football game at Jackson, Tennessee, 17 Dec. 1938. Morriss accompanied the team to Jackson on the train and filed a number of stories for the *Elizabethton Star*. Walter Stewart was a sports writer for the Memphis, Tennessee *Commercial Appeal* at the time and featured the game in his 18 Dec. 1938 column.

12. The Battle of the Tenaru (Ilu) was fought 20-21 Aug. 1942 and was the first major action on Guadalcanal of the campaign. The Ichiki Unit (a reinforced battalion of the 28th Infantry, 7th Division, named for its commander, Col. Kiyono Ichiki), which made the counterattack on Marine forces defending the airfield was utterly annihilated and the reporting of this heavy fighting formed a key part of Tregaskis's best-seller, *Guadalcanal Diary*. A fine personal account is in Robert Leckie, *Helmet For My Pillow* (Garden City, N.Y.: Nelson Doubleday, 1979), 67-80. Today, a simple monument at the Ilu marks the spot where Ichiki killed himself, and while the bodies of the Japanese have long since been recovered, the ammunition such as the dump at Hell's Point is still there. Solomons Islands Police maintains a bomb disposal team and the estimate is that it will take a quarter century more to clear the explosives that still remain. For this, "The Battle that Never Ends," *Solomons*, no. 8 (1992): 39.

13. Spelled Beau Guest in the diary.

14. Probably Lt. Corcoran Thom, an intelligence officer in S-2, Hq. 5th Bombardment Group. A letter he wrote from Espiritu Santo to Maj. Frank Brown at Pearl Harbor, 7 Dec. 1942, describing conditions in the Guadalcanal area is in USAF Collection, GP-5-SU-CO, AFHRA.

15. Lt. Walter S. Bralley, the ordnance officer for the 31st Squadron, 5th Group, on

Guadalcanal. He had graduated from Virginia Polytechnic Institute in 1941 and in addition to having relatives in Johnson City, Tennessee, a few miles from Morriss's hometown of Elizabethton, he had gone to school with boys from the area. Fifty years later he remembers Morriss coming into the camp area from time to time seeking information. Lt. Col. (ret) Walter S. Bralley to Ronnie Day, 24 Jan. 1992.

16. Morriss and Brodie got to know members of this crew very well on Guadalcanal and flew their only combat mission with them. Capt. Berton H. "Tex" Burns (who the next month would be promoted to major and made 23rd Squadron commander) was the pilot; Lt. Radar Forsberg was the navigator; Walter Sidler was the flight engineer and top turret gunner; Forrest W. Averbeck was the ball turret gunner; Basil Debnekoff was the waist gunner; Ross Henderson was the bombardier; Anton Schmidt was the radio operator; and J. W. Weaver was the tail gunner. Forest Averbeck to Ronnie Day, 20 Jan. 1992. Averbeck recalls a Captain Bradley as being a co-pilot on some missions. At the time Morriss and Brodie were on Guadalcanal, the Burns crew flew the B-17 known as "Sad Sack." By the time of the New Georgia campaign four months later, they were flying a B-17, called "Jap-Happy." Some information regarding B-17s in the South Pacific is in Steve Birdsall and Roger A. Freeman, *Claims to Fame: The B-17 Flying Fortress* (London: Arms and Armour, 1994). Also, Steve Birdsall to Ronnie Day, 15 Jan. 1994.

17. The AC eagle was the old Air Corps patch, a blue eagle on a red background. The new men were wearing the new Air Force patch with a star and wings. Col. (ret.) Burton H. Burns to Ronnie Day, 3 Nov. 1991.

18. Arthur Conradi, Jr. Colonel Burns called him a "fine officer who did his job well." Berton H. Burns to Ronnie Day, 4 Sept. 1994.

19. Colonel Burns remembers that he never did have either a co-pilot or a navigator for any length of time. The co-pilots moved up to pilot and many of the navigators were new being trained in combat on the spot. In daylight at least an inexperienced navigator posed little problem since the pilots knew the islands well "and could visually navigate when some inexperienced navigator got them off track." Berton H. Burns to Ronnie Day, 3 Apr. 1992.

20. Describing a bombing mission over Kahili at night, Averbeck wrote: "Over the target, several search lights were turned on our B-17. This becomes very very bright, especially so in a ball turret where you have a ringside seat to ground action. Then ack-ack started. Personally I did not fear this too much as it did not seem real accurate. But you would hear the shells crunch and if this happened in front and you flew through it, it would make little ticking sounds." Forrest W. Averbeck to Ronnie Day, 20 Jan. 1992.

21. Actually, some of Brodie's best-known sketches from the South Pacific came out of his association with the Burns crew. Brodie flew on a low altitude practice mission over nearby Tulagi and then made detailed sketches on the ground with members of the crew posing. Howard Brodie to Ronnie Day, 13 Oct. 1991. The finished work appeared in a two page layout, "Bomber Raid on Japs at Bougainville," *Yank*, 20 Aug. 1943. Debnekoff remembers that he and some of the others spent several very hot hours one day with the plane on the ground posing for Brodie. Basil Debnekoff to Ronnie Day, 1 Apr. 1992.

22. The safe return of the Classen crew was one of the most remarkable survival stories to come out of the Pacific. With little rest from the last mission, the crew took off in the early morning hours of 9 Feb. 1943 on a search mission to locate the Japanese fleet. Their old plane had been shot up and returned to Hawaii for overhaul, and they were flying the B-17 that had once been General Harmon's personal plane. Shortly after sunrise they sighted Nauru, a small, Japanese-held island 750 miles northeast of Guadalcanal and important for its phosphate deposits. Ten miles out, Classen turned to try to sneak by and check the harbor for enemy ships without being spotted. The check was accomplished and he had headed for home when he looked out his side window and saw two Zeros closing fast. Six others joined

and a forty-five minute battle ensued. Two Zeros were shot down, and when the remaining six broke off and headed back to base, the B-17 had one engine out and another soon to go out, seven guns out of commission (thought later to be faulty head spacings), and three men wounded, fortunately none seriously. To lighten the plane, the bomb bay gas tanks were jettisoned (one stuck and had to be drained at considerable risk), and Classen finally got the plane to about 800 feet. Ditching was inevitable because of the gasoline supply, and when some two hours later the third engine stopped, Classen brought the disabled aircraft in on top of a six foot swell. The entire crew escaped the plane safely and for the next sixteen days their raft floated southwest. On the sixteenth day, after a 640-mile journey, they made landfall in the Carteret Islands (now known on the maps as Kilinailu Islands), which lay fifty miles off Buka Island, which is separated by a narrow passage from the northern tip of Bougainville. There is an account of this in Narrative of 72nd Squadron History, 28 Feb. 1944, SQ-Bomb-72-HI, USAF Collection, AFHRA. I have followed the account, however, of Col. Thomas J. Classen, "Survival," *Combat Crew* (Strategic Air Command, May 1952). In addition, Colonel Classen explained to me the problem of the guns failing to operate in a letter, 8 Feb. 1994. The reader should be alerted to a number of exceptions Colonel Classen takes with the entries in the diary. These are discussed in the notes as each instance appears in the text.

23. The Battle of the Eastern Solomons. Wiley was the only survivor of the three man crew of the Avenger shot down by two Zero fighters due north of Malaita as it attacked what was thought to be a Japanese cruiser. During the next fifteen days, Wiley drifted four hundred miles west to the Carterets, where the natives rescued him and where months later he was to meet the Classen crew. When Wiley arrived on Guadalcanal he was taken to Adm. Marc Mitscher, *COMAIRSOLS*. "At this time," he writes, "I was taken in tow by an aide and without realizing it, and without so much as a handshake, was separated from my Air Corps friends and Goni [the native guide]." Next day he was aboard a DC-3 bound for Noumea. (And this explains why Wiley disappeared so quickly from the accounts Morriss recorded in this diary.) I am indebted to Del Wiley for sending me his book about his incredible adventure, *Wiley's Island, or Island Blong Wiley* (privately printed, 1986).

24. Colonel Classen is adamant that there was no memorial erected. There is a photograph of a "Roll of Honor" that Morriss used in his article that lists the Classen crew as missing in action. This may be what Morriss meant by a memorial. Thomas J. Classen to Ronnie day, 15 Apr. 1995.

25. The four airmen and Goni or Gonay (the name is spelled variously), their native guide, made the island of Choisuel after almost landing in Shortlands Harbor, a major Japanese base. Conditions on Choisuel, however, were also quite dangerous. The Japanese had a strong presence there and in addition, some of the Solomon Islanders were aiding the Japanese. The situation had grown so bad that in early February 1943, the coast watcher stationed there, Alexander "Nick" Waddell, had requested and got an air strike on Malavaga and Cape Alexander villages, 4 Feb. 1943. Radio messages and memoranda concerning this incident are in BSIP 5/I F 1/7, SINA. Nevertheless, in the midst of being hunted by Japanese ground forces and bombed by enemy planes, Waddell and his colleague, Carden Seton, still managed to arrange a PBY pickup for the Americans. Sir Alexander Waddell, "The Ancient Order of the Rubber Rafters," unpublished manuscript, courtesy of Colonel Classen. D.C. Horton also reported the story in his book, *Fire Over the Islands: The Coast Watchers of the Solomons* (Sydney: A.H. and A.W. Reed, 1970), 235-37. In general, the story of the effect of the war on the Solomon Islanders themselves has only been noted in western histories in an incidental way—that is, covered if it had some relation to the Allies effort. Recently, however, an attempt has been made to record the history of the war from the Islanders' perspective, in particular, *The Big Death: Solomon Islanders Remember World War II* (Honiara: Institute of Pacific Studies and the Solomon Islands Extension Centre of the University of the South

Pacific, 1988), and Hugh Laracy and Geoffrey White, "Taem Blong Faet: World War II in Melanesia," *'O'O: A Journal of Solomon Islands Studies,* no. 4 (1988).

26. Classen's recollection of this whole episode is quite different from Morriss's account. First, he does not remember ever having talked to Morriss and so the statements attributed to him are wrong. Second, he contradicts much of the details as given here. In regard to the paragraph above, for example, Classen said that the statement attributed to Gibson about native women was not true, the people were clean and well-kept; that the statement of the natives being "finicky" about their women is not true; that the story of the Japanese pilot who crash landed is wrong on two points—the incident happened at Choiseul not the Carterets and no one talked to the Japanese before he was shot; that the story of Peter's quest for a woman and the subsequent rape is not true; and that the question of taking Peter off the island never came up nor was any thought given to it. In his book, previously cited, Wiley mentions Peter in some detail, but says nothing about the incident involving women. Nor is it or the other incidents mentioned above recorded in Morriss's notebook, which he had at the time of the interview. On the other hand, the details of the incident that were recorded in the notebook are accurate enough. Classen annotated a copy of the pages of the diary in question here; the notebook cited is titled in ink on the cover, "Resume of Battle: the Army on Guadalcanal, Oct, '42-Feb. '43," and is in Morriss Papers.

27. With the exception of the part about the natives being pro-American, none of this paragraph is true according to Classen's recollection.

28. Colonel Classen recalls that the substance resembled salt or sugar but, contrary to the account in the diary, had no odor. The natives dipped beetle nut into it and then chewed the nut. They would become intoxicated and have hangovers in the morning. Col. Thomas J. Classen to Ronnie Day, 15 Apr. 1995.

29. Colonel Classen objects to the word argue; the crew bought the boat and later saw that the owners were paid for it. He is also certain that no women wanted to go along. The boat did capsize, however, and three natives paddled out and helped them. Col. Thomas J. Classen to Ronnie Day, 15 Apr. 1995.

30. There were no white men whatsoever on the island. Col. Thomas J. Classen to Ronnie Day, 15 Apr. 1995.

31. Colonel Classen does not recall a flight of fifteen planes. But the two patrol planes did give them a scare because they flew a 360 degree turn around them at low altitude before flying off. They could not keep the prow of the canoe pointed in the planes' direction. Col. Thomas J. Classen to Ronnie Day, 15 Apr. 1995.

32. Colonel Classen is certain that he made no statement whatsoever concerning what the coastwatchers were paid. The story that Dowart related about the battery and the parachute is not true. On the other hand, they did meet a Japanese pilot off the coast of Choiseul. The natives shot him and Colonel Classen still has his flag. Col. Thomas J. Classen to Ronnie Day, 15 Apr. 1995.

33. "The Kiwi from New Zealand," mentioned previously. John Bushemi, "Medical Commandos," *Yank,* 9 Apr. 1943. Bushemi also did the photographs for the Kiwi piece.

34. Growder was a member of the Marine combat correspondents group previously mentioned. The photo credits in *Yank* did not mention Growder by name.

35. These two planes were not lost as a result of combat action but rather through navigational error, which led to ditching at sea. Historical Data and History of 23rd Bomb Squadron, 10 May 1944, SQ-Bomb-23-HI, USAF Collection, AFHRA.

36. What *they* did with it was publish it—not a word cut or a change made—as "Guadalcanal Has Its Own Tojo Ice Plant to Say Nothing of Hotel de Gink," *Yank,* 21 May 1943. The editors did change the title, which had simply been, "Signs." The original manuscript is in Morriss Papers.

37. Maj. George E. Glober, commanding officer, 31st Bomb Squadron.

38. As of December 1942, Lt. Col. George A. Blakey was 5th Group executive and operations officer. This may have changed by April 1943, but I have found no record (admittedly records are sketchy for this unit) indicating it. History 5th Bomb Group, AFHRA. Colonel Bralley has no recollection of having ever heard the story attributed to him, much less having told it. The language is not that he used either at the time or since. Indeed, the story has all the marks of being a bit of oral apocrypha that made the rounds of the billets with the other pieces of scuttlebutt and Morriss could very well have been mistaken as to his source.

39. M. Sgt. Joe Flanagan who was a line chief.

40. The 214th Coast Artillery Regiment was an anti-aircraft unit on Guadalcanal. Morriss kept among his papers a poem written by Lucky Biddulph, Btry I, 214th C.A.A.A, 15 Apr. 1943, which begins: "We of the 214th are not boys / And what we handle are not toys." Whether the GI who had lost an eye was the author, Morriss does not indicate.

41. Corporal Ervin Bickwermert was an assistant squad leader in the First Platoon, "E" Co., 2nd Battalion, 132nd Infantry that had had the point on the attack on Hill 27, 2 Jan. 1943. He was killed by rifle fire later that day as he and Sgt. Wayne Douglas sought to reposition the platoon to meet the first of the Japanese counterattacks from the Gifu strongpoint. He was awarded the D.S.C. and Morriss wrote up the PRO release of the recommendation for this award and so knew of his last words, "Hold that hill." When the cemetery at Guadalcanal was closed and the bodies removed to the United States, Bickwermert's was evidently unclaimed since he was buried in the Punch Bowl in Hawaii. He had grown up fatherless and his only known relative had been his mother. He lies in the Punch Bowl Cemetery today, his name misspelled as B-i-c-k-w-e-r-w-e-r-m-e-r-t. Douglas interview, 19 Apr. 1991; Morriss for PRO, Award, Ervin M. Bickwermert, Morriss Papers. LST 711 carried the American search and recovery expedition that exhumed the Lunga Cemetery in 1948, using mainly Filipino labor. BSIP 1/III F. 9/66/3, SINA.

42. Entitled simply, "Ground Crews," this piece was never published in *Yank*. Later, a half century after it was written and two decades after Morriss's death, an excerpt from it appeared in the biography of a 5th Bomb Group pilot on Guadalcanal at the time—Gene Roddenberry. David Alexander, *Star Trek Creator: The Authorized Biography of Gene Roddenberry* (New York: Penguin, 1994), 73-74.

43. Maj. Ralph Wanderer, Jr., commanding officer, 23rd Squadron. In May 1943, Capt. Berton Burns was promoted to major and succeeded Wanderer as squadron commander. Twenty Third Bomb Sq. (H) Historical Data from 1 Apr. to 30 June 1943, 30 June 1943, SQ-Bomb-23-HI, USAF Collection, AFHRA.

44. What Morriss referred to previously concerning the faith the crew must have in the pilot was at work here. Classen never left the cockpit from the time of the attack until the ditching and during the action noted that he made "only a slight turn into the attacking aircraft so as to destroy his attack." After all, as he told me, he had "two engines out and we were barely staying in the air." Col. Thomas J. Classen to Ronnie Day, 15 Apr. 1995. The members of the crew picked up by the PBY were: Lt. Ernest C. Ruiz, co-pilot; T. Sgt. Donald O. Martin, engineer; Sgt. William H. Nichols, assistant engineer; Sgt. Robert J. Turnbull, tail-gunner; and Sgts. James H. Hunt and Theodore H. Edwards, radio operators.

45. The Classen crew flew Harmon's plane on seven missions before the deep-six, as Classen puts it. No photograph seems to have survived, but one of General Harmon's second plane which has, reads "My Ever . . ." and Classen remembered that the B-17 was actually called, "My Ever Lovin' Dove." Thomas J. Classen to Ronnie Day, 16 June 1994. Colonel Classen is adamant that there were no puckered lips and arched eyebrows on the B-17, for as he told me, the "Dove" was named for General Harmon's wife. Col. Thomas J. Classen to

Ronnie Day, 15 Apr. 1995. There does not seem to be any nose art on the second "My Ever Lovin' Dove." See 168.604-43 (3-4506-44K), USAF Collection, AFHRA. In the collection of photographs of B-17s Basil Debnekoff lent me, none has nose art. The name only is on the nose.

46. The 101st Medical Regiment, Americal Division (redesignated 121st Medical Battalion). The story was published as "Stretcher Bearers Can Also Carry a Swing Tune," *Yank*, 23 July 1943.

47. Morriss was probably listening to the happy celebration of the pilots who had shot down Admiral Isoroku Yamamoto that day and were enjoying a case of I.W. Harper. This passage from the diary was quoted in Burke Davis, *Get Yamamoto* (New York: Random House, 1969), 189-90. Davis seemed to think that the pilots could have been doing the singing since they tied one on and were unable to fly next day. Burke Davis to Mack Morriss 4 June 1968, Morriss Papers.

48. Carney Field, also known as Koli Field and Bomber No. 2, was built east of Henderson between the Nalimbu (now Ngalimbiu) and Metepono Rivers. Although other units took part in the construction at various times, the unit involved at the beginning was the 14th Naval Construction Battalion, which had arrived in November 1942 as part of a composite unit known as Acorn Red One, commanded by Capt. James V. Carney, USN. The 14th Seabees immediately started construction of a bridge across the Nalimbu River to link Koli and Lunga, and a hospital and emergency air strip at Koli Point. When the 7300-foot strip was completed, Captain Carney flew a SBD from Henderson and made a test landing, pronounced the strip satisfactory and gave the men a pep talk. But when he took off to return the aircraft to Henderson, the engine failed over Sealark Channel, and he and the gunner were killed. His body was recovered and following a memorial service on 19 Dec., he was buried in the cemetery at Lunga. The 14th Seabees went on to build the big airfield and petitioned Admiral Halsey to name it in honor of their fallen commander. How Carney Field got its named is based on correspondence with 14th veterans Enoch Henderson, James D. Rothermel, and William C. Fulton. In addition, Henderson provided me with a copy of Peter Frank Walz, "Overseas History of the 14th Naval Construction Battalion," a work in manuscript in which he also had a hand and Rothermel and Fulton provided me with a copy of Norris W. Woldy, "Historical Data—14th Construction Battalion." Finally, Franklin Schroer, a Navy aviation mechanic in Acorn Red One, Donald Schuette, an aviation rating, and Raymond Massey, a member of the *George Elliot's* boat crew on the beach at the time of the accident, all provided useful information. The role of the 810th Engineer Aviation Battalion in construction and maintenance at Carney complex is in The Operations of Aviation Engineers in the South Pacific, XIII Air Force Service Command Historical Monographs, Number 17, 2 vols., 15 July 1945, 753.01-1, USAF Collection, AFHRA.

49. In addition to the 5th Bomb Group (H) already discussed, elements of the 307th Bomb Group (H) were beginning to arrive, the 424th Squadron in February and the 370th Squadron in March. The 371st and 372nd were still in the New Hebrides as of 4 Mar. 1943. The 6th Night-fighter Squadron was a part of the 18th Fighter Group and a half dozen P-70s were based at Carney. The P-70 was the night fighter version of the Douglas A-20 Havoc, a twin engine plane that carried a crew of three and had been designed originally for the French air force. During the war, a number were sent to Great Britain where they were called Bostons. USAAF Aircraft Based On Guadalcanal On or About 4 Mar. 1943, Special Project File, 3-2868-40, AFHRA.

50. Morriss and Debnekoff met again in mid-August 1943 as Morriss and *Yank* photographer Johnny Bushemi traveled to New Georgia by way of Guadalcanal. Debnekoff was still flying with Berton Burns in the B-17 "Jap Happy" but with an almost totally new crew from the one Morriss and Brodie flew with in April. Morriss went down to Carney (he had

already run into Allan Jackson, recently rescued following the *Helena's* sinking at the Battle of Kula Gulf at *COMAIRSOLS*) to see Debnekoff and recorded in the new diary that he was keeping that "Jap Happy" had been shot up over Kahili three weeks back. 13 Aug. 1943 entry, Mack Morriss, New Georgia Diary, Morriss Papers. The mission Morriss mentioned was 27 July 1943 and was a night harassing raid in which two ships would make a run over the air field and attract the searchlights and AA fire and another flight of two aircraft would then make the actual bombing run. The Burns ship had dropped its bombs when searchlights fastened on it and the next instant two Japanese night fighters attacked. The B-17 on the left wing blew up and went down in a fiery ball and "Jap Happy" was raked with six 20mm cannon shots, wounding two men in the crew. Basil Debnekoff to Ronnie Day, 11 Mar. 1994.

51. The letter came from Curtis Brown, Ltd., a literary agency, dated 25 Feb. 1943; later Morriss corrects his entry on this. Morriss placed a short story with the agency in 1944 that seems to have been written in late 1943 since a copy of it is in the New Georgia Diary. It was headed, Untitled, and based on the last nights at Guadalcanal. It was never published. Untitled Article in Curtis Brown folder and letter retiring the manuscript, Mrs. Sewell Haggard, Magazine Department, to Sgt. Mack Morriss, 9 Feb. 1943, are in Morriss Papers. The Brodie piece was "Last Days at Guadalcanal," *Yank,* 19 Mar. 1943 and was the spread referred to in the introduction in connection with James Jones's work, *WWII,* in which the latter mistook Brodie's reference to the Horse's Neck front to be on the Galloping Horse, when in fact it was on the Sea Horse. The line of sheer snow is probably the following: "He was never able to complete a drawing without being interrupted by air raids, mortar bursts and Jap snipers who seemed to delight in taking pot shots at him just when he was beginning to concentrate on his model."

52. Published as "66 Days Missing in Action," *Yank,* 11 June 1943.

53. Spence's letter has not survived, but judging by Morriss's response, he had a twofold request, both parts of which were concerned with the upcoming first anniversary issue in June 1943. First he wanted suggestions on how to portray the paper's role in the first year of fighting. Regarding how to play the paper, Morriss recommended that it be kept simple—explain how the paper worked, that it was a world-wide operation, and, most important, like the rest of the Army it had a lot to learn. Borrowing an idea from AP, he suggested that pictures of the correspondents be superimposed on a world map to illustrate the global operation. Second, Spence wanted a report on "what the Army had learned in the first year of fighting." In response, Morriss drafted out five densely packed pages which he had read and corrected by a G-3 officer. It does not differ in any substantial way from what Morriss wrote in this diary, 31 Jan. and 9 Feb., or from the Army's study, *Fighting on Guadalcanal* (Washington, D.C.: Government Printing Office, 1943), which although restricted, Morriss evidently saw on his return to New Caledonia. At any rate, he recommended it to Spence, if the latter could get a release on it. Mack Morriss to Hartzell Spence, 26 and 28 Apr. 1943, McCarthy Papers. The Harmon letter was a prepared testimonial and it was eventually signed because it appeared in the anniversary issue along with those of other high-ranking officers. The reference to passing out cards to get the "required quotes" was probably a similar exercise in eliciting commentary from enlisted men. The only piece in the anniversary issue that might have been connected with this, however, was a short side-bar on "Latrine Questions," one of the questions being, "Whether Jane Russell or Betty Grable is the better pin-up." At any rate, when the 25 June 1943 *Yank* appeared with eight bonus pages of pin-ups and cartoons, Morriss had to have been pleased. As he had recommended, *Yank's* role was confined to just two pages, and these were devoted mainly to photographs of the correspondents on the battlefront around the world (Brodie and Morriss were shown by a machine gun on the Sea Horse). In addition, his analysis of the Army was used word for word in the section

"Twelve Months under Fire," including his colorful but true statement on the support the artillery gave the infantry—"You have to have plenty of faith in the accuracy of somebody else when he's shooting at an enemy 100 yards away—the same faith William Tell's little boy had." *Yank,* 25 June 1943.

54. Classen does not remember any reference to taking part in a bond-selling campaign. At any rate, they did not.

55. The new credentials were issued 19 Mar. 1943 and were definitely fancier than the old identification he had carried. With the new designation of War Correspondent No. 574, he received the War Department's Basic Field Manual, FM 30-26, *Regulations for Correspondents Accompanying U.S. Army Forces in the Field, 21 January 1942.* All three items are in Morriss Papers.

"So ends a chapter of my life"

1. The trip that reminded Morriss of driving the road from Johnson City, Tennessee, to Asheville, North Carolina, took them north along the east coast of New Caledonia.

2. Jean Oxford, nee Goodwin. Morriss had known her at the time he and the others left for the service. John Bloomer was a newspaperman and editor Morriss greatly respected, who, at this time, was with the Kingsport, Tennessee, *Times.*

3. Morriss received a handsomely designed invitation to the dance, which he saved and which is among his papers. "Maytime" was the theme for the ball, which was sponsored by the Hq. Co. USAFISPA.

4. Spence mentioned that he was "sorry the cable request for a story on the Signal Corps did not work out, but it is one way of getting stories which might not otherwise be available," and let it go at that. Hartzell Spence to Mack Morriss, 24 May 1943, McCarthy Papers.

5. The photograph is of Bob Cromie, Jack Dowling, Bill Moscowitz, the Marine driver, Morriss, Allan Jackson, Roberts Jackson, and Bob Brumby. The original is in the possession of Allan Jackson.

6. Jackson had the basic information right. The 43rd Division, which was in the Russell Islands and which would make up the main assault force, was alerted for the New Georgia operation around the middle of May. See, Harold R. Barker, *History of the 43rd Division Artillery* (Providence, R.I.: John F. Greene, 1960), 33. It was generally known that New Georgia would necessarily be the next invasion target in the drive toward Rabaul; the problem that Morriss faced was in trying to learn exactly when.

7. *The Watauga Spinnerette* was the company paper of the huge rayon manufacturing complex in Elizabethton, North American Rayon Corporation and American Bemberg Division, Beaunit Mills, Inc. Of Morriss's three friends, Robert Lee Davis has already been mentioned. Cadet Harry Nave, killed in a crash at Roswell Flying Field, had entered service with the National Guard in 1940 and had transferred to the Air Corps a month after Morriss left for *Yank.* Lt. Ben Franklin, a navigator, was lost over Europe in February 1943. Morriss's editorial was published as "The Dead," *Yank,* 18 June 1943.

8. Nina Davis, Morriss's father's half sister, lived in Chillicothe, Ohio. Morriss had misspelled Sgt. James W. Hurlbut in the text. Hurlbut was a member of the Marine combat correspondents group with Burman.

9. Brodie wrote Spence, "Sir, I am not happy to go, nor the reason why (I am assuming that malaria was your only reason) but if this will mean another *active,* combat theater, I

am eager to return." And on the subject of he and Morriss splitting up, he continued, "I hate like hell to part with Mack personally, professionally we feel it is a good move. For my part I would certainly like to see Bushemi and Mack together. . . ." Howard Brodie to Hartzell Spence, 16 May 1943, McCarthy Papers. As it turned out, Morriss and Bushemi did cover the end of the New Georgia campaign.

10. Helmuet Hammer, son of German immigrants, one of Morriss's boyhood friends.

11. "Press Conference on Guadalcanal," in "Background for Peace: Communications," *Time,* 19 Apr. 1943, 104.

12. The Burns crew landed during a heavy rainstorm. Searchlight crews manned lights on either end of the runway for Burns to use as a reference. Other than hitting a coconut palm with the left wing and losing a section of it, Burns landed the plane safely. A few weeks later, however, another crew tried the same technique during a severe storm, but landed in the trees and their bomber exploded. Berton H. Burns to Ronnie Day, 16 Aug. 1991.

13. Brodie was a very sick man when he returned to New York City and was hospitalized in the Army's Halloran General Hospital, Staten Island, for a long time with hepatitis. While there he gave up both smoking and drinking and, never one to miss an opportunity, produced a series of sketches published as "Nine Wounded Veterans," *Yank,* 22 Oct. 1943. When Morriss returned from the Pacific, the two men met once in a bar in New York City and then after both had been sent to Europe their paths crossed several times. Howard Brodie to Ronnie Day, 10 July 1991.

14. Rex Barber and Thomas Lanphier, Jr., shared credit for the kill, and that is still the official record. But a great deal of controversy has ensued over the years, especially since 1966, when Lanphier publicly claimed sole credit for the plane carrying Yamamoto. See, Carroll V. Glines, *Attack on Yamamoto* (New York: Orion Books, 1990), and R. Cargill Hall, ed., *Lightning over Bougainville: The Yamamoto Mission Reconsidered* (Washington, D.C.: Smithsonian Institution Press, 1991).

15. The incident of the tooth and the reference to it in Wolfert's review of *The Best from Yank* have both been previously cited in the introduction.

16. Left blank in the diary.

17. By March 1943, the government was running out of gas masks and the situation was complicated by the fact that in a year's time civilians in Hawaii lost over 3,000 of them. "Whereabouts of Lost Gas Masks Mystery," *Honolulu Advertiser,* 2 March 1943.

18. Ira Wolfert, the North American Newspaper Alliance writer who has been mentioned on several occasions before, was as Morriss said, a "Name" in the Pacific. His *Battle for the Solomons* (Boston: Houghton Mifflin, 1943) won the Pulitzer Prize and in addition, by war's end, he had published at least two others. Maurice Evans was a noted Shakespearean actor who was serving with Special Services in Hawaii. For this, "Thespians in Uniform," *Honolulu Advertiser,* 1 Jan. 1943. Larry McManus was a *Yank* staff correspondent who covered a number of Pacific campaigns. In his notes, Morriss listed Art Cohen as being with UP and assigned to New Guinea. Desmond, *Tides of War,* 247, lists an Art Cohn, INS, as covering the New Georgia invasion.

19. Robert Trumbull was city editor of the *Honolulu Advertiser* and a correspondent for the *New York Times.* He had published *The Raft* (New York: Henry Holt, 1942), about the adventure of three American airmen. Paul Sample was an artist with *Life* and specialized in painting scenes of life in the navy. See, John Hersey, "Experience By Battle," *Life,* 27 Dec. 1943.

20. Sesso was a B-17 pilot mentioned in *Battle for the Solomons,* 108-9.

21. Allan Jackson filled me in on the Short Snorter club. On long flights, the prospective member paid the others one dollar and in return, they each signed a bill. This signed bill became the membership card for the club and as more bills were added, they were taped

together. Allan Jackson to Ronnie Day, 13 Jan. 1994. Part of the string of bills from both the South Pacific and the ETO are in Morriss Papers.

22. George Meyers, a *Yank* correspondent.

23. The *MidPacifican* was an Army paper set up in April 1942 to serve servicemen in the Hawaiian Department. See, "Midpacifican Soldier Paper," *Honolulu Advertiser,* 6 Apr. 1943. When he returned to the South Pacific in late July, Morriss filed some pieces for the paper. The manuscripts, headed "A Yank in the MidPacific" with editorial marks, are in Morriss Papers.

24. Fred Purnell, 67th Fighter Squadron.

"I got that old feeling"

1. Perhaps W.R. Williams also of the 67th Fighter Squadron.

2. Capt. Charles W. Balthrope was coming out to Honolulu as commanding officer of the Pacific Edition.

3. Charles H. McMurtry had been badly burned during the Battle of the Santa Cruz Islands, when a Japanese plane crashed into the signal bridge of the carrier he was on. After he recovered, he became chief of the AP Bureau in Honolulu. Desmond, *Tides of War,* 244.

4. Sgt. Robert Harold Hilton, one of Morriss's friends, was killed in a bombing mission in Europe, 14 May 1943. Louis Kinch, Morriss's old scout master, survived the war.

5. Col. Vachel D. Whatley was the Hawaiian Department special services officer.

6. Sgt. Alvin L. Pierce was killed 10 May 1943.

7. Morriss has him as Grossenbecker in the May 28 entry, here as Groppenbecker. In the notes he kept, Morriss has him as Bill Groppenbecker, *MidPacifican.* Morriss Papers.

8. The Kamehameha School for Boys. See, Gwenfread Allen, *Hawaii's War Years* (Honolulu: University of Hawaii Press, 1950), 198.

9. The 16 June air battle was the biggest of the Guadalcanal campaign. George E. Jones, UP, gave the official claim as ninety-four enemy planes to a loss of six in "Allied Fliers Destroy New Type Jap Zeros," *Honolulu Advertiser,* 20 June 1943. Jones described the new Zeros as blue-gray and square winged. This could have been the "Hamp" (Mitsubishi A6M3 Type O, Model 32), which in an article Morriss did much later he described as a "sort of M-2 Zero" and noted that for recognition purposes, the "only significant difference between the two planes is the squared wing tips of the Hamp." See, Mack Morriss, "I Think It's One of Ours," *Yank,* 7 Apr. 1944.

10. Along with Gregory "Pappy" Boyington, Foss was probably the most famous Marine fighter pilot in the Pacific War. See chap. 3 of Edward H. Sims, *Greatest Fighter Missions* (New York: Ballantine, 1962).

11. "*Yank's* Pacific Edition to Make Bow Friday," *Honolulu Advertiser,* 23 June 1943.

"The Army of the Pacific"

1. The operations against the New Georgia group began 30 June. First published news of the invasion appeared in the morning edition of the *Advertiser,* 1 July 1943. The next day Henry Keyes had an eyewitness account in the *Advertiser.*

2. Spence had written in mid-June that they were debating his future movements. One idea was to send either a photographer or a sketch artist (Robert Greenhalgh who was to do such excellent work in the Bougainville campaign was mentioned as a possible artist) to work with him. Another was to allow Bushemi to go with him. Still another was that he was needed back in New York. Hartzell Spence to Mack Morriss, 14 June 1943, McCarthy Papers.

3. Cables, Hartzell Spence to Merle Miller, 5 July 1943, B.H. Morriss to Merle Miller, 5 July 1943, Mack Morriss to Helen Morriss, 6 July 1943, are in Morriss Papers.

4. Twin girls were born, 15 Feb. 1945. *Yank* flew Morriss home from the ETO for the occasion, which made Walter Winchell's column in the *Daily Mirror,* 5 Mar. 1945.

5. These are substantially the same feelings Morriss put in his first letter to Helen, 6 July 1943, Morriss Papers. He also had learned that he was to return to Noumea and await his replacement, which in effect meant that he would not return to the States as early as they had both hoped. *Yank* personnel lent their full support to Helen in Morris's absence. Telegrams, Greta Jones to Helen Morriss, 5 July 1943 and Joe McCarthy to Helen Morriss, 6 July 1943, Morriss Papers.

6. Morriss caught up with Bushemi in Suva, Fiji, and with very little authorization they headed for New Georgia. They got to Noumea 4 Aug., to Guadalcanal 11 Aug., and to Munda, New Georgia, 15 Aug. Munda Field had fallen and the American forces were mopping up resistance around Bairoko Harbor and Arundel Island. Nonetheless, working as a team, Morriss and Bushemi produced three feature pieces for *Yank*—"Story of an Infantry Battle in New Georgia," 15 Oct. 1943, "Five-Day Attack on the Japs at Hastings Ridge," 19 Nov. 1943 and "Jungle Mop-Up," 26 Nov. 1943—and of these, two featured Bushemi covers. As Morriss had planned, their adventures were set down in detail in the loose leaf diary which, as previously mentioned, is in Morriss Papers. Following their stint in New Georgia, Bushemi was ordered back to Honolulu, Morriss back to New York. Johnny Bushemi was killed on Eniwetok, 19 Feb. 1944, by mortar fire. He had become well known to millions of civilians as a result of being a principal character in another *Yank* correspondent's book about army life, Marion Hargrove's *See Here, Private Hargrove* (New York: Henry Holt, 1942), so that when the *Chicago Tribune* reported his death, 1 Mar. 1944, the leader said: "Gary Sergeant Slain; Hargrove Book Character."

Index

246 *Index*

Hitching Post, 198
Hollywood, 18, 32, 37, 55, 61, 89, 156, 209 n 23
Honolulu, 165, 194; Aloha Tower, 195; Diamond Head, 185, 194; Kam Hospital (Kamehameha School of Boys), 194-95; Moana, 185, 195, 201; Pearl Harbor, 188, 195; Royal Hawaiian, 185; Wheeler Field, 188
Honolulu, 211 n 1, 213 n 15, 215 n 27
Hotel Sevastopol, 98. *See also* Noumea
Houailou, 165-66
Hughes, L., author of *Big Sea*, 16
Hunt, Sgt. James H., 153, 236 n 44
Hurlbut, Sgt. James W., 172, 239 n 8
Hurley, Patrick J., 118, 230 n 9
Hutshing, E.E., 72

Infantry Divisions: Americal, 9, 79, 93, 130, 132, 215 n 25, 220 n 33; 4th, 4; 25th, 4, 9, 63-65, 79, 80, 93-94, 220 n 33; 27th, 192; 30th, 4, 207 n 11; 43rd, 230 n 13
Infantry Regiments: 27th (25th Div.), 73, 80, 156, 209 n 20, 210 n 23; 35th (25th Div.), 61, 223 n 6, 67, 69, 77, 79, 80, 92, 135; 117th (30th Div.), 4, 207 n 11, 80-81; 132nd (Americal Div.), 53-54, 220 n 34, 57, 221 n 1, 67, 69, 70, 72, 77, 80, 147; 147th (originally 37th Div.), 86, 227 n 6, 91; 161st (25th Div.), 91; 164th (Americal Div.), 33, 215 n 25, 79-80,93, 145, 153, 231 n 4; 182nd (Americal Div.), 79-80, 129, 231 n 4, 130, 132. *See also* Marine Regiments

Jackson, Allan, INP: on Guadalcanal, 60, 61, 62, 63, 66, 83, 87; in Auckland, 109; photo of Brodie, 160; career during war, 227 n 7
Jackson, Sgt. Roberts, 57, 58, 59, 73, 74, 74, 76, 78, 82, 85, 98, 100, 105, 112, 162, 165, 168, 176, 177, 200
Jackson, U.S. Army Fort, 1-3, 6, 13, 16, 23, 30, 42
Japanese Army, soldiers of: tooth of, 7, 184, 209 n 21; reported speaking English, 42, 92, 134; as prisoners of war, 47; superman myth, 55-56; atrocities against, 62, 65, 67, 72; fatalism of, 66; character incomprehensible, 74-75; corpses of, 77-78; as a fighter, 94; expectation of

execution if captured, 145; diary of, 154-55. *See also* prisoners of war, Japanese
Jarbel, Capt. ___, 129
Johnson, Capt. ___, 118
Johnson, Martin, 121, 230 n 10
Johnson, Osa, 121, 230 n 10
Jones George E., UP, 198, 241 n 9
Jones, Greta, *Yank*, 216 n 1, 242 n 6
Jones, James: comment on Morriss's novel, 6-7; author of *From Here to Eternity*, 6, 9; of *The Thin Red Line*, 9; of *Whistle*, 9; Appalachian characters in trilogy, 209 n 20; Brodie and Morriss on Horse's Neck; 210 n 23; author of *WW II*, 210 n 23; admiration for Brodie's work, 210 n 25
Jones, Lt. ___, 166

Kahn, E.J., *Yank*, 124, 231 n 16, 128

Kay (Auckland), 107
Kennedy, Walter, 16
Kenny, Reginald, *Yank*, 5
Kerns, Walter, 115
Keyes, Henry W. "Harry," *Daily Express*, 54, 221 n 35, 98, 177
Kinch, Louis, 68, 70, 160, 193, 241 n 4, 194
Klippfontein, 211 n 1, 213 n 15
Knapp, ___, 112-13, 123, 126-27, 178
Knox, Frank, Secretary of the Navy, 68-70
Kynett, Maj. ___, 135

L'Abbe, Col. Norris M., 117, 230 n 6, 124
Lacy, Alan, 201
Le Bec, Madame ___, 165-66
Lego, Evelyn W., 172
LeMay, Tom, 80-81
Liberty, 199
Life, 5, 8, 37, 50, 70, 124, 147, 206 n 2
Lockwood, Gen. ___, 123
Lodge, J. Norman, AP, 71, 224 n 26, 72
Long, Tom, 170
Long, Col. [William D.], 76, 225 n 33
Love, Maj. Ewell Scott, 55, 80
Lucas, Capt. Walter Y., 49, 219 n 28
Luciano, "Lucky," 20
Luker, Jerry, 185
Lynch, Lt. Joseph, 44-45, 218 n 17

MacArthur, Gen. Douglas, 16, 42, 55, 98, 177, 213 n 13
Mahon, Jack, INS, 177
Mailor, Norman, 9, 210 n 24

www.ingramcontent.com/pod-product-compliance
Lightning Source LLC
Chambersburg PA
CBHW030530100426
42813CB00001B/208